TM

BESTSELLING BOOK SERIES

eBay™
FOR
DUMMIES®
2ND EDITION

eBay™ FOR DUMMIES®

2ND EDITION

by Marsha Collier, Roland Woerner, and Stephanie Becker

Hungry Minds™

HUNGRY MINDS, INC.

New York, NY ◆ Indianapolis, IN ◆ Cleveland, OH

eBay™ For Dummies®, 2nd Edition

Published by
Hungry Minds, Inc.
909 Third Avenue
New York, NY 10022
www.hungryminds.com
www.dummies.com (Dummies Press Web Site)

Library of Congress Control Number: 00-103646

ISBN: 0-7645-0761-3

Printed in the United States of America

10 9 8 7 6 5 4 3 2

2B/RV/QS/QR/IN

Distributed in the United States by Hungry Minds, Inc.

Distributed by CDG Books Canada Inc. for Canada; by Transworld Publishers Limited in the United Kingdom; by IDG Norge Books for Norway; by IDG Sweden Books for Sweden; by IDG Books Australia Publishing Corporation Pty. Ltd. for Australia and New Zealand; by TransQuest Publishers Pte Ltd. for Singapore, Malaysia, Thailand, Indonesia, and Hong Kong; by Gotop Information Inc. for Taiwan; by ICG Muse, Inc. for Japan; by Intersoft for South Africa; by Eyrolles for France; by International Thomson Publishing for Germany, Austria and Switzerland; by Distribuidora Cuspide for Argentina; by LR International for Brazil; by Galileo Libros for Chile; by Ediciones ZETA S.C.R. Ltda. for Peru; by WS Computer Publishing Corporation, Inc., for the Philippines; by Contemporanea de Ediciones for Venezuela; by Express Computer Distributors for the Caribbean and West Indies; by Micronesia Media Distributor, Inc. for Micronesia; by Chips Computadoras S.A. de C.V. for Mexico; by Editorial Norma de Panama S.A. for Panama; by American Bookshops for Finland.

For general information on Hungry Minds' products and services please contact our Customer Care Department within the U.S. at 800-762-2974, outside the U.S. at 317-572-3993 or fax 317-572-4002.

For sales inquiries and reseller information, including discounts, premium and bulk quantity sales, and foreign-language translations, please contact our Customer Care Department at 800-434-3422, fax 317-572-4002, or write to Hungry Minds, Inc., Attn: Customer Care Department, 10475 Crosspoint Boulevard, Indianapolis, IN 46256.

For information on licensing foreign or domestic rights, please contact our Sub-Rights Customer Care Department at 650-653-7098.

For authorization to photocopy items for corporate, personal, or educational use, please contact Copyright Clearance Center, 222 Rosewood Drive, Danvers, MA 01923, or fax 978-750-4470.

For information on using Hungry Minds' products and services in the classroom or for ordering examination copies, please contact our Educational Sales Department at 800-434-2086 or fax 317-572-4005.

Please contact our Public Relations Department at 212-884-5163 for press review copies or 212-884-5000 for author interviews and other publicity information or fax 212-884-5400.

Hungry Minds™ is a trademark of Hungry Minds, Inc.

About the Authors

Marsha Collier is a multi-tasking professional who uses all aspects of graphics in her advertising business, The Collier Company. In her spare time, she's mastered the art of eBay and she has enjoyed close to 900 positive feedback comments. Using her ability to spot trends, she continues to buy and sell on eBay, while also winning awards for her achievements in advertising and for her work in the community.

Roland Woerner is an Emmy Award-nominated producer and writer for NBC's *The Today Show*. In addition to his news duties, he enjoys writing and producing segments exploring the world of technology and pop culture. In his spare time he enjoys going on adventures with his daughters, flying airplanes, driving boats, and collecting lunchboxes and T.V. memorabilia.

Stephanie Becker is an Emmy Award-nominated television producer for NBC News. Her essays as Gadget Gal have appeared both in *Gadget Guru Guide Magazine* and on the Web. She is an avid cyclist and has several unique collections, including refigerator magnets, momentos from catastrophes around the world, and dust bunnies.

Dedication

I dedicate this book to my buddy and daughter, Susan and her husband. I also dedicate this book to Beryl Lockhart, who's finally gotten into this eBay thing, and my mother, Claire Berg, who becomes more understanding as the years go by.

Author's Acknowledgments

I would like to thank my assistant and friend, Joni Lusk, for handling all the details of my business and life. I thank my clients for putting up with me sliding into deadlines at the last minute due to doing double-duty with this book. A special thank you to Roland Woerner, a very extraordinary person, who helped me believe that I could do so much myself. Thank you to John Lentz for doing what he does best, and a sincere thank you to Stephanie Becker, who worked with me on the first edition. Without her wry phrases this book wouldn't be quite as interesting. Last but not least, a very special thanks to all the eBay users out there who shared their thoughts and insights for this book.

I particularly want to thank my editors at IDG Books Worldwide, Inc., Nicole Haims, Sandy Blackthorn, Jill Mazurczyk, Beth Parlon, Sheri Replin, and Steven Hayes for helping us to take our wacky idea and turn it into a great book.

Publisher's Acknowledgments

We're proud of this book; please send us your comments through our Online Registration Form located at www.dummies.com.

Some of the people who helped bring this book to market include the following:

Acquisitions, Editorial, and Media Development

Senior Project Editor: Nicole Haims

Acquisitions Editor: Steven Hayes

Copy Editors: Bill Barton, Sandy Blackthorn, Beth Parlon

Proof Editor: Jill Mazurczyk

Technical Editors: Allen Wyatt, Kelly Braun, and Arlene Brenner

Permissions Editor: Carmen Krikorian

Editorial Manager: Leah Cameron

Media Development Manager: Laura Carpenter

Media Development Supervisor: Richard Graves

Editorial Assistant: Seth Kerney

Production

Project Coordinator: Maridee Ennis

Layout and Graphics: Beth Brooks, Amy Adrian, Jackie Bennett, Jacque Schneider, Jeremey Unger

Proofreaders: Susan Moritz, Christine Pingleton, Marianne Santy, Charles Spencer

Indexer: Liz Cunningham

Special Help
Teresa Artman, Sheri Replin, Rebecca Senninger

Special Thanks to eBay Inc., especially Kelly Braun, Arlene Brenner, Jim Davis, and George Koster

---

General and Administrative

Hungry Minds, Inc.: John Kilcullen, CEO; Bill Barry, President and COO; John Ball, Executive VP, Operations & Administration; John Harris, CFO

Hungry Minds Technology Publishing Group: Richard Swadley, Senior Vice President and Publisher; Mary Bednarek, Vice President and Publisher, Networking and Certification; Walter R. Bruce III, Vice President and Publisher, General User and Design Professional; Joseph Wikert, Vice President and Publisher, Programming; Mary C. Corder, Editorial Director, Branded Technology Editorial; Andy Cummings, Publishing Director, General User and Design Professional; Barry Pruett, Publishing Director, Visual

Hungry Minds Manufacturing: Ivor Parker, Vice President, Manufacturing

Hungry Minds Marketing: John Helmus, Assistant Vice President, Director of Marketing

Hungry Minds Online Management: Brenda McLaughlin, Executive Vice President, Chief Internet Officer

Hungry Minds Production for Branded Press: Debbie Stailey, Production Director

Hungry Minds Sales: Roland Elgey, Senior Vice President, Sales and Marketing; Michael Violano, Vice President, International Sales and Sub Rights

◆

The publisher would like to give special thanks to Patrick J. McGovern, without whom this book would not have been possible.

◆

Contents at a Glance

Introduction 1

Part I: Forget the Mall: Getting a Feel for eBay 7

Chapter 1: Why eBay Is Better Than Your Local Antique Shop 9
Chapter 2: The Bucks Start Here: Signing Up at eBay 19
Chapter 3: There's No Place Like the Home Page 31
Chapter 4: My Own Private eBay 47

Part II: Are You Buying What They're Selling? 71

Chapter 5: Seek and You Shall Find: Research 73
Chapter 6: Bidding: The Basics 93
Chapter 7: Power Bidding Strategies 117
Chapter 8: After You Win the Auction 129

Part III: Are You Selling What They're Buying? 141

Chapter 9: Selling in Your Bedroom Slippers for Fun and Profit 143
Chapter 10: Filling in the Blanks: Cyber Paperwork for the Savvy Seller 167
Chapter 11: Going, Going, Gone: Closing the Deal 191
Chapter 12: Troubleshooting Your Auction 211
Chapter 13: Using Pictures and Strategies to Increase Your Profits 231

Part IV: Oy Vay, More eBay!: Special Features 249

Chapter 14: Privacy: To Protect and Serve 251
Chapter 15: eBay's Rules & Safety Program 265
Chapter 16: The eBay Community: Playing Nice with Other eBay Members 285
Chapter 17: Charities and Special Features 297

Part V: The Part of Tens 303

Chapter 18: Ten (Or So) Golden Rules for eBay Buyers and Sellers 305
Chapter 19: Ten (Or So) Programs and Services to Ease Your Way on eBay 311

Appendix A: Computers: How High-Tech Do I Go? 321

Appendix B: Answers for the Fanatic:
Finding More Stuff to Sell 333

Index 339

Book Registration Information.......................Back of Book

Cartoons at a Glance

By Rich Tennant

The 5th Wave   By Rich Tennant

"Look, Honey – the Kiss shoes I won at eBay arrived today, and better yet – they fit!"

page 7

The 5th Wave   By Rich Tennant

"Well, if there's anywhere I'll find a pair of shoes to match my yam-hat, it'll be at eBay."

page 141

The 5th Wave   By Rich Tennant

"My gosh, Barbara, if you don't think it's worth going a couple of weeks without dinner so we can afford to bid on that small Mediterranean island we saw at eBay, just say so!"

page 71

The 5th Wave   By Rich Tennant

"What troubles me is that he spends all his time in eBay's Beanie Babies chat room."

page 249

The 5th Wave   By Rich Tennant

"Oh sure, it'll float alright, but I want to check your feedback rating before you place a bid."

page 303

Fax: 978-546-7747
E-mail: richtennant@the5thwave.com
World Wide Web: www.the5thwave.com

Table of Contents

Introduction **1**

About This Book 1
Foolish Assumptions 2
How This Book Is Organized 3
    Part I: Forget the Mall: Getting a Feel for eBay 3
    Part II: Are You Buying What They're Selling? 3
    Part III: Are You Selling What They're Buying? 3
    Part IV: Oy Vay, More eBay!: Special Features 4
    Part V: The Part of Tens 4
Icons Used in This Book 4
What Now? 5
Feedback, Please 5

Part I: Forget the Mall: Getting a Feel for eBay **7**

Chapter 1: Why eBay Is Better Than Your Local Antique Shop **9**

What Is eBay and How Does It Work? 10
All About Auctions 11
    Traditional auctions 11
    Reserve-price auctions 12
    Restricted-access auctions 12
    Private (mind-your-own-business) auctions 13
    Dutch auctions 13
So You Wanna Sell Stuff 14
So You Wanna Buy Stuff 14
Research for Fun and Profit 15
eBay's Role in the Auction Action 15
Features and Fun Stuff 16
    Chatting it up 16
    Rules & Safety (SafeHarbor) 16
Extra Gizmos You're Gonna Want 17

Chapter 2: The Bucks Start Here: Signing Up at eBay **19**

Sign In, Please — Register at eBay 19
Registering Is Free and Fun (And Fast) 20
    So, what's your sign? Putting down general information 21
    Can I get your digits? Filling in required information 22
    Getting to know you: Optional information 22
    Check your work and confirm registration 23

Do you solemnly swear to . . . ? 24
It must be true if you have it in writing 26
Sprint to the finish 26
A Quick Word about Passwords 27
A Not-So-Quick Word about Choosing a User ID 28
Your License to Deal (Almost) 30

Chapter 3: There's No Place Like the Home Page **31**

What Is the Home Page? 31
Sign In, Please! 32
This Bar Never Closes 33
Exploring Your Home Page Search Options 35
Peering through the Home page Search window 36
Going where the Search button takes you 36
Using eBay's "Welcome Mat" 38
Home Links, the Next Generation 39
Maneuvering through Categories 40
Go Global 42
Using the Featured Items Link 42
Hanging Out in the Gallery 43
Don't Miss This 44
Spotlight's On! 44
Bottoming Out 45

Chapter 4: My Own Private eBay **47**

Your My eBay Page 47
Choosing Your My eBay Preferences 50
Setting Up Your Account 51
Getting Your Favorites Area Together 54
All Sorts of Sorting: Keeping Track of Your Auction Items 57
Sorting auction items using the My eBay Sign In page 57
Staying organized on your own 58
Getting and Giving Feedback 59
How to get positive feedback 61
How to get negative feedback 62
The Feedback Profile page 62
Reading your feedback 64
You have the last word — use it! 64
Leaving feedback with finesse 65

Part II: Are You Buying What They're Selling? **71**

Chapter 5: Seek and You Shall Find: Research **73**

General Online Tips for Collectors 73
The experts speak out 74
Go, Joe: Following an expert on the hunt 76
Making the grade 77

Finding More Collecting Information 78
    Visiting eBay's online library 78
    Searching other places online 79
    Finding other sources of information 80
Looking to Find an Item? Start Your eBay Search Engine 80
    eBay's Smart Search 82
    An item number search 84
    A seller search 84
    A bidder search 86
    A completed items search 87
    An international search 88
    Narrowing down your eBay search 88
Finding eBay Members: The Gang's All Here 90

Chapter 6: Bidding: The Basics **93**
The Auction Item Page 93
Beating the Devil in the Details 97
    Read the item description carefully 97
    Get the scoop on the seller 98
Factoring in the Extras 101
    Payment methods 101
    Using an escrow service 104
    Shipping and insurance costs 105
Placing Your Bid 106
Bidding to the Max: Proxy Bidding 108
Specialized Auction Categories 110
    eBay Motors 110
    eBay Great Collections 111
    Business Exchange 111
The Agony (?) of Buyer's Remorse 112
    Retracting your bid 112
    Avoiding deadbeat (nonpaying bidder) status 113

Chapter 7: Power Bidding Strategies **117**
Get to Know the High Bidder 117
Find Out the Item's Bidding History 119
Strategies to Help You Outsmart the Competition 120
    Dutch auction strategy 120
    Bidding strategies eBay doesn't talk about 121
Time Is Money: Strategy by the Clock 122
    Using the lounging-around strategy 124
    Using the beat-the-clock strategy 124

Chapter 8: After You Win the Auction **129**
eBay Calling: You're a Winner 129
Getting Your Paperwork Together 130
Getting Contact Information 131

So, What's Your Number? 132
Talking Turkey: Communicating with the Seller 133
Sending Out the Payment Promptly and Securely 135
    Using person-to-person payment services 136
    Using i-Escrow 137
Keeping in Touch: Dealing with an AWOL Seller 138
You Get the Item (Uh-Oh! What's This?) 139
Don't Forget the Feedback 140

Part III: Are You Selling What They're Buying? 141

Chapter 9: Selling in Your Bedroom Slippers for Fun and Profit ...143

Why Should You Sell Stuff on eBay? 143
Mi Casa, Mi Cash-a: Finding Stuff to Sell 144
Know When to Sell 146
Know Thy Stuff 147
    Getting the goods on your goods 147
    Spy versus spy: Comparison selling 149
Know What You Can (And Can't) Sell 151
    Prohibited items 152
    Infringing items 155
    Questionable Items: Know the laws 157
    Forbidden auctions 157
Reporting a Problem Auction 158
VeRO to the Rescue 159
eBay Fees? What eBay Fees? Oops 160
    Insertion fees 160
    Final value fees 161
    Optional fees 162
    Keep current on your cash flow 163
Uncle Sam Wants You — to Pay Your Taxes! 164
    Two wild rumors about federal taxes 164
    State taxes 166

Chapter 10: Filling in the Blanks: Cyber Paperwork for the Savvy Seller 167

Getting Ready to List Your Item 167
Examining the Sell Your Item Page 168
Filling in the Required Blanks 170
    Item title info 171
    Choosing a category 174
    Writing your description 176
    Filling out the item location 178

Listing the payment methods you'll accept 178
Setting shipping terms 180
Listing the number of items for sale 180
Setting a minimum bid — how low can you go? 181
Setting your auction time 182
eBay Options: Ballyhoo on the Cheap 183
Your secret safety net — reserve price 185
I want to be alone: The private auction 186
Put me in the Gallery 186
Checking Your Work and Starting the Auction 186
Mid-Course Corrections: Fixing Current Auctions 188
Making changes before bidding begins 188
Making changes after bidding begins 189

Chapter 11: Going, Going, Gone: Closing the Deal **191**
Bookkeeping and Staying Organized 191
Talking to Buyers: The ABCs of Good Communication 193
Thank you! I mean it! 194
Let's keep e-mailing 196
Shipping without Going Postal 196
Shopping for a shipper 198
Getting the right (packing) stuff 204
Buying Postage Online 209
eBay's partner in postage: E-stamp 209
Stamps.com — the other guys 210

Chapter 12: Troubleshooting Your Auction **211**
Dealing with a Buyer Who Doesn't Respond 211
Going into nudge mode 212
Be a secret agent, man 213
Step up your nudge a notch 214
Try a last-ditch emergency effort 215
And Some Other Auction Problems 217
The buyer backs out of the transaction 217
Houston, we have a payment problem 218
The item you send is busted — and so are you 218
You have regrets — seller's remorse 219
Auction Going Badly? Cut Your Losses 220
Try canceling bids first 220
If all else fails, end your auction early 222
Extending your auction (not!) 223
Filing for a Final Value Fee credit 224
Déjà vu — relisting your item 227
Show me the money: Refunds 229

**Chapter 13: Using Pictures and Strategies
to Increase Your Profits** **231**

Using Images in Your Auctions 231
Choosing a digital camera 232
Choosing a digital scanner 233
Making Your Picture a Thing of Beauty .234
Get it on camera! 235
Use traditional photos? Yes, I scan 236
Software that adds the artist's touch 237
Making Your Images Web-Friendly 238
The Image Is Perfect — What Now? 239
Using an ISP to store your images .240
Using image-hosting Web sites to store images 241
Using eBay's new picture service 242
Getting Your Item Noticed 243
Putting on the hits 243
Playing the links for fun and profit .244
It's All About Me 245

Part IV: Oy Vay, More eBay!: Special Features **249**

Chapter 14: Privacy: To Protect and Serve **251**

What (And How) eBay Knows about You .251
What you tell eBay 252
What cookies gather 253
Your eBay sign-in cookie 254
What Web servers collect 254
BBBOnline and TRUSTe 255
What Does eBay Do with Information about Me, Anyway? 257
What Do Other eBay Members Know about Me? 259
Spam — Not Just a Taste Treat Anymore 260
Sending spam versus eating it 260
Trash your junk mail! 261
I Vant to Be Alone — and Vat You Can Do to Stay That Vay 262

Chapter 15: eBay's Rules & Safety Program **265**

Keeping eBay Safe with Rules & Safety .265
Abuses You Should Report to Rules & Safety 267
Selling abuses 267
Bidding abuses 268
Feedback abuses 268
Identity abuses 269
Operational abuses 269
Miscellaneous abuses 269

Reporting Abuses to Rules & Safety 270
Stuff eBay Won't Do Anything About 271
Using Mediation and Dispute Resolution Services 273
Launching a Fraud Report 274
Walking the Plank: Suspensions 275
Toss 'em a Life Saver: eBay Insurance 276
    Filing an insurance claim 277
    Docking with escrow 278
Trimming in the Sales: Authentication and Appraising 278
Verifying Your ID 280
If It's Clearly Fraud 282

**Chapter 16: The eBay Community: Playing Nice
with Other eBay Members** **285**
News and Chat, This and That 286
Hear Ye, Hear Ye! eBay's Announcements Board 287
Help! I Need Somebody 288
Community Discussion and Help Boards 289
User-to-User Discussion Boards 290
Other Message Boards 291
    Café society 291
    Wanted Board 291
    Holiday Board 292
    Giving Board 292
    Emergency Contact Board 292
    eBay International Boards 294
Category-Specific Chat Boards 294

Chapter 17: Charities and Special Features **297**
Truly Righteous Stuff for Charity 297
    Rosie's For All Kids Foundation 298
    Other charity auctions 298
And Now for Our Feature Presentation 299
    Member specials 299
    Who's minding the eBay store? 300
    Personal Shopper 301

Part V: The Part of Tens *303*

**Chapter 18: Ten (Or So) Golden Rules for eBay
Buyers and Sellers** **305**
Buyer: Investigate Your Treasure before You Buy 305
Buyer: Check the Seller's Feedback 306
Buyer: Understand Post-Auction Charges and Payment Methods 306

Buyer: Check the Item Price Tag and Bid Wisely 306
Buyer: Be a Good Buyer Bee 307
Buyer: Cover Your Assets 307
Seller: Know Your Stuff 307
Seller: Polish and Shine 308
Seller: Picture-Perfect Facts 308
Seller: Communication Is Key 309
Seller: Be a Buyer's Dream 309
Seller: Listen to the Music 309
Buyers and Sellers: Keep Current, Keep Cool 310

**Chapter 19: Ten (Or So) Programs and Services
to Ease Your Way on eBay** **311**
Online Services 312
AuctionWatch.com 312
AuctionWorks 313
ManageAuctions 313
PriceRadar 314
NetMechanic 314
Software for Offline Use 315
AuctionAssistant Classic 315
ePoster2000 316
Auction Wizard 316
TurboBid 317
Virtual Auction Ad Pro 317
eBay's Software and Services 318
eBay's Mister Lister 318
eBay Power Sellers Program 318

Appendix A: Computers: How High-Tech Do I Go? *321*
Buying a New Computer 321
Buying a Used Computer 322
Buying a Refurbished Computer 323
Upgrading Your System with the Help of eBay 324
No Computer? Connect to eBay on the Cheap 325
Libraries: From Dewey decimal to eBay 325
WebTV 325
AOLTV 325
Commercial cyber-outlets 326
Hooking up from work 326
Choosing an ISP 327
Paying for an ISP service 327
Using a free ISP 328
Going digital 328
Browsing for a Browser 329
Hooking Up on E-Mail 330

Appendix B: Answers for the Fanatic:
Finding More Stuff to Sell *333*
Knowing the Market 333
Catching Trends in the Media 334
In newspapers 334
On television 335
Catch up with youth culture 335
Check out magazines 336
The Hunt for eBay Inventory 336
The goods are out there 336
Tips for the modest investor 338

Index *339*

Book Registration Information ....*Back of Book*

Introduction

●●●

*W*elcome to *eBay For Dummies,* 2nd Edition! You've come to the right place to learn all about eBay. This book's designed to help you understand everything you need to know about buying and selling at eBay, the most successful person-to-person trading community Web site on the Internet. We give you all the tools you need to get moving at eBay, whether you're new to the Internet or a Webaholic. We show you how to turn your everyday household clutter into cold, hard cash — and how to look for items that you can sell at eBay. If you're a collector (or you'd like to be), we show you how to figure out how much you should spend, how to make smart bids, and how to win the auctions. How much money you earn (or spend) depends entirely on how *often* and how *smartly* you conduct your eBay transactions. You decide how often you want to run auctions and place bids; we're here to help you out on the *smart* part.

A Web site as complex as eBay has many nooks and crannies that may be confusing to the first-time user. Think of this book as a detailed roadmap that can help you navigate eBay, getting just as much or as little as you want from it. Unlike an actual roadmap, you won't get frustrated folding it back to its original shape. Just close the book and come back any time you need a question answered.

After you figure out the nuts and bolts of eBay, you can start buying and selling stuff. We have a ton of terrific buying and selling strategies that help you get the most out of your auctions. With this book and a little elbow grease, you can join the ranks of the millions of people who use their home computers to make friends, become part of the eBay community, have a lot of fun, and make a profit.

About This Book

Remember those open-book tests that were sprung on you in high school? Well, sometimes you may feel like eBay pop-quizzes you while you're online. Think of *eBay For Dummies,* 2nd Edition, as your open-book-test resource with all the answers. You don't have to memorize anything; just keep this book handy to help you get over the confusing parts of eBay.

With that in mind, we divided this book into pertinent sections to help you find your answers fast. We show you how to

- ✔ Get online and register at eBay.
- ✔ Navigate eBay to do just about anything you can think of — search for items for sale, set up auctions, monitor your transactions, and join the chat room circuit.
- ✔ Bid on and win eBay auctions.
- ✔ Choose an item to sell, pick the right time for your auction, market it so a ton of bidders see it, and make a profit at eBay.
- ✔ Communicate well and close deals without problems, whether you're a buyer or a seller.
- ✔ Become a part of a really unique community of people who like to collect, buy, and sell items of just about every type.

Do not adjust your eyes. To protect the privacy of eBay users, screen images (commonly called *screen shots*) in this book blur User IDs.

Foolish Assumptions

You may have picked up this book because you heard that people are making big bucks trading at eBay and you want to find out what's going on. Or you heard about the bargains and wacky stuff you can find in the world's largest garage sale. If either of these assumptions is true, this is the right book for you.

Other foolish assumptions we've made about you:

- ✔ You have, or would like to have, access to a computer, a modem, and the Internet so that you can do business at eBay.
- ✔ You have an interest in collecting stuff, selling stuff, and buying stuff, and you want to find out more about doing that stuff online.
- ✔ You want tips and strategies that can save you money when you bid and make you money when you sell. (You too? We can relate. Talk about all things to all people . . . !)
- ✔ You're concerned about maintaining your privacy and staying away from people who try to ruin everyone's good time with negligent, and some-times illegal, activity.

If you think the expression *surfing the Web* has something to do with spiders and boogie boards, then this book can get you started, but you may want to browse through *The Internet For Dummies,* 7th Edition, by John R. Levine for a crash course in Internet confidence. The book comes from IDG Books Worldwide, just like the book you're reading now. From time to time (and by astounding coincidence), we mention other titles in the *. . .For Dummies* series that you may find helpful.

How This Book Is Organized

This book has five parts. The parts stand on their own, which means that you can read Chapter 5 after you read Chapter 10 or skip Chapter 3 altogether. It's all up to you. We do think that you should at least dip into Chapter 1 and Chapter 2 to get an overview on what eBay is all about and how you can become a registered user.

If you're already conducting transactions at eBay, you certainly can jump ahead to get good tips on advanced strategies to enhance your auctions. Don't wait for permission from us — just go for it. We won't argue with you that jazzy auctions equal higher profits!

Part I: Forget the Mall: Getting a Feel for eBay

In this part, we tell you what eBay is and how you use it. We take you through the registration process, help you organize your eBay transactions and interactions using the My eBay page, and get you comfortable navigating the site from the Home page.

Part II: Are You Buying What They're Selling?

If you're pretty sure you want to start making bids on items, this part gives you the lowdown on searching, grading an item's value, researching, bidding, and winning auctions.

That old cliché, "Let the buyer beware," became a cliché because even today (maybe especially today) it's sound advice. Use our friendly, fat-free tips to help you decide when to bid and when to take a pass.

Part III: Are You Selling What They're Buying?

This part gets you up to speed on how to sell your items at eBay. Think of it as an eBay graduate course in marketing. Here, you find important information on how to conduct your auctions, what to do after you sell an item, how to ship the item, and how to keep track of all the money you make. Even Uncle Sam gets to chime in on his favorite topic: taxes. Know the rules so your friendly local tax office doesn't invite you over for a snack and a little audit.

We also show you how to jazz up your auctions by adding pictures and how to use basic HTML to link your auctions to your own Home page. (If you don't have a Home page, don't freak out — links are optional.) You can make your digital images look like high art with our tips, hints, and strategies.

Part IV: Oy Vay, More eBay!: Special Features

Check this part out to find out how to handle privacy issues relating to eBay and how you can resolve buying and selling issues with the help of Rules & Safety (SafeHarbor), eBay's problem-solving clearinghouse. Also included here are ways of having fun with the eBay community and using charity auctions to bid on great items for a good cause.

Part V: The Part of Tens

In keeping with a long tradition, this part is a compendium of short chapters that gives you ready references and useful facts. We share more great tips for buying and selling items, as well as a description of our favorite software programs that help lighten your auction load.

Appendix A tells you just what kind of computer equipment you need to get up and running at eBay. In Appendix B, we give you some insider information on how to spot a trend before the rest of the world catches on, and how to acquire items cheaply that others may spend a bundle on.

Icons Used in This Book

Time is money at eBay. When you see this shortcut or time saver come your way, read the information and think about all the moola you just saved.

Think of this icon as a sticky note for your brain. If you forget one of the pearls of wisdom revealed to you, you can go back and reread it. If you *still* can't remember something here, go ahead, dog-ear the page — we won't tell.

Don't feel our pain. We've done things wrong at eBay before and want to save you from our mistakes, so we put these warnings out there bright and bold so that you don't have a bad experience. Don't skip these warnings unless you're enthusiastic about masochism.

 When you see this icon, you know you're in for the real deal. We created this icon especially for you to give you war stories (and success stories) from eBay veterans (*learn from their experience* is our motto!) that can help you strategize, make money, and spare you from the perils of a poorly written auction item description. You can skip over these icons if you want to, but we think you may get burned if you do.

What Now?

Like everything else in the world, eBay constantly evolves. We keep you updated on all the changes occurring at eBay. At this point, you're armed with everything you need to know to join the eBay community and begin conducting transactions. If you hit rough waters, just look up the problem in the table of contents or index in this book. We either help you solve it or let you know where you can go at eBay for some expert advice.

Although eBay makes its complex Web site as easy to navigate as possible, you may still need to refer back to this book for help. Don't get frustrated if you have to keep reviewing topics before you feel completely comfortable trading at eBay.

After all, Albert Einstein once said, "Don't commit to memory something you can look up." (We forgot when he said that . . . .)

Feedback, Please

Communication makes the world go round, and we'd love to hear from you. Check out our Web site at the address below or e-mail us at dummies @collierad.com or go to

www.coolebaytools.com

Caution: Information highway
roadwork next 3 miles

You'd think that with millions of people accessing the eBay Web site every day, those Silicon Valley guys would have enough to keep them busy. As if! But hey, everybody's sprucing up for the new millennium, and eBay wants to make the site *even more* new and exciting — that means switching things around to see if you notice. For example, you may see a *link* (an image or group of words that takes you to a different part of the site after you click it) on the Home page that's here today and gone tomorrow, replaced with something else. Don't have a cow — the *main navigation bar* is like your own personal breadcrumb trail. It can get you into eBay, around the block, and out of the woods with nearly no hassles.

Part I
Forget the Mall: Getting a Feel for eBay

The 5th Wave   By Rich Tennant

"Look, Honey— the Kiss shoes I won at eBay arrived today, and better yet—they fit!"

In this part . . .

*e*Bay may feel kind of big and scary, especially if you're
new to the Internet. What you need is someone to point
out the most useful tools you need to get around, help you
find out how eBay works, and start showing you how to
do your own transactions.

In this part, you can get the information you want about
how eBay works and what it offers its members. Find out
how to become a registered user, maneuver the eBay
Home page, and customize your own private My eBay
page. You can also find out about the all-important
Feedback profile that follows every eBay user around like
a shadow.

Chapter 1

Why eBay Is Better Than Your Local Antique Shop

· ·

In This Chapter

▶ Finding out about eBay

▶ Getting the scoop on types of auctions

▶ Using features and fun stuff

▶ Getting the scoop on digital cameras and scanners

· ·

*T*ake a look around your house. Nice toaster. Great-looking TV. Spiffy microwave. Not to mention all the other cool stuff you own. The fact of the matter is, all these household appliances and collectibles are fabulous to own, but when was the last time your toaster actually turned a profit? When you connect to eBay, your PC or Mac magically turns into a money machine. Just plug in to eBay and marvel at all the collectibles that are just a few mouse clicks away from being bought and sold.

In this chapter, we tell you what eBay is and how it works. eBay is the perfect alternative to spending hours wandering through antique shops or swap meets looking for the perfect doodad. Not only can you buy and sell stuff in the privacy of your own home, but you can also meet people who share the interests that you enjoy. The folks who use the eBay site are a friendly bunch, and soon you'll be buying, selling, swapping stories, and trading advice with the best of them.

Before you can get to eBay, you need to access the Internet. To access the Internet, you need a computer — either a Personal Computer (PC) or Macintosh (Mac) — with a modem, or you can get WebTV. We know where to find new and used computers, and we give you pointers on how to set up a system on the cheap in Appendix A. If you're not quite ready to take the high-tech plunge, we can show you exactly how to start operating at eBay (and earning money) without owning a single cyber thing.

What Is eBay and How Does It Work?

The Internet is spawning all kinds of new businesses (known as *e-commerce* to Wall Street types), and eBay is one of its few superstars. The reason is simple: It's the place where buyers and sellers can meet, do business, share stories and tips, and have fun. It's like one giant online party — and instead of bringing a dish, you sell it!

eBay *doesn't* sell a thing. Instead, the site simply does what all good hosts do: eBay creates a comfy environment that brings people with common interests together. You can think of eBay like you think of the person who set you up on your last blind date — except the results are often a lot better. Your match-making friend doesn't perform a marriage ceremony but does get you in the same room with your potential soul mate. eBay puts buyers and sellers in a virtual room and lets them conduct their business safely within the rules that eBay has established.

All you need to do to join eBay is fill out a few forms online and click. Congratulations. You're a member with no big fees or secret handshakes. After you register, you can buy and sell anything that falls within the eBay rules and regulations. (Chapter 2 eases you through the registration process.)

The eBay Home page, shown in Figure 1-1, is your first step to finding all the cool stuff you can see and do at eBay. You can conduct searches, find out what's happening, and get an instant link to the My eBay page, which helps you keep track of every auction item you have up for sale or have a bid on. You can read more about the eBay Home page in Chapter 3 and find out more about My eBay in Chapter 4.

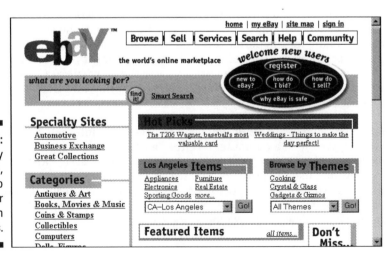

Figure 1-1: The eBay Home page, ground zero for all your auction needs.

eBay's humble beginnings

It all started with a Pez. You know, those little plastic dispensers with funny heads that flip up and present you with a rectangular piece of candy. To help out his girlfriend (who is an avid Pez collector), a Silicon Valley software engineer named Pierre Omidyar created a Web site (the original site was called Auction Web) so she could chat and trade with other Pez-collecting people online. The site was so successful that he expanded it to include other kinds of collectibles. He began charging a small fee to list items, just so he could break even. Legend has it that one day $10,000 in fees arrived in Pierre's mailbox. He quit his day job.

eBay was born on Labor Day 1995. The name *eBay* is taken from *electronic* and *bay* for the Bay Area of San Francisco, where Pierre is from. (We're glad to see *that* bit of trivia has already turned up on *Jeopardy!*)

All About Auctions

The value of an item is determined by how much someone's willing to spend to have it. That's what makes auctions exciting. eBay offers several different kinds of auctions, but for the most part, they all work the same way. An *auction* is a unique sales event where the exact value of the item for sale is not known. As a result, there's an element of surprise involved — not only for the bidder (who may end up with a great deal) but also for the seller (who may end up making a killing). A seller pays a fee, fills out an electronic form and sets the auction up, listing a *minimum bid* he or she is willing to accept for the item. Think of an auctioneer at Christie's saying, "The bidding for this diamond necklace begins at $5,000." You could bid $4,000, but it wouldn't do you any good. Sellers can also set a *reserve price* — sort of a financial safety net that protects them from losing money on the deal. We explain how this stuff all works later in this chapter.

Bidders duke it out over a period of time (sometimes three days but usually a week or even longer) until one comes out victorious. Usually, the highest bidder wins. The tricky thing about participating in an auction (and the most exciting aspect) is that no one knows the final price an item goes for until the last second of the auction.

Traditional auctions

Ever heard those motor-mouthed auctioneers who continue to raise the price of an item until they finally say, "Going once, going twice, sold!"? They're conducting *traditional* auctions, and the majority of items sold at eBay are sold this way. The beauty of eBay is that you don't have to sweat out translating what these auctioneers are saying. Everything is done very quietly. Traditional auctions are simple: The seller pays a fee and lists the item; the highest bidder takes home the prize.

Reserve-price auctions

Unlike a minimum bid, which is required in any eBay auction, a reserve price protects a seller from having to sell an item for less than the amount they want for it. You may be surprised to see a 1968 Jaguar XKE sports car up for auction at eBay with a minimum bid of only a buck, but believe us, Mr. Jag has put a reserve price on this car to protect himself from losing money. The reserve price allows sellers to set lower minimum bids, and lower minimum bids attract bidders. Unfortunately, if a seller makes the reserve price too high and it isn't met by the end of the auction, no one wins.

eBay charges a fee for sellers to run these auctions. Nobody knows (except the seller and the eBay computer system) what the reserve price is until the auction is over, but you can tell from the auction page whether you're dealing with a reserve-price auction. If bids have been made on an item, a message also appears on the page saying whether the reserve price has been met. You can find out more about bidding on reserve-price auctions in Chapter 6 and setting up a reserve-price auction in Chapter 9.

Restricted-access auctions

If you're over 18 years of age and interested in bidding on items of an adult nature, eBay has an Adults Only category, which has restricted access. Although you can peruse the other eBay categories without having to submit credit card information, you must have a credit card number on file at eBay to view and bid on items in this category. Restricted-access auctions are run the same as every other eBay auction. To bid on adult items, you first need to complete an authorization page using your User ID and password; the page pops up automatically when you attempt to access these kinds of items.

If you aren't interested in seeing or bidding on items of an adult nature, or if you're worried that your children may be able to gain access to graphic adult material, eBay's solved that problem by excluding adult-content items from easily accessible areas like the New Items and (ahem) Hot Items pages. Besides, children under the age of 18 aren't allowed to register at eBay and should be under an adult's supervision if they do wander onto the site.

Charity auctions: All for a good cause

A *charity auction* is a high-profile fund-raising auction where the proceeds go to a selected charity. Most people don't wake up in the morning wanting to own the shoes that Ron Howard wore when he put his footprints in cement at Mann's Chinese Theater in Hollywood, but one-of-a-kind items like that are often auctioned off in charity auctions. (In fact, someone did want those shoes badly enough to buy them for a lot of money at eBay.) Charity auctions became popular after the NBC *Today Show* sold an autographed jacket at eBay for over $11,000 with the proceeds going to Toys for Tots. Charity auctions are run like most other auctions at eBay, but because they're immensely popular, bidding can be fierce and the dollar amounts can go sky-high. Ron Howard, Rosie O'Donnell, and other celebrities often use eBay to help out their favorite charities. We suggest that you visit these auctions and bid whenever you can. Charity auctions are a win-win situation for everyone. You can read more about celebrity auctions in Chapter 17.

Private (mind-your-own-business) auctions

Some sellers choose to hold a private auction because they know that some bidders may be embarrassed to be seen bidding on a box of racy neckties in front of the rest of the eBay community. Others may go the private route because they are selling big-ticket items and don't want to disclose their financial status.

Private auctions are run like traditional auctions except that each bidder's identity is kept secret. At the end of the auction, eBay provides contact info to the seller and to the high bidder, and that's it.

You can send e-mail questions to the seller in a private auction, but you can't check out your competition because the auction item page shows the current bid price but not the high bidder's User ID.

Dutch auctions

Dutch auctions have nothing to do with windmills, wooden shoes, or sharing the check on a date. A *Dutch auction* allows a seller to put multiple, identical items up for sale (see Figure 1-2). Instead of holding 100 separate auctions for 100 pairs of wooden shoes, for example, a seller can sell them all together. As a buyer, you *could* elect to bid for 1, 3, or all 100 pairs. But unless you're running an alternative boutique (or know a giant centipede who needs all those clogs), you probably want to bid on just one pair. For more on Dutch auctions, see Chapter 6.

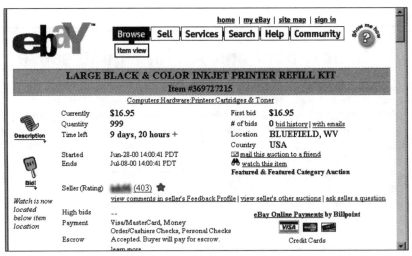

Figure 1-2:
An eBay
Dutch
Auction: If
you need
999 inkjet
refill sets,
you can buy
'em all. If
not, just type
in your bid
for 1 or 2.

A Dutch auction can't be conducted as a private auction.

So You Wanna Sell Stuff

If you're a seller, creating an auction page at eBay is as simple as filling out an online form. You type in the name of your item, a short description, add a picture if you want to, set your price, and voilà — it's auction time. eBay charges a small fee ($.25 to $2.00) for the privilege. When you list your item, millions of people from all over the world can take a gander at it and place bids. All you do is sit back and watch the bids come in. With a little luck, a bidding war can break out and drive the bids up high enough for you to turn a nice profit. After the auction, you deal directly with the buyer, who sends you the payment. Then you ship the item. Go out and meet your friendly mail carrier, courteously accept your payment, and grin wildly all the way to the bank. Abracadabra — you just turned everyday clutter into cash! And if you want to, you can run as many auctions as you want, all at the same time. To get info on deciding what to sell, leaf through Chapter 9; to find out how to set up an auction, jump to Chapter 10; and to get the scoop on advanced selling, visit Chapter 13.

So You Wanna Buy Stuff

If you're a collector or you just like to shop for bargains, you can browse 24 hours a day through the items up for auction in eBay's thousands of categories, which range from Antiques to Writing Instruments. Find the item you want, do a little research on what you're buying and who's selling it, place your bid, and keep an eye on it until the auction closes.

Take a look at Chapter 5 for info on searching for items to bid on. When you see an item you like, you can set up a bidding strategy and let the games begin. Chapter 6 gives you bidding strategies that can make you the winner. When you win the auction, you can get expert advice about completing the transaction from Chapter 7. You can bid as many times as you want on an item, and you can bid on as many auctions as you want.

Research for Fun and Profit

eBay's awesome search engine allows you to browse through countless *categories* of items up for sale. As a buyer, you can do some comparison shopping on that special something you just can't live without or just browse around until something catches your eye. If you're a seller, the search engine allows you to keep your eye on your competition and get an idea of how hot your item is. That way, you can set a competitive price. To find out more about using search options and categories, check out Chapters 3 and 5.

The search engine even lets you find out what other people are bidding on. From there, you can read up on their *feedback rating* (eBay's ingenious honor system) to get a sense of how good their reputations are — even before you deal with them.

eBay's Role in the Auction Action

Throughout the entire auction process, eBay's computers keep tabs on what's going on. When the auction is over, eBay takes a small cut of the final selling price and instructs the seller and buyer to contact each other through e-mail. At this point, eBay's job is pretty much over, and eBay steps aside.

Most of the time, everything works great, everybody's happy, and eBay never has to step back into the picture. But if you happen to run into trouble in paradise, eBay can help you settle the problem, whether you're the buyer or the seller.

eBay also regulates members with a detailed system of checks and balances known as *feedback,* which we talk about in Chapter 4. The grand plan is that the community polices itself. Don't get us wrong — eBay does jump in when sketchy activity comes to light. But the people who keep eBay most safe are the buyers and sellers who have a common stake in conducting business honestly and fairly. Every time you sell something or win an auction, eBay members have a chance to leave a comment about you. You should do the same for them. If they're happy, the feedback is positive; otherwise, the feedback is negative. Either way, feedback sticks to you like glue.

Building a great reputation with positive feedback ensures a long and profitable eBay career. Negative feedback, like multiple convictions for grand theft auto, is a real turnoff to most folks and can make it hard to do future business at eBay.

If your feedback rating becomes a −4, eBay can suspend your buying and selling privileges. You can find out more about how eBay protects you as a buyer or a seller in Chapters 15 and 16.

Features and Fun Stuff

So eBay is all about making money, right? Not exactly. The folks at eBay aren't kidding when they call it a community — a place where people with similar interests can compare notes, argue, buy and sell, and meet each other. Yes, people have gotten married after meeting at eBay. (Take a guess how friends bought them wedding gifts!)

Chatting it up

eBay has over four dozen specific chat boards whose topics range from advertising to trading cards. So if you have no idea what that old Mobil gas station sign you found in your grandfather's barn is worth, just post a message on the Advertising chat board. Somewhere out there is an expert with an answer for you. Your biggest problem is deciding whether to keep the sign or put it up for auction. Those are good problems to have!

One of our favorite chat rooms is eBay's Wanted board. If there's an item you want out there somewhere, someone at eBay knows how to find it. For more about posting messages and chat rooms, visit Chapters 5 and 16.

Rules & Safety (SafeHarbor)

Rules & Safety (SafeHarbor) is sort of the catch-all resource for information and services about making deals at eBay safer — and for what to do if deals go sour. We don't like to think about it, but sometimes — despite your best efforts to be a good eBay user — you find that buyers or sellers don't keep their word. In a small percentage of cases, unscrupulous louts sometimes do invade the site and try to pull scams, and you may buy an item that isn't as it was described, or the winner of your auction doesn't send the payment.

Sometimes even honest members get into disputes. Rules & Safety is an excellent resource when you need questions answered or you need a professional to come in and handle an out-of-hand situation. Chapter 15 tells you all about Rules & Safety.

Extra Gizmos You're Gonna Want

At some point in your eBay career, you're going to become comfortable with all the computer-related hoops you've got to jump through in order to make the eBay magic happen. At that time, you may be ready to invest in a few extra devices that can make your eBay experiences even better. Digital cameras and scanners can help make your time at eBay a more lucrative and fun adventure. (We explain how to use digital technology in your auctions in more detail in Chapter 13.)

Chapter 2

The Bucks Start Here: Signing Up at eBay

In This Chapter

▶ Using eBay's easy forms (the shape of things to come)
▶ Getting up close and personal about privacy
▶ Identifying with User IDs and passwords
▶ Learning the ropes (eBay rules and regs)

*Y*ou've probably figured out that you sign on to eBay electronically, which means you don't *really* sign on the proverbial dotted line as folks did in days of old before computers ran the world. Nowadays, the art of scribbling your signature has become as outdated as 8-track tapes (although you *can* still get 8-track tapes at eBay if you're feeling nostalgic).

Compared to finding a prime parking space at the mall in a snowstorm, signing up at eBay is a breeze. About the toughest thing you have to do is type in your e-mail address correctly.

In this chapter, you find out everything you need to know about registering at eBay. We give you tips on what information you have to disclose and what you should keep to yourself. Don't worry — this is an open-book test. You won't need to memorize state capitals or multiplication tables.

Sign In, Please — Register at eBay

No, you don't have to wear one of those tacky "Hello, My Name Is" stickers on your shirt after you sign in, but eBay needs to know some things about you before it grants you your membership. You and several other folks will be roaming around eBay's online treasure trove (or garage sale, depending on where you wind up); eBay needs to know who's who. So, keeping that in mind, sign in, please!

eBay internationale!

eBay now has Web sites in the United States, the United Kingdom, Canada, Germany, Australia, and Japan. The vast majority of eBay users are from the United States, but the international membership is growing daily. At eBay's registration page, you can see a list that has more countries on it than the United Nations. Really. eBay lists 226 nations and territories, but the United Nations has only 185 member countries. You find in the list a "Where's Where" of the world, including countries from Australia to Zimbabwe. You can even register from Jan Mayen, a Norwegian island in the Arctic Ocean. That would be a feat, because Jan Mayen is an uninhabited meteorological station. (Maybe this is where retired weathermen should go to hide out after years of wrong predictions. . . .)

You don't have to be a rocket scientist to register at eBay, but you can *buy* a model rocket or something bigger after you do. The only hard-and-fast rule at eBay is that you have to be 18 years of age or older. Don't worry, the Age Police won't come to your house to card you; they have other ways to discreetly ensure that you're at least 18 years old. (**Hint:** Credit cards do more than satisfy account charges.) If you're having a momentary brain cramp and you've forgotten your age, just think back to the *Brady Bunch* TV show. If you can remember watching the original episodes of that favorite show of the 1970s, you're in. Head to the eBay Home page and register. The entire process takes only a few minutes.

Registering Is Free and Fun (And Fast)

Before you can sign up at eBay, you have to be connected to the Web. If you're confused about what particular computer hardware, software, and Internet services you need, Appendix A can come to your rescue. If you're already connected, you're ready to sign up.

Just type **www.ebay.com** in your browser and press Enter. Your next stop is the eBay Home page. Right there, where you can't miss it, is the Registration link shown in Figure 2-1. Click it and let the sign-up begin. You can also get to the Registration form by clicking eBay's Welcome Mat links. Check Chapter 3 for details.

This part of eBay is like window-shopping: It's free until you buy something.

Figure 2-1:
Click on this
link to
register —
it's free!

So, what's your sign? Putting down general information

The Register button links you to the first of the eBay Registration pages. Follow these steps to complete the first page:

1. **Scroll down the list and choose the country you happen to be in today.**

   You have many nations to choose from; we highly recommend your homeland (it *does* have to be on this planet; Klingons are out of luck).

2. **Make sure the box that says SSL has a check mark in it.**

   SSL (Secure Sockets Layer) enables you to have a secure (encrypted) connection to eBay because a bunch of really smart techie types made it that way. We could tell you how SSL works, but instead we'll just give you the bottom line: It *does* work, so trust us and use it. The more pre- cautions you take, the harder it is for some mega-caffeinated high-school kid to get into your files.

3. **Click the button that says Continue.**

   Now you're transported through a series of registration pages. Figure 2-2 shows you the first registration page.

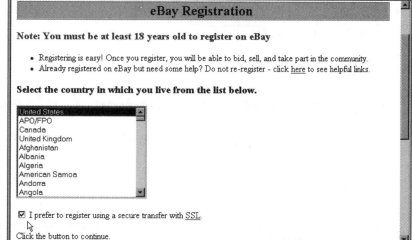

Figure 2-2:
The first
eBay
registration
page.

Can I get your digits? Filling in required information

At the top of the next page, eBay briefly outlines the registration process for you and asks you to fill out some required (and not-so-required) information (see Figure 2-3). Here's what eBay wants to know about you:

- Your e-mail address (yourname@bogusISP.com).

- Your full name, address, and primary telephone number. All this information is kept by eBay in case the company needs to contact you.

- How you first heard about eBay.

- Your *promotional priority code,* if any. If you don't have a promotional priority code, leave this area blank.

- You can also include, if you want, a secondary phone number and a fax number.

---

eBay Registration

Welcome! Let's begin.

- Please enter your required contact information below

Note: You must be at least 18 years old to register on eBay.

	Enter your contact information	
Email address	ebaydummies@collierad.com (required) Note: Enter your valid email address - including your "@serviceprovider.com" domain. For example, if your AOL screen name is joe cool, your email address is joecool@aol.com	
Full name e.g., John H. Doe	Marsha Collier (required) First M. Last	
Company	(optional)	
Address	1234 Anywhere Street (required)	
City	Los Angeles (required)	

Figure 2-3: Some of the required information on the eBay registration form.

Getting to know you: Optional information

Some optional questions allow you to fill in your self-portrait a bit for your new pals at eBay.

Although eBay doesn't share member information with anyone, you don't have to answer the optional questions if you don't want to.

The following list shows you the optional questions eBay asks. You decide what you feel comfortable divulging and what you want to keep personal.

eBay asks for this information because the company wants a better picture of who is actually using the Web site. In marketing mumbo-jumbo, this stuff's called *demographics* — statistics that characterize a group of people who make up a community. In this case, it's the eBay community.

 Hey, AOL users, this one's for you: Make sure that your Mail Controls are set to receive e-mails from eBay. If you have Internet e-mail blocked, you need to update your AOL Mail Controls. To do so, enter the AOL keyword Mail Controls.

Here is the optional information eBay asks for — and some tips on how to respond to it:

- ✔ **If a friend referred you to eBay, please enter your friend's e-mail address.** Although eBay may not be offering any freebies for referrals at the moment, it may someday — and your buddy will be the lucky beneficiary of such goodwill.

- ✔ **Do you use eBay for personal or business purposes?** Sometimes this question isn't easy to answer. If you're registering for fun but think you could turn buying and selling into a business, you may not be sure. It's okay to skip this one.

- ✔ **I am most interested in.** This is a good question to answer. eBay has the software to keep track of categories of items that you're interested in, so it doesn't hurt to let eBay know for its future planning.

- ✔ **Age.** If you feel comfortable letting your age float out into cyberspace where it's visible, go ahead and tell 'em; otherwise, you can skip this one.

- ✔ **Education: Select an education.** You get the usual choices: high school, college, graduate school, and other. (Hmm, does Starfleet Academy count as *other*?)

- ✔ **Annual household income.** Fill it in *if* you want to (eBay states that this info is kept anonymous), but we think this information is too personal; if you're not comfortable with it, skip it.

- ✔ **Gender.** This is our favorite question because if you don't fill it out, it defaults to *unspecified* (which is great if you're an amoeba).

Check your work and confirm registration

Think back to your second-grade teacher, who kept saying, "Class, check your work." Remember that? She's still right! Review your answers. If everything is accurate, then click once on the Continue button at the bottom of the page. If you've made a mistake, fix it using the Edit Information button.

Don't tell anyone, but your info is safe at eBay

eBay keeps most personal information secret. The basics (your name, phone number, city, and state) go out only to answer the specific request of another registered eBay user, law enforcement, or members of Verified Rights Owners (eBay's copyright-watchdog program). Other users may need your basic access info for several reasons — a seller may want to verify your location, get your phone number to call you regarding your auction, or double-check who you really are. If somebody does request your info, you get an e-mail from eBay giving you the name, phone number, city, and state of the person making the request.

If eBay finds a glitch in your registration, like an incorrect area or zip code, you're warned with a message (see Figure 2-4). This is part of eBay's security system to ward off fraudulent registrations. Use the Back button to correct the information — if you put in a wrong e-mail address, for example, eBay has no way of contacting you. You don't hear a peep from eBay until you go through the whole registration process all over again. If all your information is correct, click Continue.

eBay Registration

Review and confirm your contact information

- To make a correction, click the Edit button to go back and edit your information
- If all the information is accurate, click the Continue button

Email address	ebaydummies@collierad.com	to be verified via email
Full name	Marsha Collier	OK
Address	1234 Anywhere Street	OK
City	Los Angeles	OK
State	CA	OK
Zip Code	91325	OK
Country	United States	OK
Primary phone #	(818) 555 - 1212	Invalid

There are problems with the information you submitted.

Figure 2-4:
If you've input invalid data, eBay will find it.

Do you solemnly swear to . . . ?

After you click the Continue button, you're taken to the eBay User Agreement page. At this page, you take an oath to keep eBay safe for democracy and commerce. You promise to play well with others, not to cheat, and to follow the golden rule. No, you're not auditioning for a superhero club, but don't ever forget that eBay takes this stuff very seriously. You can be kicked off eBay or worse. (Can you say "Federal investigation"?)

Be sure to read the User Agreement thoroughly when you register. So that you don't have to put down this riveting book to read the legalese right this minute, we provide the nuts and bolts here:

- ✔ You understand that every transaction is a legally binding contract. (Click the User Agreement link at the bottom of the Home page or in the Help section under Community Standards for the current eBay Rules and Regulations.)
- ✔ You state that you can pay for the items you buy and the eBay fees that you incur. (Chapter 8 fills you in on how eBay takes its cut of the auction action.)
- ✔ You understand that you're responsible for paying any taxes.
- ✔ You understand that if you sell prohibited items, eBay will forward your personal information to law enforcement for further investigation. (Chapter 8 explains what you can and can't sell at eBay — and what eBay does to sellers of prohibited items.)
- ✔ eBay makes clear that it is just a *venue,* which means it's a *place* where people with similar interests can meet, greet, and do business.

When everything goes well, the eBay Web site is like a school gym that opens for Saturday swap meets. At the gym, if you don't play by the rules, you can get tossed out. But if you don't play by the rules at eBay, the venue gets un-gymlike in a hurry: eBay has the right to get state and federal officials to track you down and prosecute you. But fair's fair; if you click the appropriate box on this page, eBay will keep you posted by e-mail of any updates in the user agreement.

If you're a stickler for fine print, head to this Internet address for all the *p*s and *q*s of the latest policies:

```
pages.ebay.com/help/community/png-user.html
```

Before you can proceed, you must click the four boxes indicating that you really, really understand what it means to be an eBay user. Because we know that you, as a law-abiding eBay member, will have no problem following the rules, go ahead and click on the I Accept button at the bottom of the page, which takes you to a cheery screen stating that eBay is sending you an e-mail: "Go check your e-mail now. Your eBay confirmation message may have already arrived!"

Normally, it takes eBay less than a minute to e-mail you with a confirmation notice. If you do not receive your eBay registration confirmation e-mail within the next 24 hours, there was most likely an error in your e-mail address. At this point, the customer support folks can help you complete the registration process. Go to

```
pages.ebay.com/help/basics/select-support.html
```

It must be true if you have it in writing

When you receive the eBay registration confirmation e-mail, print it out. What's most important is the confirmation code. If you lose that number, go back to the initial eBay registration page and follow Step 2. You can also click the link in your e-mail to get the confirmation number.

With your confirmation number in hand, head back to the eBay registration page by clicking on the link supplied in your e-mail browser. If your e-mail doesn't support links, go to

```
cgi4.ebay.com/aw-cgi/eBayISAPI.dll?EbayRegisterConfirm
```

Sprint to the finish

On the final registration page, shown in Figure 2-5, follow these steps:

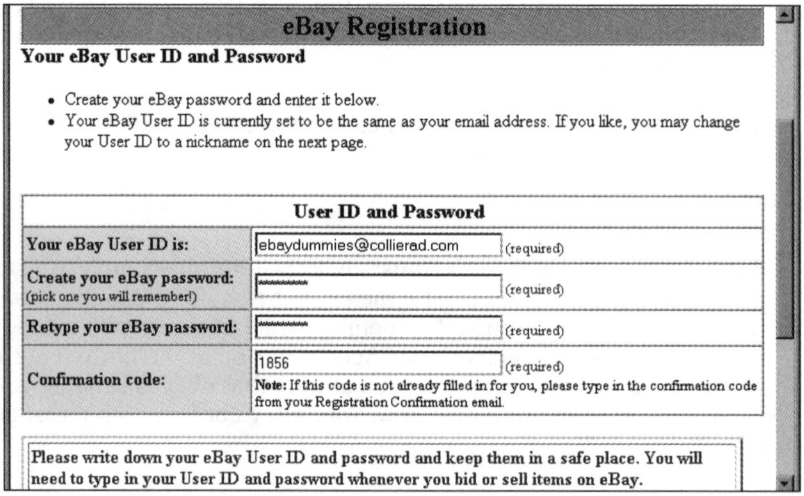

Figure 2-5:
The eBay
Email
Confirmation
page, the
final
registration
page.

eBay Registration
Your eBay User ID and Password
• Create your eBay password and enter it below.
• Your eBay User ID is currently set to be the same as your email address. If you like, you may change your User ID to a nickname on the next page.

User ID and Password		
Your eBay User ID is:	ebaydummies@collierad.com	(required)
Create your eBay password: (pick one you will remember!)	●●●●●●●●	(required)
Retype your eBay password:	●●●●●●●●	(required)
Confirmation code:	1856	(required)
	Note: If this code is not already filled in for you, please type in the confirmation code from your Registration Confirmation email.	

Please write down your eBay User ID and password and keep them in a safe place. You will need to type in your User ID and password whenever you bid or sell items on eBay.

1. **Reenter your e-mail address.**

   If you've used the e-mail link, it will already be there.

2. **Make up a permanent password and reconfirm your password by typing it again.**

   For more information on choosing a password, see the next section, "A Quick Word about Passwords."

3. **Enter the confirmation code eBay sent you and then promptly forget it.**

   Again, if you used the e-mail link, your code will already be inserted.

4. **Click the Continue button to change your e-mail address into a catchy User ID.**

You're all set (see Figure 2-6). And if you think *that* was the fun part, just wait. . . .

A Quick Word about Passwords

Picking a good password is not as easy (but *is* twice as important) as it may seem. Whoever has your password can (in effect) "be you" at eBay — running auctions, bidding on auctions, and leaving dangerous feedback for others. Basically, such an impostor can ruin your eBay career — and possibly cause you serious financial grief.

As with any online password, you should follow these common-sense rules to protect your privacy:

✔ Don't pick anything too obvious, such as your birthday, your first name, or your Social Security number. (***Hint:*** If it's too easy to remember, it's probably too easy to crack.)

✔ Make things tough on the bad guys — combine numbers and letters and create nonsensical words.

✔ Don't give out your password to anyone — it's like giving away the keys to the front door of your house.

✔ If you even suspect someone has your password, immediately change it by going to the following address:

```
pages.ebay.com/services/myebay/selectpass.html
```

✔ Change your password every few months just to be on the safe side.

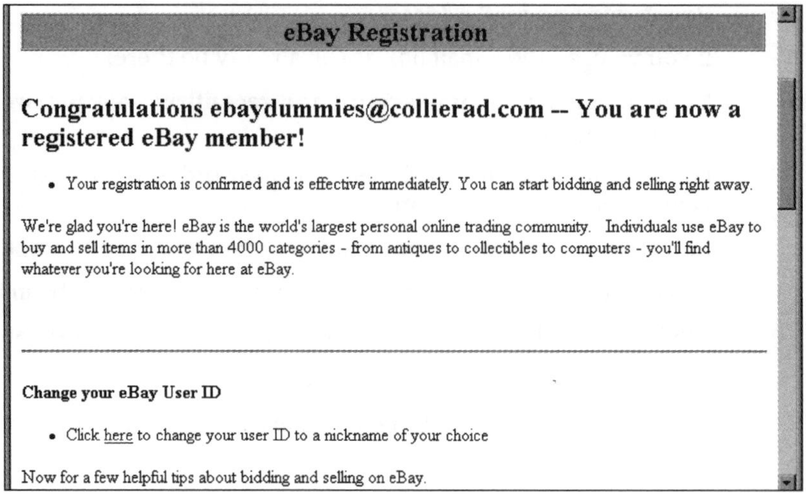

---

eBay Registration

Congratulations ebaydummies@collierad.com -- You are now a registered eBay member!

- Your registration is confirmed and is effective immediately. You can start bidding and selling right away.

We're glad you're here! eBay is the world's largest personal online trading community.   Individuals use eBay to buy and sell items in more than 4000 categories - from antiques to collectibles to computers - you'll find whatever you're looking for here at eBay.

Change your eBay User ID

- Click <u>here</u> to change your user ID to a nickname of your choice

Now for a few helpful tips about bidding and selling on eBay.

Figure 2-6:
You've completed your registration!

A Not-So-Quick Word about Choosing a User ID

eBay gives you the option of picking your User ID. (If you don't choose one, then your e-mail address becomes your default User ID.) Making up a User ID is our favorite part. If you've never liked your real name (or never had a nickname), here's the chance to correct that situation. Have fun. Consider choosing an ID that tells a little about yourself. Of course, if your interests change, you may regret too narrow a User ID.

You can call yourself just about anything; you can be silly or creative or boring. But remember, this ID is how other eBay users will know you. So here are some common-sense rules:

- Don't use a name that would embarrass your mother.
- Don't use a name that's too weird, such as scam-man. If people don't trust you, they won't buy from you.
- Don't use a name with a negative connotation.
- eBay doesn't allow spaces in User IDs, so make sure that the ID makes sense when putting two or more words together.

If you're dying to have several short words as your User ID, you can use *underscores* to separate them, as in tin_sign_king. If you sign in each time you do business on the site, typing those underscores won't slow you down.

The craze that began with AW

Back in 1994, when eBay founder Pierre Omidyar had the idea to start a Web auction, he named his first venture Auction Web. The *aw* occasionally appears in many of eBay's URL addresses and refers to the original name that eventually evolved into eBay.

The following figure shows a vintage AuctionWeb, eBay Internet auction from February 1997. There were some great deals even in those days!

Auction Web

[Menu] [Listings] [Buyers] [Sellers] [Search] [Contact]

ALL YOU NEED IS A CLICK AND A DREAM　TO PLAY GET RICH CLICK　CLICK HERE

Member of the Internet Link Exchange

Janet Reno, hand written note (pic) (item #fex4355)

Bidding is closed for this item.

Bidding history page | Other auctions by this seller | Ask the seller a question

Seller assumes all responsibility for listing this item. You should contact the seller to resolve any questions before bidding. Currency is U.S. dollars (US$) unless otherwise noted.

Current bid for this item:	**$10.00**
Quantity:	**1**
Date auction ends:	**02/05/97, 21:46:50 PST**
Date auction started:	**01/22/97, 21:46:50 PST**
Seller:	(60) ☆ (registered user)
First bid at:	**$5.00**
Number of bids made:	**7**
Current high-bidder:	**marshac@** (2) (registered user)
Item number:	**fex4355**
Location of item:	**Texas**
Category:	Autographs

Description:

View at *** This 4x6 embossed note card with Department of Justice gold imprint contains a hand-written account of the Attorney General's childhood aspirations. This is a very classy collectible, dated June 1, 1993, mounted on 8.5x11 parchament type paper. *** Buyer pays $2 shipping *** Please see the autograph offerings at under the heading Corry's Coins and Collectibles *** Happy bidding, and have a grea 1997!

Bidding is closed for this item.

[Menu] [Listings] [Buyers] [Sellers] [Search] [Contact]

eBay Internet

You can change your User ID (once every 30 days) if you want to, but we don't recommend it. People will come to know you by your User ID. If you change your ID, your past does play tagalong and attaches itself to the new ID. But, if you change your User ID too many times, people may think you're trying to hide something or you're in the Witness Protection Program.

To change your User ID, click on the My eBay link at the top of most eBay pages. From the My eBay login page, click the Change My User ID link, fill out the boxes, and click the Change User ID button. You now have a new eBay identity.

eBay also has some User ID rules to live by:

- No offensive names (like &*#@guy).
- No names with *eBay* in them. (It makes you look like you work for eBay, and eBay takes a dim view of that.)
- No names with & (even if you *do* have both looks&brains).
- No names with @ (like @Aboy).
- No case-sensitive names (like SuZiEq).
- No names of one letter (like Q).

When you pick your User ID, make sure that it isn't a good clue for your password. If you use *Natasha* as your User ID, don't pick *Boris* as your password. Even Bullwinkle could figure that one out.

Your License to Deal (Almost)

After you click the Complete Your Registration button, you get a big ol' `Welcome to eBay`. You are now officially a *newbie,* or eBay rookie. The only problem is that you're still at the window-shopping level. If you're ready to go from window shopper to item seller, just zip through a few more forms and before you know it, you can start running your own auctions at eBay.

Until you have been a member of eBay for 30 days, a picture of a pair of sunglasses is next to your User ID wherever it appears on the site. The sunglasses indicate to other eBay users that your User ID is new to eBay.

Chapter 3

There's No Place Like the Home Page

In This Chapter

▶ Getting the lay of the land

▶ Using the eBay Home page's links and icons

▶ Getting the first word on searches

▶ Checking out featured auctions and other fun stuff

*T*he writer Thomas Wolfe was wrong: You *can* go home again — and again. At least at eBay you can! Month after month, millions of people land at eBay's Home page without wearing out the welcome mat. The eBay Home page is the front door to the most popular auction site on the Internet.

Everything you need to know about navigating eBay begins right here. In this chapter, we take the grand tour through the areas you can reach right from the Home page with the help of links.

What Is the Home Page?

The eBay Home page is shown in Figure 3-1 and includes the following key areas:

✔ A navigation bar at the very top with six eBay links that can zip you straight to any of the many eBay areas, as well as four additional — and powerful — links right above the navigation bar

✔ A Search window that — like the Search link in the menu bar — helps you find the items or information that you want

✔ Five destination links (under Welcome new users) that tell you a little more about eBay, get you started on selling or buying items, and get you registered at eBay

✔ A list of links to auction categories

✔ Links to featured auctions, Hot Picks, Local Trading, browsing by themes, fun stuff like charity auctions, and information about what else is happening at eBay

Figure 3-1: The eBay Home page.

Do not adjust your computer monitor. You're not going crazy. You may notice that a link was on the eBay Home page yesterday and is gone the next day. The links on the eBay Home page change often to reflect what's going on — not just on the site but in the world.

Sign In, Please!

Sign In is possibly the most powerful of all the links on the eBay pages, and it should be your first stop if you plan on doing any business at eBay (see Figure 3-2).

By going to the Sign In page and signing in, you don't have to enter your user name when you bid or post items for sale. The Sign In page also takes you to a link that allows you to change your sign in or My eBay preferences. (See Chapter 4 for info on My eBay.) sign in places a temporary *cookie* (a techno-related thingy — see Chapter 14) on your computer that remains a part of your browser as long as you remain on the site. If there's no activity for 40 minutes — or if you close your browser — the cookie expires.

eBaY™

home | my eBay | site map | sign in

| Browse | Sell | Services | Search | Help | Community |

Welcome to eBay! Please sign in.

eBay members, sign in to save time for bidding, selling, and other activities. If you're not an eBay member yet, click here to register - it's free and fast.

Your User ID: [   ]
You can also use your email address.

Your Password: [   ]
Forgot your password?

Click here to sign in using SSL.

Note: By signing in, you'll get a temporary "cookie" which will (1) remember your User ID while your browser is open and (2) allow you to select for which activities you want your password remembered. If there is no activity for 40 minutes or you close your browser, then the cookie will expire. For more information about cookies, click here.

Figure 3-2:
The eBay
Sign In
page.

Here's how to get to the eBay Sign In page and, well, sign in:

1. **Click the Sign In link at the upper right of any eBay page.**

2. **Type in your User ID and password.**

3. **Be sure to sign in with the option to use SSL.**

   Using SSL keeps your personal information even more secure than usual (see Chapter 2 for details about SSL).

4. **Click the Sign In box.**

   You're now signed in to eBay and can travel the site with ease. You may now click the My eBay link that appears in the upper right-hand corner to enter your My eBay page. (See Chapter 4 for more on My eBay.) You may also click the link in the center of the page to change your sign in or display preferences.

This Bar Never Closes

The *navigation bar* is at the top of the eBay Home page and lists six eBay links that take you directly to any of the different eBay areas. Using the navigation bar is kind of like doing one-stop clicking. You can find this bar at the top of every page you travel to at eBay. When you click one of the six links, you get a subnavigation bar under it with specific links to other important places.

Think of links as expressways to specific destinations. Click a link just once and the next thing you know, you're right where you want to be. You don't even have to answer that annoying old question *When are we gonna get there?* from the kids in the backseat.

Here, without further ado, are the six navigation bar links and where they take you:

- ✔ **Browse:** Takes you to the page that lists Featured auctions (see Chapter 6), Hot auctions (items that have received more than 30 bids — see Chapter 9), Grab Bag auctions (30 random items chosen from the Gallery), Big Ticket auctions (with bids over $5,000), and all the main categories at eBay (discussed in this chapter). You also find Cool Features — eBay promotions that vary from time to time. From this page, you can link to any one of the millions of items up for auction at eBay.

  Under the Browse tab, you'll find links to browse by category, geographic regions or themes.

- ✔ **Sell:** Takes you to the Sell Your Item form that you fill out to start your auctions. We explain how to navigate this form in Chapter 9.

- ✔ **Services:** Takes you to the eBay Services Overview page. Here, you can find links to pages that tell you all about buying and selling, registration pages, the Feedback Forum, eBay's Rules & Safety overview (SafeHarbor), the My eBay page, and the About Me page.

- ✔ **Search:** Takes you to the eBay main Smart Search page. Because over four million items are up for auction at any given time, finding just one (say, an antique Vermont milk can) is no easy task. The main Search page includes five specific searches (see "Exploring Your Home Page Search Options" later in this chapter). From the subnavigation bar you can click Find Members to search for other members and get information about their feedback (more on that stuff in Chapter 6). In addition, the subnavigation bar links you to Personal Shopper, eBay's way of helping you find what you're looking for (more about that in Chapter 16).

- ✔ **Help:** Takes you to the eBay Help Overview page, which offers links to buyer-and-seller guides, personal account information, community standards (rules and regulations and prohibited items), and useful information like a glossary. There's even a Search window here for help topics. You also find links for live help to the chat areas and a link to keen.com, where you can talk immediately — for a fee — to any number of eBay sellers on the phone (see Chapter 16 for more details on finding eBay help online).

- ✔ **Community:** Takes you to a huge page where you find links to eBay News and Chat pages, where you can find the latest news and announcements, chat with fellow traders in the eBay community, find charity auctions, read eBay's archived online newsletter, visit the eBay store, and find out more about corporate eBay. Chapters 16 and 17 tell you how to use these resources.

At the top of almost every eBay page, you find four small (but powerful) links that are just as important as the links on the navigation bar:

- ✔ **Home:** Takes you right back the Home page. Use this link from any other page when you need to get back to the Home page right away.

- ✔ **My eBay:** Takes you to the link that can access your personal My eBay page, where you keep track of all your buying and selling activities, account information, and favorite categories (more about My eBay in Chapter 4).

- ✔ **Site Map:** Provides you with a bird's-eye view of the eBay world. Every *top-level* (or main) link available at eBay is listed here. If you're ever confused about finding a specific area, come to the Site Map. If a top-level link isn't listed here, it's not at eBay. Yet.

- ✔ **Sign In:** It's important, and we tell you about it again and again throughout this book.

Exploring Your Home Page Search Options

There's an old Chinese expression that says, "Every journey begins with the first eBay search." Okay, so we updated it a tad. Very wise words nonetheless. You can start a search from the Home page in one of two ways:

- ✔ Use the Search window. It's right there at the top of the Home page, and it's a fast way of finding item listings.

- ✔ Use the Search button on the navigation bar. This button takes you to the main Search page, where you can do all kinds of specialized searches.

Both options give you the same results. The instructions we offer in the next two sections about using these Search methods are just the tip of the eBay iceberg. You can find more in-depth search suggestions in Chapter 5.

Any time you see the words Tips or More Tips, you know you're about to get some useful information. Just click the Tips link at eBay, and you're off to explore eBay's Search Tips page. The Search Tips page offers distilled wisdom on wording your searches so you get optimum results.

Peering through the Home page Search window

To launch a title search right from the Home page, follow these steps:

1. **Type keywords that describe the item you're looking for in the Search window.**

   Refer to Figure 3-1 to see the Search window.

2. **Click the Find It button.**

   The results of your search appear on-screen in a matter of seconds.

You can type just about anything in this box and get some information. Say you're looking for *Star Trek* memorabilia. If so, you're not alone. The television show premiered on September 8, 1966, and even though it was canceled in 1969 because of low ratings, *Star Trek* has become one of the most successful science fiction franchises in history. If you like *Star Trek* as much as we do, you can use the Search window on the eBay Home page to find all sorts of *Star Trek* stuff.

Try the Smart Search link next to the Search box to narrow down your search (see the following section for info on Smart Search).

When you search for popular items at eBay (and a classic example is *Star Trek* memorabilia), you may get inundated with thousands of auctions that match your search criteria. Even if you're traveling at warp speed, you could spend hours checking each auction individually. ("Scotty, we need more power *now!*") If you're pressed for time like the rest of us, eBay has not-so-mysterious ways for you to narrow down your search so that finding a specific item is much more manageable. Turn to Chapter 5 now if you want to get some techniques that can help you slim down those searches and beef up those results.

Going where the Search button takes you

One of the most important buttons on the navigation bar is the Search button. When you click this button, you're whisked away to the main Search page, which promptly presents you with six different search options. Each option enables you to search for information in a different way. Here's how the search options on the menu can work for you:

- **Old Search Method:** Next to the Find Items headline, you see a link that takes you to the old search method. The new Smart Search feature is far more efficient, though, so we recommend that you stay right where you are and use the new, improved Smart Search. Type in the name of an item (for example, **Superman lunchbox** or **antique pocket watch**) and click Search, and you can see how many are available at eBay.

- **Smart Search:** This option is eBay's new search method, and it's really smart: Smart Search enables you to define your search without the use of a bunch of code. It works pretty much the same as the old search method, but you can exclude certain words from your search. You can also take advantage of eBay's regional trading and find items for sale in your neighborhood. Figure 3-3 shows the Smart Search options.

- **By Item Number:** Every item that's up for auction at eBay is assigned an item number, which is displayed under the item name on the auction page. To find an auction by item number, just type the number and click Search, and away you go. To find out more about how individual auction pages work at eBay, spin through Chapter 6.

- **By Seller:** Every person at eBay has a personal User ID (the name you use to conduct transactions). Use a By Seller search if you liked the merchandise from a seller's auction and want to see what else the seller has for sale. Type the seller's User ID or e-mail address, and you get a list of every auction that person is running.

- **By Bidder:** For the sake of practicality and convenience, User IDs help eBay keep track of every move a user makes at eBay. If you want to see what a particular user (say, a fellow *Star Trek* fan) is bidding on, use the By Bidder search. Type in a User ID in the By Bidder search window, and you get a list of everything the user is currently bidding on, as well as how much he or she is bidding. We show you how to use the By Bidder search option as a strategic buying tool in Chapter 6.

- **Completed Items:** To find an item that sold at eBay in the past, use the Completed Items search. Type in the name of an item, and you get a list of items of this type that have been sold in the last 30 days, as well as what they sold for. You can use this type of search to strategize your asking price before you put an item up for auction.

- **International Search:** Here's your chance to locate items from other countries or to find out which auctions are available to your country if you're located outside the United States.

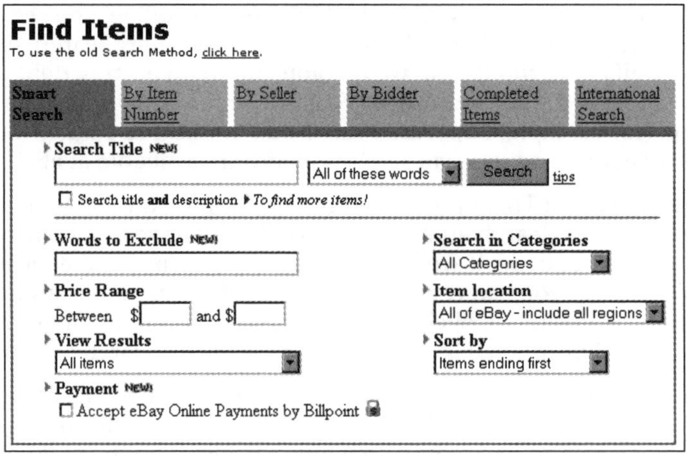

Find Items
To use the old Search Method, click here.
Smart Search
By Item Number
By Seller
By Bidder
Completed Items
International Search
Search Title NEW!
All of these words
Search
tips
Search title and description To find more items!
Words to Exclude NEW!
Search in Categories
All Categories
Price Range
Between $ and $
Item location
All of eBay - include all regions
View Results
All items
Sort by
Items ending first
Payment NEW!
Accept eBay Online Payments by Billpoint

Figure 3-3: The Smart Search section of eBay's Search page.

Using eBay's "Welcome Mat"

eBay welcomes new users to its Home page with a homespun blue welcome mat — reminiscent of your very own welcome mat at the front door of your home. We're talking about the five links on the eBay Home page that are shown in Figure 3-4. A click on one of these links takes you to some of the most important places at eBay. (Of course, if you happen to be looking for a new welcome mat, you've come to the right Web site — generally, you can find around 80 of them up for bid.)

welcome new users
register
new to eBay?
how do I bid?
how do I sell?
why eBay is safe

Figure 3-4: The eBay "welcome mat" Home page links.

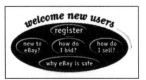

- The **New to eBay?** link takes you to the page that gives you a basic eBay overview and leads to additional links and information. There's also a nifty help window: you type in your questions and click the Find Help button at the bottom of the page, and then faster than the Amazing Kreskin, eBay comes up with helpful answers for you. This help window is also found on the other welcome mat Home page links.
- The **How Do I Bid?** link takes you to a four-point checklist on how to place bids at eBay.

✔ The **How Do I Sell?** link takes you to a three-point selling checklist; in addition, you find a quick link to the Sell Your Item form (which you have to fill out to begin your auctions) and a page itemizing eBay's fees. You also find a very handy link that takes you to a short photo tutorial on how to use pictures in your auction. If you want to jump-start your selling career, go to Chapter 9 and see how to fill out this form. Flip to Chapter 12 for the complete rundown on auction photos.

✔ The **Register** link takes you to the new user registration pages. If you haven't been there yet, turn to Chapter 2 to get the quick and painless facts about the easy eBay registration process.

✔ The **Why eBay Is Safe** link takes you to a page that lists eBay's built-in safeguards. You find a link to the Feedback Forum to familiarize you with the importance of feedback, as well as links to insurance, I-escrow, Rules & Safety, and the Square Trade resolution service. Visit Chapter 15 for in-depth descriptions of your safety nets at eBay.

Home Links, the Next Generation

If you look carefully, you can see several other links on the Home page, and they give you express service to several key parts of the site. Here are the highlights:

✔ **Specialty Sites:** Here's where clicking a link gets you to eBay's new specialty sites. A click on Automotive brings you to ebaymotors.com, a new area dedicated to the sale of almost everything with a motor and wheels. Business Exchange takes you to an area with business-related items, and Great Collections takes you to incredible fine art auctions. Chapter 17 is the place to go for more info on these sites.

✔ **Regional Items**: Click the down arrow to be swept to the local trading area of your choice. eBay has divvied up close to 60 United States regions into mini-eBays. Although these items are found at regular eBay, you can find items that would cost too much to ship from a distance. You can also narrow your search down to items near you. Just select the closest major metropolitan area to your home and click Go.

✔ **Browse by Themes:** This is a new way to find your favorite interests at eBay. It's taken over 50 themes — from Animation to Weddings — and put the appropriate auctions into groups based on your interests. (You can find out more about eBay's new areas in Chapter 17.)

✔ **Hot Picks:** Selected themes that tie in with current trends and seasons.

✔ **Featured Auctions:** Visit the featured auctions. (Translation: sellers paid more to have them featured in this section and on the top of each category.)

✔ **Don't Miss:** This link takes you to the many charity auctions that benefit worthwhile organizations.

✔ **Spotlight's On:** This link takes you to special promotions and happenings at eBay.

✔ **Global Sites:** Links to eBay's international auction sites.

You may notice that the links in Don't Miss and Spotlight's On change from day to day — even hour to hour. If you are interested in this area, click the More link to see the entire array of special happenings at eBay.

Maneuvering through Categories

So how does eBay keep track of the millions of items that are up for auction at any given moment? The brilliant minds at eBay decided to group items into a nice, neat little storage system called categories. The Home page lists around a dozen categories at any given time, but currently eBay lists thousands of categories, ranging from Antiques to Writing Instruments. And don't ask how many subcategories (categories within categories) eBay's got — we can't count that high.

Well, okay, we *could* list all the categories and subcategories currently available at eBay — if you wouldn't mind squinting at a dozen pages of really small, eye-burning text. But a category browse is an adventure that's unique for each individual, and we wouldn't think of depriving you of it. Suffice it to say that if you like to hunt around for that perfect something, you're in browsing heaven now.

Here's how to navigate around the categories:

1. **Click the category that interests you, such as Books, Movies & Music.**

   You're transported to the category's page. You see categories and sub-categories listed next to each heading. Happy hunting.

If you don't find a category that interests you among the dozen on the Home page, simply click the All Categories link and you're off to the main categories page. Not only do you get a pretty impressive page of main categories, but you also get a list of featured auctions. If you're ready to get really serious, click the Category Overview link to see *every* category and subcategory available at eBay — on a page loaded with small type like an eye chart's last lines. We recommend reading it with both eyes open.

2. **After the category page appears, find a subcategory that interests you and keep digging until you find what you want.**

   For example, if you're looking for items honoring your favorite television show, click the Books, Movies, Music category. The page that comes up includes subcategories of Books, Magazines, Memorabilia, Movies, Music, and Musical Instruments. Click the Memorabilia category, and it takes you to a page with many links, including the Television subcategory. If you click Television, you're off to the Books, Movies, Music: Memorabilia: Television page. There, you find featured auctions at the top of the page and all the current TV auctions under them. Little *icons* (pictures) next to the listings tell you more about each item — whether it's pictured (the camera), it's a hot item (the flaming match), it's a new item (the sunrise), or it shows up in eBay's Gallery (the picture frame).

   By the way, we have lots more to say about featured auctions and hot items in Chapter 10.

3. **When you find an item that interests you, click the item and the full Auction page pops up on your screen.**

   Congratulations — you've just navigated through several million items to find that *one* TV-collectible item that caught your attention. You can instantly return to the Home page by clicking its link at the top of the page (or return to the Listings page by repeatedly clicking the Back button at the top of your browser).

Near the bottom of every subcategory page you can see the line `For more items in this category, click these pages.` The page numbers can fast-forward you through all the items in that subcategory. So, if you feel like browsing around page 120 without going through 120 pages individually, just click number 120; you're presented with the items on that page (their listings, actually). Happy viewing.

If you're a bargain hunter by habit, you may find some pretty weird stuff while browsing the categories and subcategories of items at eBay — some of it super-cheap and some of it (maybe) just cheap. Remember that (as with any marketplace) you're responsible for finding out as much as possible about an item before you buy — and definitely before you bid. So, if you're the type who sometimes can't resist a good deal, ask yourself what you plan to *do* with the pile of garbage you can get for 15 cents — and ask yourself *now*, before it arrives on your doorstep. Chapters 6 and 7 offer more information on bidding with savvy.

Excuse me, do you have any Don Ho cocktail glasses?

As a matter of fact, yes! eBay adds new categories all the time to meet the needs of its users. For example, some specialized categories have popped up — with some interesting items:

- **Cultural:** Tribal masks, Kenyan drums, a Mexican turtle planter, an ebony walking cane, and a Persian camel seat.

- **Firefighting:** A firehose nozzle, an antique leather fireman's helmet (sorry, no antique leather firemen — yet), a West Virginia Fire Department badge, and a German fireman-shaped beer stein.

- **Vanity Items:** An Art Deco nail buffer, a child's hairbrush from the 1950s, a set of vintage hat pins, an antique curling iron, and a lady's compact made by Hudnut.

- **Weird Stuff:** Gag lotto tickets, an antique artificial arm, a skeleton wedding cake couple, a genuine hummingbird nest, a 1960s lava lamp, and a stuffed chicken collection.

- **Hawaiiana:** A coconut monkey bank, a hula-girl table lamp, a set of Don Ho cocktail glasses (See? They do exist!), an antique Hawaiian wedding shirt, and a Diamond Head surfing trivet.

Go Global

Listed below the Categories listing are links to eBay's international auction sites. You may enter eBay Australia, Canada, Germany, Japan, or United Kingdom: Click one of these links, and you jet off to eBay sites in these countries. Remember that once you leave eBay USA, you're subject to the contractual and privacy laws of the country you're visiting.

Using the Featured Items Link

Here at eBay, money talks pretty loudly. In the center of the Home page, you see a list of the auctions eBay is featuring at the moment. eBay usually posts six featured items at any given time and rotates items throughout the day; as many sellers as possible get a shot at being in the spotlight. When you click the featured auctions All Featured Items. . . link, you're instantly beamed to eBay's Home Page Featured Items section, as shown in Figure 3-5.

Figure 3-5:
The Home
Page
Featured
Items.

Status	Featured Items ~ Current	Price	Bids	Ends PDT
	They'll Swear You Had Liposuction -GUARANTEED	$18.95	-	07/03 08:56
	BONSAI STARTER KIT~~A FOREVER GIFT~~Live Tree	$14.95	-	07/03 08:48
	2 ROUND TRIP TICKETS ANYWHERE YOU WANT TO GO!	$22.00		
	DIGITAL VIDEO CAM BLOWOUT WIRELESS $49.99	$49.99	-	07/03 08:22

You can find everything from Las Vegas vacations to Model-T Fords to diet products in the Home Page Featured Items. Home Page Featured auctions are not for mere mortals with small wallets. They've been lifted to the exalted *featured* status because sellers shelled out more money to get them noticed. All you need to get your auction featured is $99.95, plus a second or two to click Home Page Featured Item on the Sell Your Item form. (See Chapter 10 if you have an item that all eyes must see.)

Note that bidding on these items works the same way as on regular items.

The Home Page Featured Items page contains many expensive items, also called *big-ticket* items. (You can reach all big-ticket items by clicking Categories under Browse.) Sellers who put up high-priced items have been around the block a few times and make it clear that they will verify each bid on the item. That means if you place a bid on that 1997 GMC Suburban with 36,000 miles and no dents, be prepared to get a phone call from the seller. The seller may ask you to prove that you can actually pay for the car — or insist that you go through an escrow service. Nothing personal; it's strictly business.

Hanging Out in the Gallery

When you get far enough into a category (for example, Antiques: Musical Instruments), you see some gold tabs just above the auction listings. These tabs offer you three viewing options to browse:

- ✓ The default setting is **All Items**; this option delivers on its promise.

- ✓ Click the **Gallery Items** link above the Featured Items heading to be taken to eBay's version of an auction catalog, the Gallery.

  The Gallery features pictures, also called *thumbnails,* of auction items. The seller paid extra for them to appear here, so scan the thumbnails until you find an item that interests you. Click the thumbnail, and you're taken to that item's auction page.

- ✓ Click the **All Items Including Gallery Preview** link to see all items — including those in the Gallery. Gallery thumbnail previews appear in the status column to the left of the item's title. If your Internet connection is fast, this is the way to go.

You bid on Gallery items the same way as you would at traditional auctions. The only difference is that eBay charges the seller an extra $.25 to hang up an item in the Gallery or $19.95 to have a featured auction in the Gallery. (Jump over to Chapter 10 to find out how to get your item in the door of this exclusive club.)

Don't Miss This

Below the Don't Miss heading you see links to eBay charity auctions, such as those hosted by Rosie O'Donnell. Charity auctions are a great way for memorabilia collectors to find one-of-a-kind (and authentic) items. Winning bids contribute to programs that help charities. (Chapter 6 tells you more about what you can bid on — and the good you can do with your checkbook.)

Spotlight's On!

The eBay community is constantly changing. To help you get into the swing of things right away, eBay provides a special link (shown in Figure 3-6) that takes you right to the current word on the latest eBay changes and special events.

Figure 3-6:
Get the
latest news
on eBay
events by
clicking
these links.

You *can* get there from here — lots of places, in fact:

- ✔ A rotating list of special-interest links changes at least once a day. (Half the fun is getting a closer look at pages you haven't seen.)
- ✔ Special money-saving offers from third-party vendors can be a boon if you're on the lookout for a bargain.

Bottoming Out

At the very bottom of the page is an unassuming group of links that provide more ways to get to some seriously handy pages.

- ✔ **Announcements:** Visit the Announcements Board when you want to know about any fast-breaking news. eBay also uses this venue to update users about technical glitches.
- ✔ **About eBay:** Click this link to find out about eBay the company and to get its press releases, company overview, and stock information. You can also find out about eBay community activities and charities — and even apply for a job at eBay.
- ✔ **Rules & Safety (SafeHarbor):** This link takes you to the Rules & Safety Overview page, where concerns about fraud and safety are addressed. It's such an important eBay tool that we dedicate an entire chapter to this program. Before buying or selling, it's a good idea to check out Chapter 15.
- ✔ **eBay Store:** This link enables you to browse and buy eBay merchandise.
- ✔ **Affiliates Program:** If you have your own Web site and want to make a few bucks, click this link. If you sign up for the program and put a link to eBay on your Web page, eBay pays you $3 for any new user that signs up directly from your Web site.
- ✔ **Feedback Forum:** This link takes you to one of the most important spots at eBay. The Feedback Forum is where you can find out if you've forgotten to place feedback on a transaction, place feedback, and respond to feedback left for you, all in one friendly location.
- ✔ **Jobs:** Click here if you want to work *for* eBay instead of *through* eBay.

On other eBay pages, the bottom navigation bar looks a little different. It includes even more links so that you can cruise the site quickly without necessarily having to use the navigation bar.

Chapter 4

My Own Private eBay

In This Chapter

▶ Making the My eBay page: a space to call your own

▶ Keeping tabs on what you're buying and selling

▶ Rolling with the feedback that makes the eBay world go 'round (*all* 'round)

*W*e know eBay is a sensitive kind of company because it gives all users plenty of personal space. This space is called the My eBay page, and it's your private listing of all your activities on eBay — sort of a "This is your eBay life." We think it's the greatest organizational tool around and want to talk to somebody about getting one for organizing life outside of eBay.

In this chapter, we show you how you can use the My eBay page to keep tabs on what you're buying and selling, find out how much money you've spent, and add categories to your own personalized list so you can get to any favorite eBay place with just a click of your mouse. We give you the ins and outs of feedback — what it is, why it can give you that warm, fuzzy feeling, and how to manage it so all that cyber-positive reinforcement doesn't go to your head.

Your My eBay Page

Using your My eBay page makes keeping track of your eBay life a whole lot easier. And getting there is easy enough. After you register at eBay, you have two easy ways to get to your My eBay page. The most practical way to enter eBay is always through the Sign In link (see Chapter 3). If you haven't signed in, you can access your My eBay page by following these steps:

1. **On the top of any eBay page, click the My eBay link in the upper-right corner of the page.**

    You're sent to the My eBay Sign In page (see Figure 4-1).

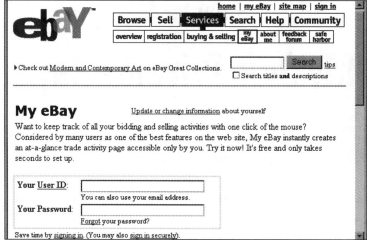

Figure 4-1:
The My
eBay Sign In
page.

You don't have to be on the eBay Home page to find My eBay or Sign In. As you maneuver around the Web site, the links follow you like Mona Lisa's eyes.

2. Type in your User ID and password.

If you forget your eBay User ID, you can type in your e-mail address instead. Your User ID appears in any search results, posts, or pages that come up using your e-mail address.

Before moving on to the next step, you may want to scroll down to the area that enables you to update your eBay information. At the bottom of the My eBay Sign In page are some extremely handy links. Although (as a new eBay member) you don't need to do all this stuff right away, links are available to

- Change your User ID
- Change your password
- Change your registration information (if you change your address or phone number)
- Report a change of e-mail address
- Change your notification parameters (what e-mails and/or notifications you want eBay to send to your mailbox)
- Create your own About Me page

3. Click the Enter button to enter My eBay.

You've arrived at your My eBay page (see Figure 4-2).

My eBay - Welcome marsha_c (818) ★

| Bidding / Watching | Selling | Recent Feedback | Account | Favorites | All | Preferences |

Show current items and items ending within the last [7] days *(30 days max)* [submit]

See items I'm watching...

Items I'm Bidding On
See item details...

Item	Start Price	Current Price	My Max Bid	Quantity	# of Bids	Start Date	End Date PDT	Time Left
MAGAZINE: FLAIR FEBRUARY 1950								
362020187	$9.95	$23.45	$26.52	N/A	6	Jun-19-00	Jun-26-00 09:44:19	**Ended**
"Le Parasol" by Rene Gruau! (reserve met)								
359596857	$150.00	$340.02	$335.02	N/A	9	Jun-15-00	Jun-25-00 21:27:52	**Ended**
BELL SCIENCE - UNCHAINED GODDESS								
364962999	$7.99	$7.99	$9.99	N/A	1	Jun-22-00	Jun-25-00 15:33:24	**Ended**

Figure 4-2:
Your very own My eBay page.

The My eBay page consists of seven tabs: Bidding/Watching, Selling, Recent Feedback, Account, Favorites, All, and Preferences. Table 4-1 gives you a little scoop about each of the tabs.

Table 4-1	The Display Tabs on Your My eBay Page
Click Here	*To See This on Your My eBay Page*
Bidding/Watching	Every auction you're currently bidding on items. Further down the page, you find every auction that you've marked to watch.
Selling	Every auction in which you're currently selling items.
Recent Feedback	The last five feedback comments about you and links that send you to all your feedback, all the feedback you've left, and an area where you can respond to feedback.
Account	What you currently owe eBay and links you to locations where you can get info on payment terms, fees and credits, and refunds. It also links to your My Billpoint Account.
Favorites	Links to your favorite item listings.
All	All the tab items from your My eBay page seen in one scrollable page.
Preferences	Lets you select the activities in which you want eBay to remember your password so that you don't have to type it every time (like when selling, bidding, managing items, and so on). It also gives you the option to display e-mail addresses while browsing eBay.

Houston, we don't have a problem

Here's an item we wish we'd sold: a Neil Armstrong signed NASA portrait w/COA (Certificate of Authenticity). It was a very clean 8-x-10-inch color NASA portrait signed and inscribed by Neil Armstrong, the first human on the moon. In recent years, Armstrong has been very reclusive, and his autographs are difficult to obtain in any form. Many forgeries are being offered, so buyer beware. This portrait came with a lifetime COA. The starting price was $10, and the portrait sold on eBay for $520!

Many believe (including us) that Neil Armstrong's autograph will be among the most important of the twentieth century. Just think of it. He was the first human to step onto another celestial body. This feat may never happen again, and certainly not in our lifetimes.

Save yourself time and bookmark this page. eBay lets you view your page from a bookmark. But note that to take advantage of the Sign In feature, you still have to (you guessed it) sign in.

Don't confuse the My eBay page with the About Me page. The About Me page is a personal home page that you can create to let other eBay members know about you. (You don't have to have an About Me page if you don't want to.) We tell you all about the About Me page in Chapter 13.

Choosing Your My eBay Preferences

One of the tabs at the top of your My eBay page is Preferences. eBay created the Preferences feature to help you avoid having to type your password every time you do certain activities, such as bid, check your account balance, and participate in auctions. The only catch is that you have to sign in before you can set your preferences.

The first time you enter the Preferences page (by clicking the Preferences tab on the My eBay page), you see that eBay requires you to sign in before going any further. So, click on the link above the navigation bar and sign in. After you do so with your User ID and password, a link appears, offering to send you back to the Preferences tab. Click the link, and you're presented with the Sign In and Display Preferences page. The options boxes have checks in them. You can customize those options by clearing the checks from the boxes (one click per box does it). Choosing your options by pointing and clicking is a little like ordering dinner at a Chinese restaurant: Choose what you want and pass the soy sauce.

When you finally get to your My eBay page, save yourself a lot of work — use your browser to bookmark your My eBay page as a favorite. Doing so saves you a lot of keystrokes later on. Some folks make their My eBay page their browser home page so they can see it the minute they log in. That's dedication. You still have to Sign In to avoid inputting your User ID and password at every turn.

Setting Up Your Account

When you first explore your My eBay page, you'll see that your eBay account has not been activated. The eBay folks only charge you a fee when you list something to sell. Even if the item doesn't sell, eBay keeps the fee. It doesn't cost you a nickel in fees to look around or sign up — or even to buy. (For details on how eBay charges you for its services, see Chapter 9.)

Even though you've already become a registered eBay user (if you haven't registered see Chapter 2), you don't have to submit your credit card information until you plan to list an item for auction or until you bid in an auction that has special rules requiring a credit card. You can provide eBay with this credit card information right from your My eBay Account page. Figure 4-3 shows you what the Account section of the My eBay page is all about.

You can look up every detail of your account history, as well as make changes to your personal preferences (such as how and when you want to pay fees). If you think eBay owes you money, you can do a refund request from here as well. Before you jump into the money game, you may want to review the links eBay gives you to manage your money:

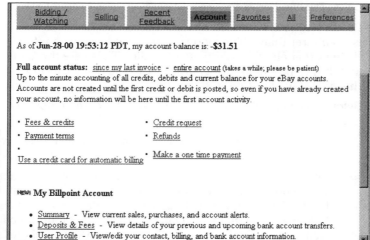

Figure 4-3:
The
Account
section of
the My eBay
page.

Nice shades!

For the first 30 days after you change your User ID (which you can do anytime, as Chapter 2 shows) — eBay gives you a pair of sunglasses that stays next to your User ID every time it appears on eBay (when you bid, run an auction, or post a message on any of the chat boards).

So why the sunglasses? eBay calls them *shades.* They're sort of a friendly heads-up to others that you are a new user or have changed your User ID. You still have all the privileges that everybody else has on eBay while you're breaking in your new identity. Remember: The shades are nothing personal, just business as usual.

✔ **Fees and Credits.** Click here to get a complete explanation of the eBay fee structure.

✔ **Payment Terms.** Click here to get a complete explanation of how eBay collects its fees.

✔ **Use a Credit Card for Automatic Billing.** Although all sellers must provide a credit card, you don't have to use this credit card to pay your monthly fees — unless you're using one of eBay's international sites, which require credit-card payment. You may pay with a check or money order if you wish. Click here and fill in the information. Even though eBay welcomes Visa, you may also use your American Express, Discover, or MasterCard. You can also change credit cards here at any time. Every month, eBay charges your card for fees you incurred the previous month. You can see these charges on your credit card statement as well as on your eBay account.

When you give eBay your credit card information, eBay attempts to authorize your card immediately. Your credit company's response, either Declined or Approved, appears on your Account Status page.

✔ **Credit Request.** If you sell an item and the buyer backs out (usually, this is even rarer than a blue moon), you can at least get a refund on some of the fees that eBay charges you as a seller. These are the *final value fees,* and they're based on the selling price of the item. This link takes you to the Final Value Fee Credit Request page.

Before you can collect a Final Value Fee refund, the following conditions must apply:

- After your auction, you have to allow bidders at least seven business days to contact you.

- After the seven days have elapsed and you have the feeling that you're not going to see your money, you must file a Non-Paying Bidder Alert. After you file this notice, eBay sends you and the bidder a very ominous e-mail reminding the bidder to complete the transaction. You have up to 45 days from the end of the auction to file this alert — and you can't get a Final Value Fee credit without filing this alert.

- • The next ten days after you file the Non-Paying Bidder Alert are your "work out" period — the period where you and the bidder hopefully complete your transaction. You may try to give the bidder a call to resolve the situation during this time.

- • After the 10 days have passed but no more than 60 days have elapsed since the end of the auction, you may file for a Final Value Fee credit.

✔ **Refunds.** If your account has a credit balance in it of $1 or more that you're not planning to use, you can get it back by clicking the Refund link. If you've used the Sign In feature, you merely click the box to get to a printable refund request coupon. If you haven't used the Sign In feature, you have to type your user name and password to access the personalized form. Print out the form on the page, fill it out, and then either fax it or send it by mail to eBay.

✔ **Make a One-Time Payment.** If you're about to hit your credit limit or you don't want eBay making monthly charges on your credit card, you can make a one-time payment. Click the link to make a payment. To pay by check, you need an eBay payment coupon, which you can get by typing in your User ID and password (if you'd have used the Sign In feature, you wouldn't have to do this), clicking either the Check or Money Order payment button, printing out the coupon page, and following the directions. If you want to make a one-time credit card payment, click the credit card box and get to an SSL-secured area to type in your information. Click Submit, and the stuff is sent to eBay for processing. Just that easy, just that simple.

The downside of paying eBay fees by check or money order is that you are charged if you bounce a check, miss a payment, or use Canadian dollars instead of U.S. dollars. You're supposed to get an e-mail invoice at the end of the month, but even if you don't, eBay expects to be paid on time. A word to the wise: Keep close tabs on your account status if you choose to pay this way.

No matter what payment option you choose, you can check your account status at any time. Your account status lists all your transactions with eBay over the last two months. If you want a more detailed account, you can click the Entire Account link on your Account page and see a record of every transaction you've ever done.

When you choose to see your entire account, eBay may take a little while to put all your transactions on-screen. How long depends on the number of auctions you've run at eBay. Don't be alarmed. eBay's just sifting through the endless list of completed auctions that have been run on the site. Just another example of why people say the *www* in Web addresses really stands for *World Wide Wait.*

Note that the Account page also has a new feature called Online Payments by Billpoint. If you use the Billpoint service for transactions at eBay, you can use the following links:

- ✔ **Summary.** To see the current sales and purchases on your My Billpoint account.

- ✔ **Deposits & Fees.** For details of your previous and upcoming bank transfers.

- ✔ **User Profile.** To view and edit your personal information.

Check out chapter 10 for more on the Billpoint service.

Getting Your Favorites Area Together

Part of the fun of eBay is actually searching around for stuff that you'd never in a million years think of looking for. Wacky stuff aside, most eBay users spend their time hunting for specific items — say, Barbies, Elvis memorabilia, or U.S. stamps. That's why eBay came up with the Favorites area of your My eBay page. Whenever you view your My eBay Favorites page, you see a list of four of your favorite categories. Because eBay isn't psychic, you have to tell it what you want listed.

You can only choose four categories to be your favorites, so with over 4,000 categories to choose from, you need to make your choices count. If you're having a hard time narrowing down your category picks, don't worry: Your choices aren't set in stone. You can change your Favorites list whenever you want. (Chapter 3 offers details on eBay categories.)

To choose your favorite categories and list them on your My eBay Favorites page, follow these steps:

1. **Click the Favorites tab and click the Here link further down the page.**

   The link takes you to the User Preferences page.

2. **Scroll down the User Preferences page to the Favorite Category 1 heading.**

   You see four separate windows, each containing category listings. These windows contain all of eBay's categories and subcategories and sub-subcategories and sub-sub-subcategories.

3. In the far left column, click the category you want.

Automatically, the column to the right changes to reflect more choices based on the main category you selected. Be sure to highlight the categories and subcategories you want, as shown in Figure 4-4.

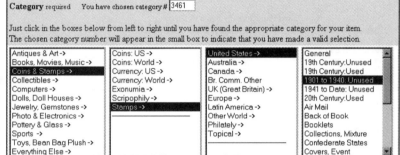

Figure 4-4:
Choosing
your favorite
categories.

4. Continue across from left to right.

Depending on your choices, you may have to scroll through each window to find the subcategory you're looking for. Once you've completed your choice, a number appears in the window at the top. That's your category number.

5. Repeat this process for Favorites Category 2 through Category 4.

If you don't want to use all four choices, just delete any numbers in the chosen category window.

6. Click the Submit button at the bottom of the page.

You get an acknowledgment that your changes have been made. Just click the My eBay link at the top of the page, and you see that your new favorite categories are waiting for you.

Remember, if you're not signed in you have to enter your User ID and password.

How specific to get when choosing your favorites depends on how many items you want to see. The more you narrow down your focus, the fewer items you have to wade through. The more general your favorite, the broader the range of items you have to view. Just below each of your favorites are five options for screening your favorites (see Figure 4-5). Which link you choose to view auctions depends on what kind of information you're looking for. Whether you're doing some preliminary searching on a category or monitoring the last few days (or minutes) of an auction, there's a link that sorts auctions and meets your needs best.

Figure 4-5:
The
Favorites
category
display
option on
the My eBay
page shows
a few of our
favorite
places.

Here's a list of the sorting options and when to use them:

- ✔ **Current:** Shows you every item currently being auctioned in the category, with the newest items shown first. If you want to look at all the current auctions for a category, you end up with a gazillion pages of items awaiting sale in a particular category for the next week.

- ✔ **New Today:** Shows you every item that was put up for auction during the past 24 hours. The little rising sun *icon* (picture) next to the item tells you that the item was listed today.

- ✔ **Ending Today:** Shows you every auction that is closing today. The ending time is printed in red if the auction closes within five hours.

If you're pressed for time, we suggest that you use either the category link New Today or Ending Today. Both of these links automatically narrow down the number of listed auctions to a manageable number. For more information on narrowing down searches at eBay, see Chapter 5.

- ✔ **Completed:** Shows you every auction that ended in the last two days. The Completed link gives you a good idea of how the market is going for an item, which helps you plan your own buying.

- ✔ **Going, Going, Gone:** Shows you every auction that's ending in the next five hours, all the way down to the last few seconds. This link offers a great way to find items you can bid on down to the wire.

When you view auctions from the Going, Going, Gone link, remember that eBay only updates this page every hour or so, so be sure to read the Auction End time. (Use the eBay time conversion chart on our Web site, www.coolebaytools.com, to decipher time differences.) Due to this same hourly update, sometimes the Going, Going, Gone items actually *are* gone — the auction has ended.

Got the time? eBay does. Click eBay Official Time (you can find it on the far left column of the Site Map or on the page with results of any search). The eBay clock is so accurate that you can set your watch to it. And you may want to, especially if you plan to get a last-second bid in before an auction closes. After all, eBay's official time is, um, *official*. A quick link to the eBay current date and time that you may want to bookmark is

```
cgi3.ebay.com/aw-cgi/eBayISAPI.dll?TimeShow
```

All Sorts of Sorting: Keeping Track of Your Auction Items

If you want to keep tabs on the items you're selling and bidding on (and why wouldn't you?), start thinking about how to sort them *before* you start looking for the first item you want to bid on. That's also pretty good advice for planning your own first auction.

Sorting auction items using the My eBay Sign In page

Sometimes it seems that eBay gives you too many options. There are eight — count 'em, *eight* — ways to sort items you're selling and bidding on from the My eBay page. That gives you a lot of options to think about, dwell on, and ponder. Each sorting method does pretty much the same thing, so pick the one that catches your eye and don't lose any sleep over your choice. After all, life's too short — and here you can change anything by clicking your mouse on the option titles. (Wish the rest of life were like that?) Table 4-2 goes into more detail about sorting methods.

Table 4-2	Sorting Methods and What They Do
Sort by	*Does This*
Item	Lists items alphabetically by what they're called.
Start Price	Lists items by their opening prices.
Current Price	Lists items by current highest bid. This listing changes often.

(continued)

Table 4-2 *(continued)*

Sort by	Does This
Reserve	Lists items by the secret reserve price you set when you started the auction (only for items you're selling). For more on reserve auctions, turn to Chapter 10.
Quantity	Lists items according to how many are available. For example, if you're bidding on an item in a Dutch auction, anywhere from 2 to 100 of exactly the same item may be auctioned at the same time (see Chapters 7 and 10 to see how Dutch auctions work).
# of Bids	Lists items by the number of bids they've received.
Start Date	Lists items based on when the auction began.
End Date PDT	Lists items based on when the auction finishes. This is one option that eBay automatically chooses for you if you don't select one on your own. This is the way most people view their lists.

All auctions at eBay are based on Pacific Daylight or Standard Time, depending on the time of year. This is true whether you live in sunny California or Vitamin-C-rich Florida or anywhere else in the world.

One thing you must decide is how long you want eBay to show the information about the items you're buying and selling on your My eBay page. You can show an item's history for as long as 30 days. There's a box on the My eBay page where you can type in how many days of eBay history you want to show on your pages (see Figure 4-6). Just type in the number of days you want to display information and click the Submit button.

Staying organized on your own

Yeah, we're going to bug you about printing stuff out — not because we're in cahoots with the paper industry but because we care. The best way to protect yourself is to keep good records on your own. Don't depend on eBay to cover you — not that eBay *doesn't* care. But this is *your* money, so keep a close eye on it.

Now don't become a pack rat and overdo it, but here's a list of important documents we think you should print and file whether you're a buyer or a seller:

- ✔ Auction pages as they appear when they close

- ✔ Bank statements indicating any payment you receive that doesn't clear

- ✔ Insurance or escrow forms

- ✔ Refund and credit requests
- ✔ Receipts from purchases you make for items to sell on eBay

Always, always, *always* save any and every e-mail message you receive about a transaction, whether you buy or sell. Also save your *EOAs* (End of Auction e-mails) that eBay sends. For more information about EOAs and correspondence etiquette after the auction is over, see Chapters 8 and 11.

Why should you save all this stuff? Here are some reasons:

- ✔ Even if you're buying and selling just a couple of items a month on eBay, you need to keep track of who you owe and who owes you money.

- ✔ Good e-mail correspondence is a learned art, but if you reference item numbers, your e-mail is an instant record. If you put your dates in writing — and follow up — you've got yourself a nice, neat paper trail.

- ✔ Documenting the transaction through e-mail will come in handy if you ever end up in a dispute over the terms of the sale.

- ✔ If you sell specialized items, you can keep track of trends and who your frequent buyers are.

- ✔ Someday the IRS may come knocking on your door, especially if you buy stuff for the purpose of selling it on eBay. Scary but true. For more on where you can get tax information, take a look at Chapter 9.

When it comes to keeping records via e-mail and documents about transactions, we say that after you've received your feedback (positive, of course), you can dump it. If you get negative feedback (how could you?), hang on to your paperwork for a little longer. Use your discretion, but generally you can toss the paperwork from a bad transaction after it's reached some sort of resolution. (You can find out more about feedback in the very next section.)

Once a month, we do a seller search on ourselves and print out our latest eBay history. You can also check your selling history on eBay by using My eBay and printing out items on selling item details by using the Details link. Chapter 5 tells you more about doing seller searches, organizing your searches, and starting files on items you want to track.

Getting and Giving Feedback

You know how they say you are what you eat? At eBay, you are what your feedback says you are. Your feedback is made up of comments — good, bad, or neutral — that people leave about you (and you leave about others). In effect, folks are commenting on your overall professionalism. (Even if you're an eBay hobbyist with no thought of using it professionally, a little business-like courtesy can ease your transactions with everyone.) These comments are the basis for your eBay reputation.

When you get your first feedback, the number that appears next to your User ID is your feedback rating, which follows you everywhere you go at eBay, even if you change your User ID. It's stuck to you like glue. Click the number next to any User ID and get a complete look at his or her feedback profile. The thinking behind the feedback concept is that you wouldn't be caught dead in a store that has a lousy reputation, so why on Earth would you want to do business on the Internet with someone who has a lousy reputation?

You're not required to leave feedback, but because it's the benchmark by which all eBay users are judged, we think whether you're buying or selling you should always leave feedback comments. Get in the frame of mind that every time you complete a transaction — the minute the check clears if you're a seller and the minute an item you've bid on and won arrives — you should go to eBay and post your feedback.

Every time you get a positive comment from a user who hasn't commented before, you get a point. Every time you get a negative rating, this negative cancels out one of your positives. Neutral comments rate a zero — they have no impact either way. eBay even has what it calls the Star Chart, shown in Figure 4-6, which rewards those with good-and-getting-higher feedback ratings.

Figure 4-6:
Ready for
your close-
up? Become
a star with
The Star
Chart.

The Star Chart
Stars are awarded for achieving a particular Feedback Profile.
A "Yellow Star" ( ) represents a Feedback Profile of 10 to 99.
A "Turquoise Star" ( ) represents a Feedback Profile of 100 to 499.
A "Purple Star" ( ) represents a Feedback Profile of 500 to 999.
A "Red Star" ( ) represents a Feedback Profile of 1,000 to 9,999.
A "Shooting Star" ( ) represents a Feedback Profile of 10,000 or higher.

The flip side (or Dark Side to you fans of *Star Wars*) of the star system is negative numbers. Negative comments deduct from your total of positive comments, thereby lowering the number beside your User ID. If you get nailed with enough negative feedback comments, your star is swiped by eBay and you're condemned to hang out with Darth Vader and his gang.

eBay riddle: When is more than one still one? Gotcha, huh? The answer is, when you get more than one feedback message from the same person. Confused? This should help: You can sell one person a hundred different items, but even if the buyer gives you a glowing review 100 times, your feedback rating doesn't increase by 100. In this case, the other 99 feedback comments appear in your Feedback Profile, but your rating only increases by one. There's one other thing: Say you sell to the same eBay user twice.The user could give you positive feedback in one case and negative feedback in another case — neutralizing your feedback by netting you a 0 feedback rating from this person. eBay set the system up this way to keep things honest.

Anyone with a –4 rating has his or her eBay membership terminated. Remember, just because a user may have a 750 feedback rating, it doesn't hurt to click the number after the name to double check the person's eBay ID card. Even if someone has a total of 1,000 feedback messages, 250 of them *could* be negative.

You can get to your personal Feedback Profile page right from your My eBay page by clicking the link that says See All Feedback about Me in the Feedback area.

Feedback comes in three exciting flavors:

- ✓ **Positive feedback.** Someone once said, "All you have is your reputation." Reputation is what makes eBay function. If the transaction works well, you get positive feedback; whenever it's warranted, you should give it right back.

- ✓ **Negative feedback.** If there's a glitch (for instance, it takes six months to get your *Charlie's Angels* lunchbox or the seller substitutes a rusty thermos for the one you bid on or you never get the item), you have the right — some would say *obligation* — to leave negative feedback.

- ✓ **Neutral feedback.** Neutral feedback can be left if you feel so-so about a specific transaction. It's the middle-of-the-road comment. Say you bought an item that had a little more wear and tear on it than the seller indicated, but you still like it and want to keep it.

How to get positive feedback

If you're selling, here's how to get a good rep:

- ✓ Establish contact with the buyer (pronto!) after the auction ends (see Chapter 11).
- ✓ After you've received payment, send out the item quickly (see Chapter 11).
- ✓ Make sure that your item is exactly the way you described it (see Chapter 10).
- ✓ Package the item well and ship it with care (see Chapter 11).
- ✓ React quickly and appropriately to problems — say, the item's lost or damaged in the mail or the buyer is slow in paying (see Chapter 11).

If you're buying, try these good-rep tips:

- ✓ Send your payment out fast (see Chapter 8).
- ✓ Keep in touch via e-mail with the seller (see Chapter 8).
- ✓ Work with the seller to resolve any problems in a courteous manner (see Chapters 8 and 11).

How to get negative feedback

If you're selling, here's what to do to tarnish your name big time:

- Tell a major fib in the item description. (Defend truth, justice, and legitimate creative writing — see Chapter 10.)
- Take the money but "forget" to ship the item. (Who did you say you are? See Chapter 16.)
- Package the item poorly so that it ends up smashed, squashed, or vaporized during shipping. (To avoid this pathetic fate, see Chapter 11.)

If you're buying, here's how to make your rep a serious mess:

- Bid on an item, win the auction, and never respond to the seller. (Remember your manners and see Chapter 6.)
- Send a personal check that bounces and never make good on the payment. (See Chapter 16 — and don't pass Go.)
- Ask the seller for a refund because you just don't like the item. (Remember how to play fair and see Chapter 8.)

The Feedback Profile page

At the bottom of the feedback section is a link called See All Feedback about Me. Click it, and you end up at the Feedback Profile page (see Figure 4-7). Think of the Feedback Profile page as your eBay report card. Your goal is to get straight "A"s — in this case, all positive feedback. Unlike a real report card, you don't have to bring it home to be signed.

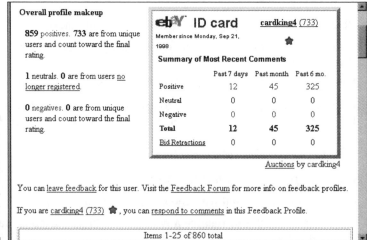

Figure 4-7: The Feedback Profile page — your eBay report card.

Overall profile makeup

859 positives. **733** are from unique users and count toward the final rating.

1 neutrals. **0** are from users <u>no longer registered</u>.

0 negatives. **0** are from unique users and count toward the final rating.

eb **ID card**   cardking4 (733)

Member since Monday, Sep 21, 1998

Summary of Most Recent Comments

	Past 7 days	Past month	Past 6 mo.
Positive	12	45	325
Neutral	0	0	0
Negative	0	0	0
Total	**12**	**45**	**325**
Bid Retractions	0	0	0

Auctions by cardking4

You can <u>leave feedback</u> for this user. Visit the <u>Feedback Forum</u> for more info on feedback profiles.

If you are <u>cardking4</u> (733) ⭐, you can <u>respond to comments</u> in this Feedback Profile.

Items 1-25 of 860 total

Extra, extra, read all about it

Normally, we say, "Keep your business private." But not when it comes to feedback. The default setting is for public viewing of your feedback. This way, everyone at eBay can read all about you.

If you want to make your feedback a private matter, you need to go to the Feedback Forum, click the link Make Feedback Changes Public or Private, and reset it to Private.

We think hiding your feedback is a bad idea. You want people to know that you're trustworthy;

being honest and up-front is the way to go. If you hide your Feedback Profile, people may suspect that you're covering up bad things. It's in your best interest to let the spotlight shine on your feedback history.

It's your rep, your money, and your experience as an eBay member. It's wise to keep in mind that all three are always linked.

Here's what's on the Feedback Profile page:

- ✔ **Your User ID.** Your eBay nickname appears, followed by a number in parentheses — the total number of the feedback comments you've received, minus any negative feedback you may have gotten (but that wouldn't happen to you . . .).

- ✔ **Your overall profile makeup.** This area sums up the positive, negative, and neutral feedback comments people have left for you.

- ✔ **Your eBay ID card with a summary of most recent comments.** This area is a scorecard of your feedback for the last six months. At the bottom of the feedback tote board is a summary of your bid retractions — the times you have retracted bids during an auction.

Be careful when you retract a bid. All bids on eBay are binding, but under what eBay calls "exceptional circumstances," you may retract bids — very sparingly. Here are the circumstances in which it's okay to retract a bid:

- ✔ If you've mistakenly put in the wrong bid amount — say, $100 instead of $10

- ✔ If the seller adds to his or her description after you've placed your bid, and the change considerably affects the item

- ✔ If you can't authenticate the seller's identity

You can't retract a bid just because you found the item elsewhere cheaper or you changed your mind or you decided that you really can't afford the item. See Chapter 6 for more information on retracting bids.

Reading your feedback

Your eBay reputation is at the mercy of the one-liners the buyers and sellers leave for you in the form of feedback comments.

Each feedback box contains these reputation-building (or -trashing) ingredients:

✔ The User ID of the person who sent it. The number in parentheses next to the person's name is the number of feedback comments he or she has received.

✔ The date and time the feedback was posted.

✔ The item number of the transaction that the feedback refers to.

✔ Feedback comes in different colors: praise (in green), negative (in red), or neutral (in black).

✔ The feedback the person left about you.

You have the last word — use it!

After reading feedback you've received from others, you may feel compelled to respond. If the feedback is negative, you may want to defend yourself. If it's positive, you may want to say *thank you*.

To respond to feedback:

1. **In the feedback section of your My eBay page (or from the Feedback Forum), click on the Review and Respond to Feedback about Me link.**

   You're transported to the Review and Respond to Feedback Comments Left for You page (see Figure 4-8).

2. **When you find the feedback you want to respond to, click the small icon of an envelope with an arrow.**

3. **If you have not signed in, type your User ID and password into the appropriate boxes.**

   Always keep your password a secret. If you suspect somebody may know your password, change it before that person has a chance to sign in as you and ruin your reputation. (For more on selecting and protecting your level of privacy, see Chapters 1 and 14.)

4. **Type in your response.**

Figure 4-8:
The page
where you
respond to
comments
left by
others.

Leaving feedback with finesse

Believe it or not, writing feedback well takes some practice. It isn't a matter of saying things; it's a matter of saying *only the appropriate things*. Think carefully about what you want to say because once you submit feedback, it stays with the person for the duration of his or her eBay career. We think you should always leave feedback, especially at the end of a transaction, although doing so isn't mandatory. Think of leaving feedback as voting in an election: If you don't leave feedback, you can't complain about lousy service.

eBay says to make feedback "factual and emotionless." You won't go wrong if you comment on the details (either good or bad) of the transaction. If you have any questions about what eBay says about feedback, click the Services link at the top of every eBay page; then click Feedback Forum on the subnavigation bar that automatically appears (or go to the user agreement by clicking the link at the bottom of almost every eBay page).

In the Feedback Forum, you can perform six feedback-related tasks:

- ✔ **See feedback about an eBay user.**
- ✔ **Leave feedback for many auctions at once**. Here, you see all pending feedback for all transactions within the past 60 days. You are presented with a page of all your transactions for which you haven't left feedback. Fill them in, one at a time, and with one click, you can leave as many as 25 feedback comments at once.

> ✔ **Review and respond to existing feedback about you**.
>
> ✔ **Review the feedback you have left for others**.
>
> ✔ **Make your Feedback Profile public or private**. Remember, if you make your Feedback Profile private, you may hinder your future business on eBay.
>
> ✔ **Check the Feedback FAQ to review any changes in the feedback system**.

In the real world (at least in the modern American version of it), anybody can sue anybody else for slander or libel at any time; this fact holds true on the Internet, too. It's a good idea to be careful not to make any comments that could be libelous or slanderous. eBay is not responsible for your actions, so if you are sued because of negative feedback (or anything else you've written), you're on your own. The best way to keep yourself safe is to stick to the facts and don't get personal.

Mincing words: The at-a-glance guide to keeping feedback short

eBay likes to keep things simple. If you want to compliment, complain, or take the middle road, you have to do it in 80 characters or less. That means your comment needs to be short and sweet (or short and sour if it's negative, or sweet and sour if you're mixing drinks or ordering Chinese food). If you have a lot to say but you're stumped about how to say it, here are a few examples for any occasion. String them together or mix and match!

Positive feedback:

✔ Very professional

✔ Quick e-mail response

✔ Fast service

✔ A+++

✔ Exactly as described

✔ Wonderful merchandise

✔ Smooth transaction

✔ Would deal with again

✔ An asset to eBay

✔ Highly recommended

Negative feedback:

✔ Never responded

✔ Deadbeat

✔ Steer clear!

✔ BAD!

✔ Beware track record

✔ Do not do business here

✔ Not as described

✔ Watch out — you won't get paid

Neutral feedback:

✔ Slow to respond but item as described

✔ Item not as described but seller made good

✔ Paid w/MO (money order) after check bounced

✔ Lousy communication but item came OK

If you're angry, take a breather *before* you type out your complaints and click the Leave Comment button. If you're convinced that negative feedback is necessary, try a cooling-off period before you send comments. Wait an hour or a day; see whether you feel the same. Nasty feedback based on pure emotion can make you look vindictive (even if what you're saying is perfectly true).

Safety tips for giving feedback

And speaking of safety features you should know about feedback, you may want to study up on these:

- Remember that feedback, whether good or bad, is (above all) *sticky*. eBay won't remove your feedback comment if you change your mind later. Be sure of your facts and consider carefully what you want to say.

- Before you leave feedback, see what other people had to say about that person. See whether what you're thinking is in line with the comments others have left.

- Your feedback comment can be left as long as the transaction remains on the eBay server. This is usually within 60 days of the end of the auction. After 60 days have passed, you must have the transaction number to leave feedback.

- Your comment can only be a maximum of 80 letters long, which is really short when you have a lot to say. Before you start typing, organize your thoughts and use common abbreviations to save precious space.

- Before posting negative feedback, try to resolve the problem by e-mail or telephone. You may discover that your reaction to the transaction is based on a misunderstanding that can be easily resolved.

- eBay users generally want to make each other happy, so use negative feedback *only as a last resort*. See Chapters 8 and 10 for more details on how to avoid negative feedback.

If you do leave a negative comment that you later regret, you can't remove it. You *can't* go back and leave an explanation or a more positive comment (unless you're responding to feedback this person has left about you), so think twice before you blast.

The ways to leave feedback

Several ways are available to leave feedback comments:

- If you're on the user's Feedback Profile page, click the Leave Feedback link (refer to Figure 4-7). The Leave Feedback page appears (see Figure 4-9).

- Go to your auction and click the Leave Feedback icon. Then click the To Bidder or the To Seller link. Click the To Seller or To Bidder link below the Leave Feedback icon. Click the Leave Feedback icon to see a list of all your completed auctions from the last 60 days for which you haven't yet left feedback.

✔ Click on the Feedback Forum link at the bottom of almost any eBay page.

✔ Click the Services link in the main navigation bar and then click Feedback Forum. On the next page that appears, click the link that says Use the Feedback Forum.

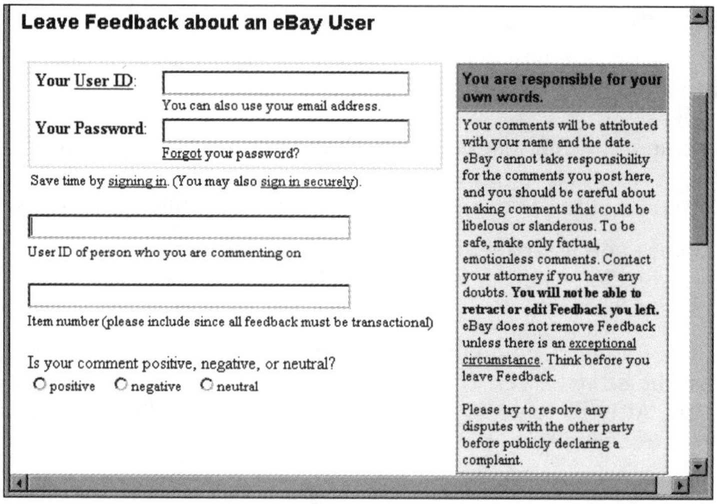

Figure 4-9:
The Leave
Feedback
page.

Leave Feedback about an eBay User

Your User ID:

You can also use your email address.

Your Password:

Forgot your password?

Save time by signing in. (You may also sign in securely).

User ID of person who you are commenting on

Item number (please include since all feedback must be transactional)

Is your comment positive, negative, or neutral?
○ positive   ○ negative   ○ neutral

You are responsible for your own words.

Your comments will be attributed with your name and the date. eBay cannot take responsibility for the comments you post here, and you should be careful about making comments that could be libelous or slanderous. To be safe, make only factual, emotionless comments. Contact your attorney if you have any doubts. **You will not be able to retract or edit Feedback you left.** eBay does not remove Feedback unless there is an exceptional circumstance. Think before you leave Feedback.

Please try to resolve any disputes with the other party before publicly declaring a complaint.

To leave feedback:

1. **Enter the required information.**

   Note that your item number is usually filled in, but if you're placing feedback from the user's Feedback Profile page, you have to have the number at hand.

2. **Choose whether you want your feedback to be positive, negative, or neutral.**

eBay will consider removing feedback if ...

✔ eBay is served with a court order stating that the feedback in question is slanderous, libelous, defamatory, or otherwise illegal. eBay will also accept a settlement agreement from a resolved lawsuit submitted by both attorneys and signed by both parties, as well as a ruling by a certified arbitrator where both parties agreed to submit the issue for binding arbitration.

✔ The feedback in question has no relation to eBay — such as comments about transactions outside of eBay or personal comments about users.

✔ The feedback contains a link to another page, picture, or Javascript.

✔ The feedback is comprised of profane or vulgar language.

✔ The feedback contains any personal identifying information about a user.

✔ The feedback refers to any investigation, whether by eBay or a law-enforcement organization.

✔ The feedback is left by a user who supplied fraudulent information when registering at eBay.

✔ The feedback is left by a person who can be identified as a minor.

✔ The feedback is left by a user as a part of harassment.

✔ The feedback is intended for another user, when eBay has been informed of the situation and the same feedback has been left for the appropriate user.

Part II
Are You Buying What They're Selling?

The 5th Wave   By Rich Tennant

©RICHTENNANT

"My gosh, Barbara, if you don't think it's worth going a couple of weeks without dinner so we can afford to bid on that small Mediterranean island we saw at eBay, just say so!"

In this part . . .

After you have an idea how to get around the eBay site, you'll probably want to get started. You've come to the right place. Here you can find all the information you need to start bidding on (and winning) auctions.

Although eBay is a lot more fun than school, you still have to do your homework. After you've registered to become an eBay member (in Part I), you can place a bid on any item you see. But first you have to find the item that's right for you . . . and then maybe find out what it's worth. And what happens when you do win?!

In this part, we show you how to find the items you want without sifting through every single one of eBay's millions of auctions. We also give you an insider's look at determining the value of a collectible, determining how much you're willing to spend, and using the right strategy to win the item at just the right price. When the auction is over, follow our advice to make closing the deal go smooth as silk. Watch the positive feedback come pouring in.

Chapter 5

Seek and You Shall Find: Research

In This Chapter

▶ Getting sound real-world buying advice

▶ Getting solid online buying advice

▶ Checking out other information sources for savvy buyers

▶ Conducting a narrow-minded search at eBay

*T*hink of walking into a store and seeing thousands of aisles of shelves with millions of items on them. Browsing the categories of auctions at eBay can be just as pleasantly boggling, without the prospect of sore feet. Start surfing around the site, and you instantly understand the size and scope of what's for sale here. You may feel overwhelmed at first, but the clever eBay folks have come up with lots of ways to help you find exactly what you're looking for. As soon as you figure out how to find the items you want to bid for at eBay, you can protect your investment-to-be by making sure that what you find is actually what you're looking for.

Of course, searching is easier if you have an idea of what you're looking for. In this chapter, we offer first-time buyers some expert collecting tips and tell you how to get expert advice from eBay and other sources. We also show you tips for using the eBay turbo search engine from a buyer's perspective.

The best advice you can follow as you explore any free-market system is *caveat emptor* ("let the buyer beware"). Although nobody can guarantee that every one of your transactions will be perfect, research items thoroughly before you bid so you don't lose too much of your hard-earned money — or too much sleep.

General Online Tips for Collectors

If you're just starting out at eBay, chances are you like to shop and you also collect items that interest you. You'll find out pretty early in your eBay adventures that a lot of people online know as much about collecting as they do about bidding — and some are serious contenders.

The ultimate family station wagon for sale

Need a lift? Drive in style in a 1977 Cadillac Fleetwood Hearse. Only 91K miles! Fully loaded: V8, P/S, P/B, P/W. Gray & Black w/Black interior. Good engine, good brakes, five extra tires, and a stereo system. Buyer must pick up after check clears.

This hearse sold at eBay for $600, and now the Addams family has a new set of wheels!

How can you compete? Well, in addition to having a well-planned bidding strategy (covered in Chapter 7), knowing your stuff gives you a winning edge. We've collected the opinions of two collecting experts to get the info you need about online collecting basics. (If you're already an expert collector but want some help finding that perfect something at eBay so you can get ready to bid, you've got it. See "Looking to Find an Item? Start Your eBay Search Engine" later in this chapter.) We also show you how one of those experts puts the information into practice, and we give you a crash course on how items for sale are (or should be) graded.

The experts speak out

Bill Swoger closed his collectibles store in Burbank, California, and sells his GI Joes and Superman items at eBay. His Web site (www.tvandmoviestuff. com) plays a big role in his business. And Lee Bernstein, an antiques-and-collectibles dealer who operates Lee Bernstein Antiques and Collectibles from her home base in Schererville, Indiana, not only frequents eBay but also has her own Web site (www.eLee.com). Bill and Lee offer these tips to collectors new to eBay:

- ✔ **Get all the facts before you put your money down.** Study the description carefully. It's your job to analyze the description and make your bidding decisions accordingly. Find out whether all original parts are included and whether the item has any flaws. If the description says that the Fred Flintstone figurine has a cracked back, e-mail the seller for more information.

- ✔ **Don't get caught up in the emotional thrill of bidding.** First-time buyers (known as *Under-10s* because they have fewer than ten transactions under their belts) tend to bid wildly, using emotions instead of brains. If you're new to eBay, you can get burned if you just bid for the thrill of victory without thinking about what you're doing.

We think that determining an item's value is important. But because values are such flighty things (values depend on supply and demand, market trends, and all sorts of other cool stuff), we recommend that you get a general idea of the item's value and use this ballpark figure to set a maximum amount of money you're willing to bid for that item. Then *stick* to your maximum and don't even think about bidding past it. If the bidding gets too hot, there's always another auction. To find out more about bidding strategies, Chapter 7 is just the ticket.

✔ **Know what the item should cost.** Buyers used to depend on *price guides* — books on collectibles and their values — to help them bid. Bill says that price guides are becoming a thing of the past. Sure, you can find a guide that says a *Lion King* poster in excellent condition has a book price of $75, but if you do a search at eBay, you'll see that they're actually selling for $40 to $50.

When your search at eBay turns up what you're looking for, average out the current prices that you find. Doing so gives you a much better idea of what you need to spend than any price guide can.

✔ **Timing is everything, and being first costs.** In the movie-poster business, if you can wait three to six months after a movie is released, you get the poster for 40 to 50 percent less. The same goes for many new releases of collectibles. Sometimes you're wiser to wait and save money.

✔ **Be careful of pre-sell items.** Sometimes you may run across vendors selling items that they don't have in stock at the moment but that they'll ship to you later. For example, before *Star Wars Episode I: The Phantom Menace* came out, some vendors ran auctions on movie posters they didn't have yet. If you had bid and won, and for some reason the vendor had a problem getting the poster, you'd have been out of luck. Don't bid on anything that can't be delivered as soon as your check clears.

✔ **Being too late can also cost.** Many collectibles become more difficult to find as time goes by. Generally, as scarcity increases, so does desirability and value. Common sense tells you that if two original and identical collectibles are offered side by side, with one in like-new condition and the other in used condition, the like-new item will have the higher value.

✔ **Check out the seller.** Check the feedback rating (the number in parentheses next to the person's User ID) a seller has before you buy. If the seller has many comments with very few negative ones, chances are good that this is a reputable seller. For more on feedback, check out Chapter 4.

Although eBay forbids side deals, an unsuccessful bidder may (at his or her own risk) contact a seller after an auction is over to see if the seller has more of the item in stock. If the seller is an experienced eBay user (a high feedback rating is usually a tip-off) and is interested in the bidder's proposition, he or she may consider selling directly to a buyer. See Chapter 7 for more details, but don't forget that eBay strictly prohibits this behavior. If you conduct a side deal and are reported to eBay, you can be suspended. Not only that, but buyers who are ripped off by sellers in away-from-eBay transactions shouldn't look to eBay to bail them out. You're on your own.

✔ **If an item comes to you broken in the mail, contact the seller to work it out.** The best bet is to request insurance (you pay for it) before the seller ships the item. But if you didn't ask for insurance, it never hurts to ask for a refund (or a replacement item, if available) if you're not satisfied. Chapter 11 offers the lowdown on buying shipping insurance, and Chapter 15 provides pointers on dealing with transactions that go sour.

Go, Joe: Following an expert on the hunt

Bill looks for specific traits when he buys GI Joe action figures. Although his checklist is specific to the GI Joe from 1964 to 1969, the information here can help you determine your maximum bid on other collectibles (or whether an item is even *worth* bidding on) before an auction begins. As you find out in Chapter 7, the more you know before you place a bid, the happier you're likely to be when you win.

Bill's checklist can save you considerable hassle:

✔ **Find out the item's overall condition.** For GI Joe, look at the painted hair and eyebrows. Expect some wear, but overall, a collectible worth bidding on should look good.

✔ **Be sure the item's working parts are indeed working.** Most GI Joe action figures from this period have cracks on the legs and arms, but the joints should move, and any cracks should not be so deep that the legs and arms fall apart easily.

✔ **Ask if the item has its original parts.** Because you can't really examine actual items in detail before buying, e-mail the seller with specific questions relating to original or replacement parts. Many GI Joe action figures are rebuilt from parts that are not from 1964 to 1969. Sometimes they even have two left or right hands or feet! If you make it clear with the seller before you buy that you want a toy with only original parts, you'll be able to make a good case for a refund if the item arrives rebuilt as the Six Million Dollar Man. Chapter 7 has plenty of tips on how to protect yourself before you bid, and Chapter 15 has tips on what to do if the deal goes bad.

✔ **Ask if the item has original accessories.** A GI Joe from 1964 to 1969 should have his original dog tags, boots, and uniform. If any of these items are missing, you will have to pay around $25 to replace each missing item. If you are looking to bid on any other collectible, know in advance what accessories came as standard equipment with the item, or you'll be paying extra just to bring it back to its original version.

✔ **Know an item's value before you bid.** A 1964 to 1969 vintage GI Joe in decent shape, with all its parts, sells for $125 to $150 without its original box. If you're bidding on a GI Joe action figure at eBay and you're in this price range, you're okay. If you get the item for less than $125, congratulations — you've nabbed a bargain.

> ✔ **If you have any questions, ask them *before* you bid.** Check collectors'
> guides, research similar auctions at eBay, and visit one of eBay's cate-
> gory chat boards.

Making the grade

Welcome to our version of grade school without the bad lunch. One of the
keys to establishing value is knowing an item's condition, typically referred to
as an item's *grade*. Table 5-1 lists the most common grading categories used
by collectors. The information in this table is used with permission from (and
appreciation to) Lee Bernstein (www.eLee.com) and can also be found at the
eBay Web site.

Table 5-1	Grading Categories	
Category (also known as)	*Description*	*Example*
Mint (M, Fine, 10, Mint-In-Box [MIB])	A never-used collectible in perfect condition with complete packaging (including instructions, original attachments, tags, and so on) identical to how it appeared on the shelf in the original box.	Grandmother got a soup tureen as a wedding present, never opened it, and stuck it in her closet for 50 years.
Near Mint (NM, Near Fine, Like-New, 9)	The collectible is perfect but no longer has the original packaging, or the original packaging is less than perfect. Possibly used but must appear to be new.	Grandmother used the soup tureen on her 25th anniversary, washed it gently, and then put it back in the closet.
Excellent (EX, 8)	Used but barely. Close to and often mistakenly interchanged with Near Mint. May have very *minor* signs of wear.	Grandma liked to ring in the New Year with a cup of soup for everyone.
Very Good (VG, 7)	Looks very good but has defects, such as a minor chip or light color fading.	If you weren't looking for it, you might miss that Grandma's tureen survived the '64 earthquake, as well as Uncle Bob's infamous ladle episode.

(continued)

Table 5-1 *(continued)*

Category (also known as)	Description	Example
Good (G , 6)	Used with defects. More than a small amount of color loss, chips, cracks, tears, dents, abrasions, missing parts, and so on.	Grandma had the ladies in the neighborhood over for soup and bingo every month.
Poor (P or G-, 5)	Barely collectible, if at all. Severe damage or heavy use.	Grandma ran a soup kitchen.

Grading is subjective. Mint to one person may be Very Good to another. Always ask a seller to define the meaning of the terms used. Also, be aware that many amateur sellers may not really know the different definitions of grading and may arbitrarily add Mint or Excellent to their item descriptions.

Finding More Collecting Information

Hey, the experts have been buying, selling, and trading collectible items for years. But just because you're new to eBay doesn't mean you have to be a newbie for decades before you can start bartering with the collecting gods. We wouldn't leave you in the cold like that — and neither would eBay. You can get information on items you're interested in, as well as good collecting tips, right at the eBay Web site. You can also search the rest of the Web or go the old-fashioned route and check the library (yes, libraries are still around).

Visiting eBay's online library

eBay's free public library offers online buying and collecting tips from experts. You can see what they have to say from the Inside Scoop (a primer on your item) and Front Page (which has timely articles on your subject) in the Library section.

To find Inside Scoop, go to the eBay Home page and follow these steps:

1. **Click the Community link on the navigation bar at the top of the page.**

   You're taken to the Community Overview page.

2. **Click the Library link on the subnavigation bar to see listings for all the categories offering collecting information.**

A list of categories appears, each with links to articles from Inside Scoop or Front Page (or both).

3. **Click the Inside Scoop or Front Page link for a category you're interested in and start reading.**

Searching other places online

If you don't find the information you need at eBay, don't go ballistic — just go elsewhere. Even a site as vast as eBay doesn't have a monopoly on information. The Internet is filled with Web sites and Internet auction sites that can give you price comparisons and information about cyber-clubs.

Your home computer can connect to powerful outside servers (really big computers on the Internet) that have their own fast-searching systems called *search engines*. At this moment, if something is out there and you need it, you can find it right from your home PC in just a matter of seconds. Here are some of the Web's most highly regarded search engines or multi-search-engine sites:

- ✔ AltaVista (www.altavista.com)
- ✔ Dogpile (www.dogpile.com)
- ✔ Excite (www.excite.com)
- ✔ Infoseek (www.infoseek.com)
- ✔ Lycos (www.lycos.com)
- ✔ WebCrawler (www.webcrawler.com)
- ✔ Yahoo! (www.yahoo.com)

The basic process of getting info from an Internet search engine is pretty simple:

1. **Type the address of the site you want to go to into the Address box of your Web browser.**

   You're taken to the Web site's Home page.

2. **Find the text box next to the button labeled Search or something similar.**

3. **Click in the text box.**

   You see a blinking cursor.

4. **Type in a few words indicating what you're interested in.**

   Be specific when typing in search text. The more precise your entry, the better your chances of finding what you want. Look for tips, advanced search, or help pages on your search engine of choice for more information about how to narrow your search.

5. **Click the Search (or similar) button or press Enter on your keyboard.**

   The search engine presents you with a list of how many Internet pages have the requested information. The list includes brief descriptions and links to the first group of pages. You'll find links to additional listings at the bottom if your search finds more listings than can fit on one page (and if you ask for something popular, like *Star Wars,* don't be surprised to get thousands of hits).

Always approach information on the Web with caution. Not everyone is the expert they'd like to be. Your best bet is to get lots of different opinions and then boil 'em down to what makes sense to you. And remember — *caveat emptor.* (Is there an echo in here?)

For more on using Internet search engines, try *Internet Searching For Dummies,* by Brad Hill, or *Researching Online For Dummies,* by Reva Basch (both published by IDG Books Worldwide, Inc.).

Finding other sources of information

If you're interested in collecting a particular item, you can get a lot of insider collecting information without digging too deep:

✔ **Go to other places at eBay.** eBay's chat boards and message boards (covered in detail in Chapter 16) are full of insider info. The eBay community is always willing to educate a newbie.

✔ **Go to the library.** Books and magazines are great sources of info. At least one book or one magazine probably specializes in your chosen item. For example, if old furniture is your thing, *Antiquing For Dummies,* by Ron Zoglin and Deborah Shouse (IDG Books Worldwide, Inc.), can clue you in to what antique collectors look for.

If you find a specialty magazine in the library that looks interesting, try entering the title in your search engine of choice. You may just find that the magazine has also gone paperless: You can read it online.

✔ **Go to someone else in the know.** Friends, clubs, and organizations in your area can give you a lot of info. Ask your local antique dealer about clubs you can join and see how much info you end up with.

Looking to Find an Item? Start Your eBay Search Engine

NEWS FLASH! Dateline: Silicon Valley, 2000: It's official. Through billions of dollars of research and development, millions of man- (and woman-) hours, incredible advances in miniaturization, and really good rebate programs, people around the world can now actually find a needle in a haystack with a personal computer that costs under a thousand bucks. The needle that has been lost for centuries has now been found, and we can finally put that threadbare cliché to rest. In a related story, haystacks are now tragically missing. They are golden yellow in color, stand about 5 feet tall, and have straw-like features. Check your local television station for more details.

Okay, we made up that news flash, but when you've done your research and you're ready to buy, the powerful eBay search engine can help you find whatever you're collecting — even if it's a needle in a haystack.

eBay has lots of cool ways for you to search for items (sample 'em in Chapter 3). The six main options are

- Search Title (Smart Search)
- Search by Item Number
- Search by Seller
- Search by Bidder
- Searching Completed Auctions
- International Search

You can access the six search options by clicking the Search link on the navigation bar at the top of any eBay page. Each search option can provide a different piece of information to help you find the right item from the right seller at the right price.

Testing, testing . . . how long *does* a search take at eBay?

Having a massive search engine is a matter of necessity at eBay — millions of items are up for auction at any given time — and often, an easy, fast search makes all the difference between getting and not getting. After all, time is money, and eBay members tend to be movers and shakers who don't like standing still.

So how long do searches really take at eBay? We put it to the test. In the Search window of the eBay Home page, we typed in **1933 Chicago World's Fair Souvenir Pennant** and let 'er rip.

The search engine went through 4 million general items and 860 World's Fair items and gave us our one specific item in just 4 seconds. (Now, if the wizards at eBay could only figure out a way to find that sock that always escapes from clothes dryers, they'd really be on to something.)

By the way, that slightly wrinkled felt pennant got four bids and sold for $17.50, in case you're in the market for one.

If you want to be thorough in your eBay searches, we recommend that you conduct searches often. And when you find a particularly juicy item or sub-category, bookmark it, or if it's an item click Watch This Item, (a link on the auction page just beneath the Mail This Auction To a Friend link), or use Personal Shopper. (See Chapter 7 for more info on keeping a paper trail and see Chapter 17 for more on Personal Shopper.)

eBay's Smart Search

When you use the Smart Search feature, the search engine looks for every auction at eBay that has the words you're looking for in the title or the description. The title (as you might expect) is just another word or group of words for what you call the item. For example, if you're looking for an antique silver ice tea spoon, just type **silver ice tea spoon** into the search window (see Figure 5-1). If there's someone out there selling a silver ice tea spoon who used exactly those words in his or her title or description, you're in Fat City.

Find Items
To use the old Search Method, click here.

| Smart Search | By Item Number | By Seller | By Bidder | Completed Items | International Search |

▶ **Search Title** NEW!

| silver ice tea spoon | All of these words ▾ | Search | tips |

☐ Search title **and** description ▶ *To find more items!*

▶ **Words to Exclude** NEW!   ▶ **Search in Categories**

| plated | | All Categories ▾ |

▶ **Price Range**   ▶ **Item location**

Between $[   ] and $[   ] | All of eBay - include all regions ▾ |

▶ **View Results**   ▶ **Sort by**

| All items ▾ | | Items ending first ▾ |

▶ **Payment** NEW!

☑ Accept eBay Online Payments by Billpoint 🗎

Figure 5-1: Using Smart Search to find a silver ice tea spoon.

Before you click the Search button, narrow your search down further. When you type in your search title, you have the option of choosing how you want the search engine to interpret your search entry. You can have the search engine search the title and description for

- ✔ All the words you type
- ✔ Some of the words you type
- ✔ The exact phrase in the order you've written it

In addition, you can choose other criteria:

✓ **What price range you want to see:** Type in the price range you're look-ing for, and eBay searches the specific range between that low and high price. If money is no object, then leave this box blank.

✓ **Words to exclude:** If you want to find a silver ice tea spoon, but you do not want it to be plated silver, exclude the word *plated*.

✓ **The payment:** You may find items that accept online payments by Billpoint.

✓ **The category:** Use this option if you want to limit your search to a par-ticular main (or *top-level*) category, for example, instead of searching all categories of eBay.

✓ **The item location:** You can narrow your search into over 50 eBay Local Trading regions.

✓ **The order you want your results to appear:** If you indicate "Items ending first" the search engine gives you the results so that auctions closing soon appear first on the list. "Newly listed items first" lists all the newly listed auctions, "Lowest prices first" and "Highest prices first" lists them just that way.

✓ **Whether you want the search engine to check through item titles alone or check *both* item titles *and* item descriptions:** We suggest that you select Search Title and Description. You get more information that way.

Okay, *now* click the Search button. In a few seconds, you see the fruits of all the work you've been doing. (Wow, you're not even perspiring.)

Figure 5-1 shows the Smart Search page with title information filled out, and Figure 5-2 shows the results.

Figure 5-2:
The Smart
Search
results of a
quest for a
silver ice
tea spoon.

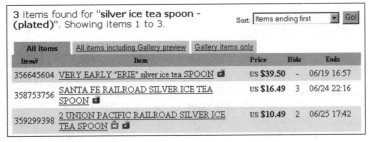

Next to item listings you often see pictures, or *icons*. A golden yellow rising sun picture means the listing is brand new (this icon stays on for the first 24 hours an item is listed), a small camera means the seller has included a digi-tal picture along with the item description, a flaming match means the item is hot and has over 30 bids, a picture frame indicates that the item is listed with a photo in the Gallery, and a small lock with a dollar sign in it means that the seller accepts online payments by Billpoint.

An item number search

All items put up for auction at eBay are assigned an item number. Using an item number is extremely handy if you don't want to wade through a title search again as you follow an auction or find out about auctions that have closed. Sure, you can type **LARGE ESTATE TANZANITE & PAVÉ DIAMOND RING** into the Title Search field again and again, but once you've found one, all you have to do is enter the nine-digit item number in the Item Number (#) search box to find it again, which is a lot simpler. Trust us. All you have to do is click the By Item link from the main Search page.

The page that appears, shown in Figure 5-3, is simple to use. Just type the item number in the Item Number (#) box and click Search.

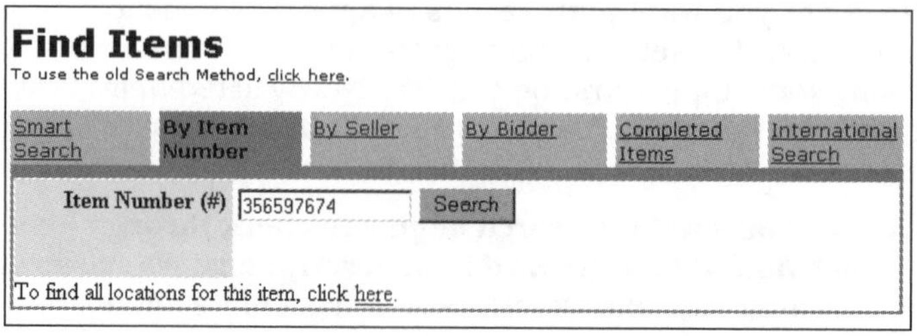

Figure 5-3:
Use the Item
Number (#)
search box
to find a
specific
item.

Find Items
To use the old Search Method, click here.

| Smart Search | By Item Number | By Seller | By Bidder | Completed Items | International Search |

Item Number (#) [356597674] [Search]

To find all locations for this item, click here.

Below the Item Number field is a message that says To find all locations for this item, click here. When you click there, you are taken to a Where Is An Item page. This page shows you exactly in which category the item is listed.

A seller search

The By Seller page, shown in Figure 5-4, gives you a list of all the auctions a seller is running, and it's a great way for you to keep a list of people you have successfully (or unsuccessfully, if you're trying to avoid them) done business with in the past. The By Seller page is also a strategy that eBay users use to assess the reputation of a seller. You can find out more about selling strategies in Chapter 8. To use the By Seller search option, follow these steps:

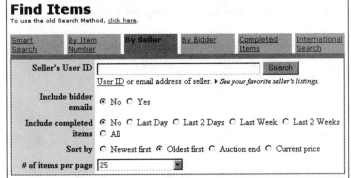

Figure 5-4:
The By
Seller
Search
page.

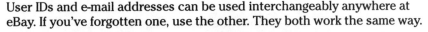

1. **In the Search field, type the eBay User ID or e-mail address of the person you want to learn more about.**

   User IDs and e-mail addresses can be used interchangeably anywhere at eBay. If you've forgotten one, use the other. They both work the same way.

2. **On the Include Bidder Emails line, tell eBay whether you want to see the e-mail addresses of other people who are bidding on auctions posted by the person you're searching for.**

   If you want these addresses, click the Yes option button. If not, click No. If you click Yes and have not already signed in, you have to fill out the User ID History and Email Address Request Form (shown in Figure 5-5). Type your User ID and password and click the Submit button.

3. **If you don't want to see auctions that this specific user has conducted in the past, click No on the Include Completed Items line.**

   You can choose to see all current and previous auctions, as well as auctions that have ended in the last day, last two days, last week, or last two weeks.

   eBay only keeps past auction results active for 30 days; if you're looking for something auctioned 31 days (or longer) ago, sorry — no dice.

4. **Choose an order to control how you want the results of your search to appear on-screen. If you want to see the auctions that are closing right away, click Sort by Auction End.**

5. **Choose the number of results you want to see per page.**

   If the person you're looking up has 100 auctions up and running, you can keep from getting swamped by sheer quantity if you limit the number of results to 25 listings, spread over four separate pages. Doing so allows you to narrow down what you want to see.

6. **Click Search.**

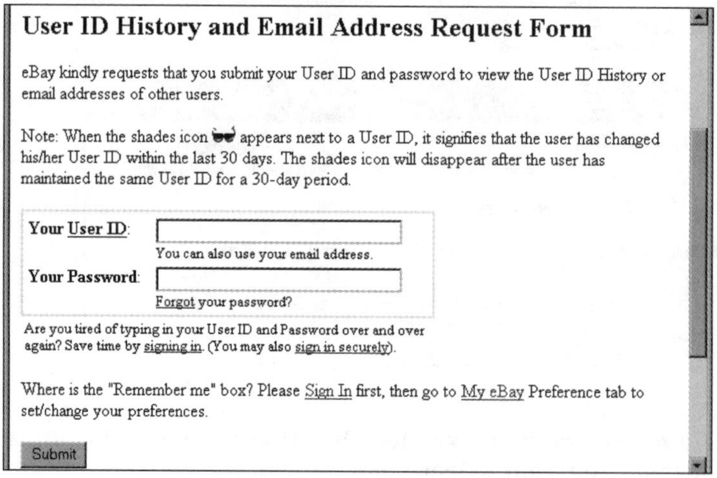

Figure 5-5:
The User ID
History and
Email
Address
Request
Form. If you
don't sign in
when you
enter eBay,
you'll be
seeing this
page many
times.

User ID History and Email Address Request Form

eBay kindly requests that you submit your User ID and password to view the User ID History or email addresses of other users.

Note: When the shades icon 👓 appears next to a User ID, it signifies that the user has changed his/her User ID within the last 30 days. The shades icon will disappear after the user has maintained the same User ID for a 30-day period.

Your User ID: [   ]
You can also use your email address.

Your Password: [   ]
Forgot your password?

Are you tired of typing in your User ID and Password over and over again? Save time by signing in. (You may also sign in securely.)

Where is the "Remember me" box? Please Sign In first, then go to My eBay Preference tab to set/change your preferences.

[Submit]

Figure 5-6 shows the results page of a By Seller search.

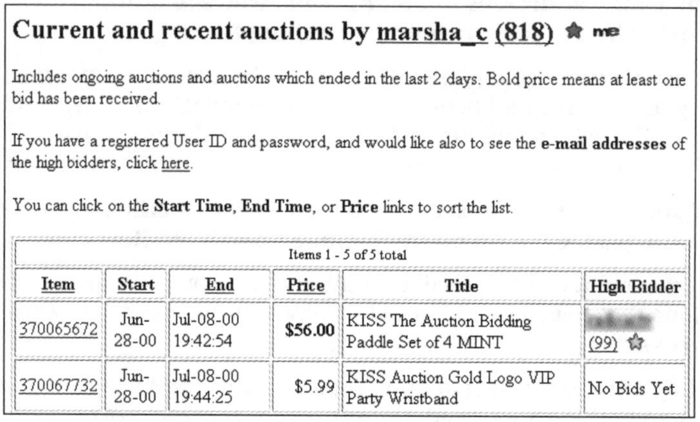

Current and recent auctions by marsha_c (818) ☆ me

Includes ongoing auctions and auctions which ended in the last 2 days. Bold price means at least one bid has been received.

If you have a registered User ID and password, and would like also to see the **e-mail addresses** of the high bidders, click here.

You can click on the **Start Time**, **End Time**, or **Price** links to sort the list.

Figure 5-6:
The results
page from a
By Seller
search.

Items 1 - 5 of 5 total					
Item	Start	End	Price	Title	High Bidder
370065672	Jun-28-00	Jul-08-00 19:42:54	**$56.00**	KISS The Auction Bidding Paddle Set of 4 MINT	▓▓▓▓▓ (99) ☆
370067732	Jun-28-00	Jul-08-00 19:44:25	$5.99	KISS Auction Gold Logo VIP Party Wristband	No Bids Yet

A bidder search

The By Bidder search option is unique because sellers and buyers alike use it when an auction is going on — to figure out their best strategies. After all, money is the name of the game. For information on conducting a By Bidder search, take a look at Chapter 7.

A completed items search

A Completed Items search returns results of auctions that have already ended. This is our favorite search option at eBay because you can use it as a strategic bidding tool. How? If you're bidding on an item and want to know if the prices are likely to go too high for your pocketbook, you can use this search option to compare the current price of the item to the selling price of similar items from auctions that have already ended.

You can also use this tool if you want to sell an item and are trying to determine what it's worth, how high the demand is, and if this is the right time to list the item. (Chapter 10 offers the nuts, bolts, and monkey wrenches you need to set up your auction.)

Figure 5-7 shows the Completed Items search page. And here's how to do a Completed Items search:

Figure 5-7:
The Completed Items search page.

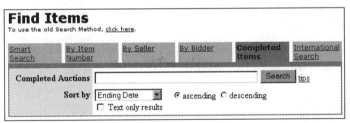

1. **In the title search field, type in the title name or the keywords of the item you want to find.**

2. **Tell eBay how you want the results arranged.**

   You have four options:

   - Select Ending Date to see your search results listed by the date the auction ended.

   - Select Starting Date to see your search results listed by the date the auction started.

   - Select Bid Price to see a list of the final auction prices paid for an item.

   - Select Search Ranking to see how many of your keywords in the title were hit during the search.

   When you've made your choice, you see an Order by option.

3. **Select how you want your results ordered.**

   Click the Descending button to see the most recent or most expensive items first. Click the Ascending button to see the last recently completed auctions, least expensive selling prices, or least whatever else first.

4. **Click Search.**

   The search results appear in just a few seconds.

An international search

You can select any country (from Afghanistan to Zimbabwe, no kidding!) or narrow your search down to the United States or Canada. Don't forget that you have to pay for shipping, so if you don't want to pay to ship a heavy ice-shaving machine from Hungary to Hoboken, New Jersey, stick close to home. The International Search feature (see Figure 5-8) is pretty much an international version of Smart Search and it's done the same way. You also have the choice of narrowing down your Country search with Located In and Available To selections. If you select Located In, the search engine looks for items from the specific country you entered in the box. Selecting the Available To option gets you search results for items within your own country or from international sellers willing to ship to you.

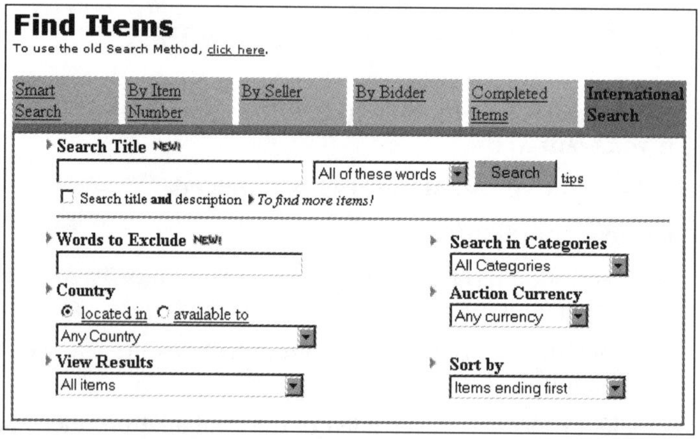

Figure 5-8:
The
International
Search
page.

Find Items

To use the old Search Method, _click here._

| Smart Search | By Item Number | By Seller | By Bidder | Completed Items | International Search |

▸ **Search Title** NEW!

[   ] [All of these words ▾] [Search] tips

☐ Search title **and** description ▸ _To find more items!_

▸ **Words to Exclude** NEW!

[   ]

▸ **Country**
  ⦿ located in ⦾ available to
  [Any Country   ▾]

▸ **View Results**
  [All items   ▾]

▸ **Search in Categories**
  [All Categories   ▾]

▸ **Auction Currency**
  [Any currency   ▾]

▸ **Sort by**
  [Items ending first ▾]

Narrowing down your eBay search

After you become familiar with each of eBay's search options, you need a crash course in what words to actually type into those nice little boxes. Too little information and you may not find your item. Too much and you'll be overwhelmed with information. If you're really into bean-bag toys, for example, you may be looking for Ty's Tabasco the Bull. But if you just search for *Tabasco*, you'll get swamped with results ranging from hot sauce to advertisements.

Some simple tricks can help narrow your eBay searches when you're making them from pages other than the main Search page (where they don't offer all the searching bells and whistles). Table 5-2 has the details.

Table 5-2	Symbols and Keywords for Conducting Searches with the eBay Search Engine	
Symbol	*Impact on Search*	*Example*
No symbol, multiple words	Returns auctions with all included words in the title	**reagan letter** might return an auction for a mailed message from the former U.S. president, or it might return an auction for a mailed message from Boris Yeltsin to Ronald Reagan.
Quotes ""	Limits the search to items with the exact phrase inside the quotes	**"Wonder Woman"** returns items about the comic book/ TV heroine. Capital and lower-case letters are regarded the same by the search engine. Using either gets you the same results.
Asterisk *	Serves as a wild card	**budd*** returns items that start with budd, such as Beanie Buddy, Beanie Buddies, or Buddy Holly.
Separating comma without spaces (a,b)	Finds items related to either item before or after the comma	**(kennedy,nixon)** returns items with descriptions that relate to either Kennedy or Nixon.
Minus sign –	Excludes results with the word after the –	Type in **box –lunch,** and you'd better not be hungry because you may find the box, but lunch won't be included.

(continued)

Table 5-2 *(continued)*

Symbol	Impact on Search	Example
Minus symbol and parentheses	Searches for auctions with words before the parentheses but excludes those with word(s) inside the parentheses	**midge –(skipper,barbie)** means that auctions with the Midge doll won't have to compete for Ken's attention.
Parentheses	Searches for both versions of the word in the parentheses	**political (pin,pins)** searches for political pin or political pins.

Here are additional tips to help you narrow down any eBay search:

✔ **Don't worry about capitalization:** You can capitalize proper names or leave them lowercase — the search engine doesn't care.

✔ **Don't use *and, a, an, or,* or *the:*** Called *noise words* in search lingo, these words are interpreted as part of your search unless you enclose them in quotes. So if you want to find something from *The Sound of Music* and you type in **the sound of music,** you may not get any results. Most sellers drop noise words from the beginning of an item title when they list it, just as libraries drop noise words when they alphabetize books. So make your search for **sound music.**

✔ **Search within specific categories:** This type of search further narrows down your results because you only search one niche of eBay — just the specific area you want. For example, if you want to find Tabasco the Bull, start at the Home page and, under the Categories heading, click Toys and Bean Bag. The only problem with searching in a specific category is that sometimes an item can be in more than one place, like a Mickey Mouse infant snuggly. If you look for it in Disney items, you may miss it. It might be listed in infant wear.

Finding eBay Members: The Gang's All Here

With millions of eBay users on the loose, you may think it's hard to track folks down. Nope. eBay's powerful search engine kicks into high gear to help you find other eBay members in seconds.

Here's how to find people or get info on them from eBay:

1. **From the main navigation bar at the top of most eBay pages, click the Search link.**

   This action takes you to the main Search page where three links pop up on the subnavigation bar: Find Items, Find Members, and Personal Shopper.

2. **Click the Find Members link.**

   This link takes you to the main Find Members page, where you can search for specific About Me pages (see Chapter 13 to find out how to create your own personal eBay Web page). Here, you can also get a look at the Feedback Profile of a user (see Chapter 4 for details about feedback) or find the e-mail addresses and User ID histories of fellow eBay members (which comes in handy when you're bidding on items, as Chapter 7 avows) or get contact information.

3. **Fill in the appropriate boxes with what you're looking for and click the Search (or, in some cases, the Submit) button to get the info you want.**

   If you're looking for e-mail addresses or contact information and you haven't signed in, you have to do so at this point (Refer to Figure 5-7).

 Clicking the Personal Shopper link on the subnavigation bar takes you to the Personal Shopper login page, where you start the process of registering for this free service. You tell eBay what items you're looking for, and Personal Shopper does automatic searches for you. Then Personal Shopper lets you know when auctions that match your descriptions crop up. (Chapter 17 tells the tender story of signing up and getting the Personal Shopper link to unite you with the item of your dreams.)

Chapter 6

Bidding: The Basics

- -

In This Chapter

▶ Getting your plan together before you bid

▶ Knowing the ins and outs of the item page

▶ Watching an auction

▶ Knowing the seller

▶ Avoiding bidder's remorse

- -

*B*rowsing different categories of eBay, looking for nothing in particular, you spot that must-have item lurking among other Elvis paraphernalia in the Collectibles category. Sure, you *can* live without that faux gold Elvis pocket watch, but life would be so much sweeter *with* it. And even if it doesn't keep good time, at least it'll be right twice a day.

When you bid for items on eBay, you can get that same thrill that you would at Sotheby's or Christie's for a lot less money, and the items you win are likely to be *slightly* more practical than an old Dutch masterpiece you're afraid to leave at the framer's. (Hey, you have to have a watch, and Elvis *is* the King.)

In this chapter, we tell you about the types of auctions available on eBay, run down the nuts and bolts of bidding strategies, and give you some tried-and-true tips that'll give you a leg up on the competition.

The Auction Item Page

Because at any given point you have more than a million pages of auction items that you can look at on eBay, auction item pages are the heart (better yet, the skeleton) of eBay auctions. Figure 6-1 shows a conventional item page.

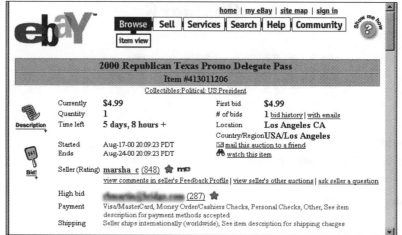

Figure 6-1:
How a
typical
auction item
page looks.

Next to the navigation bar at the top of the page, you'll notice a Show Me How icon. This is an ingenious little piece of technology installed by eBay to help you through the bidding process. If you get confused at any point — although we assume you'll be an expert after you read this chapter — click this icon. When you click it, small windows open up on your screen and step-by-step tips guide you through the process.

Here's a list of other stuff you see on a typical auction item page:

- ✔ **Item title and number:** The title and number identify the item. Keep track of this info for inquiries later on.

    If you have an interest in a particular type of item, take note of the key words used in the title (you're likely to see them again in future names). Doing so will help you in narrowing down your searches.

- ✔ **Item category:** Located just below the Item title and number bar, you can click the category listing and do some comparison shopping. (Chapter 5 gives more searching strategies.)

- ✔ **Currently:** This field indicates the dollar amount the bidding has reached, which changes throughout the auction as people place bids. Sometimes, next to the current dollar amount, you see Reserve Not Yet Met or Reserve Met. This means the seller has set a *reserve price* for the item — a secret price that must be reached before the seller will sell the item.

    If you don't see this listing on an auction item page, don't be alarmed. Not all auctions have reserve prices.

✔ **Quantity:** This field tells how many items are available. If you see a number other than 1 in this place, you're looking at a Dutch auction, which we explain later in this chapter. But, if a seller is selling two Elvis watches for the price of one, the item quantity still shows up as 1 (as in 1 set of 2 watches).

✔ **Time Left:** Although the clock never stops ticking at eBay, you must continue to refresh your browser to see the time remaining on the official clock. This field tells you the time remaining in this particular auction.

✔ **Started:** The date and time the seller began the auction. By checking this field, you can gauge interest in the auction by comparing the number of bids (or hits on a seller installed counter) to how long the auction has been running.

✔ **Ends:** Duhhh. This is the date and time the auction ends.

Timing is the key in an eBay bidding strategy (covered in Chapter 7), so don't forget that because eBay world headquarters is in California, eBay uses Pacific Standard Time or Pacific Daylight Time as the standard, depending on the season.

✔ **First Bid:** This is the starting price set by the seller (sometimes called *the minimum bid*). This is the lowest price somebody can bid to get the auction going.

✔ **# of Bids:** How many bids have been placed. To use the number of bids to your advantage, you have to read between the lines. You can determine just how "hot" an item is by comparing the number of bids the item has received over time. Based on the amount of interest in an item, you can create a time strategy (which we talk about later in this chapter). Next to the # of Bids are two links: Bid History and With Emails. Click Bid History to find out who is bidding and what date and time bids were placed on this item. The dollar amount of each bid is kept secret until the end of the auction. Click the With Emails link if you want to get the e-mail addresses of bidders.

Bidding is more an art than a science. Sometimes an item gets no bids because everyone's waiting until the last minute. You see a flurry of activity as they all try to outbid each other (called *sniping,* which we explain in Chapter 7). But that's all part of the fun of eBay.

✔ **Location:** This field tells where the item is. Factor in the geographic location of a seller when you consider bidding on an item. Knowing exactly where the item is can help you calculate what the shipping charges will be. (We tackle that subject in Chapter 10.)

✔ **Country/Region:** This field tells what country the item will ship from. If the item is in Australia, for example, and you're in Vermont, you may decide that you don't need that wrought-iron doorstop. (Remember, you pay the shipping charges.) The region lets you know if the item is included in eBay's regional auction areas.

✔ **Mail This Auction to a Friend:** You can tip off a friend on a good find, get some advice from an antique or collecting expert, or run it by a friend who's been around the eBay block a few times and ask for strategy advice.

✔ **Watch this Item:** Click the link next to the teeny binoculars, and you're taken to a page that allows you to add the item to the Bidding/Watching tab of your My eBay page so you can keep track of the auction — without actually bidding. If you haven't signed in, you'll have to type in your User ID and password before you can save the auction to your My eBay page.

✔ **Seller (Rating):** Gives you information about the seller. *Know thy seller* ranks right after *caveat emptor* as a phrase that pays at eBay. As we tell you a nearly a million times in this book, *Read the feedback rating!* (Okay, maybe not a million — it would drive the editors bonkers.) Human beings come in all shapes, sizes, and levels of honesty, and like any community, eBay has its share of good folks and bad folks. Your best defense is to read the seller's feedback. To the right of the seller's name is a number in parentheses. Click the number to view his or her eBay ID card and entire feedback history just below it. Read, read, and reread all the feedback (hey, we're one closer to a million!) to make sure you feel comfortable doing business with this person. Just below the seller's name is a link to see other auctions he or she may be running — and another link that pops up an e-mail window so that you can send a question. We give you a step-by-step guide on how these links work later in this chapter.

✔ **High Bid:** This one shows you the User ID and feedback rating of the current high bidder. It could be you if you've placed a bid!

✔ **Payment:** This field tells you the payment terms the seller has set. It lets you know if the seller accepts checks, money orders, credit cards, or online payments by Billpoint. Often, it tells you to read the item description for more details. We explain how to read item descriptions later in this chapter.

✔ **Shipping:** Check here to see if the seller is willing to ship to your area. Sometimes sellers will not ship internationally, and they'll let you know here before you place a bid. Also, always check the item description for shipping charges and terms (which, except in rare instances, buyers have to pay).

✔ **Description icon:** This icon shoots you directly to the item description, but because you want to know all about the auction, you more than likely won't use this option.

✔ **Bid icon:** With a click, the small blue bidding paddle brings you to the bottom of the page — to the bidding form.

Be sure to use the Watch This Item feature. Organization is the name of the game at eBay, especially if you plan to bid on multiple auctions while you're running auctions of your own. We figure you're in the bidding game to win, so start keeping track of items now.

Beating the Devil in the Details

As with any sale — whether you find it at Joe's Hardware, Bloomingdale's, or Kmart — carefully check out what you are buying. The auction page gives you links to help you know what you're bidding on — and who you're potentially buying from. If you take advantage of them, you won't have many problems. But, if you ignore these essential tips, you may end up unhappy with what you buy, the person you buy it from, and how much you spend.

Read the item description carefully

The *item description* is the most critical item on the auction item page. This is where the seller lists the details about the item being sold. Read this page carefully and pay close attention to what is, and isn't, written.

Don't judge a book by its cover — but do judge a seller by his or her item description. If the sentences are succinct, detailed, and well structured, you're most likely dealing with an individual who planned and executed the auction with care. It takes time and effort to post a good auction. If you see huge lapses in grammar, convoluted sentences, and misspellings, *you maybe gonna get burnt!* Make sure you feel comfortable dealing with this person; decide for yourself whether he or she is out to sell junk for a quick buck or is part of eBay for the long term.

If a picture is available, take a good look. The majority of eBay sellers jazz up their auctions with photos of their items. The seller should answer a few general questions in the item description. If these questions aren't answered,

---

Does the horse know?

One seller offered a bracelet from the mid-1800s — 8 inches in diameter and made from links of woven horsehair (some rather worn but generally in good condition). A horsehair charm dangled from a foot-long chain of links; the clasp was a woven ball and loop. The opening bid was $8, and this bracelet sold for $103.50!

that doesn't necessarily mean that the seller's disreputable — only that if you're really interested, you should e-mail the seller and get those answers before you bid. In particular, ask questions like these:

✔ Is the item new or used?

✔ Is the item a first edition or a reprint? An original or a reissue? (See Chapter 5 for tips on how to assess what you're buying.)

✔ Is the item in its original packaging?

✔ Is the item under warranty?

Most sellers spell out in their item descriptions exactly how the item should be paid for and shipped. Check to see whether an actual shipping charge applies — and if so, how much it'll cost you.

✔ If you're in a hurry to get the item, are delays likely? If so, what sort and how long?

✔ Can the seller guarantee you a refund if the item is broken?

✔ What condition is the item in? Is it broken, scratched, flawed, or Mint?

Most experienced collectors know that, depending on the item, a tiny scratch here or there may be worth the risk of making a bid. But a scratch or two may affect your bidding price. (Look at Chapter 5 for more expert collecting advice.)

✔ Is this item the genuine article or a reproduction, and if it's the real deal, does the seller have papers certifying its authenticity?

✔ What size is the item? (That fiberglass whale may not *fit* in your garage.)

If you win the item and find out the seller lied in the description, you have the right to return the item. But, if you win the item and discover that you overlooked a detail in the description, the seller isn't obligated to take the item back.

The seller is obligated to describe the item honestly and in detail, so if your questions aren't answered in the item description, then for goodness' sake, e-mail the seller for the facts. If a picture is available, is it clear enough that you can see any flaws?

Get the scoop on the seller

We can't tell you enough that the single most important way you can make an auction go well is to *know who you're dealing with*. Apparently, the eBay folks agree with us; they help you get info on the seller right from the auction item page. We recommend that you take advantage of the links offered there. (Chapter 5 demonstrates how to conduct a thorough By Seller search.)

✔ Click the number beside the seller's User ID to get his or her feedback history.

or

✔ Click the Me link next to Seller to view the seller's About Me page.

and

✔ Click View Seller's Other Auctions to take a look at what else that person's selling. (If you win more than one auction from a seller, they will often combine the shipping costs).

Check the seller's feedback (message sound familiar?)

Check the seller's eBay ID card and feedback history. All together now — *check the feedback.* (Is there an echo in here?) What you find are (for the most part) the honest thoughts and comments of buyers from previous transactions. No eBay user has control over the comments others make, and feedback sticks to you like your high school permanent record.

Read the feedback — the good, the bad, and the neutral — and unless you're prepared to kiss your money good-bye, we recommend that you stay away from anyone with a large percentage of negative comments.

eBay, like life, is full of shades of gray. Some sellers are unfairly hit with negative comments for something that wasn't their fault. If you suspect that a seller's received a bum rap (after you've read all his or her positive feedback), be sure to read the seller's response. (Look at Chapter 4 for more on reading and leaving feedback.)

Although scoping out an eBay member's ID card is *just that fast, just that simple,* you still need to take the time to read the feedback. (There's that echo again. Good thing it's a wise echo.) Someone with 500 positive feedback messages may look like a good seller, but if you take a closer look, you may find that his or her most recent 10 feedback messages are negative.

View the seller's other auctions

To find out what other auctions the seller has going at eBay, all you have to do is click the corresponding link on the item page; you're whisked away to a list of the other auction pies the seller has a finger in. If the seller has no other auctions going and has no current feedback, you may want to do a more thorough investigation and conduct a By Seller search that will show you all that person's completed auctions in the last 30 days (see Chapter 5 for details).

How Swede it is!

A savvy eBay user we know benefited from a major seller error. The seller titled his auction "Swede Star Trek Cast Jacket." Our friend checked out the item description and found that it was written with bad spelling and incoherent grammar, so she e-mailed the seller for more information. The seller explained that the jacket was a suede cast jacket given to the crew of the movie *Star Trek: Generations*. He had won it in a local radio contest, and it was brand new.

Because of the seller's mistake, there was only one bidder for this lovely green suede (silk-lined!) jacket, which our friend picked up for $150. Because of its *Star Trek* connection, the jacket is worth upwards of $400 to collectors. So study the item page carefully. You may get lucky and find that errors can work to your benefit. (And a word to the wise: Check your own spelling and grammar carefully when you put an item up for sale.)

Ask the seller a question

If anything about the auction is unclear to you, remember this one word: *ask*. Find out all the details about that item before you bid. If you wait until you've won the item before you ask questions, you may get stuck with something you don't want. Double-checking may save you woe and hassle later.

You can find out more about payment options, shipping charges, insurance, and other fun stuff in Chapters 8 and 11.

If you're bidding on a reserve-price auction, don't be afraid to e-mail the seller and ask what the reserve is. Yeah, reserves are customarily kept secret, but there's no harm in asking — and some sellers may even tell you.

To ask a seller a question, follow these steps:

1. **Click the Ask Seller a Question link on the item page.**

   If you *haven't* already signed in, you're automatically taken to the User ID request page (This is beginning to sound as repetitive as checking feedback!) After you fill in your User ID and password and click Enter, you're presented with the seller's e-mail address history.

   You can always change your User ID, but your past life (in the form of feedback messages) stays with you at eBay. Along with your feedback from your previous User ID, all your previous User IDs are listed as well.

   If you *have* already signed in, a preaddressed e-mail window opens for you.

2. **Click the seller's current e-mail address, fire off your questions, and send the e-mail.**

   Expect to hear back from the seller within a day. If it takes the seller more than a day or two to respond, and you get no explanation for the delay, think twice before putting in a bid.

Extend your scam antennae if a seller's reply to your question comes from an e-mail address that's *different* from the one you sent your question to. The seller should include an explanation for a difference in addresses. If you don't see an explanation, ask for one. Fraudulent sellers often use several e-mail addresses to hide their true identity. There may be nothing wrong with having several e-mail addresses, but if you're getting a gut feeling that the seller is playing hide and seek with addresses all over the place, *thank* your gut very much and rethink doing business with that person.

Factoring in the Extras

Before you think about placing a bid on an item, you should factor in the financial obligation you have to make. In every case, the maximum bid you place *won't* be all you spend on an item. We recommend that you look closely at the payment methods the seller's willing to accept and also factor in shipping, insurance, and escrow costs. If you only have $50 to spend, you shouldn't place a $50 bid on a fragile item that will be shipped a long distance because often the buyer (that would be you) pays for shipping and insurance. In addition, if you live in the same state as the seller, you may have to pay sales tax if the seller is running an official business.

Payment methods

Several payment options are available, but the seller has the right to refuse some forms of payment. Usually, the form of payment is laid out in the item's description. If it isn't, e-mail the seller and get a clear idea of your additional costs *before* you place a bid.

The forms of payment available to you are these:

✔ **Credit card:** Paying with a credit card is our favorite payment option, one that's mainly offered by businesses and dealers. We like paying with credit cards because they are fast and efficient. In addition, using a credit card offers you another ally, your credit card company, if you're not completely satisfied with the transaction.

✔ **eBay Online Payments by Billpoint:** The Billpoint service is a subsidiary of eBay, and Billpoint payments are processed securely through Wells Fargo Bank. Billpoint sellers are identified with a special secure payments icon (a small yellow padlock) and accept Visa, MasterCard, and Discover as well as electronic checks. The Billpoint service is integrated directly into eBay auctions, so paying is a mouse click away (see Chapter 9 for more information about online payments by Billpoint). Some international bidders can pay for their eBay auctions from sellers in the United States. To see a current list of Billpoint's international services go to `www.billpoint.com/services/international.html`.

Billpoint deposits the money directly into the seller's account. The service charges the seller a small transaction fee, so the seller has to absorb the cost.

Your credit card information is only known to the Billpoint service. The seller never sees your credit card info. Another major advantage is that you have your full credit card protection behind you when you use the Billpoint service. And you have the right to dispute charges if the item arrives damaged or doesn't show up at all. Also, if your credit card company offers extended warranties and protections, they are also covered when you use the Billpoint service.

Sometimes sellers use a friend's company to run credit card payments for eBay auctions. So don't be surprised if you buy a vintage Tonka bulldozer and your credit card is billed from Holly's Hair-o-Rama.

✔ **PayPal:** With over three million users, x.com's PayPal is currently the largest Internet-wide payment network. After you register with PayPal to pay for an auction item, PayPal debits your Visa or MasterCard (or your account — if you have earned some money from sales) and sends the payment to the seller's account. There's no charge for the buyer or seller to use the service. It can be used to pay any seller within the United States (although PayPal plans to expand its service internationally in the near future). The service can be accessed through a computer, a Palm device, or a Web-ready telephone.

A benefit of using an online payment system is that the seller never sees your credit card information; it's securely held by the service. Each PayPal customer is protected from unauthorized transactions from Travelers Casualty and Surety Company's SafeWeb Remote Banking Insurance for up to $100,000. In addition to offering insurance, you're protected with a Buyer Protection Guarantee. If you buy from a Verified PayPal member through the service, your purchase is guaranteed against fraud.

For more details, check out the PayPal Web site (`www.paypal.com`).

✔ **Money order:** Our second-favorite method of payment — and the most popular at eBay — is the money order. Sellers love money orders because they don't have to wait for a check to clear.

Money orders are the same as cash. As soon as the seller gets your money order, there's no reason to wait to send the item. You can buy money orders at banks, supermarkets, convenience stores, and your local post office. The average cost is about a dollar. If you're purchasing an item that's being shipped internationally, you can pay with an international money order from the U.S. Post Office, which costs about three dollars. International buyers may purchase a Western Union money order; www.westernunion.com provides locations in different cities around the world. The United Kingdom alone has hundreds of Western Union agents ready to receive your payment. Western Union money orders are also available online through BidPay.com for $5.00. The amount is charged to your credit card and BidPay mails the money order to the seller for you.

✔ **Personal or cashier's check:** Paying by check is convenient but has its drawbacks. Most sellers won't ship you the goods until after the check clears, which means a lag time as long as a couple of weeks. If a seller takes personal checks, it usually says in the item's description how long the check will be held before the item gets shipped. Unfortunately, that means that while the seller is waiting for your check to clear, your merchandise is collecting dust in a box somewhere. This is no fun for you or for the seller. Cashier's checks are available at your bank but often cost many times more than a money order. It's not worth the extra money — buy more eBay items instead.

Before you send that check, make sure that you have enough money to cover your purchase. A bounced check can earn you negative feedback — too many will bounce you off eBay.

The good news about checks is that you can track whether they've been cashed or not. Personal checks leave a paper trail that you can follow if there's a problem later.

✔ **C.O.D.:** No, we're not talking about codfish. We're talking about *Cash on Delivery.* As a buyer, you may like the idea that you only have to pay for an item if it shows up. But paying C.O.D. has two problems:

- You have to have the money on hand — the exact amount. When was the last time any of us had exact change for anything?

- Even if you have exact change, if you're not around when the item's delivered, you're out of luck.

If you miss Mr. C.O.D., the shipment heads back to Bolivia or Oblivion or wherever it came from, never to be seen again. And what do you get? A lot of angry e-mails and maybe some bad feedback. No wonder sellers rarely use this option.

Most business at eBay is conducted in U.S. dollars. If you happen to buy an item from an international seller, you may need to convert American dollars into another currency. eBay has a currency converter. Go to Site Map and click the Buyer Guide section in the Help area. On the Buyer Guide page, click International Trading. Then click Buy Globally. Click (in the right column) Currency. You have your choice of two converters. We suggest that you try them both to compare.

Never use a form of payment that doesn't let you keep a paper trail. If a seller asks for cash, quote Nancy Reagan — just say no. Occasionally, we hear of international buyers sending U.S. greenbacks in the mail. But, if a seller asks for cash, chances are that you may never see the item or your money again. And, if a seller asks you to send your payment to a post office box, get a phone number. Many legitimate sellers use post office boxes, but so do the bad guys.

Using an escrow service

Even though about half of all sales at eBay are for items that cost $25 or less, occasionally, using an escrow service comes in handy — like when you buy a big-ticket item or something fragile. *Escrow* is a service that allows a buyer and seller to protect a transaction by placing the money in the hands of a third party until a specified set of conditions are met. Sellers note in their item descriptions if they're willing to accept escrow. If you're nervous about sending a lot of money to someone you don't really know (like a user named Clumsy who only has two feedback comments and is shipping you bone china from Broken Hill, Australia), consider using an escrow company.

Using an escrow company is only worthwhile if the item you're bidding on is expensive, fragile, or going a long distance. If you're spending less than $200 for the item, we recommend that you purchase insurance from your shipper instead — just in case.

eBay has a partnership with an escrow service, i-Escrow. After an auction closes, the buyer sends the payment to the escrow company. After the escrow company receives the money, it e-mails the seller to ship the merchandise. After the buyer receives the item, he or she has an agreed-on period of time (normally two business days) to look it over and let the escrow service know that all's well. If everything's okay, the escrow service sends the payment to the seller. If the buyer is unhappy with the item, he or she must ship it back to the seller. When the escrow service receives word from the seller that the item has been returned, the service returns the payment to the buyer (minus the escrow company's handling fee, equal to between 2 and 4 percent of the item's selling price).

Before you start an escrow transaction, make sure that you and the seller agree on these terms (use e-mail to sort it out). Here are three questions about escrow that you should know the answers to before you bid:

✔ Who pays the escrow fee? (Normally, the buyer does, though sometimes the buyer and seller split the cost.)

✔ How long is the inspection period? (Routinely, it's two business days after receipt of the merchandise.)

✔ Who pays for return shipping if the item is rejected? (The buyer, usually.)

If you use a credit card or bank wire, you can pay return shipping costs right from your computer. If you're not comfortable giving your credit card number online, you can print out the escrow company's credit card form and fax it to the company.

Shipping and insurance costs

Don't let the sale go down with the shipping. Most auction descriptions end with "buyer to pay shipping charges." If the item is not an odd shape, excessively large, or fragile, experienced sellers calculate the shipping based on Priority Mail at the U.S. Post Office, which is the unofficial eBay standard. Expect to pay $3.20 for the first 2 pounds and another 35 cents to pay for tracking the item.

It's also become somewhat routine for the seller to add a dollar or so for packing materials like paper, bubble wrap, tape, and such. The cost of these items can run up over time.

You may come across sellers trying to nickel-and-dime their way to a fortune by jacking up the prices on shipping to ridiculous proportions. If you have a question about shipping costs, ask before you bid on the item.

Before bidding on big stuff, like a barber's chair or a sofa, check for something in the item description that says "Buyer Pays Actual Shipping Charges." When you see that, always e-mail the seller prior to your bid to find out what those shipping charges would be to your home. On larger items, you may need to factor in packing and crating charges. The seller may also suggest a specific shipping company.

As the bumper sticker says, (ahem) *stuff* happens. Sometimes to the stuff you buy. But before you give up and just stuff it, consider insuring it. eBay transactions sometimes involve two types of insurance that may have an impact on your pocketbook:

✔ **Shipping insurance:** This insurance covers your item as it travels through the U.S. Postal Service, the United Parcel Service, Federal Express, or any of the other carriers.

Although many sellers offer shipping insurance as an option, others don't bother because if the price of the item is low, they'd rather refund your money and keep you happy than go through all that insurance paperwork. Don't forget that if you want shipping insurance, you pay for it. (Chapter 11 is where to look for details on shipping insurance.)

✔ **Fraud insurance:** eBay has some nominal insurance against fraud. eBay has a deal with the world-famous insurer Lloyds of London. eBay insurance pays up to $175 (a maximum of $200 minus a $25 deductible). So if you file a $50 claim, you get $25. If you file a $5,000 claim, you still only get $175. (All the details of this type of insurance are covered in Chapter 15.)

Placing Your Bid

Okay, you've found the perfect item to track (say a classy Elvis Presley wristwatch), and it's in your price range. You're more than interested — you're ready to bid. If this were a live auction, some stodgy-looking guy in a gray suit would see you nod your head and start the bidding at, say, $2. Then some woman with a severe hairdo would yank on her ear, and the Elvis watch would jump to $3.

eBay reality is more like this: You're sitting home in your fuzzy slippers, sipping coffee in front of the computer; all the other bidders are cruising cyberspace in their pajamas, too. You just can't see 'em. (Be thankful for little favors.)

When you're ready to jump into the eBay fray, you can find the Bidding form (shown in Figure 6-2) at the bottom of the auction item page (or click the Bid paddle icon at the top of the auction page). The Bidding form restates some vital info that's always good to review before you commit yourself.

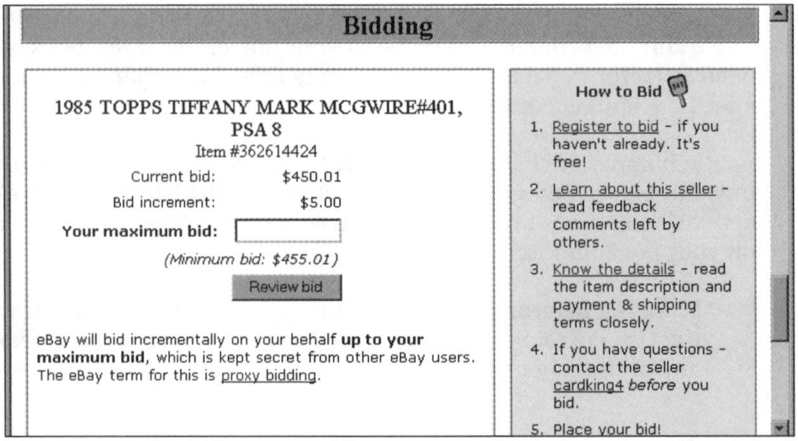

Figure 6-2:
You can find the Bidding form at the bottom of every auction page.

Bidding

1985 TOPPS TIFFANY MARK MCGWIRE#401, PSA 8
Item #362614424

Current bid: $450.01
Bid increment: $5.00

Your maximum bid: [＿＿＿＿＿]

(Minimum bid: $455.01)

[Review bid]

eBay will bid incrementally on your behalf **up to your maximum bid,** which is kept secret from other eBay users. The eBay term for this is <u>proxy bidding</u>.

How to Bid

1. <u>Register to bid</u> – if you haven't already. It's free!

2. <u>Learn about this seller</u> – read feedback comments left by others.

3. <u>Know the details</u> – read the item description and payment & shipping terms closely.

4. If you have questions – contact the seller <u>cardking4</u> *before* you bid.

5. Place your bid!

To fill out the Bidding form and place a bid, first make sure that you're registered (see Chapter 2 for details) and then follow these steps. After you make your first bid on an item, you can instantly get to auctions you're bidding on from your My eBay page. (If you need some tips on how to set up My eBay, see Chapter 4.)

1. **Enter your maximum bid in the appropriate box.**

   The bid needs to be higher than the current minimum bid.

2. **In a Dutch auction, enter the quantity of items that you are bidding on.**

   (If it's not a Dutch auction, the quantity is always 1.) Figure 6-3 shows a Dutch auction Bidding form.

   You don't need to put in the dollar sign but *do* use a decimal point — unless you really *want* to pay $104.90 instead of $10.49. If you make a mistake with an incorrect decimal point, you can retract your bid (see "Retracting your bid" later in this chapter).

3. **Click Review Bid.**

   The Review Bid page appears on your screen, filling it with a wealth of legalese. This is your last chance to change your mind: Do you really want the item, and can you really buy it? The bottom line is this: If you bid on it and you win, you buy it. eBay really means it.

4. **Type in your User ID and password in the boxes provided.**

5. **If you agree to the terms, click Place Bid.**

   After you agree, the Bid Confirmation screen appears.

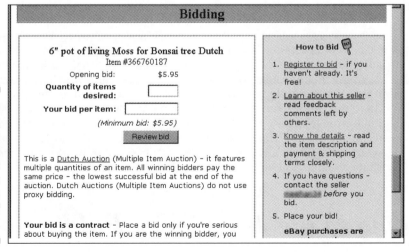

Figure 6-3: The Dutch auction Bidding form requires you to enter the quantity of the items.

Bidding

6" pot of living Moss for Bonsai tree Dutch
Item #366760187

Opening bid: $5.95

Quantity of items desired:

Your bid per item:

(Minimum bid: $5.95)

Review bid

This is a Dutch Auction (Multiple Item Auction) - it features multiple quantities of an item. All winning bidders pay the same price - the lowest successful bid at the end of the auction. Dutch Auctions (Multiple Item Auctions) do not use proxy bidding.

Your bid is a contract - Place a bid only if you're serious about buying the item. If you are the winning bidder, you

How to Bid

1. Register to bid - if you haven't already. It's free!

2. Learn about this seller - read feedback comments left by others.

3. Know the details - read the item description and payment & shipping terms closely.

4. If you have questions - contact the seller ▪▪▪▪▪▪▪ before you bid.

5. Place your bid!

eBay purchases are

When you first start out on eBay, we suggest that you start with a *token bid* — a small bid that won't win you the auction but that can help you keep tabs on the auction's progress.

After you make a bid on an item, the item number and title appear on your My eBay page, listed under (big surprise) Items I'm Bidding On (see Figure 6-4). (See Chapter 4 for more information on My eBay.) The Items I'm Bidding On list makes tracking your auction (or auctions, if you're bidding on multiple items) easy.

Figure 6-4:
Keep track of items you're bidding on right from your My eBay page.

						See items I'm watching...		
			Items I'm Bidding On				See item details...	
Item	Start Price	Current Price	My Max Bid	Quantity	# of Bids	Start Date	End Date PDT	Time Left
MAGAZINE: FLAIR FEBRUARY 1950								
362020187	$9.95	$23.45	$26.52	N/A	6	Jun-19-00	Jun-26-00 09:44:19	**Ended**
"Le Parasol" by Rene Gruau! (reserve met)								
359596857	$150.00	$340.02	$335.02	N/A	9	Jun-15-00	Jun-25-00 21:27:52	**Ended**
BELL SCIENCE - UNCHAINED GODDESS								
364962999	$7.99	$7.99	$9.99	N/A	1	Jun-22-00	Jun-25-00 15:33:24	**Ended**
BELL SCIENCE - ALPHABET CONSPIRACY								
364961904	$7.99	$7.99	$10.02	N/A	1	Jun-22-00	Jun-25-00 15:31:58	**Ended**
American Girl *HEART* Locket Necklace-Alaskid								
363134559	$1.99	$3.25	$5.05	N/A	2	Jun-20-00	Jun-25-00 15:19:23	**Ended**
85 - 89 Corvette Original GM Air Coupler								
361360030	$3.00	$3.25	$5.50	N/A	2	Jun-18-00	Jun-25-00 14:57:45	**Ended**
Item	Start Price	Current Price	My Max Bid	Quantity	# of Bids	Start Date	End Date PDT	Time Left
Totals: 6	$180.92	$385.95	-	N/A	21	-	-	-
Totals: 5	$30.92	$45.93	-	N/A	12	-	-	-

eBay sends you an e-mail confirming your bid. However, eBay's mail server can be as slow as a tree-sloth marathon (yours would be too if you had a few million auctions to keep track of), so don't rely on eBay to keep track of your auctions. After all, this is your money at stake.

eBay considers a bid on an item to be a binding contract. You can save yourself a lot of heartache if you make a promise to yourself — *never bid on an item you don't intend to buy* — and keep to it. Don't make practice bids, assuming that because you're new to eBay you can't win; if you do that, you'll probably win simply because you've left yourself open to Murphy's Law. Therefore, before you go to the Bidding form, be sure that you're in this auction for the long haul and make yourself another promise — *figure out the maximum you're willing to spend* — and stick to it. (Read the section "The Agony (?) of Buyer's Remorse," later in this chapter, for doleful accounts of what can happen if you bid idly or get buyer's remorse.)

Bidding to the Max: Proxy Bidding

When you make a maximum bid on the Bidding form, you actually make several small bids — again and again — until the bidding reaches where you told it to stop. For example, if the current bid is up to $19.99 and you put in a maximum of $45.02, your bid automatically increases incrementally so that you're ahead of the competition — at least until your maximum bid is exceeded by someone else's bid. Basically, you bid by *proxy*, which means that your bid rises incrementally in response to other bidders' bids.

No one else knows for sure whether you're bidding by proxy, and no one knows how high your maximum bid is. And the best part is that you can be out having a life of your own while the proxy bid happens automatically. Buyers and sellers have no control over the increments (appropriately called *bid increments*) that eBay sets. The bid increment is the amount of money by which a bid is raised, and eBay's system can work in mysterious ways. The current maximum bid can jump up a nickel or a quarter or even an Andrew Jackson, but there is a method to the madness, even though you may not think so. eBay uses a *bid-increment formula*, which uses the current high bid to determine how much to increase the bid increment. For example:

- ✔ A 5-quart bottle of cold cream has a current high bid of $14.95. The bid increment is 50 cents — meaning that if you bid by proxy, your proxy will bid $15.45.

- ✔ But a 5-ounce can of top-notch caviar has a high bid of $200. The bid increment is $2.50. If you choose to bid by proxy, your proxy will bid $202.50.

Table 6-1 shows you what kind of magic happens when you put the proxy system and a bid-increment formula together in the same cyber-room.

Table 6-1:		Proxy Bidding and Bid Increments		
Current Bid	Bid Increment	Minimum Bid	eBay Auctioneer	Bidders
$2.50	$0.25	$2.75	"Do I hear $2.75?"	Joe Bidder tells his proxy that his maximum bid is $8. He's the current high bidder at $2.75.
$2.75	$0.25	$3	"Do I hear $3?"	You tell your proxy your maximum bid is $25 and take a nice, relaxing bath while your proxy calls out your $3 bid, making you the current high bidder.

(continued)

Table 6-1: *(continued)*

Current Bid	Bid Increment	Minimum Bid	eBay Auctioneer	Bidders
$3	$.025	$3.25	"I hear $3 from proxy. Do I hear $3.25?"	Joe Bidder's proxy bids $3.25, and while Joe Bidder is walking his dog, he becomes the high bidder.
A heated bidding war ensues between Joe Bidder's proxy and your proxy while the two of you go on with your lives. The bid increment inches from 25 cents to 50 cents as the current high bid increases.				
$7.50	$.50	$8	"Do I hear $8?"	Joe Bidder's proxy calls out $8, his final offer.
$8	$.50	$8.50	"The bid is at $8. Do I hear $8.50?"	Your proxy calls out $8.50 on your behalf, and having outbid your opponent, you win the auction.

Specialized Auction Categories

After you get the hang of bidding at eBay, you may venture to the specialized auction areas. You can purchase fine art from eBay's Great Collections, a car or car parts and accessories from eBay Motors, your own piece of land or a new home in the Real Estate category or office equipment in the Business Exchange. eBay is always adding new specialty areas, so be sure to check the announcements as well as the Home page.

Should you reach the big time bidding, be aware that if you bid over $15,000 in an auction, you *must* register a credit card with eBay. All items in the special categories are searchable in eBay's search engine, so don't worry about missing your dream Corvette when you use the Search page.

eBay Motors

Visiting the automotive area of eBay is an auto enthusiast's dream. You can also find some great deals in used cars and eBay offers some creative ways to make it easy for you.

- ✔ **Search engine:** If you want to search for cars without coming up with hundreds of die-cast vehicles, eBay motors has its own search available from the eBay Motors home page.

- ✔ **Financing:** Through an agreement with E-LOAN, you can set up your financing online directly from eBay. You can lock in interest rates, get a decision within hours, and get a check draft in a day or so.

- ✔ **Inspections:** Many sellers selling used cars take advantage of the inspection service available through eBay and Saturn. Saturn offers a comprehensive 136-point inspection covering mechanical condition and cosmetic appearance, through a good faith, honest observation by Saturn-trained technicians. Car auctions from sellers who have their cars inspected have their auctions listed with an Inspection icon.

- ✔ **Collector Car Insurance:** A link from the eBay Motors home page takes you to Hagerty Collector Car Insurance. By answering a series of questions about your car, you can purchase car collector insurance online. Your car must be at least 20 years old to qualify for this low-cost insurance.

- ✔ **Vehicle Shipping:** Dependable Auto Shippers, DAS, offers free online quotes for auto shipping. You can ship a car from Manhattan to Los Angeles for as low as $715.

- ✔ **Escrow:** Escrow.com is one of the safest ways to purchase a vehicle online. Escrow.com verifies and secures the buyer's payment and releases payment to the seller only after the buyer inspects and is completely satisfied with the vehicle.

eBay Great Collections

eBay purchased Butterfields, the famous brick-and-mortar auction house, and through them, you can participate in online auctions for quality fine arts from top auction houses and dealers. To bid in the Great Collections areas, you must change your registration by adding a credit card if you don't already have one on file with eBay.

Business Exchange

The Business Exchange is a themed area that puts all the items relating to business in one area. You can find agricultural, medical, industrial, and restaurant equipment listed here. Also, retail and office equipment is grouped here.

The Agony (?) of Buyer's Remorse

Maybe you're used to going into a shopping mall and purchasing something that you're not sure you like. What's the worst that could happen? You end up back at the mall, receipt in hand, returning the item. Not so on eBay. Even if you realize you already have a purple feather boa in your closet that's just like the one you won yesterday on eBay, deciding that you don't want to go through with a transaction *is* a big deal. Not only can it earn you some nasty feedback, but it can also give you the reputation of a deadbeat.

It would be a shame to float around eBay with the equivalent of a scarlet D (for *deadbeat*) above your User ID. Okay, eBay uses a kinder term — *nonpaying bidder* — but for many members, it boils down to the same thing. If you won an auction and had to back out of your obligation as the winner — even through no fault of your own — you need some info that can keep you in good (well, okay, *better*) standing. Look no further; you've found it.

Retracting your bid

Remember, many states consider your bid a binding contract, just like any other contract. You can't retract your bid unless some outstandingly unusual circumstances apply:

- ✔ If your bid is clearly a typographical error (you submitted a bid for $4,567 when you really meant $45.67), you may retract your bid.

  You won't get any sympathy if you try to retract an $18.25 bid by saying you meant to bid $15.25, so review your bid before you send it.

- ✔ If the seller substantially changes the description of an item after you place a bid (the description of the item changes from "can of tennis balls" to "a tennis ball," for example), you may retract your bid.

If you simply must retract a bid, try to do so long before the auction ends — and have a good reason for your retraction. eBay users are understanding, up to a point. If you have a good explanation, you should come out of the situation all right. So you admit you've made a mistake. Here's how to retract a bid while the auction's still going on:

1. **Click the Services link on the main navigation bar.**

2. **Click the Buying & Selling link on the subnavigation bar.**

3. **Scroll down to Buyer Tools and click Retract a Bid.**

   The Retracting Bid page appears.

> ## Buyer's remorse *can* pay off
>
> Sometimes buyer's remorse does pay off. We know one eBay buyer who got a serious case of remorse after winning an auction. She decided to do the right thing and pay for the item even though she didn't want it. After receiving the item, she turned around and *sold* it on eBay for triple what she paid. If you really don't want the item, think like a seller — see whether you can turn a horrible mistake into a profitable venture. For more information on the benefits of selling, have a look at Chapter 9.

4. **Read the legalese and scroll down the page; then type in your User ID, your password, the item number of the auction you're retracting your bid from, and an explanation (in 80 characters or less) in the windows provided.**

   Take a second to review what you've written because after a bid is retracted, it can't be reinstated.

5. **Click the Retract Bid button.**

   You receive a confirmation of your bid retraction via e-mail. Keep a copy of it until the auction is completed.

The seller may send you an e-mail to ask for a more lengthy explanation of your retraction, especially if the item was a hot seller that received a lot of bids. You may also get e-mails from other bidders. Keep your replies courteous. After you retract one bid on an item, all your lower bids on that item are also retracted and your retraction goes into the bidding history — another good reason to have a really good reason for the retraction. The number of bids you've retracted also goes on your feedback rating scorecard.

Avoiding deadbeat (nonpaying bidder) status

Some bidders are more like kidders — they bid even though they have no intention of buying a thing. But they don't last long on eBay because of all the negative feedback they get. In fact, when honest eBay members spot these ne'er-do-wells, they often post the deadbeats' User IDs on eBay's message boards. Some eBay members have created entire Web sites to warn others about dealing with the deadbeats . . . ahem . . . *nonpaying bidders*. (Civilized but chilly, isn't it?) Exceptions to the deadbeat (er, sorry, *nonpaying bidder*) rule may include the following human mishaps:

✔ A death in the family.

✔ Computer failure.

✔ A huge misunderstanding.

If you have a good reason to call off your purchase, make sure that eBay knows about it. Figure 6-5 shows you the Non-Paying Bidder Appeal form.

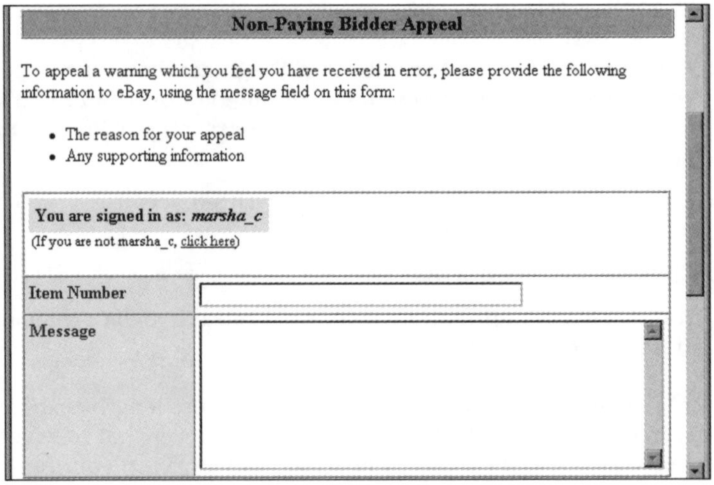

Figure 6-5:
You may succeed at appealing a deadbeat warning if you include good information on this form.

> **Non-Paying Bidder Appeal**
>
> To appeal a warning which you feel you have received in error, please provide the following information to eBay, using the message field on this form:
>
> • The reason for your appeal
> • Any supporting information
>
> **You are signed in as:** *marsha_c*
> (If you are not marsha_c, click here)
>
> | Item Number | |
> | Message | |

Here's how to plead your case from just about any eBay page:

1. **Click the Help link on the main navigation bar.**

   You're taken to the Help Overview page.

2. **Click the Rules and Safety link in the subnavigation bar.**

   You're taken to the Rules & Safety Overview page.

3. **Scroll down to the Policies heading and click the Non-Paying Bidder Policy link.**

   You're taken to the Non-Paying Bidder Program page, where you can read eBay's policy and instructions on how to make an appeal.

4. **Scroll down the page and click the Non-Paying Bidder Appeal Form link.**

   You're taken to the Non-Paying Bidder Appeal form (refer to Figure 6-5).

5. **On the Non-Paying Bidder Appeal form, fill in your e-mail address.**

6. **In the Message box, write the reasons for your appeal and also include the following information:**

   • The transaction number for the item

   • Your User ID

   • Any supporting information you have to plead your case

7. **Review the information you've given. If you have to change anything you've written, click the Clear All Data button and start over.**

8. **Click the Send Inquiry button.**

   All done. Now sit back and cross your fingers.

There's no guarantee that your nonpaying bidder appeal will be accepted. eBay will contact you after an investigation and let you know whether your appeal was successful.

eBay has a message for nonpaying bidders: The policy is *four strikes and you're out.* After the first two complaints about a nonpaying (deadbeat) bidder, eBay gives the bad guy or gal a warning. After the third offense, the nonpaying (deadbeat! deadbeat!) bidder gets a 30-day suspension. If there is a fourth offense, the nonpaying bidder is suspended from eBay for good and becomes *NARU* (Not A Registered User). Nobody's tarred and feathered, but you probably won't see hide nor hair of him or her again on eBay.

After the auction: Side deals?

If a bidder is outbid on an item that he or she really wants or if the auction's reserve price isn't met, the bidder may send an e-mail to the seller and see if the seller is willing to make another deal. Maybe the seller has another, similar item or is willing to sell the item directly rather than run a whole new auction. You need to know that this could happen — but eBay doesn't sanction this activity.

Our friend Jack collects autographed final scripts from hit television sitcoms. So when the curtain fell on *Seinfeld*, he had to have a script. Not surprisingly, he found one on eBay with a final price tag that was way out of his league. But he knew that by placing a bid, someone else with a signed script to sell might see his name and try to make a deal. And he was right.

After the auction closed, he received an e-mail from a guy who worked on the final show and had a script signed by all the actors. He offered it to Jack for $1,000 less than the final auction price at eBay. Tempted as he was to take the offer, Jack understood that eBay's rules and regulations wouldn't help him out if the deal turned sour. He was also aware that he wouldn't receive the benefit of feedback (which is the pillar of the eBay community) for the transaction.

If you even *think about* making a side deal, remember that not only does eBay *strictly* prohibit this activity but eBay can suspend you if you are reported for making a side deal. Also, if you're the victim of a side-deal scam, eBay's rules and regulations don't offer you any protection. Our advice? Watch out!

Chapter 7

Power Bidding Strategies

In This Chapter

▶ Knowing your competition

▶ Finding the hidden secrets in the bidding history

▶ Placing a token bid

▶ Using canny strategies to win your auction

*W*e speak to so many people who find an item at eBay, bid on it, and at the last minute — the last hour or the last day — are outbid. Sad and dejected, they feel like real losers.

You're not a loser if you lost at eBay. You just don't know the fine art of sneaky bidding. Sneaky bidding is our way of saying *educated* bidding.

Sports teams study their rivals, and political candidates scout out what the opposition is doing. Bidding in competition against other bidders is just as serious an enterprise. Follow the tips in this chapter and see if you can come up with a strong bidding strategy of your own. Feel free to e-mail us with any scathingly brilliant plans; we're always open to new theories.

Get to Know the High Bidder

The User ID of the person the item would belong to if the auction ended right now is listed on the auction item page. Take a look at this name because you may see it again in auctions for similar items. If the high bidder has lots of feedback, he or she may know the ropes — and be back to fight if you up the ante.

You can use the By Bidder search option, shown in Figure 7-1, to find what the bidder's recent auction experience is. If you're bidding on an item, conducting a bidder search can be a valuable asset: You can size up your competition.

Figure 7-1:
Use the
By Bidder
search
option to
get an idea
of the com-
petition's
auction
experience.

Find Items
To use the old Search Method, click here.

| Smart Search | By Item Number | By Seller | **By Bidder** | Completed Items | International Search |

Bidder's User ID [marsha_c]   [Search]

User ID or email address of bidder. ▸ *Use if you want to see what you bid on.*

Include completed items   ○ No ◉ Yes

Even if not high bidder?   ◉ Yes, even if not the high bidder   ○ No, only if high bidder

# of items per page [25 ▾]

To get the skinny on a bidder, here's the move:

1. **Type in the User ID (or e-mail address) of the bidder you want to search.**

2. **If you want to see auctions that this specific user has bid on in the past, click Yes on the Include Completed Items line.**

   We think you should check completed auctions. They give you a sense of how often the user participates in auctions.

   Remember that eBay has a 30-day limit on the auction information it pro-vides, so don't expect to see results from a year ago. By clicking the item number in the Results of your search, you can see when your main com-petition tends to bid and then bid when you know they won't be looking.

3. **Tell eBay whether you also want to see the person's bid even if he or she is not the high bidder.**

   Clicking Yes means that you want to see the bidder's activity in every auction, even if the person is not the *current* high bidder. Clicking No limits the search to auctions where the bidder is the current top dog. We think you should check all of the bidder's auctions to see how aggres-sively he or she bids on items. You can also see how badly a bidder wants specific items.

4. **Choose the number of items you want to see per page.**

5. **Click Search.**

You may be tempted to try to contact a bidder you're competing with so you can get information about the person more easily. Or you may consider requesting the bidder's contact information from eBay. Doing either is not only bad form but could also get you suspended. Don't do it.

The tale of the 3-plus-negative seller

A friend of ours took a risk and bid on an old Winchester rifle (now a banned item — see Chapter 9 for what you're allowed and not allowed to sell at eBay) without reading the seller's feedback. The seller had a (+3) next to his User ID, which is an okay rating. Good thing our friend lost the auction. It turned out that the seller had a whopping 20 negative feedback messages. He had 23 positives, mostly posted by suspicious-looking names. Repeat after us: Always read the feedback!

Find Out the Item's Bidding History

The *bidding history,* shown on the auction item page, lists everybody who is bidding on an item. You can see how often and at what time bids are placed, but you can't see *how much* each bidder bids until the auction ends. Look at Figure 7-2 to see a typical bidding history list. You can bid amounts because this auction has ended.

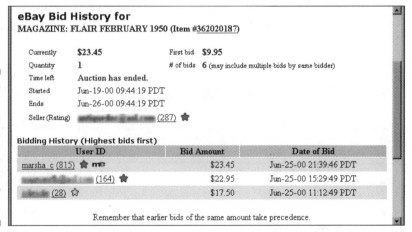

Figure 7-2: The bidding history tells you the date and time at which bidders placed their bids.

Pay attention to the times bidders are placing their bids, and you may find that, like many eBay users, the people bidding in this auction seem to be creatures of habit — making their bids about once a day and at a particular time of day. They may be logging on before work, during lunch, or after work. Whatever their schedules, you have great info at your disposal in the event that a bidding war breaks out: Just bid after your competition traditionally logs out, and you increase your odds of winning the auction.

Early in an auction, there may not be much of a bidding history for an item, but that doesn't mean you can't still check out the dates and times a bidder places bids. You can also tell if a bidder practices *sniping* (discussed later in this chapter) if his or her bid is in the last few minutes of the auction. You may have a fight on your hands if the bidder does do sniping.

Strategies to Help You Outsmart the Competition

Your two cents does matter — at least at eBay. Here's why: Many eBay members tend to round off their bids to the nearest dollar figure. Some choose nice, familiar coin increments like 25, 50, or 75 cents. But the most successful bidders at eBay have found that adding two or three cents to a routine bid can mean the difference between winning and losing. So we recommend that you make your bids in oddish figures, like $15.02 or $45.57, as an inexpensive way to edge out your competition. For the first time ever, your two cents may actually pay off!

That's just one of our many strategies to get you ahead of the rest of the bidding pack without paying more than you should. ***Note:*** The strategies in this section are for bidders who are tracking an item over the course of a week or so, so be sure you have time to track the item and plan your next moves. Also, get a few auctions under your belt before you throw yourself into the middle of a bidding war.

Dutch auction strategy

Dutch auctions (auctions in which the seller has multiple items for sale, explained in Chapter 1) are funky. Yes, that's a technical term that means that Dutch auction strategy is a little different. After all, each winner pays the same amount for the item, and Dutch auctions don't have a super-secret reserve price.

But *winning* a Dutch auction isn't all that different from winning other auctions. Therefore, wait until the closing minutes of the auction to bid and then follow our sage advice for optimum success.

Here are the key things to remember about a Dutch auction:

✔ **The seller must sell all the items at the *lowest winning price* at the end of the auction, no matter what.**

✔ **Winners are based on the *highest* bids received.** If you up the ante, you could win the auction and only pay the *lowest winning price,* which may be lower than your bid.

Confused yet? Say the minimum bid for each of ten Elvis watches is $10 and 20 people bid at $10, each person bidding for one watch. The first ten bidders win the watch. But suppose you come along at the end of the auction and bid $15 as the 21st bidder. You get a watch (as do the first nine people who bid $10), *and* you get the watch for the lowest successful bid — which is $10! Get it?

✔ **Know where you stand in the pecking order.** You can see a list of high bidders (and their bids) on the auction page, so you always know where you stand in the pecking order.

✔ **Avoid being the lowest or the highest high bidder.** The highest bidder is sure to win, so the usual bidding strategy is to knock out the lowest high bidder. The lowest high bidder is said to be *on the bubble* and on the verge of losing the auction by a couple of pennies. To avoid being the bidder on the bubble, keep your bid just above the second-lowest winning bid.

✔ **If you want to buy more than one of an item up for auction, make sure you have that number of successful high bids as the auction draws to a close.** Huh? Remember, winners are based on the *highest* bids. If you're in a Dutch auction for ten items and place five $15 bids, nothing guarantees that you'll win five of the item. Nine other people who want the item could bid $20 apiece. Then they each win one of the items at 15 bucks, and you end up with only one of the item. (At least you still pay only $15 for it.)

Most bidding at eBay goes on during East Coast work time and early evening hours, which gives you a leg up if you live out West. Night-owl bidders will find that after 11 p.m. Pacific Time (about 2 a.m. Eastern Time), lots of bargains are to be had. And believe it or not, lots of auctions end in the wee hours of the morning. Holidays are also great for bargains — especially Thanksgiving. While everyone is in the living room digesting and arguing about what to watch on TV, fire up eBay and be thankful for the great bargains you can win.

Bidding strategies eBay doesn't talk about

Here's a list of Do's and Don'ts that can help you win your item. Of course, some of these tips *are* eBay-endorsed, but we had to get you to notice what we had to say somehow.

✔ **Don't bid early and high.** Bidding early *and high* shows that you have a clear interest in the item. It also shows that you are a rookie, apt to make mistakes. If you bid early and high, you may give away just how much you want the item.

Of course, a higher bid does mean more bucks for the seller and a healthy cut for the middleman. No big mystery that many sellers recommend it. In fact, when you sell an item, you may want to encourage it too.

✔ **Do wait and watch your auction.** If you're interested in an item and you have the time to watch it from beginning to end, we say that the best strategy is to wait. Mark the auction to Watch This Item on your My eBay page and remember to check it daily. But if you don't have the time, then go ahead — put in your maximum bid early and cross your fingers.

✔ **Don't freak out if you find yourself in a bidding war.** Don't keel over if, at the split second you're convinced that you're the high bidder with your $45.02, someone beats you out at $45.50.

You can increase your maximum bid to $46, but if your bidding foe also has a maximum of $46, the tie goes to the person who put in the highest bid first. Bid as high as you're willing to go, but bid at the very end of the auction.

✔ **Do check the item's bidding history.** If you find yourself in a bidding war and want an item badly enough, check the bidding history and identify your fiercest competitor; then refer to the earlier section "Get to Know the High Bidder" for a pre-auction briefing.

To get a pretty exact picture of your opponent's bidding habits, make special note of the times of day when he or she has bid on other auctions. You can adjust your bidding times accordingly.

✔ **Do remember that most deals go through without a problem.** The overwhelming majority of deals at eBay are closed with no trouble, which means that if the auction you're bidding in is typical and you come in second place, you've lost.

However, if the winning bidder backs out of the auction, the seller *could* (but isn't obligated to) come to the second highest bidder and offer to sell the item at the second bidder's price. eBay doesn't sanction this activity, and it's grounds to get bounced from the eBay community.

Time Is Money: Strategy by the Clock

Different bidding strategies can be used depending on how much time is left in an auction. By paying attention to the clock, you can learn about your competition, beat them out, and end up paying less for your item.

Most auctions at eBay run for a week; the auction item page always lists how much time is left. However, sellers can run auctions for as short as three days or as long as ten days. So synchronize your computer clock with eBay's master time and become the most precise eBay bidder around. Figure 7-3 shows eBay's Official Time page.

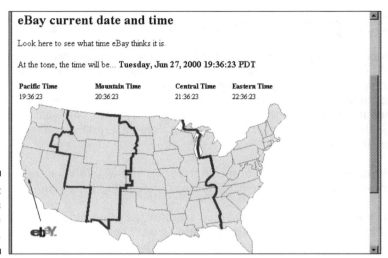

Figure 7-3:
eBay's
Official Time
page.

To synchronize your clock, make sure that you're logged on to the Internet and can easily access the eBay Web site. Then follow these steps:

1. **Go into your computer's Control Panel and double-click the icon that represents your system's date and time functions.**

2. **Go to the Site Map by clicking its link above the navigation bar on the top of every eBay page.**

   On the subcategory page, you see the eBay Official Time link.

3. **Click the eBay Official Time link.**

4. **Check your computer's time against eBay's current time.**

5. **Click the minutes in your system clock and then click the Reload button on your browser.**

6. **Type in the minutes displayed on the eBay Official Time page as soon as the newly reloaded page appears.**

7. **Repeat Steps 5 and 6 to synchronize your system's seconds display with eBay's.**

This process takes a little practice, but it can mean the difference between winning and losing an auction.

You don't need to worry about the hour display unless you don't mind your system clock displaying Pacific Time.

Using the lounging-around strategy

Sometimes the best strategy at the beginning of an auction is to do nothing at all. That's right; relax, take your shoes off, and loaf. Go ahead. You may want to make a *token bid* (a low maximum) or mark the page to watch. We take this attitude through the first six days of a week-long auction we want to bid on, and it works pretty well. Of course, we check in every day just to keep tabs on the items we're watching in our My eBay page, and we revise our strategy as time goes by.

We recommend that if you see an item that you absolutely must have, mark it to watch and plan and revise your maximum bid as the auction goes on.

As you check back each day, take a look at the other bids and the high bidder. Is someone starting up a bidding war? Look at the time that the competition is bidding and note patterns. Maybe at noon Eastern Time? During lunch? If you know what time your major competition is bidding, then when the time is right, you can safely bid after he or she does (preferably when your foe is stuck in rush-hour traffic).

If you play the wait-and-see method, then you can decide if you really want to up your bid or wait around for the item to show up again sometime. You may decide you really don't want the item after all. Or you may feel no rush because many sellers who offer multiple items put them up one at a time.

Using the beat-the-clock strategy

You should rev up your bidding strategy during the final 24 hours of an auction and decide, once and for all, whether you really *have* to have the item you've been eyeing. Maybe you put in a maximum bid of $45.02 earlier in the week. Now's the time to decide whether you're willing to go as high as $50.02.

No one wants to spend the day in front of the computer (ask almost anyone who does). You can camp out by the refrigerator or at your desk or wherever you want to be. Just stick a Post-it note where you're likely to see it, reminding you of the exact time the auction ends. You can also use TurboBid, an automatic bidding software program we tell you about in Chapter 19 to bid for you if you know you'll miss the end of an auction.

In the last half hour

With a half hour left before the auction becomes ancient history, head for the computer and dig in for the last battle of the bidding war. We recommend that you log on to eBay about 15 to 20 minutes before the auction ends. The

---

The story of the Snipe sisters

Cory and Bonnie are sisters and avid eBay buyers. Bonnie collects vases. She had her eye on a Fenton Dragon Flies Ruby Verdena vase, but the auction closed while she was at work and didn't have access to a computer. Knowing that, sister Cory decided to snipe for it. With 37 seconds to go, she inserted the high bid on behalf of her sister. Bang, she was high bidder at $63. But, with 17 seconds left, another bidder sniped back and raised the price to $73. It was, of course, Bonnie, who had found a way to get access to a computer from where she was. Bonnie got the vase, and they both got a good laugh.

---

last thing you want to have happen is to get caught in Internet gridlock and not get access to the Web site. Go to the items you're watching and click the auction title.

With 15 minutes to go, if there's a lot of action on your auction, click Reload or Refresh every 30 seconds to get the most current info on how many people are bidding.

Sniping to the finish: The final minutes

The rapid-fire, final flurry of bidding is called *sniping.* Sniping is the fine art of waiting until the very last seconds of an eBay auction and then outbidding the current high bidder just in time. Of course, you've got to expect that the current high bidder is probably sniping back.

With a hot item, we recommend that you open a second window on your browser (by pressing the Ctrl key and the N key together), keeping one open for bidding and the other open for constant reloading during the final minutes. With the countdown at 60 seconds or less, make your final bid. Then keep reloading or refreshing your browser as fast as you can and watch the time tick to the end of the auction.

Some eBay members consider the practice of sniping unseemly and uncivilized — like when dozens of parents used to mob the department store clerks to get to the handful of Cabbage Patch dolls that were just delivered. (Come to think of it, whatever happened to *those* collectibles?) Of course, sometimes a little uncivilized behavior can be a hoot.

We say that sniping is an addictive, fun part of life at eBay. And it's a blast. So our recommendation is that you try sniping. You're likely to benefit from the results and enjoy your eBay experience even more — especially if you're an adrenaline junkie.

The auction to-the-death, two-front sniping plan

If you get way far into eBay, sniping may become an everyday adrenaline rush for you, and you can increase your odds of success at the last second by viewing the auction you really want to win on *two* separate browser windows — one to reload and watch the action, and the other to bid with.

In the first browser window, click the Refresh or Reload button every few seconds to keep you up to date on where the bidding stands; use the second browser window to prepare your final bid. If you've got a slow computer, place your bid with about 45 seconds to go. If you have a very fast computer, do it in the last 20 seconds. Some people with nerves of steel wait until T-minus-15-seconds-and-counting to click Confirm on the Bidding page.

Here's a list of things to keep in mind when you get ready to place your last bid:

- Know how high you're willing to go.

  If you know there's a lot of competition, figure out your highest bid to the penny. You should have already researched the item and know its value at this point. Raise your bid only to the level where you're sure you're getting a good return on your investment and don't go overboard. Certainly, if the item has some emotional value to you and you just have to have it, bid as high as you want. But remember, you'll have to pay the piper later. You win it, you own it!

- Know how fast (or slow) your Internet connection is.

- Remember, this is a game and sometimes it's a game of chance, so don't lose heart if you lose the auction.

Although sellers love sniping because it drives up prices and bidders love it because it's fun, a sniper can ruin a week's careful work on auction strategy. The most skillful snipers sneak in a bid so close to the end of the auction that there is no chance for you to counter-bid, which means you lose. Losing too often, especially to the same sniper, can be a drag.

If your Internet connection is slower than most, and you want to do some sniping, make your final bid two minutes before the auction and adjust the amount of the bid as high as you feel comfortable so you can beat out the competition.

If you can make the highest bid with just 20 seconds left, you most likely will win. With so many bids coming in the final seconds, your bid might be the last one eBay records. Figure 7-4 shows the bidding history for a copy of a rare book of magic patents. That's some close bidding.

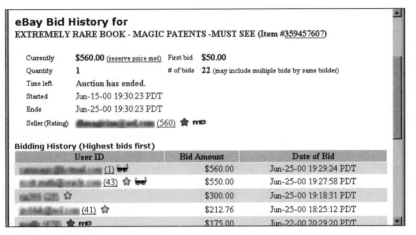

eBay Bid History for
EXTREMELY RARE BOOK - MAGIC PATENTS -MUST SEE (Item #359457607)

Currently	$560.00 (reserve price met)	First bid	$50.00
Quantity	1	# of bids	22 (may include multiple bids by same bidder)
Time left	Auction has ended.		
Started	Jun-15-00 19:30:23 PDT		
Ends	Jun-25-00 19:30:23 PDT		
Seller (Rating)	▓▓▓▓▓▓▓▓▓ (560) ⭐ me		

Bidding History (Highest bids first)

User ID	Bid Amount	Date of Bid
▓▓▓▓▓▓ (1) 👓	$560.00	Jun-25-00 19:29:24 PDT
▓▓▓▓▓▓ (43) ⭐ 👓	$550.00	Jun-25-00 19:27:58 PDT
▓▓▓▓ ⭐	$300.00	Jun-25-00 19:18:31 PDT
▓▓▓▓▓▓ (41) ⭐	$212.76	Jun-25-00 18:25:12 PDT
▓▓▓▓ ⭐ me	$175.00	Jun-22-00 20:29:20 PDT

This stuff is supposed to be fun, so don't lose perspective. If you can't afford an item, don't get caught up in a bidding war. Otherwise, the only person who wins is the seller. If you're losing sleep, barking at your cat, or biting your nails over any item, it's time to rethink what you're doing. Shopping at eBay is like being in a long line in a busy department store. If it's taking too much of your life or an item costs too much, be willing to walk away — or log off — and live to bid (or shop) another day.

Chapter 8

After You Win the Auction

In This Chapter

▶ Getting yourself organized

▶ Talking turkey with the seller

▶ Ironing out the details and sending out your payment

▶ Dealing with an AWOL seller

▶ Finishing the transaction with feedback

*T*he thrill of the chase is over, and you've won your first eBay auction. Congratulations — now what do you do? You have to follow up on your victory and keep a sharp eye on what you're doing. The post-auction process can be loaded with pitfalls and potential headaches if you don't watch out. Remember, sometimes money, like a full moon, does strange things to people.

In this chapter, you can get a handle on what's in store for you after you win the auction. We clue you in on what the seller's supposed to do to make the transaction go smoothly and show you how to grab hold of your responsibilities as a buyer. We give you info here about following proper post-auction etiquette, including the best way to get organized, communicate with the seller professionally, and send your payment without hazards. We also brief you on how to handle an imperfect transaction.

eBay Calling: You're a Winner

The Bidding/Watching section of your My eBay page highlights the titles of auctions you've won and indicates the amount of your winning bid. If you think you may have won the auction and don't want to wait around for eBay to contact you, check out this section for yourself and find out — are you a winner?

Throughout the bidding process, items that you're winning appear in green on your My eBay page. If you've been outbid, the item appears in red.

After the auction ends, there's no marching band, no visit from Ed McMahon and his camera crew, and no oversized check to duck behind. In fact, you're more likely to find out that you've won the auction from either the seller or the Items I'm Bidding On section of your My eBay page than you are to hear it right away from eBay. eBay tries to get its End of Auction e-mails (EOAs) out pronto, but sometimes there's a bit of lag time. For a look at all the contact information in the End of Auction e-mail, see Figure 8-1.

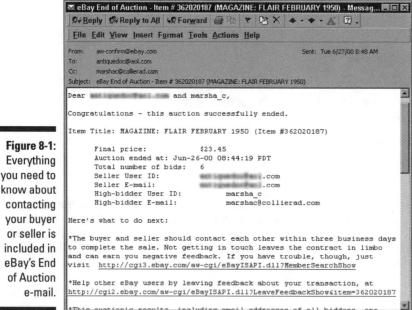

Figure 8-1:
Everything you need to know about contacting your buyer or seller is included in eBay's End of Auction e-mail.

Getting Your Paperwork Together

Yeah, we know that PCs are supposed to create a paperless society, but cars were supposed to fly by 2000 A.D., too. Maybe it's just as well that some predictions don't come true (think of the way some people drive). Paper still has its uses; printing out hard copies of your auction records can help you keep your transactions straight.

Your auction page shows the amount of your winning bid, the item's description, and other relevant information. The second you find out you've won the auction, print out *two* copies of the auction page. Keep one copy for your files. Send the second copy to the seller when you send your payment; doing so is not only efficient, but it's also polite.

An order of fries with a menu on the side

One seller offered an old menu from Howard Johnson's, estimating its era as the 1950s based on the cars pictured on the cover — and the prices (fried clams were $1.25). Also included was a separate menu card that listed fresh seafood and that had a liquor menu (with Pieman logo) on the back — plus a list of loca-tions in the New York City area. Except for a couple of staple holes at the top of the front cover (maybe evidence of daily specials past), the menu was in very good condition. The starting bid was $5; the item sold for $64.

(Wonder what they want for fried clams in New York these days . . .)

eBay only displays auctions for 30 days after they end, so don't put off printing out that final auction page for your records.

Many sellers have multiple auctions going at the same time, so the more organized you are, the more likely you will be to receive the correct item (and positive feedback) from the seller. Here's a list of the items you should keep in your auction file:

✔ A copy of your EOA e-mail from eBay. *Don't* delete the EOA e-mail. At least not until you print a copy and keep it for your records. You may need to refer to the EOA e-mail later, and there's no way to get another copy.

✔ Printed copies of all e-mail correspondence between you and the seller — especially e-mail that details payment and shipping arrangements.

✔ Two printed copies of the final auction page.

Sellers can edit and update their auctions even while they're in progress. And keep your eyes peeled for changes in the auction as you monitor it. If there are major changes in the item, you are within your rights to withdraw your bid. (Check out Chapter 6 for more on the bidding process.)

Getting Contact Information

The eBay rules and regulations say that buyers and sellers must contact each other by e-mail within three business days of the auction's end. So, if an item closes on a Saturday, you need to make contact by Wednesday.

Most sellers contact auction winners promptly because they want to complete the transaction and get paid. Few buyers or sellers wait for the official eBay EOA e-mail to contact each other. In fact, you have several ways to find contact information:

- ✔ Click the Ask Seller a Question link on the auction page, which takes you to the User ID History and E-mail Address Request Form in the Find Members section.

- ✔ Click the Site Map link, located in the top-right corner of every eBay page, and then click the Search for Members link.

- ✔ Click the Search link on the main navigation bar and then click the Find Members link on the submenu.

  All three of these options take you to Hawaii. Okay, they take you to the Find Members page, but we *wish* they would take us to Hawaii.

Within the first three business days after an auction, limit yourself to requesting the seller's e-mail address by filling out the E-mail Address and User ID History window on the Find Members page and then clicking the Submit button. The seller's User ID history and e-mail address, shown in Figure 8-2, immediately appear.

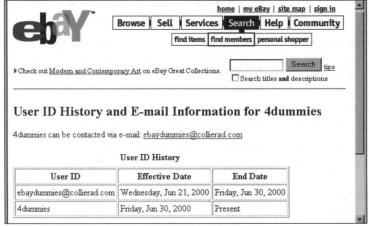

Figure 8-2:
The User ID
History and
E-mail
Information
form gives
you the
seller's
e-mail
address.

So, What's Your Number?

If you don't hear from the seller after three business days and you've already tried sending an e-mail, you need to get more contact information. Remember back when you registered and eBay asked for a phone number? eBay keeps this information for times like this.

To get an eBay member's phone number, go back to the Find Members page and fill out the Contact Info form by entering the seller's User ID, as well as your User ID and password, and then clicking the Submit button.

If all the information is correct, you automatically see a request-confirmation page and eBay automatically generates an e-mail to both you and the other user, as shown in Figure 8-3.

Figure 8-3:
After you request a user's phone number, you receive an automatic e-mail from eBay that includes the user's contact information.

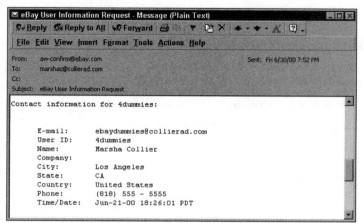

```
eBay User Information Request - Message (Plain Text)                    _ □ X
Reply   Reply to All   Forward                       ?
File  Edit  View  Insert  Format  Tools  Actions  Help

From:     aw-confirm@ebay.com              Sent:  Fri 6/30/00 7:52 PM
To:       marshac@collierad.com
Cc:
Subject:  eBay User Information Request

Contact information for 4dummies:

      E-mail:      ebaydummies@collierad.com
      User ID:     4dummies
      Name:        Marsha Collier
      Company:
      City:        Los Angeles
      State:       CA
      Country:     United States
      Phone:       (818) 555 - 5555
      Time/Date:   Jun-21-00 18:26:01 PDT
```

eBay's e-mail includes the seller's User ID, name, company, city, state, and country of residence, as well as the seller's phone number and date of initial registration. eBay sends this same information about you to the user you want to get in touch with.

Often, sellers jump to attention when they receive this e-mail from eBay and get the ball rolling to complete the transaction.

eBay doesn't tolerate any abuses of its contact system. Make sure that you only use this resource to communicate with another user about a specific transaction. If you abuse the contact system, eBay can investigate you and kick you off the site.

If the seller doesn't contact you within three business days, you may have to do some nudging to complete the transaction (see "Keeping in Touch: Dealing with an AWOL Seller," later in this chapter, and have a look at Chapter 12).

Talking Turkey: Communicating with the Seller

Top-notch sellers know that communication is the absolute key to a successful transaction, and they do everything they can to set a positive tone for the entire process with speedy and courteous e-mails.

Here's what a good e-mail from a professional eBay seller should include:

- Confirmation of the winning price
- The address for sending payment or a phone number for credit card processing
- A review of the shipping options and price (the fee you pay)
- Confirmation of escrow (if offered in the auction)
- The date the item will be shipped

When you read the seller's e-mail, be sure to compare the terms the seller's laid out in his or her e-mail with the terms laid out on the auction page. And make sure that the form of payment and where it should be sent are clear to you.

When you e-mail the seller a reply, you should

- Let the seller know what form of payment you're using. For info on payment options, see Chapter 6.
- Include your address, name, and User ID.
- Include the item's title and item number so that the seller knows exactly what you are referring to and can get your item ready to ship as soon as the payment arrives.
- Include your phone number if you plan to pay with a credit card. If there's a problem with the credit card number you've given, the seller can contact you promptly to let you know.
- Request that the seller e-mail you any shipping information, such as tracking numbers and an approximate arrival date.

The e-mail you receive from the seller after the auction is over should be a confirmation of the options laid out on the auction item page. If there are significant differences between what the seller's saying now and what you see on your printout of the auction item page, address them immediately with the seller before you proceed with the transaction. For more on clarifying payment options during the bidding process, see Chapter 6.

Sending Out the Payment Promptly and Securely

So how many times have you heard the saying "The check is in the mail"? Yeah, we've heard it about a thousand times too. If you're on the selling end of a transaction, hearing this line from the buyer but not getting the money is frustrating. If you're on the buying end, it's very bad form and also leads to bad feedback for you.

Being the good buyer that you are (you're here finding out how to do the right thing, right?), naturally, you'll get your payment out pronto.

Most sellers expect to get paid within seven business days after the close of the auction. Although this timeline isn't mandatory, it makes good sense to let the seller know payment is on the way.

Send your payment promptly. If you have to delay payment for any reason (you have to go out of town, you ran out of checks, you broke your leg), let the seller know as soon as possible. Most sellers are understanding if you send them a kind and honest e-mail. Let the seller know what's up, give him or her a date by which the money can be expected, and then meet that deadline. If the wait is unreasonably long, the seller may cancel the auction. In that case, you can expect to get some bad feedback.

Here are some tips on how to make sure that your payment reaches the seller promptly and safely:

- Have your name and address printed on your checks. A check without a printed name or address sends up a big red flag to sellers that the check may not clear. For privacy and safety reasons, though, *never* put your driver's license number or Social Security number on your check.

- Always write the item title and your User ID on a check or money order and enclose a printout of the final auction page in the envelope. The Number 1 pet peeve of most eBay sellers is that they get a payment but don't know what it's for — that buyers send checks without any auction information.

- If you're paying with a credit card without using a payment service and you want to give the seller the number over the telephone, be sure to request the seller's phone number in your reply to the seller's initial e-mail and explain why you want it.

- You can safely e-mail your credit card information over the course of several e-mails, each containing four numbers from your credit card. Stagger your e-mails so that they're about 20 minutes apart and don't forget to let the seller know what kind of credit card you're using. Also, give the card's expiration date.

Buyers routinely send out payments without their name, their address, or a clue as to what they've purchased. No matter how you pay, be sure to include a copy of the eBay confirmation letter, a printout of the auction page, or a copy of the e-mail the seller sent you. If you pay with a credit card via e-mail or over the phone, you should still send this info through the mail just to be on the safe side.

Using person-to-person payment services

Chapter 6 covers the pros and cons of using the services Billpoint and PayPal to pay for your auctions. There are other services, like ecount.com, that work in pretty much the same way. But because Billpoint and PayPal are the leaders at eBay, we want to take you step-by-step through how to pay for your auction with them:

eBay online payment by Billpoint

eBay sees to it that online payment by Billpoint is incredibly easy to use because Billpoint is the official credit card payment service at eBay. After the auction is over, a link to Billpoint appears (see Figure 8-4). If you'd like, wait until you hear from the seller. (We always like to have the seller's full name and address for our records before we send payments.)

The seller may send you a Billpoint invoice, or you can request your own. As high bidder, scroll down to find the Billpoint online payment links. Click to request and invoice, and if the seller has issued one, it will appear. If the seller has not as yet issued an invoice, you are prompted to fill out the Notify Seller Email Template. After you send the form, the seller is prompted to e-mail an invoice.

Figure 8-4:
Billpoint's
convenient
payment
link.

eBay Online Payments by Billpoint
VISA MasterCard
Credit Cards
•**High Bidder:** Click here to request an Invoice.
•**Seller:** Click here to send an Invoice.

As a Billpoint member, you can instantly pay for an auction without hassle. Your credit card information is kept with Billpoint, and your payment is deposited into the seller's Billpoint account.

PayPal

PayPal is very easy to navigate, and making a payment is fairly cut and dry. When the auction is over, you can click the PayPal logo at the bottom of the auction page to enter the PayPal site (see Figure 8-5). If the seller hasn't supplied a clickable link or has sent you a PayPal money request, just type **www.paypal.com** in your browser. Then follow these steps:

I accept payments from anyone with a credit card at PayPal – always
FREE!

PayPal

1. **If this is your first visit to the PayPal site, register.**

   If you're already a registered user, go ahead and log in by following the steps on screen.

2. **Click the Auction Tools tab and then scroll down and click Pay for an Auction.**

PayPal takes you step-by-step through how to fill out a payment form to iden-tify the auction you're paying for as well as your shipping information. You're all done. Your credit card information is held safely with PayPal, and the pay-ment is deposited into the seller's PayPal account. The seller receives notice of your payment and notifies you about how quickly he or she will ship your item.

Using i-Escrow

If you and the seller have agreed to use escrow to complete your transaction, you must first register your auction for an i-Escrow transaction.

To sign up for escrow from any eBay page, step right up:

1. **Click the Services link on the main navigation bar.**

   You're taken to the Services Overview page.

2. **On the subnavigation bar, click Buying & Selling.**

   You're taken to the Buying and Selling Tools page.

3. **Click the Escrow link under the Buyer Tools heading of the Buying and Selling Tools page.**

4. **Fill out the form with your User ID, password (*save time by signing in*), and item number to start using the escrow service.**

5. **Click the Proceed button.**

   You're taken to Step 2 of the escrow process. Review all the listed information.

6. **Click the Proceed button.**

   You're taken to Step 3 of the escrow process. Read the terms and conditions; this is the last chance for you to cancel the process. eBay sends the information to i-Escrow, an Internet escrow company, for processing.

7. **Click the I Agree button.**

   Your escrow is in the works, and i-Escrow either calls or e-mails you with information regarding the details of this transaction.

Keeping in Touch: Dealing with an AWOL Seller

The eBay community, like local towns and cities, is not without its problems. With the millions of transactions that go on every week, transactional difficulties do pop up now and then.

The most common problem is the AWOL seller — the kind of person who pesters you for payment and then disappears. Just as you're expected to hustle and get your payment off to the seller within a week, the seller has an obligation to notify you within a week of receiving your payment with an e-mail that says the item has been shipped. If you sent the money but you haven't heard a peep in awhile, don't jump the gun and assume the person is trying to cheat you.

Follow this week-by-week approach if you've already paid for the item but you haven't heard from the seller:

- ✔ **Week one, the gentle-nudge approach:** Remind the seller with an e-mail about the auction item, its number, and the closing date. "Perhaps this slipped your mind and got lost in the shuffle of your other auctions" is a good way to broach the subject. Chances are good that you'll get an apologetic e-mail about some family emergency or last-minute business trip. You'll find that the old saying "You can attract a lot more bees with honey than with vinegar" works great at eBay.

- ✔ **Week two, the civil-but-firm approach:** Send an e-mail again. Be civil but firm. Set a date for when you expect to be contacted. Meanwhile, tap into some of eBay's resources. See the section "Getting Contact Information" in this chapter to find out how to get an eBay user's phone number. After you have this information, you can send a follow-up letter or make direct contact and set a deadline for some sort of action.

> ✓ **Week three, the take-action time:** If you still haven't heard from the seller, go to Rules & Safety (SafeHarbor) and file a complaint. Explain in detail what has transpired. eBay will launch its own internal investigation. Turn to Chapter 15 to find out more about filing complaints and using other tools to resolve problems.

You Get the Item (Uh-Oh! What's This?)

The vast majority of eBay transactions go without a hitch. You win, you send your money, you get the item, you check it out, you're happy. If that's the case — a happy result for your auction — then skip this section and go leave some positive feedback for the seller!

On the other hand, if you're not happy with the item you receive, the seller may have some 'splaining to do. E-mail or call the seller immediately and politely ask for an explanation if the item isn't as described. Some indications of a foul-up are pretty obvious:

> ✓ The item's color, shape, or size doesn't match the description.
>
> ✓ The item's scratched, broken, or dented.
>
> ✓ You won an auction for a set of candlesticks and received a vase instead.

A snag in the transaction is annoying, but don't get steamed right away. Contact the seller and see if you can work things out. Keep the conversation civilized. Most sellers want a clean track record and good feedback, so they'll respond to your concerns and make things right. Assume the best about the seller's honesty, unless you have a real reason to suspect foul play. Remember, you take some risks whenever you buy something that you can't touch. If the item has a slight problem that you can live with, leave it alone and don't go to all the trouble of leaving negative feedback about an otherwise pleasant, honest eBay seller.

Of course, while we can give you advice on what you *deserve* from a seller, you're the one who has to live with the item. If you and the seller can't come to a compromise and you really think you deserve a refund, ask for one.

If you paid the post office to insure the item, and it arrives at your home pretty well pulverized, call the seller and then locate the insurance stamp or paper tag attached to the package. This tag is your proof of insurance. Then take the whole mangled shebang back to the post office and talk to the good folks there about filing a claim. Check out Chapter 11 for more tips on how to deal with a shipping catastrophe. And jump over to Chapter 15 to find out how to file your eBay insurance claim.

Don't Forget the Feedback

Good sellers should be rewarded, and potential buyers should be informed. That's why no eBay transaction is complete until the buyer fills out the feedback form. Following are some handy hints on what kind of feedback to leave for a seller. Before leaving any feedback, though, always remember that sometimes no one's really at fault when transactions get fouled up; communication meltdowns can happen to anyone. (For more info on leaving feedback, see Chapter 4.)

- ✔ Give the seller the benefit of the doubt. If the transaction could have been a nightmare, but the seller really tried to make it right and meet you halfway, that's an easy call — leave positive feedback.

- ✔ Whenever possible, reward someone who seems honest or tried to fix a bad situation. For example, if the seller worked at a snail's pace but you eventually got your item and you're thrilled with it, you may want to leave positive feedback with a caveat. Something like "Item as described, good seller, but very slow to deliver" sends the right feedback message.

- ✔ If the seller worked at a snail's pace and did adequate packaging and the item was kinda-sorta what you thought, you may want to leave neutral feedback; it wasn't bad enough for negative but didn't deserve praise. Here's an example: "Really slow to deliver, didn't say item condition was good not excellent, but did deliver." Wishy-washy is okay as a response to so-so; at least the next buyer will know to ask very specific questions.

- ✔ If the seller doesn't ship your item, or if the item doesn't match the description and the seller won't make things right, you need to leave negative feedback. But never write negative feedback in the heat of the moment and never make it personal. Do expect a response but don't get into a negative feedback war. Life's interesting enough without taking on extra hassles.

The Accidental Deadbeat might be an intriguing title for a movie someday, but being a deadbeat isn't much fun in real life. So see Chapter 6 for details on buyer's remorse and retracting a bid *before* the end of an auction.

Part III
Are You Selling What They're Buying?

The 5th Wave   By Rich Tennant

"Well, if there's anywhere I'll find a pair of shoes to match my yam-hat, it'll be at eBay."

In this part . . .

A lot of different factors are at work when a seller makes a nice profit on an item he or she has put up for auction.

If you're new to selling, you can find out all the benefits of selling and get pointed in the right direction to find items that could make you a tidy profit. In fact, you may be sitting on profits in your own home! eBay has its rules, though, so when you assess an item's value to prepare for your auction you need to make sure the item isn't prohibited from being sold at the eBay site.

In this part, we walk you through the paperwork you need to fill out to list an item for auction, and we show you how to close the deal and ship the item without any hassles. But even though we're good, we can't stop problems from occurring, which is why we walk you through every conceivable mishap. We also have a chapter for those eBay newbies out there who already know that a picture's worth a thousand words. That's right — if you really want to make money at eBay, you can't miss our advanced strategies.

Chapter 9

Selling in Your Bedroom Slippers for Fun and Profit

· ·

In This Chapter

▶ Discovering the benefits of selling

▶ Looking for inventory in your own backyard

▶ Knowing what to sell, when to sell, and how much to ask

▶ Staying out of trouble — what you can't sell at eBay

▶ Paying the piper with eBay fees

▶ Keeping the taxman happy (or at least friendly)

· ·

*F*inding items to sell can be as easy as opening up your closet and as challenging as acquiring antiques overseas. Either way, establishing yourself as an eBay seller isn't that difficult when you know the ropes. In this chapter, we show you how to look for items under your own roof, figure out what they're worth, and turn them into instant cash. But before you pick your house clean (we know eBay is habit-forming but keep a *few* things for yourself!), read up on the eBay rules of the road — like how to sell, when to sell, and what *not* to sell. If you're interested in finding out how to set up your auction page, get acquainted with Chapter 10; if you want to read up on advanced selling strategies, Appendix B is where to find them.

Why Should You Sell Stuff on eBay?

Whether you need to clear out 35 years of odd and wacky knick-knacks cluttering your basement or you seriously want to earn extra money, the benefits of selling at eBay are as diverse as the people doing the selling. For us, the biggest plus to selling at eBay is wheeling and dealing from our homes in pajamas and fuzzy slippers (every day is Casual Friday in our book). But no matter where you conduct your business or how you dress, many more important big-time rewards exist for selling at eBay.

Life lessons learned at eBay

If you have kids, get them involved with your eBay selling. They'll learn real-life lessons they can't learn in school. Give them a feel for meeting deadlines and fulfilling promises. Get them writing e-mails (if they aren't already). eBay is a great place to learn basic economics and how to handle money. We know somebody who even teaches her children about geography by using eBay. Every time she completes a transaction, she marks the city in which the buyer lives by placing a pin on a huge map of the United States.

Get creative and make eBay a profitable learning experience too. Remember, however, that eBay doesn't let anyone under the age of 18 register, buy, or sell, so make sure *you're* in charge of handling all transactions. Your kids can help out, but they need to be under your supervision at all times.

Most people starting a business have to worry about rounding up investment capital (start-up money they may lose), building inventory (buying stuff to sell), and finding a selling location like a booth at a swap meet or even a small store. Today, even a little Mom and Pop start-up operation requires a major investment. eBay's helped to level the playing field a bit; everybody can get an equal chance to start a small business with just a little money. Anyone who wants to take a stab at doing business can get started with just enough money to cover the insertion fee.

Get a few transactions under your belt. See how you like the responsibilities of marketing, collecting money, shipping, and customer service. Grow a bit more and you'll find yourself spotting trends, acquiring inventory, and marketing your items for maximum profit. In no time, you'll be making items disappear faster than David Copperfield (though you may have a little trouble with the Statue of Liberty — how'd he *do* that, anyway?).

Mi Casa, Mi Cash-a: Finding Stuff to Sell

Finding merchandise to sell at eBay is as easy as opening up a closet and as tough as climbing up to the attic. Just about anything you bought and stashed away (because you didn't want it, forgot about it, or it didn't fit) is fair game. Think about all those really awful birthday and holiday presents (hey, it was the thought that counted — and the giver may have forgotten about them, too). Now you have a place you can try to unload them. They could even make somebody happy.

In your closet, find what's just hanging around:

✔ Clothing that no longer fits or is out of fashion. (Do you really want to keep it if you wouldn't be caught dead in it or you know it will never fit?) Don't forget that pair of shoes you wore once and put away.

✔ Kids' clothes. (Kids outgrow things fast. Use profits from the old items to buy new clothes they can grow into. Now that's recycling.)

And consider what's parked in your basement, garage, or attic:

✔ Old radios, stereo and video equipment, and 8-track systems. Watch these items fly out of your house — especially the 8-tracks (believe it or not, people love 'em).

✔ Books you finished reading long ago and don't want to read again. Some books with early copyright dates or first editions by famous authors earn big money at eBay.

✔ Leftovers from an abandoned hobby. (Who knew that building miniature dollhouses was so much work?)

✔ Unwanted gifts. Have a decade's worth of birthday, graduation, or holiday gifts collecting dust? Put them up at eBay and hope Grandma or Grandpa doesn't bid on them because they think you need another mustache spoon!

Saleable stuff may even be lounging around in your living room or bedroom:

✔ Home décor you want to change. Lamps, chairs, and rugs (especially if they're antiques) sell quickly. If you think an item is valuable but you're not sure, get it appraised first.

✔ Exercise equipment. If you're like us, you bought this stuff with every intention of getting in shape, but now all that's building up is dust. Get some exercise carrying all that equipment to the post office after you've sold them at eBay.

✔ Records, videotapes, and laser discs. Sell them after you've upgraded to new audio and video formats such as DVD (Digitial Versatile Disc) or DAT (Digital Audio Tape). (Think Betamax is dead? You may be surprised.)

✔ Autographs. All types of autographs — from sports figures, celebrities, and world leaders — are very popular at eBay. A word of caution, though: A lot of fakes are on the market, so make sure that what you're selling (or buying) is the real thing.

Know When to Sell

Warning . . . warning . . . we're about to hit you with some clichés: *Timing is everything. Sell what you know and know when to sell. Buy low and sell high.*

Okay, granted, clichés may be painful to hear over and over again, but they do contain nuggets of good information. (Maybe they're well known for a reason?)

Experienced eBay sellers know that when planning an auction, timing is almost everything. You don't want to be caught with 200 Cabbage Patch Kids during a run on Furbies, and Superman action figures are good sellers unless a new Batman movie is coming out.

Some items, such as good antiques, rugs, baseball cards, and sports cars, are timeless. But timing still counts. Don't put your rare, antique paper cutter up for auction if someone else is selling one at the same time. We guarantee that will cut into your profits.

Snapping up profits

Way back in 1980, when Pac-Man ruled, our friend Ric decided to try his hand at photography. Hoping to be the next Ansel Adams or to at least snap something in focus, he bought a 1/4 Kowa 66, one of those cameras you hold in front of your belt buckle while you look down into the viewfinder. Soon after he bought the camera, Ric's focus shifted. The camera sat in its box, instructions and all, for over 15 years until he threw a garage sale.

Ric and his wife didn't know much about his Kowa, but they knew that it was worth something. When he got an offer of $80 for it at the garage sale, his wife whispered "eBay!" in his ear, and he turned the offer down.

Ric and his wife posted the camera at eBay with the little information they had about its size and color, and the couple was flooded with questions and information about the camera from knowledgeable bidders. One bidder said that the silver-toned lens made it more valuable. Another gave them the camera's history.

Ric and his wife added each new bit of information to their description and watched as the bids increased with their every addition — until that unused camera went for more than $400 in a flurry of last-minute sniping. These days, when Ric posts an auction, he always asks for additional information and adds it to the auction page.

What difference does a year make? This camera recently sold at eBay for over $600!

Timing is hardly an exact science. Rather, timing is a little bit of common sense, a dash of marketing, and a fair amount of information gathering. Do a little research among your friends. What are they interested in? Would they buy your item? Use eBay itself as a research tool. Search to see whether anyone's making money on the same type of item. If people are crazed for some fad item (say, Beanie Babies) and you have a bunch, *yesterday* was the time to sell. (In other words, if you want your money out of 'em, get crackin'.)

If the eBay market is already flooded with dozens of an item and no one is making money on them, you can afford to wait before you plan your auction.

Know Thy Stuff

At least that's what Socrates would have said if he'd been an eBay seller. Haven't had to do a homework assignment in a while? Time to dust off those old skills. Before selling your merchandise, do some digging to find out as much as you can about it.

Getting the goods on your goods

Here are some ideas to help you flesh out your knowledge of what you have to sell.

- ✔ **Hit the books.** Check your local library for books about the item. Study price guides and collector magazines.

  Even though collectors still use published price guides when they put a value on an item, so much fast-moving e-commerce is on the Internet that price guides often lag behind the markets they cover. Take their prices with a grain of salt.

- ✔ **Go surfin'.** Conduct a Web search and look for info on the item on other auction sites. If you find a print magazine that strikes your fancy, check to see whether the magazine is available on the Web by typing the title of the magazine into your browser's search window. (For detailed information on using search engines to conduct a more thorough online search, check out Chapter 5.)

- ✔ **When the going gets tough, go shopping.** Browse local stores that specialize in your item. Price it at several locations.

  When you understand what the demand for your product is (whether it's a collectible or a commodity) and how much you can realistically ask for it, you're on the right track to a successful auction.

✔ **Call in the pros.** Need a quick way to find the value of an item you want to sell? Call a dealer or a collector and say you want to *buy* one. A merchant who smells a sale will give you a current selling price.

✔ **eBay to the rescue.** eBay offers some guidance for your research on its category pages. One source eBay offers is Inside Scoop, where you can get background articles on all kinds of items. Another source, Front Page, offers timely collecting advice. Finally, eBay has category-specific chat rooms, where you can read what other collectors are writing about items in a particular category. Figure 9-1 shows Front Page in Action.

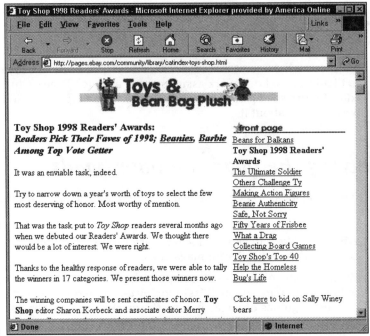

Figure 9-1:
Front Page
is ground
zero for
serious
collectors.

To get to those Inside Scoop, Front Page, and Category-Specific Chat pages from the eBay Home page, follow these steps:

1. **Click any one of the Community links on the navigation bar found on every eBay page.**

   You're taken to the Community Overview page.

2. **To get to all of eBay's chat rooms and message boards, click the Chat link on the subnavigation bar.** (Alternatively, go to the Site Map, scroll down, and click Category Specific Chat under the Community subhead.) To get to the Inside Scoop or Front Page of a specific category, click the Library link.

Assessing an item's value using price guides

The following material comes from Lee Bernstein and is also available on the eBay Web site. The opinions offered here are not eBay's, and eBay doesn't validate or endorse their accuracy. You can visit Lee Bernstein's Web site at www.elee.com.

Call it collectible-mania, but hundreds of books on collectibles and their values are out there, written by knowledgeable and responsible experts who go to great lengths to give their readers the finest information possible.

Price guides, however useful they may be, don't show the final price, the bargaining price, or even whether an item sold at book price *at all*.

Instead, they offer collectors a ballpark price — and even a good approximation is still approximate. The true value of an item can only be assessed when two or more bidders compete.

Values fluctuate, so by the time you get a book, the value it shows for an item may already be out of date.

The prices quoted in most collectors' books are intended to be flexible reference points to help guide shoppers. Check the guidelines that you'll find at the beginning of every good collecting book; they lay out how the author has determined the prices you see listed.

For information on how items are graded and valued by professional collectors, jump to Chapter 5, where we discuss grading your items.

Be certain you know what you have — not only what it is and what it's for, but also *whether it's genuine*. Make sure it's the real McCoy. You are responsible for your item's authenticity; counterfeits and knock-offs are not welcome at eBay. In addition, manufacturers are keeping an eye on eBay for counterfeit and stolen goods and may tip off law enforcement.

Spy versus spy: Comparison selling

Back in the old days, successful retailers like Gimbel and Macy spied on each other to figure out ways to get a leg up on the competition. Today, in the bustling world of e-commerce, the spying continues, and dipping into the intrigue of surveilling the competition is as easy as clicking your mouse.

Say that you're the biggest *Star Trek* fan ever and you collect *Star Trek* stuff, like posters from the movies and lunchboxes. Well, good news: That piece of tin that holds your lunchtime vittles may very well fetch a nice sum of money. To find out for sure, you can do some research at eBay. To find out the current market price for a *Star Trek* lunchbox, you can conduct a Completed Items search on the Search page and find out exactly how many *Star Trek* lunchboxes have been on the auction block in the last month. You can also find out their selling prices and how many bids the lunchboxes received by the time the auctions were over. Figure 9-2 shows the results of a Completed Items search. Chapter 5 offers specific info on conducting a Completed Items search from the Search page.

Figure 9-2:
Use the Completed Items search option to see how much an item sold for, how many bids an item received, and how many of the items sold in the last 30 days.

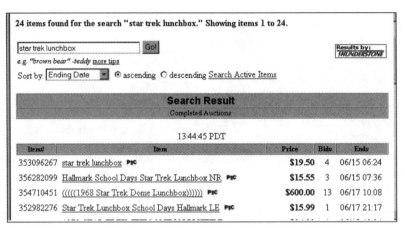

24 items found for the search "star trek lunchbox." Showing items 1 to 24.

star trek lunchbox   Go!

e.g. "brown bear" -teddy more tips

Sort by: Ending Date   • ascending ○ descending Search Active Items

Results by: *THUNDERSTONE*

Search Result
Completed Auctions

13:44:45 PDT

Item#	Item	Price	Bids	Ends
353096267	star trek lunchbox **PIC**	$19.50	4	06/15 06:24
356282099	Hallmark School Days Star Trek Lunchbox NR **PIC**	$15.55	3	06/15 07:36
354710451	(((((1968 Star Trek Dome Lunchbox)))))) **PIC**	$600.00	13	06/17 10:08
352982276	Star Trek Lunchbox School Days Hallmark LE **PIC**	$15.99	1	06/17 21:17

Sometimes sellers make errors when they write item titles. In the case of a *Star Trek* lunchbox, we suggest that you conduct a second Completed Items search. This time, though, try typing in **Star Trek lunch box** (putting a space between *lunch* and *box*). Sure enough, when we tried this tactic, we found 13 additional listings for a *Star Trek Lunch Box,* which sold for anywhere between $13.70 and $565.

Always search for the same item with different word variations. This is about the only time "creative" spelling can actually help you.

At the time of our search, a TOS *Star Trek* lunchbox was a popular item. Table 9-1 shows your how we know that.

Table 9-1	Completed *TOS Star Trek* Lunchbox Auctions		
Selling Price	**Number of Bids**	**Day & Time Auction Closed**	**Days in Auction**
$600.00	13	Saturday 10:08	7 days
$565.00	8	Sunday 19:44	10 days
$415.50	11	Wednesday 19:11	7 days

Look at the individual auction item pages for each item that your Completed Items search turns up. That way, you can confirm that the items (lunch-boxes, for example) are identical to the one you want to sell. And when you do your research, factor in your item's actual condition. Read the individual item descriptions. If your item's in better condition, expect (and ask for) more money for it; if your item is in worse condition, expect (and ask for) less. Also, note the categories the items are listed under; they may give you a clue about where eBay members are looking for items just like yours.

If you want to be extremely thorough in your comparison selling, go to one or two of eBay's competing auction sites to see whether the results of your eBay search mesh with what's going on elsewhere. If you find that no items like yours are for sale anywhere else online, and are pretty sure people are look-ing for what you have, you may just find yourself in Fat City.

Don't forget to factor in the history of an item when you assess its value. Getting an idea of what people are watching, listening to, and collecting can help you assess trends and figure out what's hot. For more about using trend-spotting skills to sniff out potential profits, take a look at Chapter 12.

Know What You Can (And Can't) Sell

The majority of auctions found at eBay are aboveboard. But sometimes eBay finds out about auctions that are either illegal (in the eyes of the state or fed-eral government) or prohibited by eBay's rules and regulations. In either case, eBay steps in, calls a foul, and makes the auction invalid.

eBay doesn't have rules and regulations just for the heck of it. eBay wants to keep you educated so you won't unwittingly bid on — or sell — an item that has been misrepresented. eBay also wants you to know what's okay and what's prohibited so that if you run across an auction that looks fishy, you'll help out your fellow eBay members by reporting it. And eBay wants you to know that getting your auction shut down is the least of your worries: You can be suspended if you knowingly list items that are prohibited. And we won't even talk about criminal prosecution.

You need to know about these three categories at eBay:

- ✔ **Prohibited** lists the items that may *not* be sold at eBay under any circumstances.
- ✔ **Questionable** lists the items that may be sold under certain conditions.
- ✔ **Potentially Infringing** lists the types of items that may be in violation of copyrights, trademarks, or other rights.

You may not even offer to give away for free a prohibited, questionable, or infringing item; giving it away doesn't relieve you of potential liability.

The items that you absolutely *cannot* sell at eBay can fit into *all three* categories. Those items can be legally ambiguous at best, not to mention potentially risky and all kinds of sticky. To find a detailed description of which items are prohibited on the eBay Web site:

1. **Click the Help link on the main navigation bar at the top of all eBay pages.**

   The subnavigation bar appears while you are simultaneously taken to the friendly Basics page.

2. **Click the Rules & Safety (Safe Harbor) link on the subnavigation bar.**

   You're taken to the Rules & Safety Overview page. You can find all the answers you need by clicking the Is My Item Allowed on eBay link, which is under the Policies heading. You can also click the Site Map, go to the Help heading, and click the Is My Item Allowed on eBay link.

Sometimes an item is okay to own but not to sell. Other times the item is prohibited from being *sold and possessed.* To complicate matters even more, some items may be legal in one part of the United States but not in others. Or an item may be illegal in the United States but legal in other countries.

Because eBay's base of operations is in California, United States law is enforced — even if both the buyer and seller are from other countries. Cuban cigars, for example, are legal to buy and sell in Canada, but even if the buyer *and* the seller are from Canada, eBay says *"No permiso"* and shuts down auctions of Havanas fast. Figure 9-3 shows an auction that was shut down soon after we found it.

Prohibited items

Even though possessing (and selling) many of the items in the following list is legal in the United States and elsewhere, you are absolutely, positively *prohibited* from buying and selling the following at eBay:

- ✔ **Firearms of all types.** This also means firearm accessories, including antique, collectible, sport, or hunting guns; air guns; BB guns; silencers; converters; kits for creating guns; gunpowder; high-capacity ammunition magazines (receptacles designed to feed ten rounds or more into a gun, not the publications about ammo); and armor-piercing bullets. You can't even sell a gun that doesn't work.

  You *can* buy and sell single bullets, shells, and even antique bombs and musket balls as long as they have nothing explosive in them.

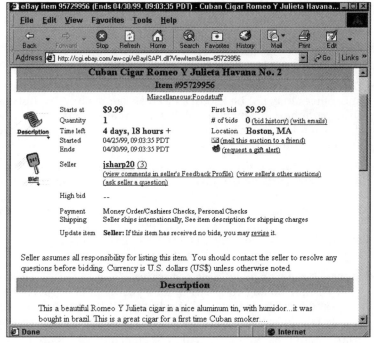

Figure 9-3:
Cuban
cigars may
be popular,
but they're
illegal to sell
in the United
States. This
auction was
canceled
by eBay.

✔ **Military weapons.** Included are bazookas, grenades, and mortars.

✔ **Police and other law-enforcement badges and IDs.** Stop in the name of the law if you're thinking about buying or selling any of these items, including actual United States federal badges or imitation badges. In fact, selling just about any U.S. government badge can get you in hot water.

You also can't own or sell those agencies' identification cards or credential cases or those really cool jackets they use in raids. Selling a copy or reproduction of any of these items is prohibited, too, because these items are copyrighted (see the section on infringing items in this chapter).

If you find a badge that's legal to sell and own, you need to provide a letter of authorization from the agency. The same letter of authorization is required for fake badges, such as reproductions or movie props.

✔ **Replicas of official government identification documents or licenses.** Birth certificates, drivers' licenses, and passports fall into this category.

✔ **Current vehicle license plates or plates that claim to resemble current ones.** Note that expired license plates are considered collectible as long as they are no longer valid for use on a vehicle.

✔ **Locksmithing devices.** These items can only be sold to authorized recipients. Federal law prohibits the mailing of such devices.

✔ **Human parts and remains.** Hey, we all have two kidneys, but if you get the urge to sell one to pay off your bills, eBay is not the place to sell it. Your can't sell your sperm, eggs, blood, or anything else you manage to extricate from your body. What's more, you can't even give away any of these items as a free bonus with one of your auctions.

✔ **Drugs or drug paraphernalia.** Narcotics, steroids, or other controlled substances may not be listed, as well as gamma hydroxybutyrate (GHB). Drug paraphernalia includes all items that are primarily intended or designed for use in manufacturing, concealing or using a controlled substance, including 1960s vintage cigarette papers, bongs, and water pipes.

✔ **Anything that requires a prescription from a doctor, dentist, or optometrist to dispense.** Listen, just because it's legal to use doesn't mean it doesn't require special permission to get. For example, even though penicillin is legal to buy in the U.S., only a doctor can prescribe it, which is why when you get sick you have to stand in that *loooong* line at the pharmacy sneezing on all the other sick people. And if you're looking for Viagra auctions at eBay, don't even *go* there.

✔ **Stocks, bonds, or negotiable securities.** Nope, you can't sell stock in your new pie baking company or an investment in property you may own. And if you're thinking of offering credit to someone, you can't do that either. Note that antique and collectible items are permitted.

✔ **Bulk e-mail lists.** No bulk email or mailing lists that contain personal identifying information. You may not even sell tools or software designed to send unsolicited commercial e-mail.

✔ **Pets and wildlife, including animal parts from endangered species.** If you've had it with Buster, your pet ferret, don't look to eBay for help in finding him a new home. And you can't sell your stuffed spotted owls or rhino-horn love potions, either. If you're in the animal business — *any* animal business — eBay is not the place for you.

✔ **Child pornography.** Note that this material is strictly prohibited at eBay, but you can sell other forms of erotica. (See the section later in this chapter about questionable items.)

✔ **Forged items.** Autographs from celebrities and sports figures are big business — and a big opportunity for forgers. Selling a forgery is a criminal act. The state of New York is taking the lead on this issue, investigating at least two dozen suspected forgery cases linked with online auctions.

If you're in the market for an autograph, don't even consider bidding on one unless it comes with a *Certificate of Authenticity* (COA). Many sellers take authenticity so seriously that they give buyers the right to a full refund if any doubt about authenticity crops up. Figure 9-4 shows an item that comes with a COA from an auction at eBay. Find out more about authentication services in Chapter 16.

✔ **Items that infringe on someone else's copyright or trademark.** Take a look at the very next section for details on infringing items.

✔ **Stolen items.** Need we say more? (Seems obvious, but you'd be surprised.) If what you're selling came to you by way of a five-finger discount, fell off a truck, or is hot, do not sell it at eBay.

Figure 9-4:
When bidding on an item with a COA, make sure that the seller is reputable (hint, hint, check for feedback).

The item you are bidding on is a 3x5 Card, Autographed by the late James Stewart ....

The card is white and in mint condition... Signed bold and clear, in black felt tip pen ...

This Autograph is 100% Genuine, and I will provide my COA that Guarantees it for life...

Infringing items

In school, if you copied someone's work, you were busted for plagiarism. Even if you've been out of school for a while, you can get busted for copying someone else's work. Profiting from a copy of someone else's legally owned *intellectual property* is an *infringement* violation. Infringement, also known as *piracy,* is the encroachment on another person's legal ownership rights on an item, trademark, or copyright. eBay prohibits the selling of infringing items at its site.

All the legal mumbo-jumbo, translated to English, comes down to this: Profiting from someone else's idea, original work, or patented invention is very, very bad and can get you in hot water.

Here's a checklist of no-no items commonly found at the center of infringement violations:

✔ Music that's been recorded from an original compact disc, cassette tape, or record.

✔ Movies that have been recorded from an original DVD, Laser Disc, or commercial VHS tape.

Hot property busted

In 1961, a young jockey named John Sellers won his first Kentucky Derby on a horse named Carry Back. He was so emotional about the victory that he was crying as he crossed the finish line. Seventeen years later, someone broke into his California home and stole his priceless trophy. But today, more than two decades after it was stolen, it's back in his possession — thanks to an observant eBay member. The prized trophy was put up for auction in 1999 by a seller who had bought it legitimately. An eBay member who knows the history of the trophy saw that it was for sale and alerted the seller. The seller stopped the auction immediately, contacted the former jockey, and personally returned the trophy to him. Now that's a great finish!

✔ Television shows that have been recorded off the air, off cable, or from a satellite service.

Selling a used original CD, tape, commercial VHS movie cassette, DVD, or CD-ROM is perfectly legal. Some television shows have sold episodes on tape; you can sell those originals as well. But if you're tempted to sell a personal copy that you made of an original, you are committing an infringing violation.

✔ Software and computer games that have been copied from CD-ROMs or disks (and that includes hard disks — anybody's).

✔ Counterfeit items (also called *knock-offs*), such as clothes and jewelry, that have been produced, copied, or imitated without the permission of the manufacturer. (Bart Simpson knock-off T-shirts abounded in the early '90s.)

If you pick up a brand-name item dirt cheap from a discount store, you can check to see whether it's counterfeit by taking a look at the label. If something isn't quite right, the item is probably a knock-off.

Trademark and copyright protection doesn't just cover software, music, and movies. Clothing, toys, sunglasses, and books are among the items covered by law. This book, for example, is copyrighted, and the eBay name is covered by a trademark and used with permission. So if you want to introduce a friend to the joys of eBay, don't photocopy this book — buy another one.

Intellectual property owners actively defend their rights and, along with help from average eBay users, continually tip eBay off to fraudulent and infringing auctions. Rights owners can use eBay's Verified Rights Owner (VeRO) program, as well as law-enforcement agencies (see "VeRO to the Rescue," later in this chapter, for info about the VeRO program).

Questionable Items: Know the laws

Because some items are prohibited in one place and not another, eBay lists a few items that you can trade but that are restricted and regulated. As a member of eBay, you're responsible for knowing the restrictions in your area as well as on the eBay Web site.

✔ **Wine and alcohol:** Selling wine and alcohol at eBay — and anywhere else, for that matter — is tricky business. For starters, you have no business in this business unless you're at least 21. eBay does not permit sales of any alcohol products unless they are sold for their "collectible" containers. Even in this case, some strict rules apply:

- The value must be in the collectible container, not in its contents. You can't auction off your uncle's Chateaux Margaux because the value is in the wine — not the bottle.

- The bottle must be unopened, and your auction must state that the contents are not meant for consumption.

- The container's value must substantially exceed the price of the alcohol in the container, and it must not be available at a retail outlet.

- You must be sure that the buyer is 21 or over.

- You must be sure that the sale complies with all laws and shipping rules. Every state has its own laws about shipping alcohol and wine. Some states require licenses to transport it; some limit the amount you can ship. You're responsible for knowing what your state laws are (and are expected to conduct your auctions accordingly).

You can find all the contact names, numbers, and links you need to keep your wine-shipping business on the good side of the law at www.wineinstitute.org/shipwine or check with the Alcoholic Beverage Control agency of your state. The ABC's telephone number is listed in the government section of your local phone book.

✔ **Erotica:** Some forms of erotica are allowed at eBay. To see what eBay allows and what it prohibits, click Help and then click Rules & Safety to get to the Policies page.

One thing that's definitely illegal, wrong, and criminal is child pornography. If someone reports that you're selling child pornography, eBay forwards your registration information to law enforcement for criminal prosecution.

Forbidden auctions

The folks at eBay didn't just fall off the turnip truck. eBay staffers have seen just about every scam to get around paying fees or following policy guidelines. Chances are good that if you try one of these scams, you'll get caught.

eBay cancels the auction and credits you for the listing fee. Do it once, and shame on you. Do it a lot, and you're out of eBay.

- ✔ **Raffles and prizes:** You need to sell something in your auction, not offer tickets or chances for a giveaway.

- ✔ **Want ads:** If you want something, make a posting on the Wanted board. Don't try to pass an ad off as an auction. We explain in Chapter 14.

- ✔ **Advertisements:** An eBay auction is not the place to make a sales pitch (other than attractive copy describing your item, that is). Some eBay bad guys list an auction name and then use the auction to send bidders to some other auction or Web site.

- ✔ **Bait-and-switch tactics:** These are a variation on the ugly old sales technique of pretending to sell what you're not really selling. Some eBay users who are selling an unfamiliar brand of item try to snag bidders by putting a more familiar brand in the title. For instance, writing *Beanie Baby — not really, but a lot like it!* is a fake-out. eBay calls it *keyword spamming*. We call it lousy.

- ✔ **Choice auctions:** These are like Dutch auctions gone crazy. Normally, sellers can offer only one item per auction in a regular auction and multiples of the same item in a Dutch auction. Choice auctions offer a mishmash of multiple items from which bidders choose. They don't work because bidders don't really know what they've bought until the auction is over.

- ✔ **Mixing apples with oranges:** This gambit tries to attract more bidders to view an item by putting it in a high-traffic category where it doesn't belong. Forget it. eBay will move it for you if necessary, but keeping that rutabaga recipe book *away* from the list of automotive repair manuals is more considerate.

- ✔ **Catalogues:** "Buy my catalogue so you can buy more stuff from me!" Uh-huh. We don't know why anyone would put a *bid* on a catalogue (unless it's a Sears-Roebuck antique). If it's only a booklet that shows off all the cool junk you're selling, then you can't offer it as an auction item.

Reporting a Problem Auction

You probably don't think that eBay can monitor millions of auctions on a daily basis. You're right. It can't. eBay relies on eBay members like you to let it know when a shady auction is afoot. If you ever smell something fishy, for goodness' sake, report it to eBay. Sometimes eBay takes a few days to cancel an auction, but rest assured that eBay invests a lot of time protecting its users from fraudulent auctions.

If you see an auction that just doesn't look right, you should report the auction via an online form at

```
cgi3.ebay.com/aw-cgi/eBayISAPI.dll?ReportInfringing
```

To get to the form, you can also click the Help link on the navigation bar, then click Rules & Safety, and then click the Items That May Not Be Allowed for Sale link. You're taken to the Community Watch department. Click the link, and you're on the report form.

eBay doesn't personally prosecute its users and wouldn't want such a huge responsibility. However, eBay does have a stake in protecting its honest users and acts as an intermediary between honest eBay users and law-enforcement agencies.

VeRO to the Rescue

If you own intellectual property that you think is being infringed upon on the eBay site, eBay has a program called the Verified Rights Owner (VeRO) program. Owners of trademarked or copyrighted items and logos, as well as other forms of intellectual property, can become members of this program for free.

You can find out more about the VeRO program by clicking the Help link of the main navigation bar. Click the Community Standards link of the subnavigation bar and then click the VeRO link under the Policies and Conduct heading of the Community Standards Overview page. Download the form, fill it out, and fax it to eBay, and you're on your way to protecting your intellectual property from being auctioned to the highest bidder. Remember, only you can stop the infringement madness. If eBay agrees with you that your intellectual property is being infringed, it invalidates the auction and informs the seller by e-mail that the auction "is not authorized." The high bidders in the auction are also notified and warned that they may be breaking the law if they continue the transaction.

eBay understands that sometimes people don't know that they're selling infringing items, but it draws a hard line on repeat offenders. eBay not only shuts down the offenders' auctions, but also suspends repeat offenders of this ilk. Also, eBay cooperates with the proper authorities on behalf of its VeRO program members.

If eBay deems your auction invalid because the item doesn't meet eBay's policies and guidelines, you can find out why by e-mailing ended@eBay.com. Be sure to include the auction item number in the e-mail.

eBay Fees? What eBay Fees? Oops . . .

The Cliché Police are going to raid us sooner or later, but here's one we're poking a few holes in this time around: *You gotta spend it to make it.* This old-time business chestnut means you need to invest a fair amount of money before you can turn a profit. Although the principle still holds true in the real world (at least most of the time), at eBay you don't have to spend much to run your business. This is one reason eBay has become one of the most successful e-commerce companies on the Internet and a darling of Wall Street. eBay keeps fees low and volume high.

eBay charges the following types of fees for conducting auctions:

✔ Regular auction insertion fees (from $.25 to $2)

✔ Real estate transaction fees ($50)

✔ Automotive fees ($25)

✔ Additional reserve auction fees, which are refundable if your item meets the reserve and sells (from .50 to $1)

✔ Final value fees (a percentage of the sales price)

✔ Optional fees (which vary)

Insertion fees

Every auction is charged an insertion fee. There's just no way around it. The insertion fee is calculated on a sliding scale that's based on the *minimum bid* (your starting price) or on the *reserve price* (the secret lowest price that you're willing to sell your item for) of your item. (Later in this chapter, we explain how the reserve price affects what you eventually have to pay.) Take a look at Table 9-2 for eBay's insertion fee structure.

Table 9-2	Insertion Fee Charges
If Your Minimum Bid Is:	*The Insertion Fee Is:*
$.01 to $9.99	$.25
$10.00 to $24.99	$.50
$25.00 to $49.99	$1.00
$50.00 to $(gazillions)	$2.00

If you're running a reserve-price auction (explained in detail in Chapter 10), eBay bases its insertion fee on the reserve price, not on the minimum bid. eBay also charges a fee to run a reserve-price auction.

Here's a little snapshot of how reserve price affects your insertion fee. If you set a minimum bid of $1 for a gold Rolex watch (say what?) but your reserve price is $5,000 (that's more like it), you're charged a $75 insertion fee based on the $5,000 reserve price plus a $1 *(refundable if the item sells)* reserve fee. You also pay a $2 listing fee.

In a Dutch auction (explained in Chapter 10), the insertion fee is based on the minimum bid — as in a regular auction — but then eBay multiplies it by the number of items you list. So if you set a minimum bid of $1 for 300 glow-in-the-dark refrigerator magnets, it costs you a $2 insertion fee for listing.

So what does the insertion fee buy you at eBay?

- ✔ A really snazzy-looking auction page of your item that millions of eBay members can see, admire, and breathlessly respond to. (Well, we can hope.)
- ✔ The use of eBay services, such as the Rules & Safety (SafeHarbor) program, that somewhat ease your auction experience. (Chapter 15 tells you how to use Rules & Safety during and after your auctions.)

Final value fees

If you follow the movie business, you hear about some big A-list stars who take a relatively small fee for making a film but negotiate a big percentage of the gross profits. This is known as a *back-end deal* — in effect, a commission based on how much the movie brings in. eBay does the same thing, taking a small insertion fee when you list your item and then a commission on the back end when you sell your item. This commission is called the final value fee and is based on the final selling price of your item.

A final value fee isn't charged on an auction in the Miscellaneous: Real Estate category. But in the Automotive category, you pay a flat $25 final value fee.

In real life, when you pay sales commissions on a big purchase like a house, you usually pay a fixed percentage. eBay's final value fee structure is different: It is set up as a three-tiered system. Table 9-3 covers final value fees.

Table 9-3	Final Value Fees
If Your Item Sells between	*You Pay a Final Value Fee of*
$.01 to $25.00	5 percent of the selling price
$25.01 to $1,000.00	5 percent on the first $25, plus 2.5 percent on selling prices of $25 to $1,000
$1,000 and up	5 percent on the first $25, plus 2.5 percent on selling prices of $25.01 to $1,000, plus another 1.25 percent on selling prices over $1,000

So how do all these percentages translate to actual dollar amounts? Take a look at Table 9-4. We calculated the final value fee on some sample selling prices.

Table 9-4	Sample Prices and Commissions	
Closing Bid Price	*Percentage*	*What You Owe eBay*
$10	5 percent of $10	$.50
$256	5 percent of $25 plus 2.5 percent of $231	$7.02
$1,284	5 percent of $25 plus 2.5 percent of $974.99 plus 1.25 percent of $248	$28.72
$1,000,000	5 percent of $25 plus 2.5 percent of $974.99 plus 1.5 percent of $999,000	$15,010.62 (ouch)

Because of the sliding percentages, the higher the final selling price, the lower the commission eBay charges. Math can be a beautiful thing.

Optional fees

You won't have to pay a license fee and destination charge, but setting up your auction can be like buying a car. eBay has all sorts of options to jazz up your auction. (Sorry, they're fresh out of two-tone metallic paint — but how about a nice pair of fuzzy dice for your mirror?) We explain how all these bells, whistles, and white sidewalls dress up your auction in Chapter 10. In the meantime, Figure 9-5 shows you what a Featured Auction listing at eBay looks like.

As a hint of things to come, Table 9-5 lists the eBay auction options and what they'll cost you.

Table 9-5	eBay Optional Fees
Option	*Fee*
Boldface Title	$2.00
Home Page Featured	$99.95
Featured Plus! (formerly Featured in Category)	$19.95
Highlight	$5.00
The Gallery	$.25 and $19.95 (Featured Auction in Gallery)

Keep current on your cash flow

When you've done all the legwork needed to make some money, do some eye-work to keep track of your results. The best place to keep watch on your eBay accounting is on your My eBay page, a great place to stay organized while you're conducting all your eBay business. We describe all the functions of the page in Chapter 4.

Here's a checklist of what to watch out for after the auction closes:

- ✔ **Keep an eye on how much you are spending to place items up for auction at eBay.** You don't want any nasty surprises, and you don't want to find out that you spent more money to set up your auction than you received selling your item.

- ✔ **If you decide to turn your eBay selling into a business, keep track of your expenses for your taxes.** (We explain Uncle Sam's tax position at eBay later in this chapter — next, in fact. Stay tuned.)

- ✔ **Make sure that you get refunds and credits when they're due.**

- ✔ **Double-check your figures to make certain eBay hasn't made mistakes.** If you have any questions about the accounting, let eBay know.

Find an error or something that isn't quite right with your account? E-mail your questions to billing@ebay.com.

Uncle Sam Wants You — to Pay Your Taxes!

What would a chapter about money be without taxes? As Ben Franklin knew (and we've all found out since his time), you can't escape death and taxes. (Hey, it's not a cliché; it's traditional wisdom.) Whether in cyberspace or face-to-face life, never forget that Uncle Sam is always your business partner.

If you live outside the United States, check the tax laws in that country so you don't end up with a real headache down the road.

As with offline transactions, knowledge is power. The more you know about buying and selling at eBay before you actually start doing it, the more savvy the impression you make — and the more satisfying your experience.

Two wild rumors about federal taxes

We've heard some rumors about not having to pay taxes on eBay profits. If you hear any variation on this theme, smile politely and don't believe a word of it. Here are two of the more popular (and seriously mistaken) tax notions running around the eBay community these days.

The U.S. government uses two laws on the books to go after eBay outlaws. One is the Federal Trade Commission (FTC) Act, which prohibits deceptive or misleading transactions in commerce. The other is the Mail or Telephone Order Merchandise Rule, which requires sellers to ship merchandise in a timely manner or offer to refund a consumer's money. The FTC is in charge of pursuing these violations. If you have a question about federal laws, you can find a lot of information online. For example, we found these three Web sites that keep fairly current lists of U.S. law and federal codes.

```
www4.law.cornell.edu/uscode
www.ftc.gov
www.fourmilab.ch/ustax/ustax.html
```

Rumor #1: E-commerce isn't taxed

One story claims that "there will be no taxes on e-commerce sales (sales conducted online) for three years." No one ever seems to know when those three years start or end.

(Right. As if Uncle Sam would pass up such an opportunity. Get real.)

Some people confuse sales tax issues with income tax issues. You don't pay Internet sales taxes, but that's not the same as not reporting income from the Internet.

Congress recently passed the Internet Tax Freedom Act. It states that until October 2001 Congress and state legislatures can't institute *new* taxes on Internet transactions. If you're betting that some custom-tailored taxation will magically appear after October 2001, we sure won't bet against you.

Rumor #2: Profits from garage sales are tax-exempt

"eBay is like a garage sale, and you don't have to pay taxes on garage sales."

(Uh-huh. And the calories in ice cream don't count if you eat it out of the carton. Who comes up with this stuff anyway?)

This notion is just an urban (or shall we say *suburban*) legend — somebody's wishful thinking that's become folklore. If you make money on a garage sale, you have to declare it as income — just like anything else you make money on. Most people never make any money on garage sales because they usually sell things for far less than they bought them for. However, the exact opposite is often true of an eBay transaction.

Even if you lose money, you may have to prove it to the government, especially if you're running a small business. You might want to have a heart-to-heart talk with your accountant if you're unsure. Our best advice? If something might look bad in an audit if you *don't* declare it, consider that a big hint.

To get the reliable word, we checked with the IRS's e-commerce office. The good folks there told us that even if you make as little as a buck on any eBay sale after all your expenses (the cost of the item, eBay fees, shipping charges), you still have to declare it as income on your federal tax return.

For the latest, up-to-date information on taxes and how they apply to e-commerce, visit:

```
ecommercetax.com
```

If you have questions about eBay sales and your taxes, check with your personal accountant, call the IRS Help Line at 1-800-829-1040, or visit the IRS Web site at www.irs.ustreas.gov. And be friendly. (Just in case.)

State taxes

Yes, it's true. Not only is Uncle Sam in Washington, D.C., looking for his slice of your eBay profits, but your state government may be hankering to join the feast.

If you have a good accountant, give that esteemed individual a call. Accountants actually do more than just process your income tax returns once a year; they can help you avoid major pitfalls even before April 15.

Here's how to find out what your responsibilities are in your home state:

✔ You may need to collect and pay state taxes, but only if you sell to someone in your state.

✔ You can get tax information online at this Web site:

```
www.kentis.com/siteseeker/taxusst.html
```

The site has links to tax information for all 50 states.

✔ You can call your state tax office and let the good folks there explain what the requirements are. They're listed in the government section of your phone book.

Chapter 10

Filling in the Blanks: Cyber Paperwork for the Savvy Seller

In This Chapter

▶ Getting ready to set up your auction

▶ Choosing your item category

▶ Writing your item description

▶ Setting up your options

▶ Making changes after your auction has started

*A*re you ready to make some money? Yes? (Call it an inspired guess.) You're on the threshold of adding your items to the hundreds of thousands that go up for auction at eBay every day. Some are so hot that the sellers quadruple their investments. Other items, unfortunately, are so stone-cold that they don't even register a single bid.

In this chapter, we explain all the facets of the Sell Your Item page — the page you fill out to get your auction going at eBay. We give you some advice that can increase your odds of making money, and we show you the best way to position your item so buyers can see it and bid on it. We also show you how to modify, extend, or end your auction whenever you need to.

Getting Ready to List Your Item

After you decide what you want to sell, find out as much as you can about it, and conduct a little market research. Then, you should have a good idea of the item's popularity and value. To get this info, check out Chapter 9.

Before you list your item, make sure that you've got these bases covered:

✔ **The specific category under which you want the item listed.** Ask your friends where they'd look for such an item and remember the categories you saw most frequently when you conducted your market research.

✔ **What you want to say in your auction item description.** Jot down your ideas. We know all about writer's block. If you're daunted by the Sell Your Item page but struggle through it anyway, then you've already done the hard work before you even begin.

✔ **Whether you want to attach a picture to your description via a uniform resource locator (URL).** Pictures help sell items, but you don't have to use them. (This information won't be on the test, but if you want to know more, see Chapter 13.)

✔ **The price at which you think you can sell the item.** Be as realistic as you can. (That's where the market research comes in.)

Examining the Sell Your Item Page

Figure 10-1 shows the Sell Your Item page, which is where your auction is born. Filling out your auction paperwork requires a couple of minutes of clicking, typing, and answering all kinds of questions. The good news is that when you're done, your auction is up and running and (hopefully) starting to earn you money.

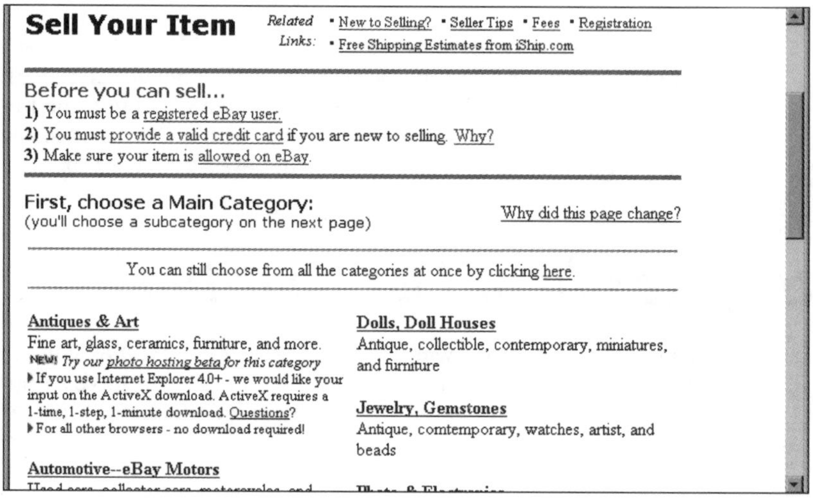

Figure 10-1:
The Sell
Your Item
page.

Within the figure:

Sell Your Item   *Related* · New to Selling? · Seller Tips · Fees · Registration
Links: · Free Shipping Estimates from iShip.com

Before you can sell...
1) You must be a registered eBay user.
2) You must provide a valid credit card if you are new to selling. Why?
3) Make sure your item is allowed on eBay.

First, choose a Main Category:
(you'll choose a subcategory on the next page)   Why did this page change?

You can still choose from all the categories at once by clicking here.

Antiques & Art
Fine art, glass, ceramics, furniture, and more.
NEW! Try our photo hosting beta for this category
▶ If you use Internet Explorer 4.0+ - we would like your input on the ActiveX download. ActiveX requires a 1-time, 1-step, 1-minute download. Questions?
▶ For all other browsers - no download required!

Automotive--eBay Motors
Used cars, collector cars, motorcycles, and

Dolls, Doll Houses
Antique, collectible, contemporary, miniatures, and furniture

Jewelry, Gemstones
Antique, comtemporary, watches, artist, and beads

Photo & Electronics

Before you begin, you have to be a registered eBay user. If you still need to register, go to Chapter 2 and fill out the preliminary cyber-paperwork. Then you're ready to set up your auction.

To find eBay's Sell Your Item page from the eBay Home page, click the Sell link on the navigation bar at the top of the page and you're whisked there immediately. eBay allows you to select your category and download the actual Sell Your Item page in less than six seconds. You can also start your auction from your My eBay page. Just click the Selling tab and scroll down the page to Related Links. Click the Add an Item link and you're whisked away to the Sell Your Item page.

Here's the info you're asked to fill out (each of these items is discussed in detail later in this chapter):

- ✔ **User ID:** Your User ID (required).
- ✔ **Password:** Your password (required).

  If you've signed in, you see a shaded notation that says: "You are signed in as: username". It will not be necessary to repeatedly input your User ID and password if you have set your My eBay Preferences to remember your password for certain activities.

- ✔ **Title:** The name of your item (required).
- ✔ **Category:** The category that best describes your item (required).
- ✔ **Description:** What you want to tell eBay buyers about your item (required).
- ✔ **Picture URL:** The Web address of any pictures you want to add (optional). Chapter 13 covers using images in your auction.
- ✔ **The Gallery:** You can add your item's picture to eBay's photo gallery (optional). This option is now available for items in every category. eBay charges $.25 extra to add the item to the Gallery and $19.95 to make your item a featured auction in the Gallery.
- ✔ **Gallery Image URL:** The Web address of the JPG image you want to place in the Gallery (optional). See Chapter 13.
- ✔ **Boldface Title:** A selling option to make your item listing stand out. eBay charges $2 extra for this feature (optional).
- ✔ **Home Page Featured** (formerly Featured Auction)**:** You can place your auction in a premium viewing section (optional). eBay charges $99.95 extra for this feature.
- ✔ **Featured Plus!** (formerly Category Featured)**:** You can have your auction appear at the top of the category in which you list it (optional). eBay charges $19.95 extra for this feature.

✔ **Highlight:** Your item title is highlighted in the auction listings and search listings with a yellow colored band, which draws eBay members eyes' right to your auction (optional). eBay charges $5 extra for this feature.

✔ **Item Location:** The region, zip code, and country from which the item will be shipped (required).

✔ **Method(s) of Payment/Shipping Terms:** How you want to be paid and who pays for shipping (optional).

✔ **eBay Online Payments by Billpoint:** Fill out this area if you'd like to offer the high bidder the option to pay through the Billpoint service (optional).

✔ **Escrow:** If using Escrow is an option you'd like to offer the high bidder, select the option as to who will pay (optional).

✔ **Where Will You Ship:** Here's where you can indicate where you are willing to ship an item. If you don't want the hassle of shipping out of the United States, just check off that option. You can individually select different countries, as well (optional).

✔ **Who Pays for Shipping:** Select the options that apply to your auction (optional).

You may want to consider whether you want to be in the international shipping business. Buyers usually pick up the tab, but you have to deal with post office paperwork. If time is money, you may want to skip it entirely — or at least have all the forms filled out before you get in line at the post office. But remember: If you don't ship internationally, you're blocking out a bunch of bidders.

✔ **Quantity:** The number of items you're offering in this auction is always one unless you plan to run a Dutch auction (required).

✔ **Minimum Bid:** The starting price you set (required).

✔ **Duration:** The number of days you want the auction to run (required).

✔ **Reserve Price:** The secret price you set that must be met before this item can be sold (optional). eBay charges you a fee for this feature.

✔ **Private Auction:** You can keep the identity of all bidders secret with this option (optional).

✔ **Remember My Selling Preferences:** With this feature, you won't constantly have to repeat your preferences when you're listing a group of items (optional). This feature is indicated with a yellow pushpin icon.

Filling in the Required Blanks

Yes, the Sell Your Item page looks daunting, but filling out its 22 sections doesn't take as long as you may think. Some of the questions you're asked aren't things you even have to think about; just click an answer and off you go — unless you forget your password. Other questions ask you to type in information. Don't sweat a thing; we have all the answers you need right here. You can find info on all the required stuff, and later in this chapter, we talk about optional stuff. After you click your main category, you land on the official Sell Your Item page.

Item title info

After you fill in your User ID and password, eBay wants to get down to the nitty-gritty — what the heck to call that thing you're trying to sell. Think of your item title as a great newspaper headline.

Give the most essential information right away. You want to grab the eye of the reader who's just browsing, and you want to be clear and descriptive enough to get noticed by eBay's search engine. Figure 10-2 shows examples of good titles.

Figure 10-2:
These item titles are effective because they're clear, accurate, and easy on the eyes.

Beautiful Summer Sophisticate Barbie-NRFB   Item #129449952

~ NEW Small Line MAYCO C-30HD Concrete Pump ~   Item #128822430

BLAIR WITCH PROJECT Original B 27x40 POSTER   Item #139285073

Here are some ideas to help you write your item title:

- ✔ Use the most common name for the item.
- ✔ If the item is rare or hard to find, mention that.
- ✔ Mention the item's condition and mention whether it's new or old.
- ✔ Mention the item's special qualities, like its style, model, or edition.
- ✔ Avoid fancy punctuation or unusual characters, such as $, hyphens, and L@@K, because they just clutter up the title — buyers rarely search for them.

Don't put any HTML tags in your title. (*HTML* stands for HyperText Markup Language, which in plain English means that it's the special code you use to create Web pages.) We don't even want to go there, so if you want to know more about designing Web pages and using HTML tags, ask a friend who's into that sort of thing or have a look at *HTML 4 For Dummies,* by Ed Tittel and Stephen Nelson James (published by IDG Books Worldwide, Inc).

Ordinarily, we don't throw out French phrases just for the fun of it. But where making a profit is an issue, we definitely have to agree with the French that picking or not picking *le mot juste* can mean the difference between having potential bidders merely see your auction and having an all-out bidding war on your hands. Read on for tips about picking *the best words* to let your auction item shine.

Look for a phrase that pays

Here's a crash course in eBay lingo that can help bring you up to speed on attracting buyers to your auction. The following words are used frequently in eBay auctions, and they can do wonders to jump-start your title:

- Very rare
- One of a kind
- Vintage
- Collectible
- Rare
- Unique
- Primitive
- Well-loved

There's a whole science (called *grading*) to figuring out the value of a collectible. You're ahead of the game if you have a pretty good idea of what most eBay members mean. Do your homework before you assign a grade to your item. If you need more information on what these grades actually mean, Chapter 5 provides a translation.

eBay lingo at a glance

Common grading terms and the phrases in the preceding section aren't the only marketing standards you have at your eBay disposal. As eBay has grown, so has the lingo that members use as shortcuts to describe their merchandise.

Table 10-1 gives you a handy list of common abbreviations and phrases used to describe items. (**Hint:** *Mint* means "might as well be brand new," not "cool chocolate treat attached.")

Table 10-1	A Quick List of eBay Abbreviations	
eBay Code	*What It Abbreviates*	*What It Means*
MIB	Mint in Box	The item's in the original box, in great shape, and just the way you'd expect to find it in a store.
MIMB	Mint in Mint Box	The box has never been opened and looks like it just left the factory.
MOC	Mint on Card	The item is mounted on its original display card, attached with the original fastenings, in store-new condition.
NRFB	Never Removed from Box	Just what it says, as in "bought but never opened."
COA	Certificate of Authenticity	Documentation that vouches for the genuineness of an item, such as an autograph or painting.
MWBMT	Mint with Both Mint Tags	Refers to stuffed animals, which have a hang tag (usually paper or card) and a tush tag (that's what they call the sewn-on tag — really) in perfect condition with no bends or tears.
OEM	Original Equipment Manufacture	You're selling the item and all the equipment that originally came with it, but you don't have the original box, owner's manual, or instructions.
NR	No Reserve Price	A reserve price is a secret price you can set when you begin your auction. If bids don't meet the reserve, you don't have to sell. Many buyers don't like reserve prices because they don't think that they can get a bargain. If you're not listing a reserve for your item, let bidders know.
HTF	Hard to Find	Out of print, only a few ever made, or people grabbed up all there were. (HTF doesn't mean you spent a week looking for it in the attic.)

Normally, you can rely on eBay slang to get your point across, but make sure that you mean it and that you're using it accurately. Don't label something MIB (Mint in Box) when it looks like it's been Mashed in Box by a meat grinder.

More title tips

Imagine going to a supermarket and asking someone to show you where the stringy stuff that you boil is instead of asking where the spaghetti is. You might end up with mung bean sprouts — delicious to some but hardly what you had in mind. That's why you should check and recheck your spelling. Buyers use the eBay search engine to find merchandise; if the name of your item is spelled wrong, the search engine can't find it. Poor spelling and incomprehensible grammar also reflect badly on you. If you're in competition with another seller, the buyer is likelier to trust the seller *hoo nose gud speling*.

If you've finished writing your item title and you have spaces left over, fight the urge to dress it up with lots of exclamation points and asterisks. No matter how gung-ho you are about your item, the eBay search engine may overlook your item if the title is encrusted with meaningless **** and ! ! ! ! symbols. If bidders do see your title, they may become annoyed by the virtual shrillness and ignore it anyway!!!!!!! (See what we mean?)

Another distracting habit is overdoing capital letters. To buyers, seeing everything in caps is LIKE SEEING A CRAZED SALESMAN SCREAMING AT THEM TO BUY NOW! All that is considered *shouting*, which is rude and tough on the eyes. Use capitalization SPARINGLY, and only to finesse a point.

Choosing a category

Choosing your item category is an important decision. eBay gives you more than 4,000 categories and subcategories, offering you this wealth of choices in a handy point-and-click way. If you're unfamiliar with the types of items you can actually *find* in those categories, however, you may want to pour over Chapter 3 before you choose one to describe *your* item. Figure 10-3 shows you the category listings on the Sell Your Item page.

To select a category, here's the drill:

1. **Click one of the main categories.**

   You see a list of subcategories.

2. **Select the most appropriate subcategory.**

3. **Continue selecting subcategories until you have narrowed down your item listing as much as possible.**

   You know you've come to the last subcategory when you don't see any more right-pointing arrows on the category list.

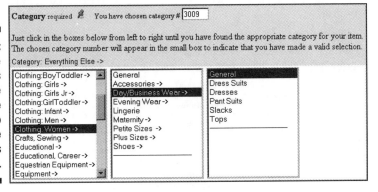

Figure 10-3: With all the categories to choose from, take the time to pick the one that best fits your item.

Most bidders scan for specific items in subcategories. For example, if you're selling a Bakelite fruit pin, don't just list it under Jewelry; keep narrowing down your choices. In this case, you can put it in a costume jewelry category that is especially for Bakelite. We guarantee that the real Bakelite jewelry collectors out there know where to look to find the jewelry they love. eBay makes it easy to narrow down the category of your item: Just keep clicking until you hit the end of the line.

If you've chosen to list an item, bid on an item, or even just browse in the Adult/Erotica category, you need to follow separate, specific guidelines because that category contains graphic nudity or sexual content that may offend some members. You must

✔ Be at least 18 years of age (but you already know that all eBay customers must be 18 or older).

✔ Have a valid credit card.

✔ Complete a waiver stating that you're voluntarily choosing to access adults-only materials. For more on how to do this (and a handy primer on privacy issues), see Chapter 14.

If you have Adult/Erotica items that you'd like to sell in a private auction, study the section later in this chapter that details the Private Auction option.

Writing your description

Once you hook potential bidders with your title, reel 'em in with a fabulous description. Don't think Hemingway here; think infomercial (the classier the better). Figure 10-4 shows a great description of some silver dollars. You can write a great description, as well — all you have to do is click in the box and start typing.

Figure 10-4:
Writing a good item description often means the difference between selling success and failure.

UNCIRCULATED MS63+ 1896 Morgan Silver Dollar

I recently purchased a group of MS63+ Morgan Silver Dollars from a long time collector to sell on ebay. The ones I've already sold have been very well received (*please look at my feedback*). This is your chance to own a beautiful 1896 Morgan Silver Dollar in Premium Quality Brilliant Uncirculated Condition. Bright and well struck, it has very clean surfaces with very sharp features and details. The picture below doesn't do justice to this striking coin. It will make a lovely addition to any coin collection or a great start towards a new one.

Bid with confidence and bid whatever you feel this coin is worth to you as it is selling with NO RESERVE! Winning bidder to pay shipping & handling of $2.50, and must submit payment within a week of winning the auction. Credit cards are accepted through Paypal.com. Good luck!
Click below to...
Win another of my auctions and Save on shipping!

Here's a list of suggestions for writing an item description:

✔ **Accentuate the positive.** Give the buyer a reason to buy your item and be enthusiastic when you list all the reasons everyone should bid on it. Unlike the title, you can use as much space as you want. Even if you use a photo, be precise in your description — how big it is, what color, what kind of fabric, what design, and so on. Refer to this chapter's "Item title info" section, as well as Table 10-1, for ideas on what to emphasize and how to word your description.

✔ **Include the negative.** Don't hide the truth of your item's condition. Trying to conceal flaws costs you in the long run: You'll get tagged with bad feedback. If the item has a scratch, a nick, a dent, a crack, a ding, a tear, a rip, missing pieces, replacement parts, faded color, dirty smudges, or a bad smell (especially if cleaning might damage the item), mention it in the description. If your item has been overhauled, rebuilt, repainted, or hot-rodded (say, a "Pentium computer" that was a 386 till you put in the new motherboard), say so. You don't want the buyer to send back your merchandise because you weren't truthful about imperfections or modifications.

✔ **Be precise about all the logistical details of the post-auction transaction.** Even though you're not required to list any special S&H (shipping and handling) or payment requirements in your item description, the majority of eBay users do. Try to figure out the cost of shipping the item in the United States and add that to your description. If you offer shipping insurance, add it to your item description.

✔ **Promote your other auctions.** The pros always do a little cross-promotion, and it works. When Jane Pauley on *Dateline NBC* tells you to tune in for the morning news, she's trying to prevent you from turning to the competition. So, if you're selling Furbies *and* Beanie Babies, say something like "Check out my Tabasco the Bull Beanie Baby auction."

✔ **While you're at it, promote yourself too.** As you accumulate positive feedback, tell potential bidders about your terrific track record. Add statements like "I'm great to deal with. Check out my feedback section." You can even take it a step further by linking your auction page to your personal Web page (if you have one) or your About Me page. (Chapter 13 gives you some tips on how to make your auction seen by a wider audience.)

✔ **Wish your potential bidders well.** Communication is the key to a good transaction, and you can set the tone for your auction and post-auction exchanges by including some simple phrases that show your friendly side. Always end your description by wishing bidders good luck, inviting potential bidders to e-mail you with questions, and offering the option of providing additional photos of the item if you have them.

Occasionally, sellers offer an item as a *pre-sell*, or an item that the seller doesn't yet have in stock but expects to. If you're offering this kind of item, make sure that you spell out all the details in the description. Don't forget to include the actual shipping date. We have found that putting an item up for sale without actually having it in hand is a practice fraught with risk. The item you are expecting may not arrive in time or arrive damaged. We've heard of one too many sellers who had to go out and purchase an item at retail for a buyer in order to preserve their feedback when caught in this position.

Like stores that hang signs that say *No shirt, no shoes, no service,* eBay members can refuse to do business with certain members. You have the right to be selective (within reason and the law, of course) about whom you want as a prospective buyer for your item. The auction is yours, and you can protect your investment any way you want. However, you can't discriminate or break any state or federal laws in your description.

Filling out the item location

eBay wants you to list the general area and the country in which you live. The idea behind telling the bidder where you live is to give him or her a heads-up on what kind of shipping charges to expect. Don't be esoteric (listing where you live as *The Here and Now* isn't a whole lot of help) but don't go crazy with cross-streets, landmarks, or degrees of latitude. Listing the city and state you live in is enough.

eBay also wants you to indicate in which of its local regions you reside. Doing so allows your auction to be listed under the Regional eBay pages. You also have the option not to be listed. We recommend that, if you live in one of the listed metropolitan areas, you use the benefits of local trading and select your area.

If you live in a big area — say, suburban Los Angeles (who, us?), which sprawls on for miles — you may want to think about narrowing down your region a little. You may find a bidder who lives close to you, which could swing your auction. We suggest that if you do a face-to-face transaction, do it in a public place.

Listing the payment methods you'll accept

Yeah, sure, eBay's loads of fun, but the bottom line to selling is the phrase *show me the money!* You make the call on what you're willing to take as money from the high bidder of your auction. Just click the payment options eBay offers that you like. They are

- **Money Orders/Cashier's Check:** The safest method of payment is a money order or cashier's check. It's the closest thing you can get to cash. As a seller, you want to get paid with as little risk as possible.

- **C.O.D. (Collect on Delivery):** We think that this option is the least attractive for both buyers and sellers. The buyer has to be home with the cash ready to go on the day that the package arrives. Odds are that on the day the item's delivered, your buyer is taking his or her sick pet goldfish to the vet for a gill-cleaning. Then the item ends up back at your door, and you have no sale.

- **See Item Description:** This option is selected for you by default. We think you should always state in your item description how you want to be paid. Why? Because there's no good reason not to.

    Standard practice is to restate and fully explain payment and shipping terms in your item description, but you don't have to.

✔ **Personal Check:** This is an extremely popular option, but it comes with a risk: The check could bounce higher than a lob at Wimbledon. If you accept personal checks, explain in your item description how long you plan to wait for the check to clear before sending the merchandise. The average hold is about five business days. Some sellers wait as long as two weeks.

Cut down on the risk of bad checks by reading the bidder's feedback when the auction's underway. Be wary of accepting checks from people with negative comments. (We explain all about feedback in Chapter 4.) Never ship an item until you're certain the check has cleared.

eBay is trying to take some of the mystery and foreboding out of accepting checks with its ID Verify program, which allows Equifax, a gigantic check-verification company, to run credit checks and present eBay members with a clean bill of health. (For more on ID Verify, see Chapter 15.)

✔ **Online Escrow:** An escrow service acts as a referee, a neutral third party. Unless you're selling an expensive item, however, offering escrow is overkill. Usually, the buyer pays for this service. Escrow companies charge 5 percent of the sale price. On big-ticket items, it may give some bidders an added sense of security. If you do offer escrow, the winning bidder should inform you right after the auction that he or she intends to use escrow. You can find more on escrow in Chapter 6.

✔ **Other:** If you're offering payment options that are not listed here, select this option. Some buyers (mostly international) like to pay in cash, but we think this is way too risky and recommend that you never, ever deal in cash. If a problem arises — for either buyer or seller — no one has evidence that payment was made or received. Avoid it.

✔ **Credit Cards (Visa, MasterCard, American Express, Discover):** If you accept credit cards, be sure to check off the little boxes next to the ones you accept. If you accept the online payment service by Billpoint or PayPal, be sure to indicate the credit card option here.

If you plan on using the Billpoint service, remember that it charges you a percentage of your final sale.

Some sellers who use credit card services try attaching an additional fee to the final payment. However, that's against the law in California, home of eBay, and therefore against eBay's rules. So forget about it.

Most sellers offer buyers several ways to pay. You can choose as many as you want. When the auction page appears, your choices are noted at the top of the listing. Listing several payment options makes you look like a flexible, easygoing professional.

Setting shipping terms

Ahoy, matey! Hoist the bid! Okay, not quite. Before you run it up the mast, select your shipping options. You've got these:

- ✓ **Ship to Home Country Only.** This option is selected by default; it means you only ship domestically.

- ✓ **Will Ship Internationally.** The world is your oyster. But make sure that you can afford it.

- ✓ **Will Ship to United States and the Following Regions**. If you are comfortable shipping to certain countries but not to others, make your selections here and they show up on your auction page.

eBay has lots of good international users, so you may want to consider selling your items around the world. If you do, be sure to clearly state in the description all extra shipping costs and customs charges. (See Chapter 11 for more information on how to ship to customers abroad.)

You're also asked who you want to pay for shipping. Choose an option:

- ✓ **Seller Pays:** You're picking up the shipping tab.

- ✓ **Buyer Pays Actual Shipping Cost:** You let the buyer know exactly how much the item costs to ship, and the buyer picks up the tab.

- ✓ **Buyer Pays Fixed Amount:** You state a fixed shipping price in your item description; the buyer agrees to include this amount in the payment for the item.

- ✓ **See Item Description:** This is another option selected by default; we see no reason not to explain your terms in the item description.

We recommend choosing the See Item Description option. Check out Chapter 11 to get more information on each of these options.

Listing the number of items for sale

Unless you're planning on holding a Dutch auction, the number of items is always 1, which means you're holding a traditional auction. If you need to change the quantity number from 1, just type the number in the box.

A matching set of cufflinks is considered one item, as is the complete 37-volume set of *The Smith Family Ancestry and Genealogical History since 1270*. If you have more than one of the same item, we suggest that you sell them one at a time.

Going Dutch

If you've got five Dennis Rodman Wedding Dolls, 37 Breathalyzers, or 2,000 commemorative pins, and you want to sell them all at once to as many bidders as possible, sell them in a Dutch auction. Dutch auctions are mainly used by dealers and businesses who want to move lots of items fast.

eBay has requirements for starting a Dutch auction. You have to be an eBay member at least 60 days with a feedback rating of ten or higher. Click on the Dutch auction link for more information on how to conduct this type of auction, and check out Chapter 1 for more info on how a Dutch auction works. If you're interested in bidding on a Dutch auction, take a look at Chapter 6.

Whether you list your items individually in auctions or together in a Dutch auction, eBay won't allow you to list the same item in more than seven auctions at one time.

Setting a minimum bid — how low can you go?

eBay requires you to set a *minimum bid,* the lowest bid allowed in an auction. What do a baseball autographed by JFK, a used walkie-talkie, and a Jaguar sports car have in common? They all started with a $1 minimum bid. You may be surprised to see stuff worth tens of thousands of dollars starting at just a buck. These sellers haven't lost their minds. Neither are they worried someone could be tooling down the highway in a $100,000 sports car for the price of a burger.

Setting an incredibly low minimum (just type it in the box *without* the dollar sign but *with* the decimal point) is a subtle strategy that gives you more bang for your buck. You can use a low minimum bid to attract more bidders, who will drive up the price to the item's real value — especially if, after doing your research, you know that the item is particularly hot. If you are worried about the outcome of the final bid, you can protect your item by using a *reserve price* (the price the bidding needs to reach before the item can be sold). Then you won't have to sell your item for a bargain-basement price because your reserve price protects your investment. The best advice is to set a reserve price that is the lowest amount you'll take for your item and then set a minimum bid that is ridiculously low. Use a reserve only when absolutely necessary because many bidders may pass up a reserve auction. (For more info about setting a reserve price, see the section "Your secret safety net — reserve price," later in this chapter.)

Starting with a low minimum is also good for your pocketbook. eBay charges the seller an insertion, or placement, fee — based on your opening bid. If you keep your opening bid low and set no reserve, you get to keep some more of your money. (See Chapter 9 for more about eBay fees.)

The more bids you get, the more people want to bid on your item because they think the item is hot. eBay actually designates every non-reserve auction item that has 31 bids or more as a Hot item and attaches a Hot icon (a flaming match) to that auction. The item is also listed in the Hot category. A designated Hot item draws bidders the way a magnet attracts paper clips.

Before you set any minimum bid, do your homework and make some savvy marketing decisions. If your auction isn't going as you hoped, you *could* end up selling your Grandma Ethel's Ming vase for a dollar. Once you set your minimum bid, you can't change it, so don't be hasty. Think about your strategy.

When putting in your minimum bid, type in only the numbers and a decimal point. Don't use dollar signs ($) or cents signs (¢).

Setting your auction time

How long do you want to run your auction? eBay gives you a choice — 3, 5, 7, or 10 days. Just click the number you want in the box.

Our auction-length strategy depends on the time of year and the item we're selling, and we have great success. If you've got an item that you think will sell pretty well, run a seven-day auction so bidders have time to check it out before they decide to bid. (We almost always run seven-day auctions.) However, if you know that you've got a red-hot item that's going to fly off the shelves — like a rare Beanie Baby or a hard-to-get Furby — choose a three-day auction. Eager bidders tend to bid higher and more often to beat out their competition if the item's hot and going fast.

No matter how many days you choose to run your auction, it ends at exactly the same time of day as it starts. A seven-day auction that starts on Thursday at 9:03:02 a.m. ends the following Thursday at 9:03:02 a.m.

Although we know the folks at eBay are pretty laid back, they do run on military time. That means they use a 24-hour clock that's set to Pacific Coast time. So 3:30 in the afternoon is 15:30, and one minute after midnight is 00:01. Questions about time conversions? Check out the Cheat Sheet at the front of this book. At ease.

Go to the Site Map for an eBay Official Time link that takes you to a nifty-looking map with the actual time in different parts of the country.

Once a week, eBay conducts a mandatory outage for database maintenance, which means that it closes up shop on Fridays from 1 a.m. to 5 a.m. Pacific Time (that's 4 a.m. to 8 a.m. Eastern Time). Never post an auction right after this outage. eBay regulars won't be around to bid on it. Also, search updates are usually 12 to 15 hours behind on Friday and Saturday following scheduled maintenance.

With auctions running 24 hours a day, 7 days a week, you should know when the most bidders are around to take a gander at your wares. Here are some times to think about:

✔ **Saturday/Sunday:** Always run an auction over a weekend. People log on and off of eBay all day.

Never start or end your auction on a Saturday or Sunday. Although this advice may seem strange, bidders are busy having lives on weekends, and their schedules are unpredictable. Some eager bidders may log on and place a maximum bid on your auction, but, you can bet they won't be sitting at a computer making a last-minute flurry of competitive bids if they have something better to do on a Saturday or Sunday.

✔ **Holiday weekends:** If a holiday weekend's coming up around the time you're setting up your auction, run your auction through the weekend.

Don't end an auction on the last day of a three-day holiday. People in the mood to shop are generally at department stores collecting bargains. If eBay members aren't shopping, they're out enjoying an extra day off.

✔ **Time of day:** We think the best time of day to start and end your auction is during eBay's peak hours of operation, which are 5 p.m. to 9 p.m. Pacific Time, right after work on the West Coast. Of course, this timing depends on the item you're auctioning and whether 5–9 p.m. Pacific Time is the middle of the night where you live.

Unless you're an insomniac or a vampire and want to sell to werewolves, don't let your auctions close in the middle of the night. There aren't enough bidders around to cause any last-minute bidding that would bump up the price.

eBay Options: Ballyhoo on the Cheap

Although eBay's display options aren't quite as effective as a three-story neon sign in Times Square, they do bring greater attention to your auction. Here are the options:

✔ **Bold.** eBay fee: $2. Bold type does catch your attention, but don't bother using it on items that'll bring in less than $20. Do use it if you're in hot competition with other similar items and you want yours to stand out.

✔ **Highlight.** eBay fee: $5. Yellow highlighter is what we use to point out the high points in books we read. (You're using one now, aren't you?) The yellow highlight feature can really make your item shine.

✔ **Home Page Featured.** eBay fee: $99.95. As with expensive real estate, you pay a premium for location, location, location. The $99.95 gives you the highest level of visibility at eBay, and it occasionally appears smack in the middle of the eBay Home page, as well as on the Special Featured auction section and on the individual category pages of the featured items (kinda hard to miss). Figure 10-5 shows the featured auctions on eBay's Home page.

Bidders do browse the Featured Auctions to see what's there, just as you might head directly to the New Releases section of your video store. But, because the vast majority of auctions found at eBay are under $25, the average seller doesn't use the Featured Auctions option.

✔ **Featured Plus!** eBay fee: $19.95. You want top billing? You can buy it here. This option puts you on the first page of your item category and on search results pages. We like this option for moving special merchandise. Often, bidders just scan the top items; if you want to be seen, you gotta be there. Ask yourself this: Is it worth $20 to have more people see my item? If yes, then go for it. Figure 10-6 shows how items are listed in the Featured in Category listings.

You need a feedback rating of at least 10 to make it to the Featured Auctions and Featured in Category Auctions.

Figure 10-5: High traffic on eBay's Home page means high visibility for featured auctions.

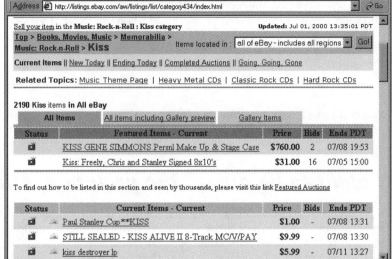

Figure 10-6:
Items at the top of the Featured in Category listings are very visible to buyers.

Your secret safety net — reserve price

Here's a little secret: The reason sellers list big-ticket items like Ferraris, grand pianos, and high-tech computer equipment with a starting bid of $1 is because they're protected from losing money with a *reserve price*. The reserve price is the lowest price that must be met before the item can be sold. It's not required by eBay but can protect you. eBay charges an additional fee for this feature that varies depending on how high your reserve is.

For example, say you list a first edition book of John Steinbeck's *The Grapes of Wrath*. You set the starting price at $1, and you set a reserve price at $80. That means that people can start bidding at $1, and if at the end of the auction the book hasn't reached the $80 reserve, you don't have to sell the book.

As with everything in life, using a reserve price for your auctions has an up side and a down side. Choosy bidders and bargain hunters blast past reserve-price auctions because they see a reserve price as a sign that proclaims *No bargains here!* Many bidders figure they can get a better deal on the same item with an auction that proudly declares *NR* (for *no reserve*) in its description. As an enticement to those bidders, you see lots of NR listings in auction titles.

On lower priced items, we suggest that you set a higher minimum bid and set no reserve. Otherwise, if you're not sure about the market, set a low minimum bid but set a high reserve to protect yourself.

If bids don't reach a set reserve price, some sellers e-mail the highest bidder and offer the item at what the seller thinks is a fair price. Two caveats:

- ✔ eBay can suspend the seller *and* the buyer if the side deal is reported to Rules & Safety (SafeHarbor). This activity is strictly prohibited.

- ✔ eBay will not protect buyers or sellers if a side deal goes bad.

You can't use a reserve price in a Dutch auction. And reserve-price auctions aren't eligible to have their goods placed in the Hot Items category.

I want to be alone: The private auction

In a private auction, bidders' User IDs are kept under wraps. Sellers usually use this option to protect the identities of bidders during auctions for high-priced big-ticket items (say, that restored World War II fighter). Wealthy eBay users may not want the world to know that they have the resources to buy expensive items. Private auctions are also held for items from the Adult/Erotica category. (Gee, there's a shocker.)

In private auctions, the seller's e-mail address is accessible to bidders in case questions arise. Bidders' e-mail addresses remain unseen.

Put me in the Gallery

The Gallery is a highly specialized auction area that lets you post pictures to a special photo gallery that's accessible from the listings. Many buyers enjoy browsing the Gallery catalog-style, and it's open to all categories. If you choose to go this route, your item is listed in both the Gallery and in the regular text listings. (We explain how to post your pictures in Chapter 13.)

Checking Your Work and Starting the Auction

When you've filled out all the blanks on the Sell Your Item page and you think you're ready to join the world of e-commerce, follow these steps:

1. Click the Review button at the bottom of the Sell Your Item page.

You waft to the Verification page (shown in Figure 10-7), the place where you can catch mistakes before your item is listed. The Verification page shows you a condensed version of all your information and tallies up how much eBay is charging you in fees and options to run this auction.

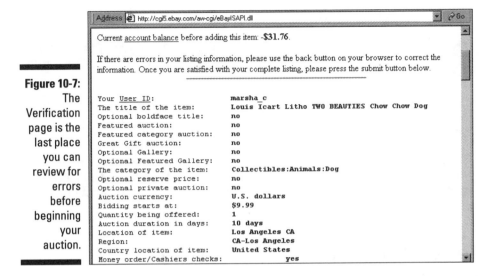

Address [🔗] http://cgi5.ebay.com/aw-cgi/eBayISAPI.dll ▾ 🔁 Go

Current account balance before adding this item: -$31.76.

If there are errors in your listing information, please use the back button on your browser to correct the information. Once you are satisfied with your complete listing, please press the submit button below.

```
Your User ID:                          marsha_c
The title of the item:                 Louis Icart Litho TWO BEAUTIES Chow Chow Dog
Optional boldface title:               no
Featured auction:                      no
Featured category auction:             no
Great Gift auction:                    no
Optional Gallery:                      no
Optional Featured Gallery:             no
The category of the item:              Collectibles:Animals:Dog
Optional reserve price:                no
Optional private auction:              no
Auction currency:                      U.S. dollars
Bidding starts at:                     $9.99
Quantity being offered:                1
Auction duration in days:              10 days
Location of item:                      Los Angeles CA
Region:                                CA-Los Angeles
Country location of item:              United States
Money order/Cashiers checks:                  yes
```

Figure 10-7:
The Verification page is the last place you can review for errors before beginning your auction.

You also may find the Verification page helpful as a last-minute chance to get your bearings. If you've chosen a very general category, eBay asks you whether you're certain there isn't a more appropriate category. You can go back to the Sell Your Item page by clicking the Back button of your browser. Make category changes or any other changes and additions, and then head for the Verification page again.

2. **Check for mistakes.**

   Nit-pick for common, careless errors; you won't be sorry. We've seen eBay members make goofs such as the wrong category listing, spelling and grammatical errors, and missing information about shipping, handling, insurance and about payment methods.

3. **When you're sure everything's accurate and you're happy with your item listing, click the Submit My Listing button.**

   An Auction Confirmation page pops up from eBay. At that precise moment, your auction begins, even though it may be a couple of hours before it appears in eBay's search and listings updates.

Print out the Auction Confirmation page and hold on to it for future reference. You also get a confirmation of your auction e-mailed to you within 24 hours. Print that out and hang on to it as well; it's handy if anybody involved in the auction has questions later.

Your auction appears in its category listing within about two hours from when you receive the Auction Confirmation page. If you want to see your auction right away and check for bids, your Auction Confirmation page provides a link for the purpose. Click the link and you're there. You can also keep track of your auctions by using the My eBay page. (To find out how, see Chapter 4.)

All auction pages come with this friendly warning:

> Seller assumes all responsibility for listing this item. You should contact the seller to resolve any questions before bidding.

Some eBay veterans just gloss over this warning after they've been wheeling and dealing for a while, but it's an important rule to remember. Whether you're buying or selling, you are responsible for your own actions.

For the first 24 hours after your auction is underway, eBay stamps the Auction item page with a funky sunrise icon next to the listing. Just a little reminder for buyers to come have a look at the latest items on auction.

Mid-Course Corrections: Fixing Current Auctions

Don't worry if you make a mistake filling out the Sell Your Item page but don't notice it until after the auction is up and running. Pencils have erasers, and eBay allows revisions. You can make changes at two stages of the game: before the first bid is placed and after the bidding war is underway. The following sections explain just what you can (and can't) correct — and when you have to accept the little imperfections of your Auction item page.

Making changes before bidding begins

Here's what you can change about your auction before bids have been placed:

- The title of your auction
- The item category
- The item description
- The URL address of the picture you're including with your auction
- Accepted payment methods, payment terms, and shipping terms

When you revise an auction, eBay puts a little disclaimer on your auction page that reads Seller revised this item before the first bid. (Think of it as automatic common courtesy.)

To revise an auction before bids have been received:

1. **Go to the auction page and click the Revise link.**

   If the item hasn't received any bids, a message appears on your screen to indicate that you may update the item.

   You're taken to the Update Item Information Request Form page, where the item number of your auction and your User ID are already entered on the form.

2. **Type your password and click the Submit button.**

   You're taken to the Update Your Item Information page.

3. **Make changes to the item information and then click the Verify button at the bottom of the page when you're finished.**

   A summary of your newly revised auction page appears on your screen.

4. **If you're happy with your revisions, click the Update button.**

   If not, click the Back button of your browser and redo the Update Your Information page.

   You're taken to your newly revised auction item page, where you see a disclaimer from eBay that says you've revised the auction before the first bid.

Making changes after bidding begins

If your auction is up and running and already receiving bids, you can still make some slight modifications to it. Newly added information is clearly separated from the original text and pictures. In addition, eBay puts a time stamp on the additional info in case questions from early bidders crop up later.

After your item receives bids, eBay allows you to

- **Change your item category:** If you think your auction isn't doing well because you listed it in the wrong category, change it. No moving vans or packing is required. You can find a new home for your item faster than you can say *Century 21*.

- **Add to your item's description:** If you feel you were at a loss for words in writing up your item's description or if a lot of potential bidders are asking the same questions, go ahead and make all the additions you want. But whatever you put there the first time around stays in the description as well.

To change your item's category from the eBay Home page after the item's received bids:

1. **Click the Services link on the navigation bar and then click Buying & Selling on the subnavigation bar.**

   You're taken to the Services Overview page.

2. **Click the Change My Item's Category link.**

   You're taken to the Changing My Item's Category page.

3. **Type in your User ID and your password, if you haven't signed in, and the item number for the auction item you want to modify; then select the item's new category.**

4. **Click the Change Category button.**

   Your auction appears in its new listings in about an hour.

You've discovered that the Apollo 11 cookie jar you thought was a reproduction is really an original? Better change that description before you sell it. To change your item's description from the eBay Home page, follow these steps:

1. **Click the Services link on the navigation bar and then click Buying & Selling on the subnavigation bar.**

   You're taken to the Services Overview page.

2. **Scroll down to Buying and Selling Tools and click the Add to My Item's Description link.**

   You're taken to the Adding To Your Item Description page.

3. **Type in your User ID, your password, and the item number of the item you want to add to; then click Submit.**

   You're taken to a page where you can add any text you want to your item's description in the description window.

4. **Click the Review button to see the additional information attached to your previous description.**

5. **If you like the changes, click the Add To Description button.**

   A message appears on your screen, bearing the glad tidings that your addition has been recorded.

Don't let an oversight grow into a failure to communicate, and don't ignore iffy communication until the auction is over. Correct any inaccuracies now to avoid problems later on.

Always check your e-mail to see whether bidders have questions about your item. If a bidder wants to know about flaws, be truthful and courteous when returning e-mails. As you get more familiar with eBay (and with writing auction descriptions), the number of e-mail questions will decrease. If you enjoy good customer service in your day-to-day shopping, here's your chance to give some back.

Chapter 11

Going, Going, Gone: Closing the Deal

In This Chapter

▶ Staying organized

▶ Communicating with the buyer

▶ Packing and sending the item

▶ Purchasing stamps online

*T*he auction's over, and you have a winning bidder who (you hope) is eager to send you money. Sounds perfect, doesn't it? It is if you watch your step, keep on top of things, and communicate like a professional.

In this chapter, we help you figure out how to stay organized by showing you what documents you need to keep and for how long. We also give you tips and etiquette on communicating with the buyer so that you're most likely to come out with positive feedback. We also show you how to pack your item, assess costs, and make sure the item reaches the buyer when you say it will (oh, yeah. . . in one piece).

Bookkeeping and Staying Organized

Although we don't recommend lining your nest with every scrap from every auction you run, you can safely keep some documents without mutating into a giant pack rat. We think you should print and file these essentials:

✔ **The auction page as it appeared when the auction closed.** This page gives you a record of the item name and number, the bidding history, every bidder's User ID, and a lot of other useful information. The page also includes the auction item description (and any revisions you've made to it), which is handy if the buyer argues that an item's disintegrating before his eyes and you honestly believe it's just well-loved.

You may think you don't need this information because you can always look it up, but here practicality rears its head: eBay trashes completed auctions after 30 days (hey, nothing lasts forever). Print your auction page *before* you forget about it; file it where you know you can find it; *then* forget about it.

✔ **The End of Auction (EOA) e-mail you receive from eBay that notifies you that the auction is over.** If you lose this e-mail, you can't get it back because eBay doesn't keep it.

✔ **E-mail between you and the buyer.** In the virtual world, e-mail is as close to having a face-to-face conversation as most people get. Your e-mail correspondence is a living record of all the things you discuss with the buyer to complete the transaction. Even if you sell just a couple of items a month at eBay, keep track of who's paid up and who owes you money. And more importantly, if the buyer says, "I told you I'd be out of town," you can look through your e-mail and say, "Nope, it doesn't show up here," or "You're right! How was Timbuktu? Is the check on the way?" Or something more polite. Be sure to keep that e-mail with the headers and date on it so that you can't be accused of (ahem) creative writing.

✔ **Any bank statements you receive that reflect a payment that doesn't clear.** Keep anything related to payments, especially payments that didn't go through. That way, if a buyer says he's sure he sent you a check, you can say, "Yes sir, Mr. X, you did send me a check, and it was made of the finest rubber." Or something kinder, especially if you want that payment.

✔ **Any insurance or escrow forms that you have.** Until the item has arrived and you're sure the customer is satisfied, be sure to keep those shipping and insurance receipts, as well as any documentation that goes along with an escrow sale.

✔ **Refund requests you make.** If you make a request to eBay for a refund from an auction that doesn't go through, hold on to it until the process is completed.

✔ **Receipts for items that you buy for the sole purpose of selling them at eBay.** This comes in handy as a reference so that you can see if you're making a profit. It can also be helpful at tax time.

Someday, the Internal Revenue Service (or government agency in your area) may knock on your door. Scary, but true. Like hurricanes and asteroid strikes, audits happen. Any accountant worth his or her salt will tell you that the best way to handle the possibility of an audit is to be prepared for the worst — even if every single eBay transaction you conduct runs smooth as silk and you've kept your nose sparkling clean. See Chapter 9 for more tax information.

If you accept online payments by Billpoint or use PayPal, and you're a Premier or Business member, you can download your transaction history for use in QuickBooks, Quicken, or Excel. These programs are excellent sources for your documentation.

Tales from the formerly Type-A

We have to confess. We used to keep all our paperwork — auctions, e-mails, the works. Now we keep the letters and receipts sent to us until we know a transaction is completed. Then they go wafting off to Recycle Heaven so that we can still find a flat surface in the house.

These days, we stay on top of our eBay finances with auction-management software that helps

us keep track of who has paid us and who hasn't. These programs also help us figure out our expenses, profits, and other financial calculations, almost painlessly. They also help jazz up the look of auctions. Ah, progress.

Once a month, we conduct a By Seller search on ourselves so that we can print out all the information we want on the bid histories of our most recent auctions. You can also join an online auction management service or purchase software that can help you organize your bidder information. We mention a few in Chapter 19.

When it comes to printouts of e-mails and documents about transactions, we say that as soon as you get your positive feedback, you can dump them. If you get negative feedback, hang on to your documentation a little longer (say, until you're sure the issues it raises are resolved and everyone's satisfied). If selling at eBay becomes a fairly regular source of income, save all receipts for items you've purchased to sell; for tax purposes, that's inventory.

If you sell specialized items, you can keep track of trends and who your frequent buyers are by saving all your paperwork. This prudent habit becomes an excellent marketing strategy if you discover that a segment of eBay users faithfully bids on your auctions. An *audience*. Imagine.

Talking to Buyers: The ABCs of Good Communication

You've heard it countless times — talk is cheap. Compared to what? Granted, empty promises are a dime a dozen, but honest-to-goodness talk and efficient e-mail are worth their weight in gold and good feedback — especially at eBay. Sometimes, *not* talking is costly.

We say that a smooth exchange of money and merchandise really starts with you (the seller). Your first e-mail, soon after the auction is over, sets the entire transaction in motion and helps set the tone for that transaction. If all goes well, no more than two weeks should elapse between getting paid and sending the item.

After the auction closes, print out a copy of both the auction page that indicates the winning bidder's final closing price and e-mail address page. Keep it handy.

Take a proactive approach and start the ball rolling yourself. We suggest contacting the buyer even *before* you get eBay's EOA. Here's how to get the buyer's e-mail address:

1. **Start on the main auction page of the item you sold.**

   If you signed in on the auction page, you can see the winner's e-mail address in parentheses next to the User ID. If you don't see the winner's e-mail address, click the winning bidder's User ID.

   This takes you to the User ID History and Email Address Request Form.

2. **Type your User ID and password; click the Submit button.**

   Signing in first puts a temporary *cookie* (a computer file that makes it easier to get around a Web site) in your computer so that you automatically get the e-mail addresses of eBay users without going through this process again. You have to set your preferences to do this on your My eBay page. The cookie is erased after you finish the current online session, or have had 40 minutes of inactivity. For more tasty info on cookies, see Chapter 14.

   You now see the user's User ID history and e-mail information. This page tells you some needed information:

   - The person's e-mail address
   - The person's User ID (or multiple User IDs if the person did any name changes in the past)
   - The date the User ID became effective
   - The end date of the User ID (if this person had others in the past)

3. **Print this information and put it in a place where you can find it again.**

Thank you! I mean it!

What do all the successful big-name department stores have in common? Yes, great prices, good merchandise, and nice displays. But with all things being equal, customer service always wins hands-down. One department store in the United States, Nordstrom, has such a great reputation that they happily took back a set of snow tires because a customer wasn't happy with them. No big deal, maybe — until you notice that Nordstrom doesn't even *sell* snow tires!

A friend of ours who owns restaurants calls this level of customer satisfaction the *Wow!* effect. If customers (no matter what they're buying) say, "Wow!" during or after the transaction — admiringly or happily — you've satisfied the customer. A good rule to go by: Give people the same level of service you expect when you're on the buying end.

The best way to start satisfying the buyer is with an introductory e-mail. Congratulate the person on winning the auction, and thank the buyer for bidding on your item. Then provide these important details:

- Item name and auction number
- Winning bid amount
- Estimated cost of shipping and packing (you'll know more exactly when you find out where the buyer lives), and any shipping or insurance restrictions. (We give pointers on determining shipping and packaging costs later in this chapter.)
- Payment options (check, money order, C.O.D., credit cards, or online payment)
- How long you will hold a check (usually seven to ten days)
- The shipping timetable

You should also mind a few vital details in the first e-mail:

- Ask for the buyer's home address (and daytime phone number if you think you need to call); ask whether this is where you should ship the item. If not, ask for the correct shipping address.
- Include your name and the address to which you want the payment sent.
- Remind your buyer to write the item name and auction number on whatever form of payment they send. You'd be surprised how many buyers forget to give you the item number. Also ask the buyer to print out and send a copy of your e-mail with the payment.
- If you are using an online payment service, such as Billpoint or PayPal, be sure to give the buyer instructions on how they can pay for the auction online.
- Include your phone number if you think it will speed up the process.
- Suggest that if all goes well, you'll be happy to leave positive feedback for the buyer. (See Chapter 4 for more on feedback.)

Keep a copy of your buyer's e-mail with a copy of the auction page that shows the winning bid.

Let's keep e-mailing

If you've got a good transaction going (and the majority of them are), the buyer will reply to your e-mail within three business days. Customarily, most replies come the next day. If your buyer has questions regarding anything you asked in your e-mail, you'll get those inquiries now. Most of the time, all you get back is, "Thanks. Payment on the way." Hey, that's good enough for us.

If any last-minute details need to be worked out, usually the buyer asks to set up a time to call or request further instructions about the transaction. Respond to this communication as soon as possible. If you can't deal with it at the moment, let the buyer know you're working on it and will shoot those answers back ASAP. *Never* let an e-mail go unanswered.

As soon as you get the hang of sending e-mail, you can actually put in an eBay link that takes the buyer right to the Feedback Forum with just a click of the mouse. We explain how to do that in Chapter 4. Buyers and sellers can also link to the Feedback Forum from the final auction page by clicking the Leave Feedback icon.

Shipping without Going Postal

Shipping can be the most time-consuming (and most dreaded) task for eBay sellers. Even if the selling portion of your transaction goes flawlessly, the item has to get to the buyer in one piece. If it doesn't, the deal could be ruined — and so could your reputation.

This section briefs you on shipping etiquette, gives you more details about the main three most popular shipping options (the U.S. Postal Service, United Parcel Service, and Federal Express), and offers tips on how to make sure your package is ready to ride.

The best way to avoid shipping problems is to do your homework beforehand, determine which method is likely to work best, and spell out on your auction page exactly how you intend to ship the item. We always say `Buyer pays actual shipping, handling, and insurance` in our item description, and that's what we charge, although we can make allowances if the buyer wants a specific method of shipment within reason. Here's how we handle the whole process:

1. **After the auction, get the package ready to ship.**

   You don't have to seal the package right away, but you should have it ready to seal because the two critical factors in shipping are weight and time. The more a package weighs and the faster it has to be delivered, the higher the charge. (We cover packing materials and tips later in this section.) The time to think about packing and shipping is actually *before* you put the item up for auction — that way, you're less likely to see last-minute surprises arise while your buyer waits impatiently for the item!

2. **Make sure you know your carrier options.**

   In the United States, the three main shipping options for most eBay transactions are the U.S. Postal Service, Federal Express, and United Parcel Service. See the section "Shopping for a shipper" (try saying *that* five times fast) for how you can get rate options from each service, painlessly and online. Compare costs and services.

3. **Before you share the cost estimate with the winner of your auction, make sure you include all appropriate costs.**

   We recommend that you charge a nominal handling fee ($1 isn't out of line) to cover your packing materials, which can add up quickly as you start making multiple transactions. You should also include any insurance costs and any delivery-confirmation costs. See the sidebar "Insuring your peace of mind (and your shipment)" for more information.

Some eBay scam artists inflate shipping and handling costs to make added profit. *Shame on them*. Purposely overcharging is tacky, ugly, and immature. And the buyer often figures it out after one look at the outrageous postage on the box.

Bidders often e-mail sellers while the auction is still going on to find out how much the shipping cost will be so that they can weigh this cost when they consider their bidding strategies. Figure out what the packed item will weigh, and then give a good guess; the online calculators can help. Be sure to say you're just giving an estimate, and that the final cost will be determined after the auction is over. Optionally, you could tell the bidder how much the item weighs and where you're shipping from (some bidders don't mind doing the math).

Occasionally, shipping calculations can be off-target, and you may not know that until after you take the buyer's money. If the mistake is in your favor and is a biggie, notify the buyer and offer a refund. But if shipping ends up costing you a bit more, take your lumps and pay it. You can always let the buyer know what happened and that you paid the extra cost. Who knows, it may show up on your feedback from the buyer! (Even if it doesn't, spreading goodwill never hurts.)

4. **E-mail the buyer and congratulate him or her on winning; reiterate what your shipping choice is and how long you expect it'll take.**

   Make sure you're both talking about the same timetable. If the buyer balks at either the price or the shipping time, try working out an option that will make the buyer happy.

5. **Send the package.**

   When should you ship the package? Common courtesy says it should go out as soon as the package and shipping charges are paid. If the buyer has held up his or her side of the bargain, you should do the same. Ship that package no more than a week after payment (or once the check clears). If you can't, immediately e-mail the buyer and explain the delay. You should e-mail the buyer as soon as you send the package and ask for an e-mail to confirm arrival after the item gets there. (Don't forget to put in a plug for positive feedback.)

Send a prompt follow-up e-mail to let the buyer know the item's on the way. In this e-mail, be sure to include when the item was sent, how long it should take to arrive, any special tracking number (if you have one), and a request for a return e-mail confirming arrival after the item gets there. We also include a thank-you note in each package we send out. We appreciate when we get one in eBay packages, and it always brings a smile to the recipient's face. It never hurts to take every opportunity to promote goodwill (and future positive feedback).

More often than not, you do get an e-mail back from the buyer to let you know the item arrived safely. If you don't, it doesn't hurt to send another e-mail (in about a week) to ask whether the item arrived in good condition. It jogs the buyer's memory and demonstrates your professionalism as a seller. Use this opportunity to gently remind your buyer(s) that you'll be leaving positive feedback for them. Ask whether they're satisfied and don't be bashful about suggesting they do the same for you. Leave positive feedback right away so that you don't forget.

Shopping for a shipper

If only you could transport your item the way they do on *Star Trek* — "Beam up that Beanie, Scotty!" Alas, it's not so. Priority Mail via the U.S. Postal Service is pretty much the eBay standard if you are shipping within the United States and Canada. Many Americans also rely on it to ship internationally as well. Federal Express and United Parcel Service are global alternatives that work well, too.

Insuring your peace of mind (and your shipment)

Sure, "lost in the mail" is an excuse we've all heard hundreds of times, but despite everyone's best efforts, sometimes things actually do get damaged or misplaced during shipment. The universe is a dangerous place; that's what insurance is for. We usually offer to get insurance from the shipper if the buyer wants to pay for it, and always get it on expensive items, one-of-a-kind items, or very fragile items. We spell it out in our item description that the buyer pays for it.

The major shippers all offer insurance that's fairly reasonably priced, so check out their rates at their Web sites. But don't forget to read the details. For example, many items at eBay are sold MIMB (Mint in Mint Box). True, the condition of the original box often has a bearing on the final value of the item inside, but the U.S. Postal Service only insures whatever is *in* the box. So, if you sold a Malibu Barbie mint in a mint box, USPS will only insure the doll and not

the original box. Pack carefully so that your buyer gets what's been paid for. Be mindful that shippers won't make good on insurance claims if they suspect you of causing the damage by doing a lousy job of packing.

We also offer our own type of *self-insurance*. No, we're not pretending we're State Farm or Allstate (though our hands *are* pretty good). Here's what we offer our buyers at no cost to them:

- ✔ On lower-priced items, we are willing to refund the buyer's money if the item is lost or damaged.

- ✔ On some items we sell, we have a *risk reserve*. That means we have more than one of the item we sold. If the item is lost or destroyed, we can send the backup item as a replacement.

Whether you're at the post office, UPS, FedEx, or your doctor's office, be ready, willing, and able to wait in line. We definitely have a "rush hour" at our neighborhood office — everybody's in a rush, so everything moves at a glacial pace. We avoid both the noontime and post-work crunches (easier on the nerves). A good time to ship is around 10:30 a.m., when everyone is still in a good mood. If we have to go in the afternoon, we go about 3:00 p.m., when the clerks are back from their lunch breaks and friendly faces (ours too — we always smile!) can take the edge off those brusque lunchtime encounters. And no matter what shipper you use, fill out the shipping forms before you get to the drop-off center. That saves time and frustration.

U.S. Postal Service

The U.S. Postal Service (USPS) is the butt of many unfair jokes and cheap shots, but when it comes right down to it, we think the USPS is still the most efficient and inexpensive way to ship items — eBay or otherwise. They also supply free boxes, labels, and tape for Priority and Express Mail packages. Here are some of the ways eBay members get their items from here to there via the USPS:

✔ **Priority Mail.** As mentioned earlier, this is the *de facto* standard method of shipping for eBay users. We love the free boxes, and we like the rate. Promised delivery time is two to three days, although we've experienced rare delays of up to a week during peak holiday periods.

Cost? As of this writing (rates are always subject to change), Priority Mail costs $3.20 for packages up to 2 pounds, and an additional $.90 for each of the next 3 pounds. Over 5 pounds, the charge is calculated according to weight and distance.

✔ **Express Mail.** If the item needs to be delivered the next day, use Express Mail. The post office promises delivery no later than noon the following afternoon (even weekends or holidays). And you can get free boxes.

Cost? Express Mail runs $11.75 for packages 8 ounces and under, $15.75 for packages 8 ounces to 2 pounds, and $2.75 for every pound over 2 (up to 70 pounds).

The post office makes a special pick-up for Priority Mail and Express Mail. The pick-up costs $8.25, no matter how many separate packages are included. If you have quite a few packages, this is an excellent option to consider, and the extra cost can be covered in your handling charge.

✔ **First-class mail.** If your item weighs 13 ounces or less, you can use first-class mail, as long as the item is flat like a letter. First class is slightly cheaper than Priority Mail — the first ounce is 33 cents, and every additional ounce is 22 cents. Unfortunately, if the envelope is an unusual size (too big, too small, too oblong), tack on another 11 cents.

✔ **Other options.** The Postal Service offers all sorts of add-ons. We always get the Delivery Confirmation service that you can add to Priority Mail, as well as other mailing services. A mere 35 cents buys you the knowledge of when and where your item was delivered. With the parcel's tracking number, you can check on whether the package was delivered (or an attempt was made to deliver it) by calling 1-800-222-1811 in the U.S. If you go online at `www.framed.usps.com/cttgate/welcome.htm`, you can get a more complete report.

Delivery confirmation also comes in handy if you try to collect insurance for an item that was never delivered, or if the buyer says it was never delivered. It gives you proof from the Postal Service that the item was sent. (We explain insuring shipments later in this chapter.) But understand that you cannot track your package. Delivery confirmation is merely proof that the package was delivered. If your package gets lost in the mail for a few weeks, this number will not act as a tracking number, and won't reveal the location of your package until it's delivered.

The USPS Web site (`new.usps.com/cgi-bin/uspsbv/scripts/front.jsp`) gives you an overview of the U.S. Postal Service rates so that you can see all of your options. Sure beats standing in that endless line! For a complete explanation of domestic rates, check out this page: `new.usps.com/cgi-bin/uspsbv/scripts/content.jsp?D=15617&B=Mail_or_Ship&A=B&U=X&U1=B&U2=H.`

✔ Even better, the USPS has a page that can help you determine exactly what your item costs to mail (after you've packaged it all up and weighed it, of course). Start at the Domestic Rate Calculator page at `postcalc.usps.gov` and follow the instructions. Rates to send packages from the United States to foreign countries can be found by going to the International Rate Calculator at `ircalc.usps.gov`.

United Parcel Service (UPS)

The folks in the brown UPS trucks love eBay. The options they offer vary, with everything from overnight service to the UPS Ground service. We use UPS for items that are heavy (say, antique barbells) or extremely large (such as a 1920s steamer trunk), because UPS ships anything up to 150 pounds in a single box — 80 more pounds than the USPS takes. UPS also takes many of the odd-shaped large boxes, such as those for computer equipment, that the Postal Service won't.

UPS makes pick-ups, but you have to know the exact weight of your package so that you can pay after the UPS driver shows up. But, the pickup service is free (our favorite price).

You can find the UPS Home page at `www.ups.com`. For rates, go to the UPS Home page and click the Quick Cost Calculator, which gives you prices based on zip codes and package weights.

Sí, oui, ja, yes! Shipping internationally

Money's good no matter what country it comes from. We don't know why, but lots of people seem to be afraid to ship internationally and list `I don't ship overseas` on the auction page. Of course, sending an item that far away may be a burden if you're selling a car or a street-sweeper (they don't fit in boxes too well), but we've found that sending a package across the Atlantic can be just as easy as shipping across state lines. The only downside: Our shipper of choice, the U.S. Postal Service, does not insure packages going to certain countries (check with your post office to find out which ones; they seem to change with the headlines).

A couple of other timely notes about shipping internationally:

✔ You need to tell what's inside the package. Be truthful when declaring value on customs forms. Be sure to use descriptions that customs agents can figure out without knowing eBay shorthand terms. For instance, instead of declaring the contents as "MIB Furby," call it a "small stuffed animal toy that talks." Some countries require the buyers to pay special duties and taxes, depending on the item and the value. But that's the buyer's headache.

✔ Wherever you send your package (especially if it's going to a country where English is not the native language), be sure to write legibly. (Imagine getting a package from Russia and having to decipher a label written in the Cyrillic alphabet. 'Nuff said.)

---

iShip, you ship, we all ship

iShip (www.iship.com), now part of Stamps.com, is an online shipping-comparison Web site that allows you to compare the charges from each of four major shipping companies (USPS, FedEx Express air service — not FedEx Ground — UPS, and Airborne Express). This handy site is easy to use, though sometimes slightly imprecise:

1. On the Price It page (enter with a click from the Home page), enter your zip code (or the zip code from the city you'll be sending the package from), the zip code of the address you're sending it to, and the size and weight of the package.

2. Click the Continue button. On the following page, you're presented with various shipping options. Leave the area asking for your handling fee blank so you can get the clearest idea of what it costs to ship.

3. Click the Continue button again, and you're taken to a page that displays rates and delivery times. This page shows you the costs of each of the four major services and how many days it will take to ship the package to its final destination. Each of the services is represented by a specific color: red for Airborne Express, purple for Federal Express, brown for United Parcel Service, and blue for the U.S. Postal Service. Click any of the color-coded rates for more information on that specific service.

We double-checked iShip's listed rates against the USPS, FedEx, and UPS online calculators and found iShip is sometimes slightly off. Even so, iShip is still a handy resource for getting the big picture of what it costs to send packages around the United States.

The Quick Cost Calculator prices online are based on what UPS charges regular and high-volume users. When you get to the counter, the price may be slightly higher than what you find on the Web.

Our favorite link on the UPS site is the transit map that shows the United States and how long it takes to reach any place in the country (based on the originating zip code). If you're really thinking of shipping that compact refrigerator to Alaska, you can check out this fun and informative page at www.ups.com/using/services/servicemaps/servicemaps.html.

If you use UPS, always buy the delivery confirmation option for $1.25. As soon as the package gets to its destination and is signed for, UPS sends you back a confirmation so that you have evidence showing it has been shipped. But what's really cool is the free UPS online tracking. Every package is barcoded, and that code is read everywhere your package stops along its shipping route. You can follow its progress by its package number at the following address: www.ups.com/tracking/tracking.html

Federal Express (FedEx)

We use FedEx Express air all the time for business in our day jobs, but Express seems rather expensive for our eBay shipping. However, if the buyer wants it fast and is willing to pay, we'll send it by FedEx overnight, you bet.

The new FedEx Ground Home Delivery service has competitive prices, and carries all the best features of Federal Express. We like the online tracking option for all packages, and FedEx Express takes packages over 150 pounds. FedEx will pick up your package for a $3 charge.

We also like the FedEx boxes, which are — like one of our favorite actors, Joe Pesci from *My Cousin Vinnie* and the *Lethal Weapon* movies, small but tough. But if you're thinking of recycling these boxes and using them to ship with another service, forget it. The FedEx logo is plastered all over every inch of the freebies, and the company may get seriously peeved about it. You can't use those fancy boxes for the Home Delivery service.

Federal Express recently launched its new FedEx Ground Home Delivery service. These rates are competitive to UPS, and FedEx offers a money-back guarantee for residential ground delivery. A two-pound package going from Los Angeles to New York City takes five days and costs $4.35. Federal Express includes online package tracking and insurance up to $100 in this price. You have to be a business to avail yourself of home delivery — but plenty of home businesses exist.

A two-pound U.S. Post Office Priority Mail package with $100 insurance and a delivery confirmation costs you $5.35. Granted, the package will arrive within two to three days, but FedEx Ground guarantees a five-day delivery. FedEx Ground will not supply boxes for you, so you're on your own there. But that $1 savings and other benefits more than make up the difference.

United Parcel Service gives you five-day service for $6.65, but there's no money-back guarantee on delivery time.

You can find the FedEx home page at `www.fedex.com/us`. The link for rates is conveniently located at the top of the page.

Rough ride

This old U.S. Post Office (Pony Rider) patch was found when I was disposing of my patch collection. This patch is a mint-condition example of the old United States post office Department uniform patch. The patch was used prior to the current U.S. Postal Service eagle's head emblem, and is in the form of the old mail rider on horse back, as seen in use in the Kevin Costner film *The Postman.* This patch is an old original, not a movie prop, and even comes with the hard-to-obtain detached Letter Carrier arc tab — so that you actually get two patches. Buyer pays shipping, with USPS money order payment preferred, checks take 10 days to clear.

The starting price was $14.99. It received no bids and did not sell. (Maybe the bidders thought it would be sent via Pony Express?)

Getting the right (packing) stuff

You can never think about packing materials too early. You may think you're jumping the gun, but by the law of averages, if you wait until the last minute, you won't find the right-size box, approved tape, or the labels you need. Start thinking about shipping even before you sell your item.

But before you pack, give your item the once-over. Here's a checklist of what to consider about your item before you call it a wrap (love that Hollywood lingo).

- ✔ **Is your item as you described it?** If the item has been dented or torn somehow, e-mail the winning bidder immediately and come clean. And if you sell an item with its original box or container, don't just check the item, make sure the box is in the same good condition as the item inside. Collectors place a high value on original boxes, so make sure the box lives up to what you described in your auction. Pack to protect it as well.

- ✔ **Is the item dirty or dusty, or does it smell of smoke?** Some buyers may complain that the item they received is dirty or smelly, especially from cigarette smoke. Make sure the item is fresh and clean, even if it's used or vintage. If something's dirty, check to make sure you know how to clean it properly (you want to take the dirt off, not the paint), and then give it a spritz with an appropriate cleaner or just soap and water. If you can't get rid of the smell or the dirt, say so in your item description. Let the buyer decide whether the item is desirable with aromas and all.

If the item has a faint smell of smoke or is a bit musty, a new product called Febreze may help. Just get a plastic bag, give your item a spritz, and keep it in the bag for a short while. *Note:* Not recommended for cardboard. And, as with any solvent or cleaning agent, read the label before you spray.

When the item's ready to go, you're ready to pack it up. The following sections give you suggestions on what you should consider using and where to find the right stuff.

Packing material: What to use

This may sound obvious, but you'd be surprised: Any list of packing material should start with a box. But you don't want just any box — you want a heavy cardboard type that's larger than the item. If the item is extremely fragile, we suggest you use two boxes, with the outer box about three inches larger on each side than the inner box that holds the item, to allow for extra padding. And if you still have the original shipping container for such things as electronic equipment, consider using the original, especially if it still has the original foam inserts (they were designed for the purpose, and this way they stay out of the environment a while longer).

As for padding, Table 11-1 compares the most popular types of box-filler material.

Table 11-1	Box-Filler Materials	
Type	*Pros and Cons*	*Suggestions*
Bubble wrap	**Pros:** Lightweight, clean, cushions well. **Cons:** Cost.	Don't go overboard taping the bubble wrap. If the buyer has to battle to get the tape off, the item may go flying and end up damaged. And for crying out loud, don't pop all the little bubbles, okay?
Newspaper	**Pros:** Cheap, cushions. **Cons:** Messy.	Seal fairly well. Put your item in a plastic bag to protect it from the ink. We like shredding the newspaper first. It's more manageable and doesn't seem to stain as much as wadded-up paper. We spent about $30 at an office-supply store for a shredder (or find one at eBay for much less).
Cut-up cardboard	**Pros:** Handy, cheap. **Cons:** Transmits some shocks to item, hard to cut up.	If you have some old boxes that aren't sturdy enough to pack in, this is a pretty good use for them.
Styrofoam peanuts	**Pros**: Lightweight, absorb shock well, clean. **Cons:** Environmentally unfriendly, annoying.	Your item may shift if you don't put enough peanuts in the box, so make sure to fill the box. Also, don't buy these — instead, recycle them from stuff that was shipped to you (trash bags are great for storing them). And never use plastic peanuts when packing electronic equipment, because they can create static electricity. Even a little spark can trash a computer chip.
Popped popcorn	**Pros:** Lightweight, environmentally friendly, absorbs shock well, clean (as long as you don't use salt and butter, but you knew that), low in calories. **Cons:** Cost, time to pop.	You don't want to send it anywhere there may be varmints who like it too. The U.S. Postal Service suggests popcorn. Hey, at least you can eat the leftovers!

Whatever materials you use, make sure you pack the item well and that you secure the box. Many shippers will contest insurance claims if they feel you did a lousy job of packing. Do all the little things that you'd want done if you were the buyer — using double boxes for really fragile items, wrapping lids separately from containers, and filling hollow breakables with some kind of padding. A few other items you need are the following:

- **Plastic bags.** Plastic bags protect your item from moisture. We once sent a MIB doll to the Northeast, and the package got caught in a snowstorm. The buyer e-mailed us with words of thanks for the extra plastic bag, which saved the item from being soaked along with the outer box. (Speaking of boxes, if you send an item in an original box, bag it.)

   For small items, such as stuffed animals, you should always protect them in a lunch baggie. For slightly larger items, go to the 1-quart or 1-gallon size. Be sure to wrap any paper or cloth products, such as clothing and linens, in plastic before you ship.

- **Address labels.** You'll need extras because it's always a good idea to toss a duplicate address label inside the box, with the destination address and a return address, in case the outside label falls off or becomes illegible.

- **Two- or three-inch shipping tape.** Make sure you use a strong shipping tape for the outside of the box. Use nylon-reinforced tape or pressure-sensitive package tape. Remember not to plaster every inch of box with tape; leave space for those *Fragile* and *Insured* rubber stamps.

- **Two-inch clear tape.** For taping the padding around the inside items. We also use a clear strip of tape over the address on the outside of the box so that it won't disappear in the rain.

- **Scissors.** A pair of large, sharp scissors. Having a hobby knife to trim boxes or shred newspaper is also a good idea.

- **Glue gun.** We use one for reconstructing cut-down boxes.

- **Handy liquids.** Three that we like are GOO GONE (which is available in the household supply section of most retail stores and is a wonder at removing unwanted stickers and price tags); WD-40 (the unstick-every-thing standby that works great on getting stickers off plastic); and Un-Du (the best liquid we've found to take labels off cardboard). If you can't find Un-Du in stores, lighter fluid also does the trick, but be careful handling it and make sure you clean up thoroughly.

- **Black permanent marker.** These are handy for writing addresses and the all-important *Fragile* all over the box. We like the thick Sharpie markers.

Taking it to the mat

1985 Rare WWF Hulk Hogan with T-shirt! One action figure you don't want to miss! Serious collectors can take advantage of this 1985 Hulk Hogan wrestling figure. This is the second Hulk Hogan figure released by LJN Toys. The first was the common one that most collectors have that depicts the Hulkster in yellow tights with no shirt. This more scarce version depicts Hulk with a white Hulkamania T-shirt. This item is sealed in original packaging. The package has very little wear around the corners, otherwise in great condition. Buyer pays shipping. U.S./Canada orders only please.

The opening bid was $10, but the item later sold at eBay for $80.98. How's that for a body slam?

Not sure how to pack your item? No problem. Just call a store in your area that deals in that kind of item and ask them how they pack for shipment. They'll probably be glad to offer you a few pointers. Or post a question to seasoned eBay veterans in the chat room for your auction's category. (We introduce you to chat rooms in Chapter 16.)

If you really plan to become an eBay mover and shaker, consider adding a five-pound weight scale (for weighing packages) to your shipping department. Why five pounds? Because that's the weight/price break for the Postal Service's Priority Mail.

When it comes to fragile items, dishes, pottery, porcelain, china, anything that can chip, crack or smash into a thousand pieces, *double box*. The boxes should be about three inches different on each side. Make sure there's enough padding so that the interior box is snug. Just give it a big shake. If nothing rattles, ship away!

Packing material: Where to find it

The place to start looking for packing material is the same place you should start looking for things to sell at eBay: your house. Between us, we've done over a thousand eBay transactions and never once paid for a carton. Because we buy most of our stuff from catalogs and online companies (we love e-commerce), we save all the boxes, bubble wrap, padding, and packing peanuts we get in the mail. Just empty your boxes of styrofoam peanuts into large plastic trash bags — that way, they don't take up much storage space. Marsha's most proud of the bubble-wrap blanket that covers her car!

If you recently got a mail-order shipment box that was only used that once — and it's a good, sturdy box with no dents or dings — there's nothing wrong with using it again. Just be sure to cover any old labels so the delivery company doesn't get confused.

Beyond the ol' homestead, here are a couple of other suggestions for places where you can rustle up some packing stuff:

- ✔ **Your local supermarket, department store, or drug store.** You won't be the first person pleading with a store manager for boxes. (Ah, fond memories of moving days past. . . .) Stores actually like giving them away because it saves the extra work of compacting them and throwing them away.

  We found that drug stores have a better variety of smaller boxes. Be careful that you don't take dirty boxes reeking of food smells.

- ✔ **The inside of your local supermarket, department store, or drug store.** Places like Kmart, Wal-Mart, Target, and office-supply stores often have good selections of packing supplies.

- ✔ **Shippers like UPS, FedEx, and the Postal Service.** They offer all kinds of free supplies as long as you use them to ship things with their service. The Postal Service also ships free boxes, packing tape, labels, and shipping forms for Express Mail, Priority Mail, and Global Priority Mail to your house. In the U.S., you can order by phone (1-800-222-1811) or online (supplies.usps.gov). A couple of rules for USPS orders:

  - • Specify the service (Priority Mail, Express Mail, or Global Priority Mail) you're using because the tape, the boxes, and the labels all come with the service name printed all over them, and you can only use it for that specific service.

  - • Order in bulk. For example, address labels come in rolls of 500 and boxes in packs of 25.

  - • The boxes come flat, so you have to assemble them. Hey, don't look a gift box in the mouth — they're free!

- ✔ **Other places online.** Many terrific online sites can offer you really good deals. We recommend the following sites:

  - • Bubblefast (www.bubblefast.com) is an eBay Power Seller with over 3,000 positive feedbacks. Bubblefast gives credit to all eBay buyers with a feedback rating of 20 or more.

  - • ShippingSupply.com (www.shippingsupply.com) is an eBay Power Seller with close to 10,000 positive feedbacks.

  - • Discount Box & The Packaging Store (www.movewithus.com).

  - • Uline Shipping Supplies (www.uline.com).

And, of course, you can rifle through the auctions at eBay in quest of shipping supplies. You can find some great deals, especially on bubble wrap.

Buying Postage Online

Isn't technology great? You no longer have to schlep to the Post Office every time you need stamps. What's even better, with the new print-it-yourself postage, you can give all your packages (up to five pounds) directly to your mailman. When you install your Internet postage, you apply for a USPS postal license that allows you to print your own *Information Based Indicia (IBI)* for your postage. IBI is a two-dimensional barcode either printed on labels or directly on an envelope that has both human- and machine-readable information about where it was printed and security-related elements. It provides you with a much more secure way of getting your valuable packages through the mail.

You can print postage for first class, priority, express, parcel post, and additional postage for delivery confirmations and insurance. If your printer mangles a sheet of labels or an envelope, you can send the printed piece to your Internet postage provider for a refund. Several vendors of Internet-based postage exist, but E-stamp and Stamps.com are the most popular.

eBay's partner in postage: E-stamp

E-stamp and eBay go hand in hand, and special offers for eBay buyers are continually offered through the eBay site. To join, check eBay's happenings at `pages.ebay.com/community/news/happenings.html` and order the starter kit. The kit includes the software on a CD, a USPS-address matching CD (which checks your typewritten address against a database to insert the complete zip code, and verifies that the address is accurate), and a piece of hardware, called a *vault*, that attaches to your printer port. The CD contains references to all deliverable addresses in the U.S.

It's often discounted for eBay members at $24.99 — regularly $49.99. If no discount is available through eBay, check with `www.estamp.com` for other special offerings.

The vault holds the information on your postage purchases and enables you to print postage whether you're online or not. Your addresses and account information are kept securely on your computer. The software integrates with Microsoft Office and Outlook, QuickBooks, Corel WordPerfect, and many other applications. You may attach the optional $99 electronic postage scale to the vault (we highly recommend this). It weighs your mail and prints exactly the amount of postage that you need — not a penny more.

After you join E-stamp (costs may vary depending on which deal of the month you get), you are only charged a convenience fee when you purchase your postage. The minimum you pay of the 10 percent convenience fee is

$4.99 and the maximum fee is $24.99 per purchase. As an eBay member, you never have to pay more than $24.99 per month, no matter how may times you purchase postage in a month. We recommend buying a minimum of $50 each time you buy postage, so that your convenience fee will never add up to more than 10 percent. E-stamp has no monthly recurring fees, so you only pay a premium when you purchase postage.

Stamps.com — the other guys

Stamps.com is truly an online postage system; you must be online to use it and to print your postage. After you accept the bargain du jour (today it's $20 or $50 in free postage) sign-up package, you may instantly download the software or request that a CD be sent to you. It's simple and convenient, and you don't have to buy a starter kit.

Stamps.com handles everything you need to do online. There's no address matching CD as with E-stamp, your addresses are confirmed online, and the complete zip code is picked up directly from the servers. Your postage purchases are also kept online, so if you have a less-than-reliable Internet connection or if you have security concerns regarding your addresses, this may not be the plan for you. The Stamps.com software integrates with all the same software programs as E-stamp, plus a few more.

Stamps.com runs more like a postage meter service and charges monthly fees. They have two levels of service: the Simple plan and the Power plan.

The Simple plan charges you a monthly service fee of 10 percent of postage printed, with a monthly minimum of $1.99 and a maximum of $19.99. No convenience fees are attached to purchasing postage, so if all the postage that you print in a month totals $19.99, all you pay is $1.99 a month. On the other hand, if you send out 20 Priority Mail packages, each with a delivery confirmation, your total postage would be $71 and your fee to Stamps.com would be $7.10. If you print no postage in a given month, you still pay $1.99 just to have the service.

The Power plan carries a $19.99 flat service fee per month, no matter how much postage you print. You also get a free digital scale to weigh your packages. (*Note:* It doesn't connect directly to your computer.) It's perfect if you ship over $200 in postage per month.

If you go on vacation, or don't run any auctions, you're still charged $19.99 per month.

Chapter 12

Troubleshooting Your Auction

In This Chapter
- ▶ Dealing with a difficult buyer
- ▶ Handling other auction mishaps
- ▶ Ending an auction early
- ▶ Canceling an auction after it ends
- ▶ Relisting an item
- ▶ Getting refunds from eBay

There's no getting around it: The more transactions you conduct at eBay, the more chances you have of facing some potential pitfalls. In this chapter, we give you pointers on how to handle an obnoxious buyer as if he or she is your new best friend (for a little while anyway). In addition, we explain how to keep an honest misunderstanding from blowing up into an e-mail war. We show you how to handle an auction that's (shall we say) on a road to nowhere, how to get some attention, and if it all goes sour, how to relist and get the money you paid eBay back. We don't think all of what we mention here will happen to you, but the more you know, the better off you'll be.

Dealing with a Buyer Who Doesn't Respond

Most of the time, the post-auction transaction between buyers and sellers goes smoothly. However, if you have difficulty communicating with the winner of your auction, you should know the best way to handle the situation.

You've come to the right place if you want help dealing with a potential non-paying bidder (more commonly known as deadbeat bidders, which is how we refer to them). Of course, you should start with good initial post-auction communications; see Chapter 11. (For more information on how to deal with a fraudulent seller, see Chapter 15.)

Going into nudge mode

Despite our best efforts, sometimes things fall through the cracks. Both buyers and sellers should contact each other within three business days of the close of the auction. Sometimes winners contact sellers immediately, which can save you some trouble, but if you don't hear from the buyer within three business days of your initial contact, our first advice is *don't panic.*

People are busy; they travel, they get sick, computers crash, or sometimes your auction may simply slip the winner's mind. After a week of not hearing from the winner, you need to get into big-time *nudge-nudge mode* — as in, "Mr. X, remember me and your obligation to buy the Tiffany lamp you won at eBay last week?"

Send a friendly-but-firm e-mail letting Mr. X know that when he bid and won your auction, he became obligated to pay and complete the transaction. If Mr. X doesn't intend to buy your item for any reason, he needs to let you know immediately.

Don't threaten your buyer. The last thing you want to do is add insult to injury in case the buyer is facing a real problem. Besides, if the high bidder goes to sleep with the fishes, you'll *never* see your money.

Here's what to include in your nudge-nudge e-mail:

- ✔ A gentle rebuke, such as, "Perhaps this slipped your mind," or "You may have missed my e-mail to you," or "I'm sure you didn't mean to ignore my first e-mail."

- ✔ A gentle reminder that eBay's policy is that every bid is a binding contract. You can even refer the buyer to eBay's rules and regulations if you want.

- ✔ A statement that firmly (but gently) explains that, so far, you've held up your side of the deal and you'd appreciate it if he did the same.

- ✔ A date by which you expect to see payment. Gently explain that if the deadline isn't met, you'll have no other choice but to consider the deal invalid.

Technically, you can nullify the transaction if you don't hear from a buyer within three business days. However, eBay members are a forgiving bunch under the right circumstances. We think you should give your buyer a one-week grace period after the auction ends to get in touch with you and set up a payment plan. If you don't see any real progress towards a closing of the deal at the end of the grace period, say goodnight, Gracie. Consider the deal kaput and go directly to the section "Auction Going Badly? Cut Your Losses" (later in this chapter) to find out what recourse you have.

Be sure you're not the one who erred. Did you spell the name right in your winner's e-mail address? If you didn't, that person may not have received your message!

Be a secret agent, man

We won't say history repeats itself; that would be a cliché. (All right, so you caught us, but clichés are memorable because they're so often true.) After you send your polite and gentle nudge-nudge e-mail, but before you decide that the auction is a lost cause, take a look at the bidder's feedback history. Figure 12-1 shows you the Feedback Profile of an eBay user with several negative feedback ratings in the last month. Beware.

Figure 12-1: You can get an indication of whether the buyer will complete the sale by looking at the user's Feedback Profile.

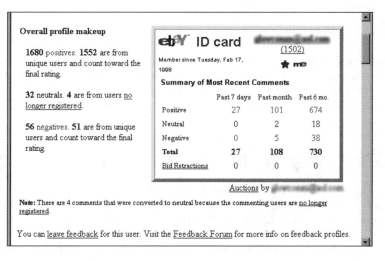

Overall profile makeup

1680 positives. **1552** are from unique users and count toward the final rating.

32 neutrals. **4** are from users no longer registered.

56 negatives. **51** are from unique users and count toward the final rating.

ID card (1502)
Member since Tuesday, Feb 17, 1998

Summary of Most Recent Comments

	Past 7 days	Past month	Past 6 mo.
Positive	27	101	674
Neutral	0	2	18
Negative	0	5	38
Total	**27**	**108**	**730**
Bid Retractions	0	0	0

Auctions by

Note: There are 4 comments that were converted to neutral because the commenting users are no longer registered.

You can leave feedback for this user. Visit the Feedback Forum for more info on feedback profiles.

To check the feedback of a bidder (starting at your auction item page), do the following:

1. **Click the number in parentheses next to your winner's User ID.**

   This takes you to the Feedback Profile page of the member.

2. **Scroll down the Feedback Profile page and read the comments.**

   Check to see if the bidder has gotten negative feedback from previous sellers. Make a note of it in case you need some support and background information.

3. **Conduct a Bidder search.**

   Click Search on the main navigation bar and do a Bidder search to see the buyer's conduct in previous auctions. How many has the buyer won? Click the item number to see the history of the auction. For more info on Bidder searches, check out Chapter 5.

When all else fails, you may want to double-check with some of the bidder's previous sellers. It's okay to e-mail previous sellers who've dealt with the bidder. They're often happy to give you details on how well (or badly) the transaction went.

If there's any indication that the buyer has gone AWOL in the past, start thinking about getting out of the transaction before too much time passes. If the buyer looks to be on the level, continue to give him or her the benefit of the doubt.

Be sure to ask previous sellers that dealt with the bidder the following questions (politely):

- ✔ Did Mr. X pay on time?
- ✔ Did his check clear?
- ✔ Did he communicate well?

When e-mailing a third party about any negative feedback left, choose your words carefully. There's no guarantee that if you trash the bidder, the third party will keep your e-mail private. Make sure you stick to the facts. Writing false or malicious statements can put you in danger of being sued.

Step up your nudge a notch

If you don't hear from the winner after a week, your next course of action is to contact the winner by phone. To get the contact information of an eBay member for transaction purposes only, do the following:

1. **Click the Search link on the navigation bar at the top of most eBay pages.**

   You see a subdirectory appear below the navigation bar.

2. **Click the Find Members link and scroll down the page to the Contact Info box.**

3. **Enter the User ID of the person you're trying to contact.**

4. **Enter your User ID (or e-mail address) and your password.**

5. **Click the Submit button.**

   eBay e-mails you the contact information of the person with whom you want to be in touch and also sends your contact information to that person.

Wait a day before calling the person. We like the last-chance e-mail sent after ten days that says you want to put the item back up at eBay if the buyer is no longer interested. Also, mention that you want to apply for any credits you can get from eBay due to an incomplete transaction. If enough money is involved in the transaction, and you feel it's worth the investment, make the call to the winner. eBay automatically sends your request and your information to the bidder, and that may be enough of a nudge to get some action.

If you do get the person on the phone, keep the conversation like your e-mail — friendly but businesslike. Explain who you are, when the auction closed, and ask if there are any circumstances that have delayed the bidder's reply. Often, the bidder will be so shocked to hear from you that you'll get the check immediately, or you'll know this person is a complete deadbeat.

Try a last-ditch emergency effort

If e-mails and phoning the winner don't work, and you really want to give the buyer one last chance to complete the transaction, check out eBay's Emergency Contact Board. Again, you should decide if the money involved in the cost of the phone call is worth the effort. The Emergency Contact Board is where members who are having trouble contacting buyers and sellers leave word. Don't worry that the buyer may miss your message. A conscientious group of eBay pros man this area and try to help by passing on e-mails to the missing parties. Jump over to Chapter 16 for more information on this Board and its group of regulars. Figure 12-2 shows you what the Emergency Contact Board looks like.

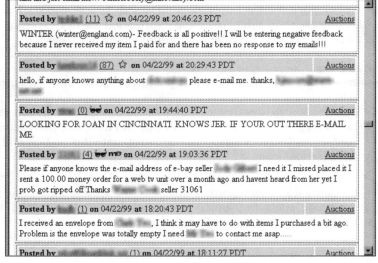

Figure 12-2:
You can make one last attempt to contact your buyer on the Emergency Contact Board.

To post a message on the Emergency Contact Board, do the following:

1. **Click the Community link on the main navigation bar at the top of most eBay pages.**

   A submenu with additional links appears.

2. **Click the Chat box on the submenu of the Navigation bar.**

   You're taken to the Discussion Help & Chat page, which lists all eBay's chat boards.

3. **Scroll down under General Chat Rooms category and click the Emergency Contact link.**

   You're taken to the Emergency User Contact Board.

   Before you post a message, scroll through the postings and look for messages from your AWOL buyer. Maybe he or she has been trying to get in touch with you, too.

4. **If you haven't already signed in, type your User ID and password in the appropriate boxes. Then type your message where you want to post it.**

   Even though you may feel like the transaction is a lost cause when you get to the point of posting a message on the Emergency Contact Board, keep your message neutral and don't make accusations.

5. **Check your message for errors and click the Click here button.**

   Your message is instantly posted.

Not sure what to post on the Emergency Contact Board? Start off by sticking to the facts of the transaction and say what you want your buyer to do. Have the item number and the buyer's User ID handy before you start your posting. Be sure not to post any personal information about the buyer, like their real name and address. That is a violation of the eBay rules.

You can send messages to specific users or post a general cry for help. Here are two examples of short-but-sweet postings that get your message across:

- ✔ Dear Mr. X, I've been trying to reach you through e-mail and phone for two weeks about Item number XXXXX and have had no response. Please contact me by (leave date) or I will invalidate the auction and leave negative feedback.

- ✔ I've been trying to contact Mr. X (mrx@completelybogusbidder.com) for two weeks now regarding an auction. Does anybody know this person or have a new e-mail address for him? Did anybody get burned by this buyer in the past? Thanks.

Your postings aren't very useful if you don't check back often and read other eBay users' postings on the Emergency Contact Board. Check the board to see whether someone has responded to your message. Also, keep your eyes open as you scroll through the board. Although we suggest you don't trash anyone on this board, many people use the Emergency Contact Board to issue an all-points bulletin about bad eBay members.

And Some Other Auction Problems

We're not quite sure why, but where money is involved, sometimes people act kind of weird. Buyers may suddenly decide that they can't purchase an item after they've made a commitment, or there may be payment problems, or shipping problems. Whatever the problem, look no farther than here to find out how to make things better.

The buyer backs out of the transaction

Every time an eBay member places a bid, he or she makes a commitment to purchase the item in question. In theory, anyway. In the real world, people have second thoughts, despite the rules. You have every right to be angry that you're losing money and wasting your time. Remind the buyer that making a bid is a binding contract. But, unfortunately, if the winner won't pay up, you can't do much except make the winner pay with negative feedback. Jump to Chapter 6 to find out more about buyer's remorse.

Keeping your cool

By all means, if the winner of one of your auctions tells you that the transaction can't be completed, no matter what the reason — remain professional, despite your anger. For one thing, at least such a would-be buyer has the heart to break the news to you instead of ignoring your e-mail and phone calls.

When Plan A fails, try Plan B, or even C

You have several options if the winner backs out. You can offer the item to the next highest bidder or relist the item and hope it sells again. In addition, you can request a full or partial Final Value Fee credit. (We give you more information on requesting a Final Value Fee credit, selling your item to the next highest bidder, and relisting your item later in this chapter.) Who knows? This bidder may actually *earn* you money in the long run.

You may feel inclined to offer the item to the next-highest bidder, but watch out — eBay doesn't sanction this activity and you will not be protected by eBay if the deal doesn't work out. If you're reported for doing a side deal you could have your eBay membership revoked.

Leaving feedback after an imperfect auction experience

If the buyer never materializes, backs out, bounces a check, or moves slower than a glacier to send your payment (but wants the item sent overnight from Boston to Khartoum at your expense), you need to think about how you want to word your feedback. You're well within your rights to leave negative feedback, but that doesn't mean you can go off the deep end. Remember to stick to the facts and don't get personal.

Here are a few feedback tips. For more information, check out Chapters 4 and 6.

✔ If the transaction was shaky but everything turned out all right in the end, go ahead and leave neutral feedback.

✔ If a blizzard stopped planes out of Chicago for three days and that's why it took a long time to get your check, take a deep breath, blame the fates, and leave positive feedback.

✔ If the buyer was a living nightmare, take a long break before leaving negative feedback — and have someone you love and trust read it before you send something into the virtual world that you can't take back.

Houston, we have a payment problem

Lots of things can go wrong where money is concerned. Maybe you never receive the money, or perhaps the check bounces. If the check bounces, contact the seller immediately. Honest winners will be completely embarrassed and make good while unscrupulous winners will offer lame excuses. Either way, insist on a more secure form of payment, like a money order.

If the buyer pays by check, hang on to the check until it clears, and then ship the item.

The item you send is busted — and so are you

Uh-oh! Could it be true? Could you have sent the wrong item? Or is it possible that the crystal vase you thought you packed so well is a sad pile of shards at the bottom of a torn box? If so, read Chapter 11 as soon as you take care of this catastrophe so that you can get some hints on packing and insurance.

It's time to do some serious problem solving. If the buyer met his or her end of the deal, you need to do your best to fix the problem. Your communication skills are your number one asset in this situation, so get to work.

Picking up the pieces

No matter how carefully you pack an item, sometimes it arrives on the buyer's doorstep mangled, broken, or squashed. News of this unfortunate event travels back to you fast. The buyer will let you know in about 30 seconds how unhappy he or she is in an e-mail. Tell the buyer to locate the insurance stamp or paper tag that's attached to the package as proof of insurance and then take the whole mangled shebang back to his or her post office.

Here's what happens at the post office:

- ✔ If the item is insured for less than $50, the buyer immediately gets a postal service money order for the value of the item.

- ✔ If the item is insured for over $50, the buyer fills out a claim form, and you're contacted to fill out additional forms. You need to show the good people at the post office your insurance receipt. You have to wait 60 to 90 days for the paperwork to be processed before you actually get paid.

- ✔ Of course, the post office won't refund the postage. Hey, they delivered the item, didn't they?

If a package is lost, you'll know it because the delivery confirmation never comes through, or the buyer tells you the package is a no-show. You need to go the post office from which you sent the item to file for insurance. Then the postal service checks around. If your item isn't located in 30 days, it's declared lost, and there's another round of paperwork and processing before you get your money. And no, you don't get a return on the postage either.

Boxed out of a claim

In our experience, neither UPS nor the United States Postal Service will pay on an insurance claim if they feel you did a lousy job of packing. So, don't be surprised if your claim is declined. Always use good products, pack carefully, and get ready to plead your case.

Every shipping company has its own procedure for complaints. But the one thing they do have in common: no procedure is hassle-free. Call your shipper as soon as a problem arises.

You have regrets — seller's remorse

You've undoubtedly heard about buyer's remorse. Here's a new one for you — *seller's remorse*. If you were selling your velvet Elvis footstool because your spouse said, "It's me or that footstool!" and in the end you realize your spouse should have known how much you revered the King when you went to Graceland on your honeymoon, you can end the auction. Read "Try canceling bids first" and "If all else fails, end your auction early," later in this chapter.

Auction Going Badly? Cut Your Losses

So your auction is cruising along just fine for a couple of days when you notice that same eBay user who didn't pay up on a previous auction is your current high bidder. You don't want to get burned again, do you? Of course not; *cancel* this deadbeat's bid before it's too late. While canceling bids — or, for that matter, entire auctions — isn't easy (you have a load of explaining to do, pardner), eBay does allow it.

If you feel you have to wash your hands of an auction that's given you nothing but grief, it doesn't mean you have to lose money on the deal. Read on to find out the protocol for dumping untrustworthy bidders or (as a last resort) laying a bad auction to rest and beginning anew.

Try canceling bids first

Face the facts: This auction is fast becoming a big-time loser. You did your very best, and things didn't work out. Before you kill an auction completely, see whether you can improve it by canceling bids first.

You may have a million reasons for thinking your auction is a bust, but eBay says your explanation had better be good. Here are some eBay-approved reasons for canceling a bid (or even an entire auction):

- ✔ The high bidder informs you that he or she is retracting the bid.
- ✔ Despite your best efforts to determine who your high bidder is, you can't find out — and you get no response to your e-mails or phone calls.
- ✔ The bidder makes a dollar-amount mistake in the bid.
- ✔ You decide mid-auction that you don't want to sell your item.

We can't drive this point home hard enough: *Say why, and your explanation had better be good.* You can cancel any bid for any reason you want, but if you can't give a good explanation why you did it, you will be sorry. Citing past transaction problems with the current high bidder is okay, but canceling a bidder who lives in Japan because you don't feel like shipping overseas after you said you'd ship internationally could give your feedback history the aroma of week-old sushi.

To cancel a bid (starting from most eBay pages), do the following:

1. **Click the Services link on the navigation bar.**

   A submenu with additional links appears.

2. **Click the Buying & Selling link on the submenu.** You're taken to the Buying & Selling Tools page, where you see the Manage Your Items for Sale heading.

3. **Click the Cancel Bids on My Item link.**

   You're taken to the Canceling Bids Placed in Your Auction page, as shown in Figure 12-3.

Figure 12-3:
You can remove a bid from one of your auctions by using the Cancel Bid form.

> **Cancelling Bids Placed in Your Auction**
>
> You should only cancel bids if you have a good reason to. Also, please remember that bids cannot be reinstated once they've been canceled. Here are a few **examples of a legitimate cancellation**:
>
> - Bidder contacts you to back out of the bid.
> - You cannot verify the identity of the bidder, after trying all reasonable means of contact.
> - You want to end your auction early because you no longer want to sell your item. **In this case you must cancel all bids on your auction before ending the auction.**
>
> Because your cancellation will be put in the bidding history for this auction, bidders may ask you to explain your cancellation. So, **please include a one-line explanation of your cancellation for the official record.**
>
> To avoid mistakes, please verify your password in order to cancel a bid. If you haven't selected a personal password, or if you've forgotten your password, please request a new temporary password before proceeding.
>
> **You are signed in as:** *marsha_c*
> (If you are not marsha_c, click here)
>
> Item number of auction

4. **Read all the fine print, and, if you haven't signed in, type your User ID, password, Item Number, and an explanation of why you're canceling a bid, as well as the User ID of the person whose bid you're canceling.**

5. **Click the Cancel Bid button.**

Be sure you really want to cancel a bid before you click the Cancel Bid button. Canceled bids can never be reinstated.

Canceling bids means you removed an individual bidder (or several bidders) from your auction, but the auction itself continues running. If you want to end the auction completely, read on.

eBay says that you can't receive feedback on a transaction that wasn't completed. So, if something in your gut says not to deal with a particular bidder, then don't.

If all else fails, end your auction early

If you put your auction up for a week and the next day your boss says you have to go to China for a month or your landlord says you have to move out immediately so that he can fumigate for a week, you can end your auction early. But, ending an auction early isn't a decision to be taken lightly. You miss all the last-minute bidding action.

eBay makes it clear that ending your auction early does not relieve you of the obligation to sell this item to the highest bidder. To relieve your obligation, you must first cancel all the bids and then end the auction. Of course, if no one has bid, you have nothing to worry about.

When you cancel an auction, you have to write a short explanation (no more than 80 characters) that appears on the bidding history section of your auction page. Anyone who bid on the item may e-mail you for a written explanation. If bidders think your explanation doesn't hold water, don't be surprise if you get some nasty e-mail.

Bidding on your own item is against the rules. Once upon a time, you could cancel an auction by outbidding everyone on your own item and then ending the auction. But some eBay users abused this privilege by bidding on their own items merely to boost the sales price. Shame on them.

To end an auction early (starting at the top of nearly any eBay page), do the following:

1. **Click the Services link on the navigation bar.**

   A submenu with additional links appears.

2. **Click the Buying & Selling link of the submenu.**

   You're taken to the Buying and Selling Tools page, where you see the Manage Your Items for Sale heading.

3. **Under the Manage Your Items for Sale heading, click the End Your Auction Early link.**

   You're taken to the Ending Your Auction form.

4. **If you haven't previously signed in, Type your User ID, password, and the Item Number; click the End Auction button.**

   A Verifying Ending Auction page appears.

5. **Click the End Auction link.**

   An Ended Auction page appears.

   eBay sends an End of Auction Confirmation e-mail to you and to the highest bidder.

If you know when you list the item that you'll be away when an auction ends, let potential bidders know when you plan to contact them in your item description. Bidders who are willing to wait will still be willing to bid. Alerting them to your absence can save you from losing money if you have to cut your auction short.

Extending your auction (not!)

Is your auction red hot? Bids coming in fast and furious? Wish you could have more time? Well, the answer is no. eBay won't extend auctions under normal conditions.

However, eBay on occasion experiences *hard outages*. That's when the system goes offline and no one can place bids. (Of course, Murphy's Law would put the next hard outage right in the thick of a furious bidding war in the final minutes of *your* auction. Or so it seems.) Outages can last anywhere from 5 minutes to a few hours. Because so many bidders wait until the last minute to bid, this can be a disaster. To make nice, eBay extends auctions by 24 hours if any of these three things happen:

- ✔ The outage is unscheduled and lasts two hours or more.
- ✔ The auction was scheduled to end during the outage.
- ✔ The auction was scheduled to end one hour after the outage.

If your auction was set to end Thursday at 20:10:09 (remember, eBay uses military time, based on the Pacific Time Zone — which would make it 8:10 p.m.), the new ending time is Friday at 20:10:09. Same Bat-time, same Bat-channel, different day.

eBay also refunds all your auction fees for any hard outage that lasts more than two hours. That means the Insertion Fee, Final Value Fee, and any optional fees. You don't have to apply for anything; all refunds are done automatically by eBay.

You can read about any hard outages at eBay's Announcements Board. To get to an outage report, check the bottom of most eBay pages; you'll find an Announcements link.

If the Announcements link isn't there, start at the navigation bar (at the top of most eBay pages) and do the following:

1. **Click Community on the main navigation bar.**

   You're taken to the Community Overview page.

2. **Click the Announcements link in the News section.**

3. **Scroll through the eBay announcements.**

We make it standard operating procedure to check the Announcements Board every time we log into eBay. Sort of like checking the obituary in the morning to make sure you're not listed. More on the Announcements Board in Chapter 16.

Filing for a Final Value Fee credit

Hard outages are not the only time you can collect a refund. If closing a successful auction is the thrill of victory, finding out that your buyer is a non-paying bidder or deadbeat is the agony of defeat. Adding insult to injury, eBay still charges you a Final Value Fee even if the high bidder never sends you a cent. But you can do something about it. You can file for a Final Value Fee credit.

To qualify for a Final Value Fee credit you must prove to eBay one of the following:

✔ The winning bidder never responded after numerous e-mail contacts.

✔ The winning bidder backed out of the sale.

✔ The winning bidder's payment did not clear or was never received.

✔ The winning bidder returned the item to you, and you refunded the payment.

So what happens if the sale goes through but for some reason you collect less than the actual listed final sale price? eBay has you covered there, too. But first you may ask, "Wait a second, how can that happen?" Let us count the ways. Here are a few of them:

✔ eBay miscalculates the final price (this doesn't happen often, but always check).

✔ You renegotiate a lower final sale price with the winning bidder, and eBay still charges you on the basis of the posted high bid.

✔ Bidder(s) in your Dutch auction back out.

To apply for a full or partial credit, you must first file a Non-Paying Bidder Alert:

1. **If 7 days elapse since the end of the auction (and no more than 45 days), click the Services link on the navigation bar at the top of most eBay pages.**

   A submenu with additional links appears.

2. **Click the Buying & Selling Tools link on the submenu.**

   You're taken to the Buying & Selling Tools page.

3. **Under the Seller Accounts heading, click the Request Final Value Fee Credit link.**

   You're taken to the Final Value Fee Credit Request page.

4. **Read the guidelines for applying for a Final Value Fee credit and click the Non-Paying Bidder Alert link.**

   You're taken to the Non-Paying Bidder Alert Form page.

5. **Since you've already signed in, just Type in the Item Number of the auction in question; click the Submit button.**

   The instant you file for Non-Paying Bidder Alert credit, eBay shoots off an e-mail to the winner of your auction (they also send you a copy) and warns the eBay user of the non-paying bidder status.

   After four non-payment warnings, eBay can boot a deadbeat from the site.

   You and your non-paying bidder now have ten days to work out your problems. If you make no progress after ten days, you may file for your Final Value Fee credit.

You need to wait *at least* seven days before you can apply for a Final Value Fee credit. We think it's jumping the gun even at seven days — try to give it two weeks unless the bidder sends you a message about backing out (or you have good cause to believe you've got a deadbeat on your hands). After your credit request is filed, eBay takes three to five business days to process it.

If you still want to file for your Final Value Fee credit after ten days, do the following:

1. **Click the Services link on the navigation bar (at the top of most eBay pages).**

   A submenu with additional links appears.

2. **Click the Buying & Selling link on the submenu.**

   You're taken to the Buying & Selling Tools page.

3. **Under the Seller Accounts heading, click the Request Final Value Fee Credit link.**

4. **Click the Final Value Fee Credit Request Form link.**

5. **If you haven't signed in, enter your User ID, password, and Item Number; click the Submit button.**

6. **Answer the following questions:**

   • **Did you receive any money from the bidder?** If you answer yes, type the amount in the box; use numerals and a decimal point.

- **Reason for refund.** eBay gives you a drop-down menu of choices. Click the small down arrow on the right of the box and all your options magically appear.

- **Bidder's e-mail address.** Type the e-mail address of the person who was the highest bidder on your auction.

7. **Click the Submit button on the bottom of the page.**

You're taken to the Credit Request Process Completed page, which confirms that your refund is being processed by eBay, as shown in Figure 12-4.

When your auction ends, you have up to 60 days after the auction closes to request a full or partial credit. After 60 days, kiss your refund good-bye; eBay won't process it.

Anyone caught applying for either a full or partial refund on a successful item transaction can be suspended or something worse — after all, this is a pretty clear-cut case of fraud.

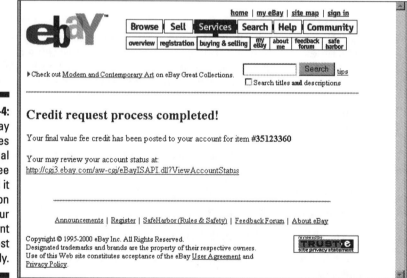

Figure 12-4:
eBay processes your Final Value Fee credit and it appears on your account almost immediately.

If you want to verify eBay's accounting, grab your calculator and use Table 12-1 to check the math. (Why couldn't we have had one of those in high-school algebra class?)

Table 12-1	Determining Your Final Value Fee
Closing Bid	*To Find Your Final Value Fee*
$.01–$25	Multiply the final sale price by 5 percent. If the final sale price is $25, multiply 25 by 5 percent. You owe eBay $1.25.
$25.01–$1,000	You pay $1.25 for the first $25 of the final sale price (which is 5 percent). Subtract $25 from your final closing bid, and then multiply this amount by 2.5 percent. Add this total to the $1.25 you owe for the first $25. The sum is what you owe eBay. If the final sale price is $1,000, multiply 975 by .025. (*Hint:* The answer is $24.38.) *Now,* add $24.38 and $1.25. You owe eBay $25.63.
$1,000.01 and over	You owe $1.25 for the first $25 of the final sale price (which is 5 percent). But you also have to pay $24.38 for the remainder of the price between $25.01 through $1,000 (which is 2.5 percent). This amount is $25.63. *Now,* subtract $1,000 from the final sale price (you've calculated those fees above) and multiply the final sale amount that is over $1,000 by 1.25 percent. Add this amount to $25.63. The sum is the amount you owe eBay. If the final sales price is $3,000, multiply $2,000 by 1.25 percent. (*Hint:* The answer is $25.) Add $25.63 to $25. The sum, $50.63, is what you owe eBay. You will not be graded on this.

Always print out a copy of any refund and credit requests you make. This paper trail can help bail you out later if eBay asks for documentation.

Déjà vu — relisting your item

Despite all your best efforts, sometimes your auction ends with no bids or bids that are not even close to your reserve price. Or maybe a buyer won your auction, but the transaction didn't go through. eBay takes pity on you and offers you the chance to pick yourself up, dust yourself off, and start all over again.

The best way to improve your chances of selling a relisted item is by making changes to the auction. eBay says the majority of all the items put up for auction sell. If you sell your item the second time around, eBay rewards you with a refund of your Insertion Fee. You receive your refund after at least one billing cycle. Accept this refund as a reward for learning the ropes.

But is she a natural blonde?

Here's an example of an item that would have made the seller a bundle if she'd done a little more strategizing up front:

Platinum Mackie Barbie: Beautiful Platinum Bob Mackie Barbie. MIB (removed from box once only to scan). The doll comes with shoes, stand, booklet, and Mackie drawing. The original plastic protects her hair and earrings. Buyer adds $10 for shipping and insurance. Payment must be made within 10 days of auction by MO

or cashier's check only. The starting price was $9.99, and even though the bidding went to $256, the seller's reserve price was not met, and the item didn't sell.

When relisting this item, the seller should lower the reserve price and add more description about the importance of the doll. (Unless, of course, $256 was far below what she wanted to make on the doll.)

To be eligible for a refund of your Insertion Fee, here's the scoop:

- ✔ You must relist no more than 30 days after closing the original auction.

- ✔ You can get credit only if you got no bids in your original auction, or if the bids you got did not equal the reserve in your reserve-price auction.

- ✔ You can change anything about your auction item description, price, duration, and minimum price, but you can't sell a different item.

- ✔ If you set a reserve price in your original auction, you must set the same reserve, lower it, or cancel the reserve altogether. If you set a higher reserve, you're not eligible for a relisting credit.

REMEMBER

eBay's generosity has exceptions. They don't offer refunds for any listing options you paid for, such as **bold lettering** or use of the Featured in Category. Also, Dutch auctions aren't covered by this offer. And if you have a deadbeat on your hands, you can relist, but you don't get a return of your Insertion Fee. More bad news: If you don't sell the second time around, you're stuck paying *two* Insertion Fees. So give it your best shot!

To get your second shot at selling, do the following (from the Items I'm Selling section of your My eBay page):

1. **Click the auction item listing that you want to relist.**

   You're taken to the main auction page of that item.

2. **Click the Relist this Item link.**

   You see a brand new auction page to fill out, following the same directions offered in this chapter (so you're already good at it).

Being as specific as possible with your item title improves your odds of being profitable. If you're selling an old Monopoly game, don't just title it **board game,** call it **1959 Monopoly Game Complete.** For more information about listing items, see Chapter 10.

Here's a list of ideas you can use to improve your auction's odds for success:

- ✔ **Change the item category.** See if the item sold better in another category (see Chapter 3).

- ✔ **Add a picture.** If two identical items are up for auction at the same time, the item with a photo gets more and higher bids. Zoom in on Chapter 13.

- ✔ **Jazz up the title and description.** Make it enticing, and grab those search engines. Breeze on over to Chapter 10.

- ✔ **Set a lower minimum bid.** The first bidders will think they're getting a bargain, and others will want a hot item. Mosey on over to Chapter 10.

- ✔ **Set a lower reserve price or cancel the reserve.** A reserve price often scares away bidders who fear it's too high. See (yup) Chapter 10.

- ✔ **Change the duration of the auction.** Maybe you need some more time. Go to (you guessed it) Chapter 10.

Long-time eBay veterans say that reducing or canceling your reserve price makes your auction very attractive to buyers.

Show me the money: Refunds

It's rare, but some folks rack up enough credits to want a refund. eBay refunds the amount in your account for anything over a buck. To get to the refund form that you must fax to eBay, click Services on the main navigation bar, click Buying & Selling on the subnavigation bar, and then click Cash Out Your Credit Balance. Fill out the form and send it in.

Chapter 13

Using Pictures and Strategies to Increase Your Profits

In This Chapter

▶ Attaching pictures to your auction

▶ Making picture-perfect images

▶ Using great photographic form

▶ Playing the links (golf cleats optional)

▶ Finding out all About Me

ou may be enjoying most of what eBay has to offer, and you're probably having some good buying adventures. If you're selling, you're experiencing the excitement of making money. But there's more. Welcome to eBay, the advanced class.

In this chapter, we take you to the head of the class by sharing some insider tips on how to jazz up the selling power of your auctions with images and spiffy text. Successful eBay vendors know that pictures (also called images) really help sell items. We show you everything you need to know to create great images. We also give you advice on linking pictures to your auctions so buyers around the world can take a gander at them. Look no further if you want to know more about spotting trends and acquiring products to sell at eBay.

Using Images in Your Auctions

Would you buy an item you couldn't see? Most people wouldn't, especially if they're interested in purchasing collectible items that they want to display. Without a picture, you can't tell whether a seller's idea of good quality is anything like yours.

Welcome to the cyberworld of *imaging,* where pictures aren't called pictures, but *images* (as in, "Excuse me, could you pass the Grey Poupon while I examine my *images*?"). With a digital camera or a scanner, you can manipulate your images — crop, color-correct, and add special effects — so that they grab viewers by the lapels. Even cooler: When you're happy with your creation, you can add it to your eBay auction for others to see.

Sellers, take heed, and read these other reasons why you should use well-made digital images in your auction pages:

- ✔ If you don't have a picture, potential bidders may wonder whether you're deliberately hiding the item from view because you know something is wrong with it. Paranoid? Maybe. Practical? You bet.

- ✔ Fickle bidders don't even bother reading an item description if they can't see the item. Maybe they were traumatized in English class.

- ✔ Everyone's doing it. We hate to pressure you, but digital images are the norm at eBay, so if you're not using them, you're not reaching the widest possible number of people who would bid on your item. From that point of view, you're not doing the most you can to serve your potential customers' needs. Hey, fads are *driven* by conformity. May as well use them to your advantage.

So which is better for capturing images: digital cameras or digital scanners? As with all gadgets, here's the classic answer: It depends. For our money, it's hard to beat a digital camera. But before you go snag one, decide what kind of investment (and how big) you plan to make in your eBay auctions. If you're already comfortable with 35mm camera equipment, don't scrap it — scan! The scoop on both these alternatives is coming right up.

Whether you buy new or used digital equipment at eBay, make sure it comes with a warranty. If you *don't* get a warranty, Murphy's Law practically ensures that your digital equipment will break the second time you use it.

Choosing a digital camera

If price isn't a factor, you should buy the highest-quality digital camera you can afford, especially if you plan to use images with a lot of your eBay auctions, and the items you plan to sell vary in size and shape.

Both Olympus and Epson make good basic cameras, starting at around $500 — we told you they can be pricey. Middle-of-the-road digital cameras sell for between $150 and $250. Compare prices at computer stores and in catalogs.

Another great place to buy digital cameras is (surprise!) eBay. Just do a search of some popular manufacturers, such as Olympus, Fujifilm, Sony, and Nikon, and you will find pages of listings — both new and used digital cameras — that you can bid on and, if you win, buy.

Look for the following features in digital cameras:

- ✔ **Resolution.** Look for a camera that has a resolution of at least 640-x-480 *pixels.* A pixel is a tiny dot of information that, when grouped together with other pixels, forms an image. The more pixels an image has the clearer and sharper the image is; the more memory the image scarfs up, the slower it shows up on-screen. A 640-x-480-pixel resolution may seem paltry next to the 1.5-million-pixel punch of a high-end digital camera, but trust us: No one bidding on your auctions will nit-pick over the difference.

- ✔ **Storage type.** The instructions with your camera explain how to transfer images to your computer. (No instructions? Write the manufacturer.)

- ✔ **Extra features.** Make sure that the camera is capable of taking close-up images; you need to be close to an item you photograph for an auction — from three inches to a foot away. A flash also comes in handy.

  If you plan to sell small or detailed items that require extreme close-ups (such as stamps, currency, coins, or Tibetan beads), look for a digital camera that lets you change lenses. Many newer, higher-end digital cameras have optional lenses for special uses, just as traditional 35mm cameras do. These cameras cost more, but if you need extreme close-ups to sell your items, this is the only way to go.

Choosing a digital scanner

Like digital cameras, digital scanners create images electronically by using pixels. Your computer stores and reads these pixels (with software supplied with the scanner), and turns them into an image that you can e-mail, print, or send to your eBay auction.

If you plan to sell flat items such as autographs, stamps, books, or documents — or if you need a good piece of business equipment that can double as a photocopier — then consider getting a digital scanner. You can pick one up, brand new, for a little under $100; you can also find scanners at eBay.

Here's what you need to look for when you buy a scanner:

- ✔ **Resolution.** As with printers and photocopiers, the resolution of digital scanning equipment is measured in *dots per inch (dpi)*. The more dpi, the greater the resolution.

    Some scanners on the market today can provide resolutions as high as 12,800 dpi, which looks awesome when you print the image, but to dress up your eBay auctions, all you need is (are you ready?) *72 dpi!* That's it. Your images will look great and won't take up much storage space on your computer's hard drive. Basic scanners can scan images up to 1,200 dpi, so even they are more powerful than you need them to be for your eBay images.

- ✔ **Flatbed.** If you're planning to use your scanner to scan pictures of documents (or even items in boxes), a flatbed scanner is your best bet. Just lay your item or box on the glass (flatbeds work just like photocopiers) and scan away.

- ✔ **Software and extras.** In addition to free photo-editing software, scanner manufacturers often include some great utilities. For example, your scanner may come with copier software so that you can make photocopies. You can also get many scanners to act like word processors, fax machines, or copiers — all with just a touch of a button.

If you're using a scanner and need to create an image of an oversize item (say, that '59 Caddy limo with the huge fins), or your flat item's just not practical to scan, even in sections (that original *Star Wars* marquee poster, for example), your film camera comes in handy. Use it to take a few good photos, get them processed on glossy paper, and scan the best picture in the bunch. The end result is often as good as if the image came from a digital camera.

Making Your Picture a Thing of Beauty

The idea of using images in your auctions is to attract tons of potential buyers. With that goal in mind, you should try to create the best-looking image possible, no matter what kind of technology you're using to capture it.

Even if you're not an expert photographer, don't be deterred if you sometimes lop off miscellaneous limbs in pictures of your family reunion. These days, plenty of terrific software programs can help make your images of auctionables look great.

Still, don't forget the old computer acronym GIGO — *garbage in, garbage out.* Even the best software program can't do much if the source image is overexposed and blurry. Help is on the way, next.

Don't forget your camcorder!

The majority of eBay users use either a digital camera or scanner to dress up their auctions with images, but some just use what they already own — their handy-dandy camcorders! Yup, after videotaping your day at the beach, point your lens at that Victorian doll and shoot. With the help of a video-capturing device, you can create a digital image right from the camera.

Although several companies offer video-capturing devices, we're most impressed with the Snappy, made by Play Incorporated. This camcorder sells for around $100 and includes everything you need to transfer and save pictures from your camcorder (or VCR) to your computer. Go to the Play Inc. Web site at www.play.com for more details about how the Snappy works.

Get it on camera!

Point-and-shoot may be okay for a group shot at a historical monument, but illustrating your auction is a whole different idea. Whether you're using a traditional film camera (so that you can scan your developed photographs later) or a digital camera to capture your item, some basic photographic guidelines can give you better results.

For more on using 35mm cameras and scanners, zoom in this chapter to the section, "Use traditional photos? Yes, I scan." Then c'mon back to these Do's and Don'ts to ensure that your digital image is a genuine enhancement to your auction:

- ✔ **Do** take the picture of your item outside, in daylight, whenever possible. That way, the camera can catch all possible details and color.

- ✔ **Do** forget about fancy backgrounds; they distract viewers from your item. Put small items on a neutral-colored, nonreflective towel or cloth; put larger items in front of a neutral-colored wall or curtain. You'll cut out almost all of the background when you prepare the picture on your computer. (We explain how to do this in this chapter.)

- ✔ **Do** use a flash, even when you're taking the picture outside. The flash acts as a *fill light* — it adds more light to the item, filling in some of the shadowed spots.

- ✔ **Don't** get so close to the item that the flash washes out (overexposes) the entire image. The clearest way to figure out the best distance is by trial and error. Start close and keep moving farther away until you get the results you want. This method can get pricey if you use film, but this is where digital cameras really shine: You can see the picture seconds after you shoot it, keep it and modify it, erase it, and start again.

✔ **Do** take two or three acceptable versions of your image; you can pick the best one later on your computer.

✔ If your item relies on detail (for example, an engraved signature or detailed gold trim), **do** take a wide shot of the entire item, and then take a close-up or two of the detailed areas that you want buyers to see.

✔ **Do** make sure you focus the camera; nothing is worse than a blurry picture. If your camera is a fixed-focus model (it can't be adjusted), get only as close as the manufacturer recommends. If you go beyond that distance, the item appears out of focus. (Automatic-focus cameras measure the distance and change the lens setting as needed.)

Some eBay creeps, whether out of laziness or deceit, steal images from other eBay members. (They simply make a digital copy of the image and use it in their own auctions. This is so uncool because the copied image doesn't really represent their actual item.) This pilfering has happened to us on several occasions. To prevent picture-snatching, you can add your User ID to all of your photos. The next time somebody lifts one of your pictures, it has your name on it.

Use traditional photos? Yes, I scan

If you use a scanner and 35mm camera to create images for your eBay auction, you've come to the right place. (Also check out the tips in "Get it on camera!") Here goes:

✔ If you're scanning already-processed photographs of your items (taken with a 35mm camera, for example), make sure to print them on glossy paper; it scans best.

✔ Avoid using incandescent or fluorescent lighting to illuminate the photos you plan to scan. Incandescent lighting tends to make your item look yellowish, and fluorescent lights lend a bluish tone to your photo.

✔ When you take traditional photos for scanning, get as close to your item as your camera allows. Enlarging photos in the scanner will only result in blurry (or, worse, jagged) images.

✔ Scan the box that the item came in.

✔ If you're scanning a three-dimensional item (such as a doll, jewelry, or a box) and you can't close the scanner lid, put a black or white tee-shirt over the item so that you will get a clean background and good light reflection from the scanner.

✔ If you want to scan an item that's too big to put on your scanner all at once, scan the item in sections and assemble the digital pieces with your image-editing software. The instructions that come with your software should explain how to do this.

Software that adds the artist's touch

After you take the picture (or scan it) and transfer it into your computer according to the manufacturer's instructions, the next step is to edit the picture. Much like a book or magazine editor, you get to cut, fix, resize, and reshape your picture until you think it's good enough to be seen by the public. If you're a non-techie type, don't get nervous. Many of the programs have one-button magical corrections that make your pictures look great.

The software program that comes with your digital camera or scanner puts at your disposal an arsenal of editing tools that help you turn a basic image of your item into something special. Although each program has its own collection of features, a few basic tools and techniques are common to all:

- ✔ **Image quality.** Enables you to enhance or correct colors, sharpen images, remove dust spots, and increase or reduce brightness or contrast.

- ✔ **Size.** Reduce or increase the size or shape of the image.

- ✔ **Orientation.** Rotate the image left or right; flip it horizontally or vertically.

- ✔ **Crop.** Trim your picture to show the item, rather than extraneous background.

- ✔ **Create an image format.** After the image is edited, you can save it as a specific format, such as .JPG, .GIF, or others. The format most preferred at eBay (and the one we strongly recommend) is .JPG (pronounced *JAY-peg*).

Every image-editing software program has its own system requirements and capabilities. Read the instructions that come with your camera or scanner. If you feel the program is too complicated (or doesn't give you the editing tools you need), investigate some of the other popular programs. Here's a quick list of programs we use and recommend, along with their Web addresses so that you can get more information online:

- ✔ **Adobe PhotoDeluxe Home Edition.** This is a popular program included with many digital cameras (or you can purchase it separately). It gives you access to quite a range of special photo effects. More importantly, however, it allows you to make your photos Internet-ready, reducing the dpi through the Send to Web Page function. You can get updates or purchase it for $49 at this Web site:

  www.adobe.com/products/photodeluxe/main.html

- ✔ **Microsoft Picture It 2000.** This program comes with some new computers and is available separately for purchase. Picture It 2000 has a full kit of features that allows you to fix the contrast, sharpen, and make your photos Web-ready — automatically. More information and lots of tips on how to improve your pictures is available at

  home-publishing.com/PictureIt/HomePages
  /ProductTips_Highlights.asp

✔ **Free image editing software** can also be found at:

```
www.tucows.com
www.shareware.com
```

Copying someone else's auction text or images without permission can constitute copyright infringement, which ends your auction and gets you suspended from eBay.

Making Your Images Web-Friendly

Because digital images are made up of pixels, and every pixel has a set of instructions that has to be stored someplace, you've got two difficulties facing you right after you take the picture:

✔ Digital images contain computer instructions, so bigger pictures take up more memory.

✔ Very large digital images take longer to *build* (to appear) on the buyer's screen, and time can be precious in an auction.

To get around both these problems, think small.

Here's a checklist of tried-and-true techniques for preparing your elegantly slender, fast-loading images to display at eBay:

✔ **Set your image resolution at 72 dpi.** You can do this with the software that comes with your camera or scanner. Although 72 dpi may seem like a low resolution, it nibbles computer memory (instead of chomping), shows up fast on a buyer's screen, and looks great at eBay.

✔ **Make the image no larger than four square inches.** When you size your picture, make it no larger than 300 x 300 pixels or four inches square, even if it's a snapshot of a classic 4 x 4 monster truck. These dimensions are big enough for people to see without squinting, and the details of your item show up nicely.

✔ **Crop any unnecessary areas of the photo.** You just need to show your item; everything else is a waste.

✔ **Use your software to darken or change the photo's contrast.** When the image looks good on your computer screen, the image looks good on your eBay auction page.

✔ **Save your image as a .JPG file.** When you finish editing your picture, save it as a .JPG. (Follow the instructions that come with your software on how to do this.) .JPG is the best format for eBay; it compresses information into a small file that builds fast and reproduces nicely on the Internet.

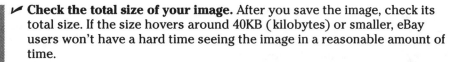

✔ **Check the total size of your image.** After you save the image, check its total size. If the size hovers around 40KB (kilobytes) or smaller, eBay users won't have a hard time seeing the image in a reasonable amount of time.

✔ **Reduce the size of your image if it's larger than 50KB.** If your image is larger than 50KB, go back into the image and reduce its size. Small is fast, efficient, and beautiful. Big is slow, sluggish, and dangerous. Impatient eBay users will move on to the next listing if they have to wait to see your image.

The Image Is Perfect — What Now?

Now that your masterpiece is complete, you want to emblazon it on your auction for all the world to see, right? Whoa, Rembrandt. You still need to make a couple of final preparations. Yes, this arty stuff *is* a lot of work, but we assure you the results are worth it — buyers are apt to pick an auction with a picture over a comparable auction item without one.

When most people first get the urge to dazzle prospective buyers with a picture, they poke around the eBay site looking for a place to put it. Trade secret: You're not actually putting pictures at eBay at all; you're telling eBay where to *find* your picture so that, like a good hunting dog, your auction *points* the buyers' browsers to the exact corner of the virtual universe where your picture is. That's why the picture has to load fast — it's coming in from a different location. (Yeah, it confused us in the beginning too, but now it makes perfect sense. Uh-huh. Sure.)

To help eBay find your image, all you have to do is type its address into the Picture URL box (shown in Figure 13-1) of the Sell Your Item form, so don't forget to write down the Web address (URL) of your image.

Figure 13-1:
To add your item's image to your eBay auction, type the image's Web address in the Picture URL box.

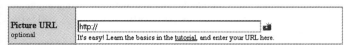

| Picture URL optional | http:// | |
| | It's easy! Learn the basics in the tutorial, and enter your URL here. | |

You can highlight your image's URL with your cursor, right-click your mouse, and copy it to your computer's clipboard. Then go to the auction page you're filling out at eBay, put your cursor in the Picture URL window, and paste the address into the box.

A typical address (for someone using AOL) looks like this:

```
members.aol.com/ebay4dummy/rolexwatch.jpg
```

Because your image needs an address, that means you have to find it a good home online. You have several options:

- ✔ **Your ISP (Internet Service Provider).** All the big ISPs — AOL, Mindspring, and Earthlink — give you space to store your Internet stuff. You're already paying for an ISP, so you can park pictures here at no extra charge.

- ✔ **An image-hosting Web site.** Web sites that specialize in hosting pictures are popping up all over the Internet. Some charge a small fee; others are free. The upside here is that they're easy to use.

- ✔ **Your server.** If you have your own server (those of you who do know who you are), you can store those images right in your own home.

- ✔ **iPIX.** You can find out about it using eBay's photo-hosting service later in this chapter.

Using an ISP to store your images

Every ISP has its own set of rules and procedures. Go to the help area of your specific ISP for directions on how to *access your personal area* and how to *upload your images*. (And those are authentic computerese phrases!)

After your images are uploaded to your ISP, get the Web address of your item's location and type it into the Picture URL box of eBay's Sell Your Item page. Now whenever someone views your auction page, the picture appears under the item description. Figure 13-2 shows you an auction page with a picture.

Don't create filenames for your images with the following symbols: ? @ # $*& ! / ~ , % or spaces. These interfere with your uploads, and your file can't successfully transfer to the ISP. (Even if you could use them, you wouldn't want total strangers to think you were cussing. . . .)

Elegant Frosted & Clear
Floral Stopper Perfume Bottle

This charming and very Lalique style
perfume bottle stands approx. 4" tall. The
base features alternating swirls of frosted
and clear cut glass and has no markings of
any kind. The ground frosted stopper has
two lovely flowers at the top. A great item
for your vanity table, or a wonderful gift.
Bid with confidence and bid whatever you feel this bottle
is worth to you as he is selling with **NO RESERVE!** *(Feel
free to check my feedback!)* I pack all my items carefully.
Winning bidder to pay shipping & handling of $4.55 and
must submit payment within a week of winning the
auction. I will accept credit cards through paypal.com
(see below). Good luck on winning!

GOOD LUCK, HAPPY BIDDING!

Click below to...
*View my other auctions - Win more than one and SAVE on
shipping!*

Figure 13-2:
Including
pictures in
your auction
takes
practice, but
the results
are well
worth it.

Using image-hosting Web sites to store images

Okay, realistically, many people are combing cyberspace looking for the next great thing. eBay's success has entrepreneurs all over the globe coming up with different kinds of auction-support businesses. As usual, a lot of junk pops up on the Internet in the wake of such trends — but one promising development caught our attention recently — *image-hosting* Web sites.

Image-hosting Web sites have changed from one-stop shops to mega-markets loaded with tons of services for your auctions. Some image-hosting sites let you post your pictures without having to use their Auction Management software — not that we think Auction Management software is a bad thing; it's great! (Flip to Chapter 19 to find more info on Auction Management software.)

Here are a few convenient image-hosting sites that allow you to post your images for free:

- **AuctionWatch.com** (www.AuctionWatch.com)
- **Honesty.com** (www.honesty.com)
- **ManageAuctions.com** (www.ManageAuctions.com)

WebTV — the easiest way to upload pictures

You can upload images to WebTV so quickly and easily that you may consider using it to upload images to the Web even if you own a computer. The restrictions? You must own (or borrow) a camcorder, and, oh yeah, WebTV Plus.

Uploading images to WebTV is simple. Our low-tech suggestions should get you through the process:

1. **Place all of your items on a kitchen counter or other flat, neutral surface and start filming.**

   Consider placing the items on a white sheet or towel to help create a background for the items.

2. **Pan your camcorder from one item to the next, zoom in and out of each item, and linger at the highlights of your collection.**

   Your camcorder's auto focus records quality images.

Don't turn your camcorder vertically, or your pictures will end up at eBay sideways. *I always wondered where sideways pictures came from.*

To load your images into your auction pages, you need to join an image-hosting site that's WebTV friendly — all the image-hosting sites we list later in this chapter are. Once you log on and register, just connect your camera to the WebTV box and follow the instructions provided by the image hosting service.

Using eBay's new picture service

In early 2000, Internet Pictures Corporation (iPIX) and eBay joined together to offer image hosting directly through eBay. eBay now hosts two images per auction — for free. If you want more images, it costs only 50 cents to add two more pictures (there's a maximum of four images per auction item).

If you use this service, your photos appear on your auction in a pre-designed template. If you use the two free photos, the first shows up in a 400 x 300 pixel format. A miniature of the first image appears to the left of the larger image.

When you prepare to list an item for auction, a page appears and you're asked whether you'd like to use the photo service. If you don't want to use it, click on the Skip this page button and go on to continue listing your item. If you do want to use the service, just follow the directions on screen.

To post your photo, either drag and drop an image file from your computer or click on the box and an open file box will appear. Find your image on your computer, click open, and the image magically appears in the image box. Add more pictures if you like and click Submit Pictures and Continue. See Figure 13-3 for the upload page.

eBay keeps an image online for the duration of your auction. After that, the image goes bye-bye. But, you can always repost the image if you need it again. (So be sure you leave a copy of the image on your computer.) *Note:* This feature doesn't support the WebTV platform.

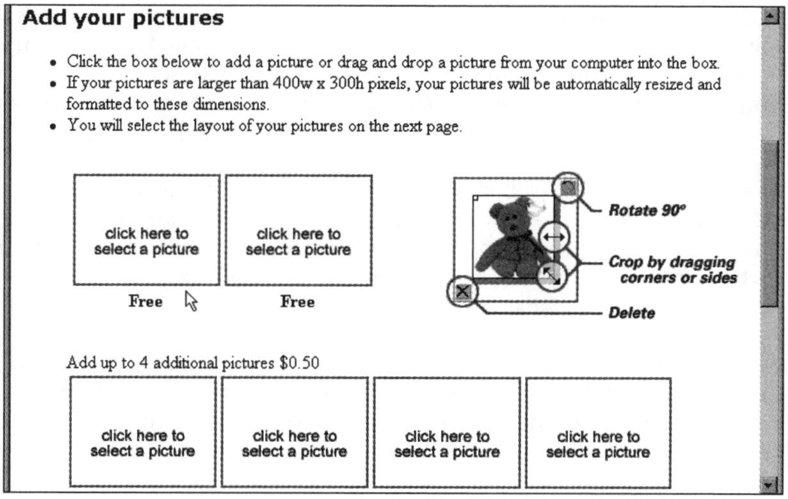

Add your pictures

- Click the box below to add a picture or drag and drop a picture from your computer into the box.
- If your pictures are larger than 400w x 300h pixels, your pictures will be automatically resized and formatted to these dimensions.
- You will select the layout of your pictures on the next page.

click here to select a picture

Free

click here to select a picture

Free

Rotate 90°

Crop by dragging corners or sides

Delete

Add up to 4 additional pictures $0.50

click here to select a picture

click here to select a picture

click here to select a picture

click here to select a picture

Figure 13-3: Using eBay's Picture Services couldn't be easier. Here's the upload page used prior to the Sell Your Item page.

Getting Your Item Noticed

Okay, you've got a great auction at eBay and great images to go with it. Now all you need is to track the number of users peeking at your items, and to attract even more people to your auction. Read the following sections to find out how to make your auction even better.

Putting on the hits

Your auction is up and running at eBay, and you're just dying to know how many people stop by to take a look. There's an easy way to monitor your auction's *hits* — the number of times visitors stop to look at the goods — if you use a free *public counter* program from an online source. A counter is a useful marketing tool; for example, you can check the number of times people have looked at, but not bid on, your auctions. If you have lots more lookie-loos than bids, you may have a problem with your auction.

If your counter indicates you're not getting many hits, consider the following potential problems so that you can resurrect your auction:

✔ Does the picture take too long to load?

✔ Is the opening bid too high?

✔ Are those neon-orange and lime-green bell-bottoms just too funky to sell?

One of the most popular counters found at eBay comes from a Web site run by Honesty Communications. You can pick the Honesty counter up for free and add it to your auction in just a few easy steps. But before you can get a public counter from Honesty Communications, you need to register — just go to `www.honesty.com`. Honesty takes it from there. Honestly.

The AuctionWatch Web site (`www.AuctionWatch.com`) also offers a service that counts how many times eBay members view your auction. The service has an "intelligent" counter that counts hits but is also smart enough to know whether somebody is continually reloading your auction page so it doesn't count the repeat visits.

ManageAuctions (`www.ManageAuctions.com`) has a really unique counter. It works much the same as other counters, but when you access your area on its site, you see an incredibly detailed status of your auction. And, how cool is this — it's free.

Playing the links for fun and profit

By linking your eBay auctions to your personal or business Web page, you can get even more people to look at what you're selling. To link your auctions to your Web page (starting at the navigation bar found at the top of most eBay pages), do the following:

1. **Click the Services link.**

   You're taken to the Services Overview page.

2. **Click the Buying and Selling link on the subnavigation bar, just below the Services link.**

   You're taken to the Buying and Selling Tools page.

3. **Scroll down the page and click the Promote your Listings with Link Buttons link.**

   You can choose to link your item to the eBay Home page, but why would you? Everyone visiting your auction already knows how to get there! Or you can choose to create a customized link that goes directly to a list of items you have for sale.

4. **Be bold; select the box that allows you to create a customized link.**

5. **Type your User ID and password into the information windows, and then type in the URL of the Web site to which you want to link your auction.**

6. **Read eBay's link agreement and click the I Agree button. It's so much more civilized that way.**

   Read the Instructions for Installing Buttons on your site page.

   eBay generates a piece of HTML code and displays it on your screen.

7. Copy the handy HTML code that eBay generated for you; use your computer's clipboard to paste it into your Web site or text editor.

An eBay icon link appears on your personal or business Web page. Anyone who clicks this link is plucked from your Web page and automatically transported to your auctions.

The instant that you or any other eBay user connects to a link that isn't owned or maintained by eBay, you're not protected by the eBay rules and regulations anymore. eBay cancels any auctions that contain links to Web sites that offer to undersell an auction by touting the same item at a cheaper price — or offer to sell items forbidden at eBay.

To add a link to your item description that takes eBay users to your Web site, type the following code at the end of your item:

```
Click below...<br>
<A HREF=http://www.bogusISP.com/~yourUserID/sale.htm>
Visit my Web site</A>
```

Check with your ISP to get the actual URL for your Web site.

It's All About Me

Want to know more about the people behind those User IDs? Thousands of eBay members have created their own personal Web pages at eBay, called About Me pages. About Me pages are easy to create and are as unique as each eBay member. The way to spot eBay users with an active About Me page is to look for a special **ME** icon next to their User ID.

Take your time when you create your About Me page. A well-done About Me page improves your sales because people that come across your auctions and check out your About Me page can get a sense of who you are, and how serious you are about your eBay activities. They instantly see that you're no fly-by-night seller.

Before you create your own About Me page, we suggest that you look at what other users have done. eBay members often include pictures, links to other Web sites (including their personal home pages), and links to just about any Web location that reflects their personality, which is why they're so entertaining. If your purpose is to generate more business, we recommend that you keep your About Me page focused on your auction listings.

Sellers with many auctions running at once often add a message to their About Me pages that indicates that they're willing to reduce shipping charges if bidders also bid on their other auctions. Subtlety, *schmuddlety*. This direct tactic may lack nuance, but it also increases the number of people who look at (and bid on) your auctions.

To create your own About Me page (starting at the main navigation bar on most eBay pages), do the following:

1. **Click the Services link; click the About Me link on the submenu.**

   You're taken to About Me: Create Your Own eBay Personal Page.

2. **If you haven't signed in, type your User ID and password in the appropriate boxes.**

3. **Click the Create and Edit your Page button.**

   You're taken to the About Me layout page. You're offered three layout options, which eBay is kind enough to show you:

   - Two-column layout
   - Newspaper layout
   - Centered layout

   The three layout options are also shown in Figure 13-4.

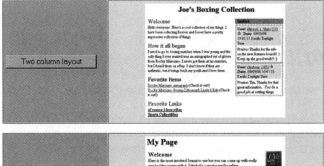

Figure 13-4:
eBay lets you choose one of the three layout options for your About Me page.

4. **Click the button that corresponds to the layout option you want.**

   You're taken to a second About Me creation page.

5. **Enter the following information:**

   - **Page Title.** Type the title of your About Me page, (for example, **Larry's Lunchboxes**).

   - **Welcome Message.** Type a personal attention-grabbing headline, such as **Welcome to Larry Lunch's Lunchbox Place.**

   - **Text.** Type a short paragraph that greets your visitors (something like, **Hey, I like lunchboxes a lot**, only more exciting).

   - **Another Paragraph.** Type in another headline for the second paragraph of the page, such as **Vintage, Modern, Ancient,** or **I Collect All Kinds of Lunchboxes**.

   - **Text.** Type in another paragraph about yourself or your collection (such as, **I used to stare at lunchboxes in the school cafeteria . . .** only more, you know, *normal*).

   - **Picture.** If you're adding a picture, type in a sentence describing it, for example: **This is my wife Loretta with our lunchbox collection.**

   - **URL.** Type in the Web site address (URL) where people can find your picture. See the section earlier in this chapter that shows you how to upload digital images.

   - **Feedback.** Select how many of your Feedback postings you want to appear on your About Me page. (You *can* opt not to show any feedback, but we think you should put in a few, especially if they're complimentary, as in, "Larry sent my lunchbox promptly, and it makes lunchtime a blast! Everybody stares at it. . . .")

   - **Items for Sale.** Select how many of your current auctions you want to appear on your About Me page. If you don't have any auctions running at the moment, you can select the Show No Items option.

   - **Caption.** Type a caption to introduce your auctions, for example: **Lunchboxes I'm Currently Selling.**

   - **Favorite Links.** Type the names and URLs of any Web links you want visitors to see, for example, a Web site that appraises lunchboxes ("It's in excellent condition except for that petrified ham sandwich. . . .").

   - **Favorite eBay Items.** Type the Item Numbers and select a comment from the options displayed to point out eBay auction items you think visitors should check out.

   These text areas are shown in Figure 13-5.

Figure 13-5:
Make your
About Me
page your
home at
eBay.

6. **Click the Preview your Page button, or, if you don't like your current layout, click the Choose New Layout button to go back to Step 1.**

   You're now looking at your final About Me page.

7. **Scroll down to the bottom of the page. You see a group of buttons:**

   • **Edit some more.** Returns you to Step 2.

   • **Save my page.** Saves your About Me page so that you're one step closer to publishing it at eBay.

   • **Edit using HTML.** If you know HTML code, you can customize your About Me page.

   • **Start over.** Takes you to a link page where you can delete what you created and begin again.

8. **When you're happy with your masterpiece, click the Save my Page button.**

   Yup, you did it — anybody in the world with access to the Internet can now find your personal About Me page at eBay.

Don't forget to update your About Me page often. A good About Me page makes bidders eager to know more about your auctions. An out-of-date About Me page turns off potential bidders. If you choose to update, you need to edit it using HTML. If you don't use HTML, you have to re-create a whole new page.

Part IV
Oy Vay, More eBay!: Special Features

The 5th Wave   By Rich Tennant

"What troubles me is that he spends all his time in eBay's Beanie Babies chat room."

In this part . . .

So you want to protect yourself from bad apples, not just at eBay but all over the Internet? We don't blame you. We want to keep safe as well, and that's why we wrote this part.

This is the place to come if you want to know just what eBay knows about you and is willing to share with other eBay members. We also introduce you to Rules & Safety (SafeHarbor), the next best thing to a superhero when it comes to protecting you from people who don't qualify for the eBay User of the Year Award.

eBay is a community, so we have to let you in on some of the ways you can commune with other collectors and get into the social scene. We also tell you about the special features that make eBay such a unique environment. Where else can you buy an item you really want and also help out a charity, all with the click of a mouse?

Chapter 14

Privacy: To Protect and Serve

- -

In This Chapter

▶ Digging up what eBay knows about you

▶ Determining how safe your information is at eBay

▶ Finding out what eBay does with your info

▶ Protecting your privacy

- -

*O*n the Internet, as in real life, you should never take your personal privacy for granted. Sure, you're ecstatic that you can shop and sell at eBay from the privacy of your own home, but remember: Just because your front door is locked doesn't mean that your privacy is being protected. If you're new to the Internet, you may be surprised to find out what you reveal about yourself to the world, no matter how many precautions you take. (Yes, we all know about that neon blue exfoliating mask you wear when you're bidding . . . just kidding . . . honest.)

In this chapter, we tell you how much eBay knows about you and who eBay shares your information with. We explain what you can do to protect your privacy and tell you some simple steps you can take to increase not only your privacy but also your safety.

What (And How) eBay Knows about You

The irony of the Internet is that although you think you're sitting at home working anonymously, third parties such as advertisers and marketing companies are secretly getting to know you. (All together now: *Get-ting-to-know all a-bout youuu*. . . .)

While you're busy collecting World's Fair memorabilia and antique toasters, eBay is busy collecting nuggets of information about you. eBay gets some of this information from you, and some of it from your computer. All the data eBay gets is stored in the eBay memory bank.

What you tell eBay

eBay gets much of what it knows about you *from* you. When you sign up, you voluntarily tell eBay important and personal information about yourself. Right off the bat, you give eBay these juicy tidbits:

- ✔ Name
- ✔ E-mail address
- ✔ Snail-mail address
- ✔ Phone number
- ✔ Password

"Okay, that's no big deal," you say, but if you're using your credit card to settle your eBay fees, you're also giving out personal financial information about yourself:

- ✔ Credit card number
- ✔ Expiration date
- ✔ Credit card billing address
- ✔ Credit card history

If you make a one-time payment with a personal check, you give eBay even more information about yourself. eBay instantly knows your bank's name and your checking account number. The bottom line is that *every time* you pay by check, you give away personal info about yourself. eBay carefully locks up this information (in a hi-tech Alcatraz, of sorts), but other companies or individuals may not be as protective. Before you put the check in the mail, make sure you're comfortable with where it's going.

If you fill in the optional questions when you sign up, eBay also knows the following information about you:

- ✔ Gender
- ✔ Interests
- ✔ Age range
- ✔ Education
- ✔ Income
- ✔ Employer

Cookie? No, thanks, I'm trying to diet

All of the cookies that eBay uses are known as *session cookies*, meaning that the second you log off the eBay site, any cookies that you pick up go away. We think these cookies are fine (and really useful, even if they aren't tasty). But if you still don't feel comfortable with them on your computer, you can put a lid on the cookie jar by setting your browser *not* to accept cookies, or you can set it to warn you and let you decide whether to accept a particular cookie.

What cookies gather

Web sites collect information about you by using *cookies*. No, they don't bribe you with chocolate-chip goodies. Cookies are nothing more than small files put on your hard drive by outside companies (such as eBay) that store data on your surfing habits.

Most Web site designers install cookies to help you navigate their sites — sometimes the cookie becomes sort of an "admission ticket" so that you don't need to register every time you log on.

eBay has a partnership with two advertising companies, Link Exchange and DoubleClick, allowing the two companies to display advertising banners on the site, whether you want to see the banners or not. If you click a banner, a cookie from the particular advertiser goes onto your computer. Figure 14-1 shows you a theme banner found at eBay.

Figure 14-1:
Here's a
typical
banner you
may see
at eBay.

Cookies have no fingers, sticky or otherwise; they can't steal information from other files on your computer. A cookie can access only the information that you already provide to its Web site.

So how do you do all this? Well, you could make a big batch of your favorite technical guru's favorite cookies (the old-fashioned kind — tangible and yummy) and ask him or her to show you the ropes.

DoubleClick says that it uses your information to limit the number of times that you see the same advertisement. DoubleClick also measures the kinds of ads that you respond to. DoubleClick tracks which member Web sites you visit and how often. The bottom line is that DoubleClick is just trying to sell you stuff with ads based on your personal interests. The upside is that you get to see stuff that you may like.

You can learn lots more about cookies in general at www.cookiecentral.com.

You may choose to keep your information private. To remove yourself from the DoubleClick cookie system, go to this Web site:

```
www.doubleclick.net/company_info/about_doubleclick/privacy/
                 privacy2.htm
```

Your eBay sign-in cookie

When you visit eBay and sign in, eBay gives you a special kind of cookie — not pecan shortbread — but an *end of session* cookie. This type of cookie remains on your computer as long as you remain on the eBay site. It also disappears if you haven't been active on the site for over 40 minutes.

We think that eBay's sign-in cookie is a good thing. It prevents the previously repetitive task of typing your User ID and password at every turn. This cookie simplifies your participation in chats, bidding, watching items, viewing e-mail addresses, and so on. Because you don't have to sign in every time you do business at eBay, it's a real time-saver.

What Web servers collect

Every time that you log on to the Internet, you leave an electronic trail of information. eBay, like zillions of other Web sites, uses *servers,* which are really immense programs that do nothing but collect and transfer bits (and bytes) of information day and night, night and day.

Web servers all over the Internet track some or all of the following information:

- What Web site you came in from
- The ISP (Internet Service Provider) that you use

✔ Auctions that you're running

✔ The Web sites you linked your auctions to

✔ Your favorite Web sites (if you link them to your About Me page)

eBay collects the following information while you visit the eBay site. After you log off, the server discards the data:

✔ What you do while logged on to the site

✔ What times you log on and log off

Like an incredible Internet archivist, eBay's server keeps a record of everything you bid on, win, and sell, which is great news if you have a problem with a transaction and need eBay to investigate. Also, eBay couldn't display feedback about you and other users if its server didn't store all the feedback you write and receive. Gosh, eBay's computers must be huge! And busy. Very busy.

Have you ever sent an e-mail to eBay? eBay's server records it and keeps it in some murky recess of eBay's memory. Remember, we live in the age of electronic commerce, and the people at eBay run a serious business that depends on e-commerce. They have to keep everything in case they need to find it later.

For an example of the type of information that can be gleaned from your computer as you surf the Internet, visit this Web site:

```
www.anonymizer.com.
```

BBBOnline and TRUSTe

If you feel a little apprehensive about all the information Web servers can collect about you while you innocently roam the Internet, we understand. But before you start looking out for Big Brother watching over your shoulder, consider this: On the Web, everybody's doing it.

The odds are excellent that all the information that eBay knows about you is already in the hands of many other folks, too — your bank, your grocer, the staff of any magazine you get by subscription, clubs you belong to, any airlines you've flown, and any insurance agencies you use. That's life at the turn of the millennium. And if you're thinking, "Just because everybody knows all this stuff about me, that doesn't make it right," all we can say is, "You're right." But maybe you'll sleep a little better knowing that eBay is one place where folks take the privacy issue seriously.

Do seals bite back?

Because eBay pays to display the TRUSTe Trustmark and the BBBOnline seal, some online critics say that the seals are nothing more than window-dressing. These critics wonder whether it would be in the Web watchdogs' best financial interest to bite the hand that feeds them all those display fees. They complain that the seals offer a false sense of security — and suggest that you view these seals as nothing more than a disclaimer to be careful in your Internet dealings.

Technically, TRUSTe and BBBOnline can pull their seals whenever a Web site becomes careless in its handling of privacy issues. However, the critics make a good point: *Always be careful in your Internet dealings*, no matter how much protection a site has.

---

eBay had a privacy policy for all their users before privacy policies were even in vogue. Now eBay maintains the safety standards set forth by two pioneers in online safeguarding: the Better Business Bureau Online and TRUSTe, as shown in Figure 14-2.

Figure 14-2:
The BBBOnline and TRUSTe icons indicate that eBay takes security seriously.

TRUSTe (www.truste.org) and the Better Business Bureau (www.bbbonline.org) set a list of standards that their member Web sites have to follow to earn a "seal of approval." The hundreds of Web sites that subscribe to one or both of these watchdog groups must adhere to their guidelines and set policies to protect privacy. eBay has been a member of both BBBOnline and TRUSTe since each privacy watchdog group was founded.

To review the policy that's earned eBay the TRUSTe and BBBOnLine seals of approval, click the Privacy Policy link that appears at the bottom of every eBay page.

The eBayla virus

In March 1999, eBay users detected a hacker who turned a covert grab for passwords into a somewhat baffling problem. On selected auctions, an unexpected window would pop up, prompting the bidder to type in his or her password. Smart eBay users knew better and dubbed this window the *eBayla virus* (a take-off on the deadly Ebola virus).

These same members started spreading the word on message boards and in chat rooms. eBay solved the problem but, unfortunately, correcting it took over a month, and some eBay users were stung by this privacy invasion. This was a valuable lesson for eBay about hacking — and probably not the last time something like this will happen.

In addition to setting and displaying a privacy policy, eBay follows these guidelines as well:

- ✔ eBay must make the TRUSTe and BBBOnline links easily accessible to users. You can find either logo at eBay's Home page. Click one of 'em, and you're taken to the site for more information. Take advantage of this opportunity to find out how your privacy is being protected.

- ✔ eBay must disclose what personal information it collects and how it's using the info.

- ✔ Users must have an easy way to review the personal information that eBay has about them.

- ✔ Users must have an option — *opting out* — that lets them decline to share information (we explain this in this chapter).

- ✔ eBay must follow industry standards to make its Web site and database secure so that hackers and nonmembers have no access to the information. eBay uses *Secure Socket Layers (SSL),* which is an encryption program that scrambles data until it gets to eBay. Unfortunately, however, no Web site, including the CIA's Web site, is completely secure, so you still have to stay on guard while you're online.

If you ever have any questions about security at eBay, send an e-mail to privacy@eBay.com or safeharbor@ebay.com.

AUCTION ANECDOTE

Grateful Dead cookie jar

This is one of the grooviest jars I have ever come across — a real find for the die-hard Grateful Dead fan or for the cookie jar collector who has it all. Made by Vandor, this Grateful Dead bus cookie jar looks like something the Dead *would* drive. Beautiful detailing on the peace signs; the roses are running lights. Painted windows. You have just got to see this piece. Only 10,000 made and I have only seen one other. Comes with box that has Grateful Dead logos on it. Buyer pays all shipping and insurance.

The cookie jar started at $1 and sold at eBay for $102.50.

Oh wow, dude, that's some far-out cookie jar. (Cue the band: *Keep truck-in'.* . . .)

What Does eBay Do with Information about Me, Anyway?

Although eBay knows a good chunk of information about you, it puts the information to good use — the fact that it knows so much about you actually helps you in the long run.

Here's what eBay uses personal information for:

- **Upgrading eBay.** Like most e-commerce companies, eBay tracks members' use and habits to improve the Web site. For instance, if a particular item generates a lot of activity, eBay may add a category or a subcategory.

- **Clearing the way for transactions.** If eBay didn't collect information such as your e-mail address, your snail-mail address, and your phone number, after an auction was over, you couldn't complete the transactions you started. Bummer.

- **Billing.** You think it's important to keep track of your merchandise and money, don't you? So does eBay. It uses your personal information to keep an eye on your account and on your paying habits. And on everybody else's. (Call it a gentle encouragement of honest trading habits.)

- **Policing the site.** Never forget that eBay tries to be tough on crime, and if you break the rules or regulations, eBay will hunt you down and boot you out. Personal information is used to find eBay delinquents, and eBay makes it clear that it cooperates with law enforcement and with third parties whose merchandise you may be selling illegally. For more about this topic, read up on the VeRO program in Chapter 9.

Periodically, eBay runs surveys asking specific questions about your use of the site. It uses your answers to upgrade eBay. In addition, eBay asks whether it can forward your information to a marketing firm. eBay says that no information that can be used to personally identify you is forwarded, which means that any info you provide is given to third parties as raw data. However, if you're nervous about privacy, we suggest that you make it clear that you don't want your comments to leave eBay should you decide to participate in eBay surveys. If you don't participate in the surveys, you won't have any hand in creating new eBay features, though, so you can't complain if you don't like how the site looks. Sometimes, however, eBay advertises surveys that users can take part in at the eBay Home page.

What Do Other eBay Members Know about Me?

eBay functions under the premise that eBay's members are buying, selling, working, and playing in an honest and open way. That means that anyone surfing can immediately find out some limited information about you:

✔ Your User ID.

   If your User ID is the same as your e-mail address, anyone with Internet access (not just eBay users) can go to the eBay site, see your e-mail address, and e-mail you.

✔ Your feedback history.

✔ All the auctions you run.

✔ Your current bids and any bids you've made within a given 30-day period.

✔ Your e-mail address. (Only registered eBay users can access it, but that still means that several million people can e-mail you.)

eBay clearly states in its policies and guidelines that e-mail addresses are to be used only for eBay business. If you abuse this policy, you can be suspended or even kicked off for good.

eBay provides limited eBay member registration information to its users. If another member wants to know the following facts about you, they're available:

✔ Your name

✔ The city, state, and zip code that you provide eBay

✔ The telephone number that you provide eBay

Following the auction, buyers and sellers exchange some real-world information. As we explain in Chapters 6 and 11, members initiate the exchange of merchandise and money by e-mail, providing personal addresses for both payments and shipments. Make sure that you're comfortable giving out your home address. If you're not, we explain alternatives in this chapter.

Spam — Not Just a Taste Treat Anymore

Although you can find plenty of places to socialize and have fun at eBay, when it comes to business, eBay is . . . well, all business.

eBay's policy says that requests for e-mail addresses and registration information can be made only for eBay business. What constitutes "business" is subject to wide interpretation by both eBay (the company) and eBay members. We suggest that you communicate at eBay as you do in any professional place of business.

Here's a list of "business" reasons for e-mail communication, generally accepted by all at eBay:

- ✔ Responding to feedback that you left
- ✔ Responding to feedback that you received
- ✔ Communicating with sellers or buyers during and after transactions
- ✔ Suggesting to other eBay members items that buyers may be interested in
- ✔ Leaving chat-room comments
- ✔ Discussing common interests with other members, such as shared hometowns, interesting collections, and past or current auctions

Sending spam versus eating it

Sending e-mail to other members is a great way to do business and make friends. But don't cross the line into spam. *Spam,* a Hormel canned meat product (we've given Spam its own sidebar), now has an alternate meaning. When you spell it with a small *s, spam* is unsolicited e-mail — most often, advertising — sent to multiple e-mail addresses gleaned from marketing lists. Eventually, it fills up your inbox the way "Spam, Spam, Spam, and Spam" filled up the menu in an old *Monty Python* restaurant skit.

> # Spam I am
>
> Spam, the unwanted electronic junk mail, is named after Spam, the canned meat product (Spam collectibles at eBay are another matter entirely). According to the Spam Web site (www.spam.com), more than five billion cans of Spam have been consumed worldwide. (By the way, Hawaiians eat more Spam than any other state in the union.) It's made from a secret recipe of pork shoulder, ham, and special spices. It was first produced in 1937 and got its name from the *SP* for spice and the *AM* from ham.
>
> It's widely believed that spam (junk e-mail) got its name from the old *Monty Python* sketch because the refrain "Spam-Spam-Spam-Spam" drowned out all other conversation. Others say that it came from a bunch of computer geeks at USC who thought the junk e-mail was about as satisfying as a Spam sandwich. Perhaps they've never enjoyed a Spam luau in Hawaii under the moonlight — aloha!

Think of spam as the electronic version of the junk mail that you get in the real world. Spam may be okay for eating (if you're into that kind of thing), but sending it can get you banned from eBay.

Ninety-nine percent of the time, spam is completely annoying and mostly worthless. If you send it, it won't be opened or answered.

If you send an e-mail that advertises a product or service to people you don't know, you're guilty of spamming.

Trash your junk mail!

Don't open e-mail from anyone you don't know, especially if there's a file attached to it. Sometimes, if a spammer is really slick, it's hard to tell that you've received spam. If you receive an e-mail with no subject line, however — or if it has an addressee name that isn't yours, or is coming in from someone you never heard of — delete it. You never know; it could be just annoying spam — or worse, it could contain a computer virus as an attachment, just waiting for you to open and activate it. (A virus that you don't open won't infect your computer.)

If you receive spam that you believe is linked to eBay or is being generated by a member, alert eBay by e-mail at timesenstive@ebay.com and safeharbor@ebay.com.

Speaking of e-mail, if you're new to the technology, we recommend getting a good antivirus program that can scan e-mail attachments and rid your system of some annoying — and increasingly dangerous — computer bugs.

For some interesting general anti-spam tips, drop in at `www.spam.abuse.net`. This Web site offers helpful advice for doing battle with spamsters.

I Vant to Be Alone — and Vat You Can Do to Stay That Vay

The Internet has a long reach. Don't be surprised when you furnish your personal information freely on one Web site, and it turns up someplace totally different. If you don't mind people knowing things about you (your name, your hobbies, where you live, your phone number), by all means share. But we think you should give only as much information as you need to do business.

Privacy is not secrecy. You shouldn't feel obligated to reveal anything about yourself that isn't absolutely necessary. (Some personal facts are in the same league as body weight — private, even if hardly a secret.)

Although you can't entirely prevent privacy leaks, you can take some precautions to protect yourself. Here are some tips to keep your online information as safe and secure as possible:

- ✔ **User ID.** When eBay first started, members used their e-mail addresses to buy and sell. Some still do. But your first line of defense against everyone who surfs through eBay is to choose a User ID that's different from your e-mail address. Non-members can't find out who you are, and members at least have to make the effort to get your e-mail address. Choose an ID that doesn't reveal too much about you. We offer pointers on how to choose your User ID in Chapter 2.

- ✔ **Passwords.** Guard your password as if it were the key to your home. Don't give any buyers or sellers your password. If a window requesting your password pops up in an auction, skip it — it's somebody who is up to no good. Use your password *only* on official eBay screens. (See Chapter 2 for more tips on choosing passwords.)

 If you're concerned that someone may have your password, change it:

 1. **Click Services on the main navigation bar.**

 2. **Scroll down to Change my Password under the My eBay section.**

 3. **Click it and follow the instructions.**

 Your password is immediately changed.

✔ **Credit card information.** Whenever you use your credit card at eBay, you can make sure your private information is safe. Look for an SSL (*SSL* stands for Security Sockets Layer) link or checkbox. Sometimes you may see a link that says You may also sign in securely. This is an encryption program that scrambles the information so that hackers have almost no chance of getting your information. We explain how to use SSL in Chapter 2. When buying from an auction that accepts credit cards, check the seller's feedback and carefully weigh the risks of giving your credit card number to someone who you don't know versus the added time of paying by money order or personal check.

Never give anyone your Social Security number online. These numbers didn't start out as national ID numbers, but they sure work that way now. Guard yours as if it were your bank account number.

✔ **Registration information.** When you first register, eBay requests a phone number and address for billing and contact purposes. We have never had a problem with anyone requesting our registration information and then misusing it. However, many people want an added measure of anonymity. You can give eBay the information it wants in several ways without compromising your privacy:

- Instead of your home phone number, provide eBay with a cell phone number, a work phone number, or the phone number hooked up to your computer. Screen your calls with an answering machine. You can also use your beeper number.

- Use a post office box instead of your home address.

- Start a bank account solely for eBay transactions. Make it a *TA* account — as in Trade As — so that you can use an alternate name. Your bank can help you with this.

✔ **Chat rooms.** eBay has more than two dozen chat rooms where members exchange information and sometimes heated arguments. We explain all about chat rooms in Chapter 16. But heed this advice: Be careful what you reveal about yourself in a chat room. Don't expect that "just between us" means that at all. Chat rooms can be viewed by anyone who visits the eBay site, not just eBay members.

Never say anything online that you wouldn't feel comfortable saying to the next person who passed you on the street. Basically, that's who you're talking to. You can find stories of romances blossoming at eBay — and we're delighted for the happy couples, we swear — but come on, that doesn't mean that you should lose your head. Don't give out any personal information to strangers; too often, that's asking for trouble. Have fun at eBay, but hang on to your common sense.

Skim some of the category chat rooms, especially the board called Discuss eBay's Newest Features, for warnings about security problems on these boards — and how to avoid 'em.

Fighting back

Robbin was minding her own business, selling software at eBay, when she ran into one of the world's nastiest eBay outlaws. He was a one-stop-shopping outlet of rule-breaking behaviors. First, he ruined her auctions by bidding ridiculously high amounts and then retracting bids at the last minute. He e-mailed her bidders, offering the same item but cheaper. He contacted Robbin's winning bidders to say he was accepting her payments. Then he started leaving messages on her answering machine. When she finally had enough, she contacted Rules & Safety (SafeHarbor), which suspended him.

But like a bad lunch, he came back up — with a new name. So Robbin fought back on her own. She got his registration information and sent him a letter. She also informed Support at his ISP what he was doing — and because he used his work e-mail address, she also contacted his boss.

Her efforts must have done the trick. He finally slipped out of eBay and slithered out of her life. The lesson: Don't rely completely on eBay to pick up the pieces. If you're being abused, stand up for your rights and fight back through the proper channels!

> ✔ **Check feedback.** Yep, we sound like a broken record, but there it is again: *Check feedback.* eBay works because it's policed by its participants. The best way to learn about the folks whom you're dealing with is to see how others felt about the person or company.

In the virtual world, as in the real world, cyberstalking is scary and illegal. If you think someone is using information from eBay to harass you, contact eBay immediately — as well as your local police.

Chapter 15

eBay's Rules & Safety Program

- -

In This Chapter

▶ Keeping eBay members safe

▶ Staying away from eBay no-no's

▶ Filing complaints against eBay bad guys

▶ Docking with escrow companies

▶ Knowing your items through authentication

▶ Saving yourself: Where to go when eBay can't help

- -

Millions of people enjoy smooth sailing at eBay. If you're new to the Internet, however, you may need a reality check. With two million items selling every week, the law of averages dictates that you're bound to run into some rough seas. If you do, know that you can get the answers you need from the Rules & Safety Overview page (this dock is also known as SafeHarbor). In this chapter, we take you through all Rules & Safety resources — from reporting eBay abuses to resolving insurance issues. We explain how eBay enforces its rules and regulations, how you can use third-party escrow and mediation services, and even how to go outside of eBay if you run into some really big-time problems.

Keeping eBay Safe with Rules & Safety

The Rules & Safety Overview page (as shown in Figure 15-1) is where eBay focuses on protecting the Web site from members who aren't playing by the rules. Through this page, eBay issues warnings and suspensions, and in some cases, it gives eBay bad guys the old heave-ho.

To get to the Rules & Safety Overview page, click the SafeHarbor (Rules & Safety) link that you can find at the bottom of every eBay page.

Figure 15-1:
Here's a
look at the
Rules &
Safety
Overview
page.

The Rules & Safety Overview page is more than just a link to policies and information. It also connects you with a group of eBay staffers who handle complaints, field incoming tips about possible infractions, and dole out warnings and suspensions. The folks here investigate infractions and send out e-mails in response to tips. eBay staffers look at complaints on a case-by-case basis, in the order they receive them. Most of the complaints they receive are about these problems:

- Shill bidders (see the section on selling abuses in this chapter)

- Feedback issues and abuses (see the section on feedback abuses in this chapter)

Keep in mind that eBay is a community of people, most of whom have never met each other. No matter what you buy or sell at eBay, don't expect eBay transactions to be any safer than buying or selling from a complete stranger. If you go in with this attitude, you can't be disappointed.

If you've been reading previous chapters in this book, you probably know about eBay's rules and regulations. For a closer online look at them, click Help on the main navigation bar, click Community Standards, and then click the link User Agreement. (The agreement is revised often, so check it often. We're waiting for the next User Agreement to be called *Revised User Agreement: The eBay User Strikes Back, Again.*)

Gilligan, Ginger, and Marianne sold separately

Here's a classic example of an honest, accentuate-the-positive-but-point-out-the-negative auction description:

34-foot Sailboat, SEB Aloa — Fast & beautiful! This boat is sea-ready but needs some cosmetic work: retouching the fiberglass work, painting down below, covering the brand-new foam cushions, and so on. Recently painted, bright-work in the process of being redone. No engine, but if you have a VW or other small diesel, you can drop its engine in; all engine electronics, gearing, etc., in great shape. I've lived aboard this boat for a few years, sailing her from the U.S. to the Caribbean during that time. This boat is fast, beautiful, seaworthy, and seakindly and will take you through any kind of weather.

The starting price was $7,000; it sold at eBay for $8,100. The seller of this boat came clean and it paid off big-time.

Another helpful link is the FAQ for the User Agreement, which explains the legalese in clearer English. To find it, click User Agreement Frequently Asked Questions and then click User Agreement Revision Frequently Asked Questions. (Coming soon: *Son of . . . ?*) To get there quickly, click the User Agreement link, located at the bottom of every eBay page.

Abuses You Should Report to Rules & Safety

Before you even consider blowing the whistle on the guy who (gasp!) gave you negative feedback by reporting him to Rules & Safety, make sure that what you're encountering *is* actually a misuse of eBay. Some behavior isn't nice (no argument there), but it *also* isn't a violation of eBay rules — in which case, eBay can't do much about it. The following sections list the primary reasons you may start SafeHarbor investigations.

Selling abuses

If you encounter any of these selling abuses, fire off an e-mail to SafeHarbor Rules & Safety at SafeHarbor@ebay.com:

- ✔ **Shill bidding:** A seller uses multiple User IDs to bid or has accomplices place bids to boost the price of his or her auction items. eBay investigators look for six telltale signs, including a single bidder putting in a really high bid, a bidder with really low feedback but a really high number of bids on items, or lots of bids between two users.

- **Auction interception:** An unscrupulous user, pretending to be the actual seller, contacts the winner to set up terms of payment and shipping in an effort to get the buyer's payment.

- **Fee avoidance:** A user reports a lower-than-actual final price and/or illegally submits a Final Value Fee credit. We explain how Final Value Fee credits work in Chapter 12.

- **Hot bid manipulation:** A user, with the help of accomplices, enters dozens of phony bids to reach the 30 bids needed to reach the Hot category. Let the experts at eBay decide on this one; but you may wonder if loads of bids come in rapid succession but the price moves very little.

If a user is conducting auctions of prohibited, questionable, or infringing items, report the conduct to Community Watch: ctywatch@ebay.com. See Chapter 9 for more information.

Bidding abuses

If you want to know more about bidding in general, see Chapter 6. Here's a list of bidding abuses that eBay wants to know about:

- **Bid shielding:** Two users working in tandem: User A, with the help of accomplices, intentionally bids an unreasonably high amount and then retracts the bid in the closing moments of the auction — leaving a lower bid (which the offender or an accomplice places) as the winning bid.

- **Bid siphoning:** Users send e-mail to bidders of a current auction to offer the same merchandise for a lower price elsewhere.

- **Auction interference:** Users warn other bidders through e-mail to stay clear of a seller *during a current auction,* presumably to decrease the number of bids and keep the prices low.

- **Bid manipulation:** A user bids a ridiculously high amount, raising the next highest bidder to maximum bid. The manipulator then retracts the bid and rebids *slightly* over the previous high bidder's maximum.

- **Non-paying bidder:** We call 'em deadbeats, and the bottom line is that these people win auctions but never pay up.

- **Unwelcome bidder:** A user bids on a specific seller's auction despite the seller's warning that he or she won't accept that user's bids. Impolite and obnoxious.

Feedback abuses

All you have at eBay is your reputation, and that reputation is made up of your Feedback history. eBay takes any violation of its Feedback system very seriously. Because eBay's instituted transaction-related feedback only, unscrupulous eBay members now have less opportunity to take advantage of this system. Here's a checklist of feedback abuses that you should report to Rules & Safety:

- ✔ **Feedback extortion:** A member threatens to post negative feedback if another eBay member doesn't follow through on some unwarranted demand.

- ✔ **Personal exposure:** A member leaves feedback for a user that exposes personal information that doesn't relate to transactions at eBay.

- ✔ **–4 Feedback:** Any user reaching a Net Feedback score of –4 is subject to suspension.

Identity abuses

Who you are at eBay is as important as what you sell (or buy). eBay monitors the identities of its members closely — and asks that you report any great pretenders in this area to Rules & Safety. Here's a checklist of identity abuses:

- ✔ **Identity misrepresentation:** A user claims to be an eBay staff member or another eBay user, or he or she registers under the name of another user.

- ✔ **False or missing contact information:** A user deliberately registers with false contact information or an invalid e-mail address.

- ✔ **Under age:** A user falsely claims to be older than the age of 18. (You must be 18 to enter into a legally binding contract.)

- ✔ **Contact information:** One user publishes another user's contact information on the eBay site without the user's consent.

Operational abuses

If you see somebody trying to interfere with eBay's operation, eBay staffers want you to tell them about it. Here are two roguish operational abuses:

- ✔ **Hacking:** A user purposely interferes with eBay's computer operations (for example, by breaking into unauthorized files).
- ✔ **Spamming:** The user sends unsolicited e-mail to eBay users.

Miscellaneous abuses

The following are additional problems that you should alert eBay about:

- A user is threatening physical harm to another eBay member.

- A person uses racist, obscene, or harassing language in a public area of eBay.

For a complete list of offenses and how eBay runs each investigation, go to the following address:

```
pages.ebay.com/services/safeharbor/safeharbor-
               proc.html#feedback
```

Reporting Abuses to Rules & Safety

If you suspect someone of abusing eBay's rules and regulations, send an e-mail to SafeHarbor@ebay.com.

Make your message clear and concise by including everything that happened, but don't editorialize. (Calling someone a "lowdown mud-sucking cretin" doesn't tell anyone who can help you anything useful and doesn't reflect well on you either.) Keep it businesslike — just the facts, ma'am. Do include all pertinent documentation, such as e-mails, receipts, canceled checks, and, of course, the auction number.

Here's a checklist of what you should include in your e-mail to Rules & Safety:

- Write only the facts as you know them.

- Attach all e-mails with complete headers. (*Headers* are all the information found at the top of an e-mail message.) Rules & Safety uses the headers to verify how the e-mail was sent and to follow the trail back to the author.

- In the subject line of your e-mail message, make sure that you name the violation and indicate whether the matter is time-sensitive. If the clock *is* running out on your case (for example, you suspect bidding offenses in a current auction), we suggest that you send a copy of your e-mail to timesensitive@ebay.com.

After eBay receives your e-mail, you get an automatic response that your e-mail was received, although in practice, several days may go crawling by before eBay actually investigates your allegations. (They must look at a *lot* of transactions.)

Depending on the outcome of the probe, eBay may contact you with the results. If your problem becomes a legal matter, eBay may not let you know what's going on. The only indication you may get that some action was taken is that the eBay member you reported is suspended — or NARU (Not A Registered User).

If your complaint doesn't warrant an investigation by the folks at Rules & Safety, they pass it along to someone at the overworked Customer Support staff, who then contacts you. (Don't bawl the person out if the attention you get is tardy.)

Unfortunately, NARU members can show up again on the eBay site. They just use a different name. In fact, this practice is fairly common, so beware! If you suspect that someone who broke the rules once is back under another User ID, alert Rules & Safety. If you're a seller, you can refuse to accept bids from that person. If the person persists, alert Customer Support with e-mail.

As eBay has grown, so has the number of complaints about slow response from Rules and Safety and Customer Support. We don't doubt that eBay staffers are doing their best. But slow response can get frustrating. You can grin and bear it, or you can plunge ahead. Several eBay users report that the best way to get a reaction out of eBay is an e-mail blitzkrieg — sending e-mail over and over until they can't ignore you. This practice is risky at best, however, and inconsiderate at worst; hitting eBay with constant e-mails about the same issue just slows down the process for everyone.

You can also call Customer Support (phone 408-369-4830), but don't expect to hear the voice of a live human being. You hear a recording promising that someone will phone you back. Don't forget to leave your name and phone number.

If you're desperate for help, you can also post a message with your problem in one of the eBay chat rooms. eBay members participating in chat rooms often share the names of helpful staffers. Often, you can find some eBay members who faced the same problem (sometimes with the same member) and can offer advice — or at the very least, compassion and a virtual ear. (Jump to Chapter 16 for more info on bulletin boards and chat rooms.)

Make sure that you don't violate any eBay rules by sharing any member's contact information as you share your story in a chat room. In addition, make sure that you don't threaten or libel (that is, say untrue things or spread rumors) the person in your posting.

If you have a few hours to burn, eBay has a Customer Support e-mail response form that will get you an answer within 12 to 36 hours. You can find Customer Support creatively hidden at

```
pages.ebay.com/help/basics/select-support.html
```

Stuff eBay Won't Do Anything About

People are imperfect everywhere, even online. (Whoa, what a shock!) You probably won't agree with some of the behavior that you run into at eBay (ranging from slightly annoying to just plain rotten). Although much of that conduct is detestable, it can (and does) go on as long as it doesn't break eBay rules.

In some cases, you may need to bite your tongue and chalk up someone's annoying behavior to ignorance of the unwritten rules of eBay etiquette. Just because people have computers and some things to sell or buy doesn't mean that they possess grown-up social skills. (But you knew that.)

Here's a gang of annoying issues that crop up pretty regularly but that *aren't* against eBay's rules and regulations:

- ✔ **You receive unwarranted or retaliatory feedback:** The biggest fear that haunts members who consider leaving negative feedback is that the recipient will retaliate with some more negative feedback. Remember that you can respond to negative feedback. Remember, however, that eBay will not remove a negative comment — no matter how unjustified you may think it is. The good news is that the comment becomes neutral if the writer is no longer a member of eBay.

  Often, people who leave retaliatory feedback are also breaking some heftier eBay rules and (sooner or later) disappear from the site, never to rant again.

- ✔ **A seller sets astronomical shipping costs:** eBay policy says that shipping costs must be reasonable. Basically, eBay is wagging its finger and saying, "Don't gouge your buyers." Some sellers are trying to avoid fees or may be disappointed that a sale didn't make enough money, so they jack up shipping costs to increase their profit.

  Under its rules, eBay can't really stop someone from charging too much for shipping. Bidders should check shipping terms in the Auction Item description. Bidders must decide whether to agree to those terms before they bid. The best way to protect yourself from being swindled is to agree with a seller on shipping costs and terms in writing — *before* you bid.

- ✔ **A seller or buyer refuses to meet the terms that you mutually set:** eBay has the power only to warn or suspend members. It can't make anyone do anything — even someone who's violating a policy. If you want to make someone fulfill a transaction, you're more or less on your own.

  We heard one story of a seller who refused to send a product after being paid. The seller said, "Come and get it." The buyer happened to be in town on business and did just that!

  Often, reluctant eBay users just need a nudge from eBay in the form of a warning to comply. So go ahead and file a Final Value Fee Credit request (we explain how to do this in Chapter 12) and a fraud report (more on fraud reports later in this chapter).

✔ **E-mail spam:** An eBay bidder whose e-mail address and User ID are the same can receive unwanted e-mail from nonmembers who offer to sell similar items outside of eBay. eBay sees this as spam, but because these spamsters are not eBay members, eBay has no way to punish them. And although the items these spammers are selling may be perfectly good, eBay won't offer you any protection in these deals. We suggest that you either ignore these folks or report them to their ISP.

The best (and most obvious) solution to this problem is to choose a User ID that's distinctly different from your e-mail address. Doing so displays your creativity, helps insulate you from great slabs of spam, and helps block lazy unsavories from cramming your e-mail with reasons to send them money. (Without even looking up your address. The nerve.)

New eBay users are often the unwitting perpetrators of annoying behavior, but you're ahead of the pack now that you know what *not* to do. You can afford to cut the other newbies some slack and help them learn the ropes before you report them.

Using Mediation and Dispute Resolution Services

Even the best of friends sometimes have misunderstandings that can escalate to all-out war if they don't resolve their problems early enough. If the going gets tough, you need to call in the heavy artillery: a *mediator*. Just as pro boxing has its referees, auctions may need a level head to intervene in any squabble. eBay is now partnering with SquareTrade, an online problem-solving service, and the service is available on the eBay Web site. Acting as a third party with no axe to grind, a mediator such as Square Trade can often hammer out an agreement or act as judge to resolve disputes.

If you file a complaint through the SquareTrade link, the service asks you to supply information regarding the offending transaction on an online form. SquareTrade then sends an e-mail to the offending party, outlining the situation. Both the complaint and the response from the other party appear on a secure Web page that only the offender, the mediator, and you can access.

SquareTrade uses a patent-pending technology to help smooth the mediation process. The mediator listens to both points of view and, if the parties can't reach an agreement, suggests a solution that he bases on the rules of fair play and good conduct. The use of a mediator doesn't, however, preclude the use of a lawyer if things truly hit an impasse.

To find SquareTrade at eBay, click the SafeHarbor (Rules & Safety) link at the bottom of any eBay page. After you arrive at the Rules & Safety overview page, scroll to the bottom and click Dispute Resolution.

Square Trade offers online sellers the opportunity to get a Square Trade Seal to post with your auctions. The Square Trade Seal represents that the seller is committed to participating in online problem-solving, dedicated to superior customer service, is in compliance with SquareTrade standards and has been verified by SquareTrade. Find out more about obtaining the Square Trade Seal by going to squaretrade.com.

Launching a Fraud Report

The second that you complain about a seller who's taken money but hasn't delivered the goods, a SafeHarbor Rules & Safety investigation automatically starts.

If you've clearly been ripped off, use eBay's Fraud Reporting program to file a complaint by clicking the SafeHarbor Rules & Safety link at the bottom of any eBay page. After you arrive at the Rules and Safety Overview page, scroll to the bottom and click the Investigations link.

The Rules and Safety Overview page can give you a lot of good general information that can help you prevent something from going wrong in a future auction, so feel free to use this page as a resource that can help prevent problems.

If you've got a troubled auction and need to launch a report, follow these steps:

1. **Read all the information on the Investigations page before filing a new complaint.**

2. **Click any of the many Report Offenses to Investigations Here links.**

   No matter which link you click, you're taken to an area that instructs you further and provides information about what offenses can and cannot be investigated by eBay.

3. **After you've found out if you have a legitimate case that should be investigated, click the** safeharbor@eBay.com **link.**

   An e-mail window automatically opens with the safeharbor@eBay.com e-mail address already entered.

   Before you send your e-mail, be sure to review what you've written to confirm that your report is accurate.

4. **Send the e-mail.**

   Be sure you only send one e-mail per case — one case per e-mail — to safeharbor@eBay.com.

To file an insurance claim with eBay, you must register a fraud report within 30 days of the close of the auction. Be careful not to jump the gun and register a complaint too soon. We suggest waiting about two or three weeks before you register your complaint; double-check first to make sure that your e-mail is working and that you have the correct address of the person with whom you're having difficulties. After all, neither eBay nor your ISP is infallible.

Even if your insurance claim isn't worth a nickel after 30 days, you can still register a fraud report and help the investigation of a lousy, terrible, *allegedly* fraudulent eBay user. That's payment enough, ain't it?

After you register a complaint, eBay informs the other party that you're making a fraud claim. eBay says that it will try to contact both parties and help reach a resolution. *Registering* the complaint is not the same thing as *filing* a complaint. Registering starts the process; filing comes after a month-long grace period if the situation isn't resolved by then.

If the accusation you're registering refers to a clear violation, eBay gives you information on the kind of third-party assistance you can get to help resolve the problem. If eBay deems the problem a violation of the law, it reports the crime to the appropriate law-enforcement agency.

Walking the Plank: Suspensions

Playing by eBay's rules keeps you off the Rules & Safety radar screen. If you start violating eBay policy, the company's going to keep a close eye on you. Depending on the infraction, eBay may be all over you like jelly on peanut butter. Or you may safely lurk in the fringes until your feedback rating is lower than the temperature in Nome in November.

Here's a docket of eBay no-no's that can get members flogged and keel-hauled — or at least *suspended:*

- ✔ Feedback rating of –4.
- ✔ Four instances of deadbeat bidding.
- ✔ Repeated warning for the same infraction.
- ✔ Feedback extortion.
- ✔ Bid shielding.
- ✔ Unwelcome bidding after a warning from the seller.
- ✔ Shill bidding.
- ✔ Auction interception.
- ✔ Fee avoidance.

> ✔ Fraudulent selling.
>
> ✔ Identity misrepresentation.
>
> ✔ Younger than 18 years old.
>
> ✔ Hacking.
>
> ✔ Physical threats.

If you get a suspension but think you're innocent, respond directly to the person who suspended you to plead your case. Reversals do occur. Don't broadcast your suspicions on chat boards. If you're wrong, you regret it. Even if you're right, it's oh-so gauche.

Be careful about accusing members of cheating. Unless you're involved in a transaction, you don't know all the facts. Perry Mason moments are great on television, but they're fictional for a reason. In real life, drawing yourself into a possible confrontation is senseless. Start the complaint process, keep it businesslike, and let eBay's staff figure out what's going on.

Toss 'em a Life Saver: eBay Insurance

One thing's for sure in this world: Nothing is for sure. That's why insurance companies exist. Two types of insurance are available for eBay users:

> ✔ Insurance that buyers purchase to cover shipping (see Chapter 11).
>
> ✔ Insurance through eBay against fraud, which we discuss here.

To cover loss from fraud, eBay has a deal with the world-famous insurer, Lloyd's of London. The insurance covers money that you pay for an item you never receive (as a result of fraud, not shipping problems) or receive but find to be materially different from the auction item's description.

eBay insurance pays up to $175 (a maximum of $200 minus a $25 deductible). So if you file a $50 claim, you get $25. If you file a $5,000 claim, you still get only $175. Hey, it's better than nothing.

To qualify for an eBay insurance payment:

> ✔ The buyer and seller must be in good standing (no negative feedback ratings).
>
> ✔ The buyer must have proof that the item costs more than $25.
>
> ✔ The buyer must prove that the payment was sent.

✔ The buyer must prove that the seller didn't send the item.

OR

✔ The buyer must prove that the item sent is substantially different from the auction description.

To be eligible for insurance, you must register a complaint with the Fraud Reporting System no more than 30 days after the auction closes. eBay then e-mails the seller that a complaint has been lodged. eBay hopes that, by the time the 30 days are up, the differences are resolved and you can withdraw your complaint.

Filing an insurance claim

To file an insurance claim at eBay, begin at the Rules & Safety Overview page. Get there by clicking the SafeHarbor (Rules & Safety) link at the bottom of every eBay page. Then just follow these steps:

1. **On the Rules & Safety Overview page, click either the Insurance link or the Fraud Prevention & Insurance link.**

   You're now at the Fraud Prevention & Insurance page.

2. **Scroll down the page to the Fraud Report link and click it.**

   You go to the Fraud Reporting and Insurance Claim Form page.

3. **Follow the step-by-step directions.**

4. **Click either the File a New Complaint button or the View a Complaint in Progress button.**

5. **On request, enter your User ID and password and Click to move to the next page.**

6. **Verify your name and address and contact info by clicking Yes or No.**

7. **Click the appropriate button (I was a Bidder or I was a Seller).**

8. **At this point, sellers need to enter the item number and the buyer's User ID, while buyers simply enter the auction number.**

9. **After you finish, print out the final page with the provided claim number.**

   Lloyd's promises to get back to you within six weeks to tell you the results of its investigation.

   You can't file more than one claim a month.

Lloyd's of London

Lloyd's of London is eBay's official insurer. The company is named for Edward Lloyd who opened a coffee shop in London in 1689. Lloyd never insured anything. But his wealthy clientele pooled their resources insuring local shippers. In the last 400 years or so, the company has insured a list of items even more eclectic than eBay's auctions: the "car" that set the land speed record of 763 miles per hour, a 2,000-year-old Chinese wine jar, the Ringling Brothers Circus, Betty Grable's "million-dollar legs," Frank Sinatra, the Rolling Stones — and the world's longest cigar, which is 12½ feet long. (That cigar would take 339 days to smoke. It's still unlit; the owner's spouse is probably grateful.)

Docking with escrow

Escrow is a relatively new concept for online trading. Escrow services act as the go-between between the seller and the buyer. We spell out all the details of using escrow in Chapter 6.

eBay has a direct link to i-Escrow (an online escrow service). From the Rules & Safety Overview page, click the Escrow link. This action takes you to the Escrow Overview page. On this page, click the Begin Escrow link and follow the directions on the page that appears next.

Trimming in the Sales: Authentication and Appraising

Despite eBay's attempts to keep the buying and selling community honest, some people just refuse to play nice. After the New York City Department of Consumer Affairs launched an investigation into counterfeit sports memorabilia sold on the Web site, errant eBay outlaws experienced some anxious moments. We can always hope they mend their ways, while at the same time advising *Don't bet on it.* Fortunately, eBay is offering a proactive approach to preventing such occurrences from happening again.

Topmost among the countermeasures is easy member access to several services that can authenticate specific types of merchandise. The good news here is that you know what kind of item you're getting; the bad news is that, as does everything else in life, it's going to cost you money.

Have a good working knowledge of what you're buying or selling. Before you bid, do some homework and get more information. And *check the bidder's feedback*. (Does this advice sound familiar?) See Chapters 5 and 9 for more information about conducting research.

Before you spend the money to have your item appraised and authenticated, ask yourself a few practical questions (regardless of whether you're buying or selling):

- ✓ **Is this item quality merchandise?** Am I selling/buying merchandise whose condition is subjective but important to its value — as in, *Is it really well-loved or just busted?* Is this item graded by some profession-ally accepted standard that I need to know?

- ✓ **Is this item the real thing?** Am I sure that I'm selling/buying a genuine item? Do I need an expert to tell me whether it's the real McCoy?

- ✓ **Do I know the value of the merchandise?** Do I have a good understand-ing of what this item's worth in the marketplace at this time, considering its condition?

- ✓ **Is the merchandise worth the price?** Is the risk of selling/buying a counterfeit, a fake, or an item I don't completely understand worth the cost of an appraisal?

If you answer "yes" to any of these questions, consider calling in a profes-sional appraiser.

In the case of *selling* a counterfeit item — otherwise known as a knock-off, phony, or five-finger-discount item, that's a no-brainer: No way. Don't do it.

If you need items appraised, eBay offers links to various appraising agencies:

- ✓ The **PCGS** (Professional Coin Grading Service) serves coin collectors.

- ✓ **PSA/DNA** (a service of Professional Sports Authenticators), authenti-cates your autographs and keeps an online database of thousands of certified autographs for you to compare your purchases against.

- ✓ **PSE** (Professional Stamp Experts) authenticates your postal stamps.

- ✓ **CGC** (Comics Guaranty) grades and restores comic books.

- ✓ **PSA** (Professional Sports Authenticators) helps guard against counter-feiting and fraud with sports memorabilia and trading cards. eBay's teamed up with PSA to grade and authenticate trading cards. PSA offers a 10 percent rebate to eBay members who use its service. The money is credited to your eBay account after the job is done.

To find links to these appraising agencies, click the SafeHarbor (Rules & Safety) link at the bottom of any eBay page. From the Rules & Safety Overview page, follow these steps:

1. **Click the Authentication Services link.**

   You go to the Opinions, Authentication & Grading overview page, where eBay offers good information about third-party appraisers.

2. **Click the link that best suits your authentication purposes.**

   You go to a page that describes how the process works. You also see links to the Web site of the agency you've chosen.

3. **Complete the information the page requests to find a professional appraiser in your area.**

Even if you use an appraiser or an authentication service, do some legwork yourself. Often, two experts can come up with wildly different opinions on the same item. The more that you know, the better are the questions you can ask.

If a seller isn't sure whether the item someone's auctioning is authentic, you may find an appropriate comment (such as *Cannot verify authenticity*) in the auction item description. Knowledgeable eBay gurus always like to share what they know, and we have no doubt that someone can supply you with scads of helpful information. But be careful — some blarney artist (one of *those* is born every minute, too) may try to make a sucker out of you.

Verifying Your ID

During the later years of the Cold War, Ronald Reagan said, "Trust but verify." The President's advice made sense for dealing with the Soviet Union, and it makes good sense with your dealings at eBay, too! (Even if you're not dealing in nuclear warheads.)

Walk the plank, ye scurvy swab!

17-inch high sea pirate sword with leather sheath. 17 inches — wood and brass handle, stainless-steel blade, hand-tooled custom leather sheath. Not for sale to anyone under the age of 18. Shipping is $5.99 CONT U.S. Cashiers Check/Money Order, same day shipping. Personal check, 2 week wait. THANKS FOR LOOKING AND HAPPY BIDDING!!!

The starting price of this "high-sea" sword was $9.99; it didn't sell at eBay. We're not sure, but we think that the words "stainless steel" may have tipped some bidders off that this item wasn't *really* a pirate's sword.

To show other eBay members that you're an honest type, you can buy a "trust but verify" option, known as *ID Verify*, from eBay for five bucks. The giant credit verification service, Equifax, verifies your identity by asking for your *Wallet information*, including the following:

- ✔ Name
- ✔ Address
- ✔ Phone number
- ✔ Social Security number
- ✔ Driver's license information
- ✔ Date of birth

Equifax matches the info you give to what's in its database and presents you with a list of questions from your credit file that only you should know the answer to. Equifax may ask you about any loans you have, for example, or what kinds of credit cards you own (and how many).

Equifax sends only the results of its Identity Test to eBay (whether you pass the test) and *not* the answers to the private financial questions it asks you. Equifax doesn't modify or add the information you provide to any of its databases.

Equifax's questions are meant to protect you against anyone else who may come along and try to steal this information from you and assume your identity. The questions aren't a credit check, and your creditworthiness is never called into question. This info simply verifies that you are who you say you are.

If you pass the test and Equifax can verify that you are who you say you are and not your evil twin (can you say "Mini Me"?), you get a cool icon by your name for a year. If, after a year, you like the validation that comes from such verification, you can pay another fee and renew your seal.

Although you can feel secure knowing that a user who's verified is indeed who he or she claims to be, you still have no guarantee that he or she's not going to turn out to be a no-goodnik (or, for that matter, a well-meaning financial airhead) during auction transactions.

Even if an eBay member gets Equifax verification, what makes this program so controversial is twofold:

- ✔ Many members object to giving out Social Security numbers. They see it as an unwarranted invasion of privacy.
- ✔ Some users also fear that this system creates a two-tiered eBay system, with verified users occupying a sort of upper class and anyone who's not verified stuck in the lower class. They're afraid that sellers may refuse to do business with *un*verified users.

You should consider all of eBay's current and future programs for protecting you from problematic transactions and people, but we think the "undisputed heavyweight champ" for finding out who someone *really is* and keeping you out of trouble is the first program eBay created. That's right, folks, *feedback* can show you other eBay members' track records and give you the best information on whether you want to do business with them or take a pass. Feedback is especially effective if you analyze it in conjunction with eBay's other protection programs. We suggest taking the time to read all about feedback in Chapter 4.

If It's Clearly Fraud

After filing either a fraud report or a Final Value Fee credit request, you can do more on your own. If the deal involves the post office in any way — if you mail a check or the seller sends you merchandise that's completely wrong and refuses to make good — file a mail-fraud complaint with the postal inspector.

In the United States, you can call your local post office or dial 800-275-8777 for a form to fill out. After you complete the form, the USPS sends the eBay bad guy a notice that you've filed a fraud complaint. Perhaps *that* will get his or her attention.

If you're interested in learning about mail-fraud law, go to the following Web site:

```
www.usps.com/websites/depart/inspect/usc18
```

Along with the post office, you can turn to some other agencies for help:

- ✔ **The National Fraud Information Center.** NFIC has an online site devoted to combating fraud on the Internet. NFIC works closely with legal authorities. File a claim at `www.fraud.org/info/repoform.htm` or call toll free at 800-876-7060.

- ✔ **Law enforcement agencies.** Contact the local district attorney or state Attorney General's office and local and state Consumer Affairs Department in the other person's state and city. (Look online for contact information or try your local agencies for contact numbers.)

- ✔ **Federal Trade Commission.** The FTC accepts complaints and investigates repeated cases of fraud. File a claim at `www.ftc.gov/ftc/complaint.htm`.

- ✔ **Internet service provider.** Contact the member's ISP. You can get this bit of info from the person's e-mail address, just after the @ symbol. (See? This easy access to information does have its advantages.) Let the ISP know whom you have filed a complaint against, the nature of the problem, and the agencies that you've contacted.

Any time that you contact another agency for help, keep Rules & Safety up to date on your progress by e-mailing them at safeharbor@ebay.com. And write them at eBay ATTN: Fraud Prevention, 2005 Hamilton Ave., Ste. 350, San Jose, CA 95125.

A very thin line separates alerting other members to a particular person's poor behavior and breaking an eBay cardinal rule by interfering with an auction. Don't make unfounded and/or vitriolic accusations — especially if you were counting on them never to get back to the person they were about (or, for that matter, if you hoped they *would*). Trample the poison out of the gripes of wrath before you have your say. We recommend that you hunt for facts, but don't do any finger-pointing on public message boards or chat rooms. If it turns out that you're wrong, you can be sued for libel.

Communication and compromise are the keys to successful transactions. If you have a difference of opinion, write a polite e-mail outlining your expectations and offer to settle any dispute by phone. See Chapters 7, 11, and 12 for tips on communicating after the auction ends — and solving disputes *before* they turn wicked, aggressive, or unprintable.

Chapter 16

The eBay Community: Playing Nice with Other eBay Members

In This Chapter

▶ Looking at announcements and other important messages

▶ Using eBay message boards

▶ Finding help when you need it

▶ Chatting it up

*e*Bay thinks of itself as more than just an Internet location for buying and selling great stuff. eBay makes clear that it's created (and works hard to maintain) a community. It's not a bad deal actually — prime real estate in *this* community costs only pennies! As in real-life communities, you participate as much as works for you. You can get involved in all sorts of neighborhood activities, or you can just sit back, mind your own business, and watch the world go by. eBay works exactly the same way.

As you've probably heard by now, one of the main ways to participate in the eBay community is through feedback (which we explain in detail in Chapter 6). In this chapter, we show you some other ways to become part of the community. You can socialize, learn from other members, leave messages, or just read what everybody's talking about through eBay's message boards, chat boards, and the corporate Announcements Board. We offer you tips on how to use all these places to your benefit and then give you a change of scenery by surfing through some off-site message boards that can help you with your buying and selling.

Anyone who browses the eBay site can see your User ID and messages on any of the community boards. Make sure that your User ID is different from your e-mail address, and see Chapter 13 for more cyber safety tips.

News and Chat, This and That

It's not quite like *The New York Times* ("All the News That's Fit to Print"), but you can find all the news, chat boards, and message boards links from the Community Overview page. Figure 16-1 shows you what the page looks like.

Here's a list of all the main headings of the main Community page. Each heading offers you links to the following specific eBay areas:

- ✔ News
- ✔ *eBay Insider* (which we cover in Chapter 17)
- ✔ Charity (which we also cover in Chapter 17)
- ✔ eBay Foundation
- ✔ Discussion, Help, & Chat
- ✔ Library (which we cover in Chapter 5)
- ✔ eBay Store (which we cover in Chapter 17)
- ✔ About eBay

Figure 16-1:
The main Community page features links to all the fun places at eBay, including areas to chat and post messages.

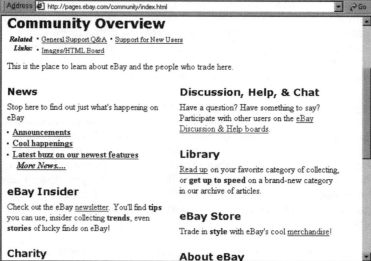

Address 🔲 http://pages.ebay.com/community/index.html

Community Overview

Related Links: • General Support Q&A • Support for New Users
• Images/HTML Board

This is the place to learn about eBay and the people who trade here.

News

Stop here to find out just what's happening on eBay

- Announcements
- Cool happenings
- Latest buzz on our newest features
  More News....

eBay Insider

Check out the eBay newsletter. You'll find **tips** you can use, insider collecting **trends**, even **stories** of lucky finds on eBay!

Charity

Discussion, Help, & Chat

Have a question? Have something to say? Participate with other users on the eBay Discussion & Help boards.

Library

Read up on your favorite category of collecting, or **get up to speed** on a brand-new category in our archive of articles.

eBay Store

Trade in **style** with eBay's cool merchandise!

About eBay

Hear Ye, Hear Ye! eBay's Announcements Board

If you were living in the 1700s, you'd see a strangely dressed guy in a funny hat ringing a bell and yelling, "Hear ye, hear ye!" every time that you opened eBay's Announcements Board. (Then again, if you were living in the 1700s, you'd have no electricity, computers, fast food, or anything else you consider fun.) In any case, eBay's Announcements Board is the most important place to find out what's going on (directly from headquarters) on the Web site. And no one even needs to ring a bell.

Here is where eBay reports outages and critical changes in policies and procedures. eBay also uses this board to update users on glitches in the system and when those may be rectified. eBay also lists any new features and charity work auctions. Figure 16-2 shows you eBay's Announcements Board with information that could affect your auctions.

Make stopping at the Announcements Board a vital part of your eBay routine.

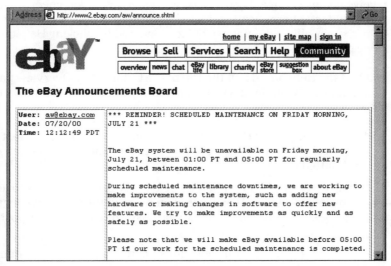

Figure 16-2:
Keep up to date about eBay by checking out the Announcements Board.

Keep your eye out for the outages listing in the Announcements Board to see whether an outage may affect your auctions. Also on this board, you can discover any new procedures and rules that could affect what you're selling.

Whenever eBay introduces new features, explanations or links sometimes appear in Cool Happenings, which is below the Announcements link in the News area of the Community Overview page.

eBay has several million members — a bigger population than some cities — but it can still have that small-town feel through announcement boards, chat boards, and message boards. Start on the main Chat page by clicking Community on the main navigation bar and then click Chat on the subnavigation bar. Now you can access more than four dozen chat boards, support sites, and message boards.

Help! I Need Somebody

If you ever have specific eBay questions to which you need answers, two eBay Customer Support message boards on the main Community page can help you.

In this area you also find a link, Support for New Users, which takes you to an online form that sweeps your question directly to Customer service. You will receive an answer in a day or so, so we recommend you check the boards if you want instant gratification. Most questions can be answered by going to eBay's super-efficient database of facts, located by clicking Help on the main navigation bar.

You find the Help boards on the top of the Community Overview page. Just click Community on the navigation bar and you can see boards on the following topics:

- **General Support Q&A:** To submit a question on a board, post it in the box at the top of the site. eBay staffers edit and post only some of the submitted questions.

   eBay newbies often find that these boards are good places to add to their knowledge of eBay. As you scroll on by, read the Q & A postings from the past; your question may already be answered in an earlier posting.

- **Images/HTML Board:** The third support board in this group is the critical *Images/HTML Board*. Questions posted here are most often answered by other very knowledgeable eBay users who really know how to explain posting a picture (in a lot fewer words than a thousand). You can even ask someone on this board to look at your auction listing and provide an opinion on your picture.

Rating the member help boards

You know you need help, but you don't know which help board is best for you. Here's our take on which boards are most helpful.

✔ **The eBay Q&A:** Good help for newbies from fellow members.

✔ **Images/HTML Board:** Good help from other eBay members for those with specific questions about using HTML.

✔ **Discuss eBay's Newest Features** (known as DNF): Many of the folks who use this board

are devoted to protesting eBay's policies and new features. Brace yourself a bit — conversation on this board can become nasty at times. However, many of the regulars on this board are extremely knowledgeable about eBay.

You can access a new board from any other board by scrolling down the drop-down list at the top of each Board page.

Community Discussion and Help Boards

Because eBay's Customer Service people get bombarded with a gazillion questions a day, they're sometimes frustratingly slow if you need an answer right away. You may get a faster answer by posting your question on one of the Community message boards.

Knowledgeable veteran eBay members generally answer posted questions as best as they can. The answers are the opinions of members and are certainly not eBay gospel. But you get a fast and honest answer; often you get more than one response. Most questions are answered in about 15 minutes. If not, repost your question. Make sure that you post your question on the appropriate board, because each board has a specific topic of discussion.

Members who post on these boards often share helpful tips and Web sites and alert other members to scams. Newbies may find *lurking* (reading without posting) on some of these boards helpful to learn more about how eBay works. Occasionally, an eBay staffer shows up, which is kinda like inviting Bill Gates to a Windows 98 new users' meeting. eBay staff members are usually hounded with questions.

You can always tell if an eBay staff member is on a board because the top border line is in pink (not gray, as with regular users). They've earned the nickname "Pinks" on the boards.

If a new policy or some sort of big change occurs, the boards are most likely going to quickly fill with discussion about it. On slow days, however, you may need to wade through personal messages and "chat" with no connection to eBay. Many of the people who post on these boards are long-time members

> ## Stone egg fossils — no reserve
>
> Fossil Egg with fossilized worms and crynoids.   Starting price was $5; sold at eBay for $11.01.
> This egg will look special anywhere (. . . except
> maybe in a frying pan).

with histories (as well as feuds) that can rival any soap opera. On rare occasion, the postings can get rather abusive. Getting involved in personality clashes or verbal warfare gains nothing.

No matter how peeved the users of a chat room or message board may get — and no matter how foul or raunchy the language may get — no one at eBay ever sees it. eBay uses a built-in "vulgarity checker" that deletes any (well, okay, *as many as possible*) words or phrases that eBay considers offensive or obscene.

One cardinal rule for eBay chat boards and message boards exists: no business. No advertising items for sale! Not now. Not ever. eBay bans repeat offenders who break this rule from participating on these boards.

Remember that you're visiting eBay and that you're a member. It's not Speakers' Corner, that London park where protesters are free to stand on a soapbox and scream about the rats in government. If you feel the need to viciously complain about eBay, take it outside, as the bar bouncers say. See our suggestions in the sidebar, "Going off-site to chat" later in this chapter. Better yet, click the Suggestion link on the Community Home page!

User-to-User Discussion Boards

eBay has three other boards that take a different tack on things. They're *discussion* boards as opposed to *chat* boards, which basically means that the topics are deliberately open-ended — just as the topics of discussions in coffee houses tend to vary depending on who happens to be in them at any given time. Check out these areas and read ongoing discussions about eBay's latest buzz. It's a lot of fun, and good reading. Post your opinions to the category that suits you. Each discussion board carries as many topics as you can imagine.

   ✔ **The eBay Town Square** is a potpourri of various subjects and topics.

   ✔ **The Soapbox** is the place to voice your views and suggestions to help build a better eBay.

   ✔ **Current Issues** discusses eBay and online auction industry news and current events.

Other Message Boards

About a dozen message boards at eBay specialize in everything from pure chat to charity work. The following sections describe these boards.

Café society

The eBay Café (eBay's first message board from back when they were just selling Pez candy dispensers) and AOL Café message boards attract mostly regulars chatting about eBay gossip. Frequent postings include the sharing of personal milestones and whatever else is on people's minds. You can also find useful information about eBay and warnings about potential scams here.

Wanted Board

One of the coolest things about eBay is how many people actually find and buy that one whatchamacallit-thingamabob-doohickey they had as a kid. If a constant search of auction sites can't help you, post a "wanted" on the Wanted Board. (But try to remember the item's real name!)

Coca-Cola soda-jerk hat from the early '60s

Soda Jerk hat from the early 1960s. The hat is adjustable to fit any size head. The Coca-Cola theme during this era was "Things go better with Coke." This hat was never worn and condition is near mint. Buyer pays S&H.

Starting price was $8; the item did not sell at eBay. Maybe everybody already had logo sweatshirts from the cola wars.

Holiday Board

Although eBay suggests that this is the place to share your favorite holiday memories and thoughts, it's really a friendly place where people meet and chat about home and family. Stop by for cyber milk and cookies next time you've got a few minutes and want to visit with your fellow auction addicts.

Giving Board

eBay isn't only about making money. On the Giving Board, it's also about making a difference. Members in need post their stories and requests for assistance. Other members with items to donate post offers for everything from school supplies to clothing on this board.

If you feel like doing a good deed, conduct a member benefit auction. You link your auction to the Giving Board so that the proceeds of that auction go to someone in need. For information on starting a member benefit auction, go to www.givingboard.com.

Emergency Contact Board

It's no *Rescue 911,* but if your computer crashes and you lose all your info, this board is the place to put out an all-points bulletin for help. If your ISP goes on vacation, your phone line is on the fritz, or you're abducted by aliens and can't connect to your buyers or sellers, use a friend's computer to post a message on the Emergency Contact Board. There's a dedicated group of eBay users who frequent this board; they will try to help you by passing on your e-mails to the intended parties. Talk about a bunch of *givers*!

Recently, a bidder posted saying that her computer had crashed *and* that she was in the process of moving. She asked her sellers to be patient and she would get to them as soon as possible. The friendly regulars of the Emergency Contact Board looked up her bidding history and e-mailed the sellers whose auctions she'd won in the last week. Then they forwarded her the e-mails they'd sent on her behalf. The sellers understood the situation and did not leave negative feedback for the user for lack of communication.

If you're having trouble contacting another eBay member, posting for help from other members to track 'em down often gets the job done.

If you think you may be the victim of a rip-off, check the Emergency Contact Board. The buyer or seller may have left word about an e-mail problem. On the flip side, you may find out that you're not alone in trying to track down an eBay delinquent who seems to have skipped town. Posting information about a potentially bad eBay guy is at least bad manners on most boards. If you wrap it in the guise of an emergency contact, however, you can clue in other members about a potential problem. Figure 16-3 shows some of the postings that you find on the Emergency Contact Board.

To access the Emergency Contact Board, follow these steps:

1. **From the eBay Home page, click the Community link.**

   A subnavigation bar appears.

2. **Click the Chat link.**

   You are now on the main Chat page.

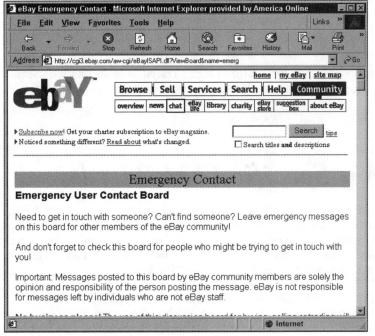

Figure 16-3:
Posting
messages
on the
Emergency
Contact
Board
usually gets
fast results
from other
eBay
members
willing to
help.

3. **Scroll down the Chat page and click Emergency Contact.**

   You see a message board full of messages from all the desperate sellers and buyers trying to locate each other. It's really quite touching, isn't it?

If you like to keep your Chit-Chat in a box . . .

An old 12-terminal Chit-Chat box from the 1920s in pristine condition. This box was found along with many other items in the attic of an old upstate office building that was being gutted.

The wood has a beautiful finish and the brass a satisfying patina.

Starting price was $29; sold at eBay for $92.

eBay International Boards

People from all around the world enjoy eBay. If you're considering buying or selling globally, visit the International Boards. It's a great place to post questions about shipping and payments for overseas transactions. Along with eBay chat, the International Boards turn up discussions about current events and international politics.

Got a seller in Italy? Spain? France? Translate your English messages into the appropriate language through the following Web site:

```
babelfish.altavista.digital.com
```

Category-Specific Chat Boards

Want to talk about Elvis, Louis XV, Sammy Sosa, or Howard the Duck? Currently about two dozen category-specific chat boards enable you to tell eBay members what's on your mind about merchandise and auctions. You reach these boards by clicking Community on the main navigation bar and then clicking Chat on the subnavigation bar.

Of course, you can buy and sell without ever going on a chat board, but you can certainly learn a lot from one. Discussions mainly focus on merchandise and the nuts and bolts of transactions. Category-specific chat boards are great for posting questions on items that you don't know much about.

At eBay, you get all kinds of responses from all kinds of people. Take some of the help you get with a grain of salt, because some of the folks who help you may be buyers or competitors.

Going off-site to chat

As you may guess, eBay is chock-full of information about, well, eBay. Sometimes, however, going outside to get other views of the Web site (or online auctions in general) is helpful. We suggest that you visit a terrific Web site called AuctionWatch (www.auctionwatch.com). One of the benefits of AuctionWatch is an image-hosting service, which we discuss in Chapter 13.

AuctionWatch's message center is a terrific place to hear from eBay gadflies — the folks who love to use eBay but hate some of its policies. They feel freer to speak their minds because they're not on eBay's home turf. Those who post here take eBay seriously. This site is not the place for questions that are easily answered on eBay message boards. A few eBay cheerleaders hang around, but you can find lots of solid information and even a few conspiracy theories.

Visit AuctionWatch and speak your mind. To find specific information about eBay on the AuctionWatch site, click the Message Center link on the site's navigation bar. Scroll down the Message Center page that appears and click The eBay Outlook link. When you arrive in The eBay Outlook, you will find a slew of topics to voice your opinion on.

These boards are also great for finding out where to go for more research and information on specific items. You can also find helpful sources for shipping information about items in that category (such as large furniture in the Antiques section or breakable items on the Glass chat board).

Don't be shy. As your second-grade teacher said, "No questions are dumb." Most eBay members love to share their knowledge of items.

Chapter 17

Charities and Special Features

● ●

In This Chapter

▶ Bidding for a good cause

▶ Using eBay's member specials

▶ Buying souvenirs at the eBay store

▶ Getting your own personal cyber-shopper

● ●

*O*ver and over, eBay members show what big hearts they have. Yes, you actually can pocket some nice-sized profits from selling at the eBay Web site, but (just as in real life) people usually take the time to give a little back for worthy causes. But because we're talking about eBay, giving back means getting something fabulous in return.

In this chapter, we not only tell you about the terrific charity auctions, we show you how eBay members can get great inside deals from manufacturers; and we open the door of the eBay store where you can get stuff with the official logo on it.

Truly Righteous Stuff for Charity

Most of us have donated to charity in one form or another. But here at eBay, charities really rock. Do you need a *Jurassic Park* helmet signed by Steven Spielberg to round out your collection (and deflect the odd dino tooth)? Post a bid on Rosie O'Donnell's charity site. How about a signed original photograph of Jerry Seinfeld from *People* magazine? Yup, you can get that, too. All these and more have turned up in charity auctions. In short, having a big heart for charities has gotten a whole lot easier — thanks to eBay.

Rosie's For All Kids Foundation

Rosie O'Donnell took TV by storm with her popular talk show, and now she's putting her high visibility to good use with her For All Kids Foundation. The foundation awards grants to help support disadvantaged kids throughout the country. In the past, Rosie's donated profits from books, a Rosie O'Donnell doll, and other projects to For All Kids. Now she's joined forces with eBay and is running auctions, with all proceeds going to her foundation.

To get to Rosie's For All Kids auctions, just click Rosie's own link on the Home page under the Don't Miss headline. Bid as you would on regular auctions. (We explain bidding in detail in Chapters 6 and 7.)

Here's a sampling of some of the neat items Rosie put up for auction, along with their selling prices:

- ✔ *Ally McBeal* pilot script, signed by the cast ($6,100).
- ✔ Movie poster of *The Graduate*, signed by Dustin Hoffman ($1,150).
- ✔ A shirt signed by Rosie and Bill Cosby ($565).
- ✔ Princess Leia action figures signed by Carrie Fisher ($205).

You can catch up with current auctions by doing a Seller Search using Rosie's User ID: **4allkids**. (See Chapter 5 for details on searches.)

Other charity auctions

New charities are popping up all the time at eBay. To see what temporary auctions they're running, go to the Charity page. To get there, start at eBay's Home page and click the Charity link, just below Rosie under the Don't Miss link or go to the Community page and click the Charity Auctions at eBay link there. Among some of the recent charity auctions held at eBay are the following:

- ✔ A March of Dimes auction of limited edition, signed Mattel toys. We participated in this auction and won a few items for this wonderful cause.
- ✔ A *People* magazine auction that offered signed and limited-edition celebrity photographs. The proceeds of this auction went to the Until There's A Cure Foundation. The foundation's goal is to help raise millions of dollars to fund HIV/AIDS youth education programs, scientific research, and care services for those who have the disease.
- ✔ An auction from the folks at MTV, which in keeping with its irreverent tone was called MTV Cool Crap. If the name implies silliness, the cause was dead serious. MTV donated all of the proceeds of the auction to Take A Stand Against Violence — a charity whose mission is to educate

the public about violence in our society. The Cool Crap auction featured all kinds of fun stuff, from supermodels' bathing suits (one size fits none), to all kinds of sports and music memorabilia.

✔ Athletes Direct is a company that runs eBay auctions of major sports stars memorabilia, such as game-worn uniforms. Each athlete who puts an item up for auction donates the sum of the item's selling price to a charity of his or her choice. When we last checked in, Karl Malone, Dennis Rodman, and Chris Webber had all donated clothing and signed items. Click Charity on the Home page and then click the Athletes Direct link for more information on current auctions. *Note:* The Athletes Direct link disappears regularly, just to keep you on your toes. Actually, it appears when an Athletes Direct auction is running — about once a month.

If you go to the About Me pages, by clicking on the link from the Charity page, of any of the charities in the preceding list, you can find out exactly where the money that eBay users bid goes. You can also get to the Charities auctions by going to `pages.ebay.com/charity`.

Charity isn't just for the big guys. Individual users can also run charity auctions. For rules and regulations, click Community on the main navigation bar and then click Charity on the subnavigation bar. eBay doesn't authorize or verify individual charities; however, 80 percent of the final selling price of an item in a charity auction *must* go to charity.

And Now for Our Feature Presentation

As an eBay member, you're entitled to some features offered on the Web site. The perks aren't quite as high-end as you may receive with, say, a country club membership, but hey — your membership dues are a lot less! With about 15.8 million registered users, eBay can get outside companies and manufacturers to listen up to what it has to say. You know the old saying about power in numbers? At eBay, you find "savings in numbers" on items or services that you can buy outside the Web site.

The following sections explain some of the savings and other services you can find at eBay.

Member specials

As eBay gains popularity, more and more outside companies are offering special deals exclusively for members. These deals aren't auctions but are conventional "pay the price and get the item or services" transactions.

To find the member specials, start at eBay's Home page and click the Spotlight's On link. Click the eBay Power Trading link, and you're there. You may also find these specials under Seller Services.

The special deals change all the time, but here's a small sampling of things available to you:

- ✔ **E-stamp:** E-stamp offers exclusive discounts on their starter kits for eBay members. There's also a new flat monthly postage plan — print all the postage you want for $9.95 a month!

- ✔ **eBay Anywhere Wireless:** Enables you to reach eBay with your web enabled cellular phone, eBay-a-go-go paging service, or on your Palm wireless connected organizer.

- ✔ **eBay Online Payments by Billpoint:** Online payments integrated directly into your eBay auctions.

- ✔ **Keen.com:** Get live answers to your urgent questions from eBay experts.

- ✔ **Authentication services:** Get a special discount (usually 10 percent) if you authenticate coins through Professional Coin Grading Service (PCGS) or trading cards through Professional Sports Authenticator (PSA). See Chapter 15 for tips on authenticating your items.

As time passes, you'll see additional benefits and programs eBay creates for the community. The folks at eBay are aggressively searching out new and helpful affiliations to help you take care of your auction business. But don't leave the task of maintaining your auctions entirely to eBay — take it upon yourself to find new ways to make your auctions easier.

A succesful seller takes advantage of every program and service he or she can. The less time you spend tied to your computer, the more time you have to plan new auctions and find new items to sell. Investigate these programs and try them out for yourself.

Who's minding the eBay store?

eBay's minding the eBay store, of course (and freshening up its window-dressing from time to time). If you can't find the perfect item for your favorite eBay member with more than two million auctions running at any given time, go browse around the eBay store. You don't find any auctions here — just eBay logo items, such as shirts, bags, coffee mugs, and even an eBay clock. (We don't know whether it can help you become a better sniper!)

To get to eBay's online store, start at the Home page. Scroll down to the very bottom and click the eBay Store link.

Just pick and choose what you like, add it to your shopping cart, and then check out when you're done. They ask you for specific billing information, so keep your credit card handy.

Personal Shopper

If you're too busy to explore the nooks and crannies of eBay on your own (or you're the type who wants to cut to the chase), sign up for eBay's Personal Shopper.

We think that this service is one of eBay's better ideas. Personal Shopper enables you to find what you're looking for *and* have a life, because it sifts through the new listings for you, 24 hours a day, looking for the items that meet your personalized description. Sniffs 'em out like a bloodhound. Then Personal Shopper sends you an e-mail containing a list of items that you may want to bid on, complete with links that take you right to them. Hey, best of all — it's free!

To register for the Personal Shopper, begin on the navigation bar at the top of most eBay pages and follow these steps:

1. **Click Search on the navigation bar.**

   The subnavigation bar appears.

2. **Click the Personal Shopper link.**

   You go to the Personal Shopper page.

3. **If you haven't signed in, you'll have to type your User ID and password in the appropriate text boxes and click the Submit button.**

   You're now at the Personal Shopper Existing Searches page.

4. **Click the Add a New Search button.**

   This action takes you to the Add a New Search information page.

5. **Complete the following information:**

   • **Search:** Type the title of the item that interests you and select the Search Item Title and Description option.

   Searching item descriptions adds to the possibility of finding exactly what you're looking for.

   • **Price Range:** Enter the dollar amount (range) you're willing to spend.

   If you leave this blank, Personal Shopper searches all price ranges.

- **e-mail Frequency:** Select how often you want to receive notification about new items that Personal Shopper finds for you.

- **e-mail Duration:** Select how long you want Personal Shopper to search for this specific item. The longer you choose, the better are your chances of coming across the item you're looking for.

6. **After completing the page, click one of the following buttons:**

- **Preview:** You see a description of your actual search, along with current search results, based on the criteria you specified. If you're happy with the results, click the Save button, and your Personal Shopper begins hunting for your item.

- **Undo:** Deletes the information you entered in the search description line.

- **View:** You see an itemized list of searches that are currently active for your Personal Shopper search.

The sincerest form of flattery

They say imitation is the greatest form of flattery, or maybe it's just really good e-commerce sense, but another company, Price Radar, is now competing with eBay's Personal Shopper. Price Radar recently started its own version of the service, offering even more features than eBay.

In addition to searching eBay, PriceRadar also searches Yahoo! Auctions, Amazon Auctions, and more than 40 additional auction sites. PriceRadar then notifies you if the item you're searching for comes up. The Find & Notify service contacts you via ICQ, e-mail, or a Web-enabled telephone. The company also provides amazing price guides that statistically show how many units of any particular item sell and how much they sell for on the various sites. This tool is great to use in pricing your own items for sale — or just for figuring out whether you've got a bargain. Best of all, these services are free. You can find the PriceRadar site at the following URL: www.priceRadar.com.

Part V
The Part of Tens

The 5th Wave   By Rich Tennant

"Oh sure, it'll float alright, but I want to check your feedback rating before you place a bid."

In this part . . .

In keeping with a long tradition, we give you the short version in this part. Check here for the golden rules every eBay user needs to know, whether you buy or sell (or, like most eBay members, do both).

We also give you information on some of the best third-party software programs available to help simplify your auction experience — from creating a catchy auction item page to helping you snipe the final bid while you're sleeping, walking Fido, washing your hair, or otherwise occupied. The best thing about some of these programs is that the price is right — you can get started for free.

Appendix A gives you the technological lowdown, telling you everything you need to soup up your computer so that you can buy low and sell high. And Appendix B gives you eBay fanatics exactly what you've been looking for — tips to help you acquire stock and take your auction habit to the next level by thinking strategically.

Chapter 18

Ten (Or So) Golden Rules for eBay Buyers and Sellers

• •

In This Chapter

▶ Investigating your treasure

▶ Checking feedback

▶ Understanding charges and payment methods

▶ Researching an item's value

▶ Covering your assets

▶ Being a buyer's dream

▶ Keeping current, keeping cool

• •

*N*o matter how much experience an airplane pilot may have, he always keeps a checklist to go over. The same is true at eBay (although the only crashing that you need to worry about is on your computer). No matter how many times you buy, the advice in this chapter can help you survive and thrive at eBay.

While conducting business at eBay is relatively smooth overall, any venture is bound to have a few bumps here and there. Here are ten (or so) easy, important Golden Rules for eBay buyers and sellers. We've noted which tips are geared toward buyers or sellers. Happy hunting and gathering!

Buyer: Investigate Your Treasure before You Buy

In the excitement of finding just what you want, you may develop a tendency to leap before you look. Even if the item is closing soon, carefully read the item description. Does the item have any flaws? Can you live with it? Is something missing from the description that should be there? Did you read the terms of payment and shipping?

You can also communicate with the seller of the item you're longing for. Don't be too shy or embarrassed. If you have any questions, send an e-mail! You're better off covering your bases before you place a bid than facing disappointment after making a purchase. Make sure that parts are original and check for a warranty or return policy. Clarify everything up front. If the seller doesn't answer back, consider that nonresponse an early warning that dealing with this person may be a mistake!

Buyer: Check the Seller's Feedback

Never bid without checking the seller's feedback. You need to be able to trust the person you're buying from. Checking some of the seller's other auctions, past and present, to get an idea of the seller's history also can't hurt. As badly as you may want something, sending money to someone with a high feedback rating but who recently got a bunch of negatives could be risky business.

Buyer: Understand Post-Auction Charges and Payment Methods

Before you bid on an item, make sure that you and the seller agree on shipping and handling, insurance, and escrow fees. Buying a $10 item and finding out that shipping and handling are going to cost more than your closing bid is a real bummer. You can figure out shipping costs yourself by using online rate calculators (see Chapter 11). Don't forget to ask about any "handling charges." Many sellers don't want the added hassle of an escrow service; make sure that they're agreeable if you want to use that option.

Also, make sure that you and the seller can agree on the form of payment before the deal closes. Is the seller willing to accept a personal check? Are you willing to wait to receive your purchase until a check clears? Is credit card payment available? Is the seller using a secure method of accepting credit cards?

Buyer: Check the Item Price Tag and Bid Wisely

Before you bid, make sure that you have some knowledge of the item, even if you limit your search to completed auctions to get an idea of how much the item went for in the past. If a deal sounds too good to be true, it may well be.

We love eBay! — but not for every single thing that we buy. Make sure that you can't get the item cheaper at the store or from an online seller.

Beware getting caught up in the frenzy of last-minute bidding: It's an easy thing to do. Whether you choose proxy bidding or sniping (see Chapter 7 for our discussion on sniping), decide how much you're willing to pay before bidding. If you set a limit, you aren't overcome with the urge to spend more than an item's worth — or, worse, more than you have in your bank account.

Although eBay is lots of fun, it's also serious business. Bidding is a legal and binding contract. Don't get a bad reputation by retracting bids or becoming a deadbeat.

Buyer: Be a Good Buyer Bee

Always leave feedback after you put the finishing touches on a transaction. Leaving feedback, and thereby helping other members, is your responsibility.

Remember your manners, too, when sending off your payment. You like to be paid on time, right? And, speaking practically, the sooner you send in the dough, the sooner you get your stuff.

Buyer: Cover Your Assets

Remember — just because you're conducting transactions from the privacy of your own home doesn't mean that you're doing everything you can to protect your privacy. Legitimate buyers and sellers never need to know your password or Social Security number. If anyone does ask, contact eBay's SafeHarbor, safeharbor@eBay.com, to report the person. You can also post your concerns on one of the eBay chat boards.

To fight back against computer viruses — which can spread through e-mail attachments and ruin your day, your auction, and maybe your computer — purchase a good antivirus software program and update it often. McAfee VirusScan (at www.mcafee.com) and Symantec's Norton AntiVirus (at www.nortonutilities.com) are both excellent antivirus programs, and Norton boasts international Web pages if you live outside the United States.

Seller: Know Your Stuff

Do some homework. Know the value of your item. At the very least, get an idea of your item's value by searching completed auctions of similar items. Knowing your product also means that you can accurately describe what you have and never, ever pass off a fake as the real McCoy. Make sure that your item isn't prohibited, illegal, questionable, or infringing. It's your responsibility!

Before posting your auction, you should take the following actions:

✔ Establish what kinds of payment you're willing to accept.

✔ Set your check-holding policy (usually seven to ten days).

✔ Spell out your shipping and handling charges.

Add each of the preceding pieces of info to your item's description to avoid any unnecessary disputes later on.

Seller: Polish and Shine

Make sure that your title is descriptive enough to catch the eye of someone browsing a category and detailed enough for eBay's search engine to identify. Don't just write *1960s Board Game*. Instead, give some details: *Tiny Tim Vintage '60s Board Game MIB*. That gets 'em tiptoeing to your auction.

Also, play editor and scrutinize your text for grammar mistakes and misspellings. Typos — in either your title or description — can cost you money. For example, a search engine will keep skipping over your *Miky Mouce Cokie Jare*. Spelling counts — and pays. Double-check your work!

Seller: Picture-Perfect Facts

Photos can be a boon or a bust at eBay. Double-check the photo of your item before you post it. Is the lighting okay? Does the photo paint a flattering image of the item? Crop out unnecessary backgrounds. Would *you* buy this item?

Make sure that your image actually appears on your auction page (and that it's not lost in Cyberspace) and that it doesn't take too long to download. And just because you add an image doesn't mean that you can ignore a detailed item description.

Be factual and honest, too. At eBay, all you have is your reputation, so don't jeopardize it by lying about your item or your terms. Tell potential buyers about any flaws. Give as complete a description as possible with all the facts that you can include about the item.

Seller: Communication Is Key

Respond quickly and honestly to all questions and use the contact to establish a good relationship. If a bidder makes a reasonable request about payment or shipping, going along with that request is usually worth it to make a sale. *Remember:* The customer is always right! (Well, some of the time, anyway.)

Also, be upfront and fair when charging for sending merchandise to your buyer. You don't make a fortune overcharging for shipping and handling. The buyer sees after the item arrives what it cost to ship. Unreasonable charges inevitably lead to bad feelings and negative feedback.

Seller: Be a Buyer's Dream

Just because you're transacting through the computer doesn't mean that you must lose your manners. Live by the golden rule: Do unto others as you would have others do unto you. Contact the buyer within three business days. And keep all your correspondence polite.

Ship the goods as soon as you can (in accordance with the shipping terms you outline in the item description, of course). An e-mail stating that the item is on its way is always a nice touch, too. That way, buyers can eagerly anticipate the arrival of their goods.

And, when shipping your items, use good packing materials and sturdy boxes to prevent disaster. Broken or damaged items can lead to reputation-damaging, negative feedback. Pack as if someone's out to destroy your package (or as if *you* had made this purchase). Your buyers are sure to appreciate the effort.

Seller: Listen to the Music

As we state in our golden rules for buyers, don't underestimate the power of positive feedback. Your reputation is at stake. Always generously dole out feedback when you complete a transaction. Your buyers will appreciate it and should, in turn, return the favor.

If you get slammed with negative feedback, don't retaliate. *Do*, however, add a response to your own feedback, explaining your side of the story.

What should you do if you get negative feedback? Don't freak out! Don't retaliate. Do, however, post a response to the feedback by using the Respond to Feedback link on your My eBay page. Those who read your feedback can often see past a single disgruntled message.

Buyers and Sellers: Keep Current, Keep Cool

You'd be surprised at the number of users who get suspended even though they have automatic credit card payment. Maybe they move. Or they change Internet service providers. Regardless, if you don't update your contact and credit card information, and eBay and other users can't contact you as a result, you can be suspended.

If you have any major moves (home address, billing address, ISP provider), let eBay know this new contact information. As soon as you know your new credit card number, your mailing address, e-mail address, or contact phone number, click Services on the main navigation bar. Scroll down to My eBay and update the appropriate information.

Keep these buyer and seller Golden Rules at the heart of all your dealings at eBay. After a while, posting auctions and bidding becomes rote. You can all too easily forget the basics, so look at this chapter every now and again and remember that, as an eBay member, you're part of a very special person-to-person community.

Chapter 19

Ten (Or So) Programs and Services to Ease Your Way on eBay

● ●

In This Chapter

▶ AuctionWatch

▶ AuctionWorks

▶ ManageAuctions

▶ PriceRadar

▶ AuctionAssistant Classic

▶ ePoster2000

▶ Auction Wizard

▶ TurboBid

▶ Virtual Auction Ad Pro

▶ eBay's Software and Services

● ●

Ready to take your auctions to the next level? Are you looking for cool text or fancy layouts to make your auctions scream out, "Buy me!"? Need to slip in a bid in the middle of the night without losing sleep? If so, here's a list of ten (or so) software programs and services to make your bidding life easy and help put your auctions ahead of the pack.

As online auctions grow in popularity, software developers are constantly upgrading and developing new auction software to meet eBay's changes. Many of these programs even look for new versions of themselves — and update themselves as you start them. (Aladdin never had things so good.)

I list several auction-management Web sites in the following sections. Each has its own distinct, different personality. Whenever you've got the time, go over each one and see whether it suits your style. You may just decide that you'd rather handle things on your own — and that's okay, too! You can always just use a site's image hosting or counters; they don't all require that you use all their features.

I also provide you the names and descriptions of some great offline software programs you can use to help you manage your auctions, make your e-auctions elegant and eye-catching, find the best prices, and snatch up that bargain at the last minute.

Online Services

Since you're comfortable transacting your auctions online, why not manage them online as well? These sites offer incredibly useful services, that save time in both posting your auctions and wrapping them up.

AuctionWatch.com

AuctionWatch.com began as a great place to exchange ideas and information among a community of online auction users. It now has a mega site, which many eBay users visit often, that includes online auction management, daily news and features about the auction industry, an appraisal gallery to gather information on your items, and what's still one of the most active message boards in the online community. You can use the site's image hosting and counters even if you don't use the management services. AuctionWatch.com also offers the following services for buyers and sellers:

- ✔ **Seller Services:** Auction Manager Pro Bulk upload software is free software that enables you to input your auctions offline and send them in a batch to eBay. It has the ability to launch your auctions from their site, and your listings automatically integrate into the AuctionWatch online Auction Manager. The online Auction Manager can launch auctions, track the progress of your auctions, provide inventory management, host images, place counters, and manage shipping, payment, and insurance.

- ✔ **Buyer Services:** AuctionWatch provides universal search for items across multiple auction sites, and with a single click, the auction you want to bid in opens in a new window. You may also use the online Auction Manager to retrieve information on current auctions and track your bids and coordinate your payments.

Most of all, visiting this site is fun. It offers so much to see and visit. Check it out at the following Web address:

```
www.auctionwatch.com
```

AuctionWorks

"Power Tools for Power Sellers" proclaims the AuctionWorks home page, and indeed, that's just what the site delivers. It offers a complete answer for the professional seller. By using the downloadable software that integrates with this secure site, sellers can manage inventory, images, customers, financial data, and post-auction tasks. If you're not yet a Power Seller at eBay, however, don't shy away from the site. It's a professional and automated way to handle your auctions that may help you eventually become a Power Seller — it even provides live online help 24 hours a day. Among its services for sellers and buyers you find the following:

- **For Sellers:** AuctionWorks has an easy-to-use inventory-management system that enables you to post your items in your own area on the site and list them at eBay whenever you want. You use Traction, an AuctionWorks utility, for tracking functions relating to the selling or bidding process. It also tracks notifications, payments, shipments, and feedback — all of which the system automates to save you time. AuctionWorks also maintains an affiliation with the eBay Online Payments by Billpoint system and PayPal to facilitate auction payments and offer professionally designed description templates, image hosting, and a wide variety of counters. All sellers can get a storefront, too — your very own e-commerce site.

    Note: Image hosting, counters, and other services are free. AuctionWorks charges a two percent commission on auctions that you launch through the site (with a 75 cent maximum), as well as a flat two-percent fee on any sales that you generate through the storefronts.

- **For Bidders:** AuctionWorks offers a handy utility — ClickBid — that enables you to automatically increase a bid by one increment on auctions where you're outbid. The Traction utility also automatically helps bidders track payments, shipments, and feedback online. The site has also licensed "Ask The Appraiser" from CollectingChannel.com, which enables users to get a professional appraisal on an item.

Make sure that you check out what's new on this Web site; visit it at the following URL:

```
www.auctionworks.com
```

ManageAuctions

How you manage your auctions is a very personal choice. ManageAuctions provides complete, free auction-management services, as well as easy-upload image hosting and the most intensive counters available. You not only can determine how many people view your auctions, but also when they view them.

You don't need to post your auctions through the site, although it offers a patent-pending process for bulk launching at eBay. ManageAuctions can also retrieve your existing auctions from eBay and perform its services from any point in the auction's progress.

The following list describes a few of the site's other services:

- ✔ Payment services through the eBay Online Payments by Billpoint
- ✔ E-mail management, and label and postage printing through its partner stamps.com for after-the-auction shipping
- ✔ Bulk feedback posting

Check out the site's services at the following Web address:

```
www.manageauctions.com
```

PriceRadar

PriceRadar is predominantly a buyers' site, and was designed to help you get the best deal that you can. It's a full-featured shopping site that helps you search, research, and evaluate your item instantly. It also tracks deals and notifies you as new items come up for auction. If you have a Web-enabled cell phone, PriceRadar can notify you through your phone; or, PriceRadar can notify you through e-mail.

The site has its own search engine, PinPoint, which searches for your item across many auction sites in seconds. Its Price Guides enable you to know how much the item has sold for in the past so that you can see in a flash whether a deal is a good one or not. You also find a lot of current information on what's hot . . . and what's not.

PriceRadar gives you all the tools to make sensible buying decisions. Visit the site at the following URL:

```
www.priceradar.com
```

NetMechanic

This site boasts, "Power Tools for Your Web Site," and provides an absolute arsenal of tools to help you make your Web site elegant and efficient. Many of these tools are free and you can apply them to your eBay auctions. The following list describes two of the tools that the site offers you:

✔ **GifBot:** Just input the URL of your image for eBay, and the GifBot compresses the size of the image to make it load quicker online. The free GifBot enables you to compare the before and after versions of the image so that you can select the image that best fits your needs before you make any changes to it.

✔ **HTML Toolbox:** This tool checks the HTML on your Web site and alerts you to any problems such as long loading times, misspellings, broken links, and more. You can fix all common errors with just one click.

Many other Web utilities are available on the site, some free and some for a minimal charge. Check the site out at the following URL:

```
www.netmechanic.com
```

Software for Offline Use

Software for offline use can handily reside on your computer after a simple download from a Web site. As with online services, this software comes in a variety of flavors, so take a look and decide which works best for you. Downloadable software may be available from Web sites that offer other services, and can be used whether you are online or not. Offline software makes the drudgery of handling auctions one that you can incorporate into your spare time, without limitations of ISPs or servers.

AuctionAssistant Classic

AuctionAssistant Classic helps you design your auction-item pages, upload your images, fill in forms automatically, place your auctions, and track them at eBay. Its management forms keep you up-to-date on the progress of your transactions with the help of its Auto Fetch feature, downloading auction info directly from eBay. It became part of eBay in late 1999. Following are some of its other talents:

✔ The Ad Studio enables you to design your own auction with interesting typefaces, sizes, and colors. You can use the predesigned themes to customize the look of your auctions with decorative graphics, animation, backgrounds, and music files!

✔ An internal FTP (File Transfer Protocol) program enables you to get your images onto your server.

✔ After the auction, the program creates custom e-mails to send to winners.

✔ After you finish with your transactions, you can use the software to place feedback at the click of a button.

Download a free trial version of AuctionAssistant Classic (which is fully operational, minus a few features) at the following Web site:

```
www.blackthornesw.com
```

ePoster2000

ePoster2000 has become an integral part of the growing Auctiva.com website. It's a downloadable software that can ease your auction posting. Enter your profile information once, and you're on your way to simplifying posting eBay auctions. ePoster2000 enables you to perform the following actions:

- ✔ Automatically create your HTML for your auction description offline, check your spelling, insert your photo, fill in the default information on eBay's forms, and with one click, preview and post your auctions.

- ✔ Put a free counter in your ad without cutting and pasting code.

- ✔ Save auctions so that you can post them again at any time.

- ✔ Store your photos on their site (for a per-photo fee) if you don't have an FTP site.

Service options range from $6.95 for one month to $29.95 for a year. Download and try the software for free; you receive a 30-day posting pass and 20 tokens, which you can use for future postings, and free image hosting or counters. You find it at the following Web address:

```
www.auctiva.com
```

Auction Wizard

Auction Wizard is a full-service professional auction-management software package, developed by eBay sellers. The software is fairly simple and amazingly powerful. It expedites all the seller functions for running and completing auctions, including automating the following tasks:

- ✔ Inputting your inventory on the software's HTML templates and uploading auctions in bulk onto eBay.

- ✔ Automatically updating the software with the current status of your auctions, including who won, who is a runner-up, and auction bidding history. The preformatted e-mail and feedback files automatically fill in the values from each auction and send them to the people you do business with directly through the software.

- ✔ Tracking income and expenses, as well as creating a full set of reports.

We can't say enough about the importance of record keeping, and this program enables you to track your inventory and keep a ledger on your sales. Download a fully functional 30-day test drive with no inactive features and no restrictions from the following URL:

```
www.standingwavesoftware.com/aw/
```

TurboBid

Here's our kind of software — a sniping software! Not that we practice sniping (ahem), but using a program such as this one makes bidding and winning even more entertaining. By such last-minute bidding (sniping), you can successfully win auctions and pay less than if you constantly bid up the price during the course of the auction. (See Chapter 7 for more on bid strategies.) TurboBid places your bid so close to the end of the auction that your adversary has no time to counterbid and win the item from you. To use the software, you take the following simple actions:

✔ Bookmark your favorite auctions. After you start TurboBid, it reads all the auction information from your browser's bookmarks.

✔ Type the maximum you're willing to pay for each item, and TurboBid automatically dials up eBay before the time that you need to place the bid.

TurboBid then synchronizes your computer's clock with eBay's and places the snipe bid all by itself.

The software comes with a guarantee and updates are free. For $10.95, it's a valuable piece of artillery. Download it at the following URL:

```
www.etusa.com/auction/robobid.htm
```

Virtual Auction Ad Pro

Virtual Auction Ad Pro takes you through an easy-to-use, step-by-step process that helps spruce up your eBay auctions with great-looking auction descriptions. We like Virtual Auction Ad Pro's simple approach, and it's easy for beginners to use. Virtual Auction Ad Pro enables you to perform the following tasks:

✔ Design auction descriptions in four different fonts with seven different sizes in millions of colors.

✔ Create auction titles and subtitles in your description in three different sizes.

✔ Create descriptions in a snap with six templates (layout designs).

✔ Easily add up to two photos with your description.

Download Virtual Auction Ad Pro for less than $12.50 at the following Web site:

```
www.virtualnotions.com/vadpro/index.htm
```

Don't forget to check our Web site for updated news on software and tools! Visit us at the following address:

```
www.CoolEbayTools.com
```

eBay's Software and Services

When the users call, eBay answers! As eBay grew there was a need for users to have additional services and software. eBay answered the need with Mister Lister Software and their Power Seller Program. Read on to see how these services tailored for the eBay user might benefit you.

eBay's Mister Lister

Mister Lister is free software available for download on the eBay site that enables you to upload many auctions simultaneously. After you prepare your auctions offline, the software uploads your auctions to a special area at eBay with just the click of a button. You can then edit, preview, and (whenever you're ready) launch all your auctions at once.

The software is also very convenient to use even if you have only a few auctions at a time but want them to all start and end at the same time.

To use Mister Lister, eBay requires that you have a credit card on file, a Feedback rating of 10 or more, and have been registered at eBay for 60 or more days. It's free and very easy to use. If you qualify, download it at the following URL:

```
pages.ebay.com/services/buyandsell/mr.html
```

eBay Power Sellers Program

eBay offers an elite club of its own for Power Sellers who fulfill the following requirements:

- Maintain a 98-percent positive feedback average with 100 or more feedback comments.

- Guarantee buyers that items are exactly as you describe them.

- Maintain minimum monthly gross sales of $2,000 (Bronze level).

- Maintain an account in good standing.

No, you don't need to wear an ugly tie. Power Sellers get a special icon next to their User IDs on the eBay site, thereby giving potential bidders the assurance that they're dealing with a seller of good reputation who stands behind each sale. Power Sellers also can access a special squad of eBay staff experts for e-mail support 24 hours a day, 7 days a week. Serious business! Power Sellers who meet or exceed eBay's requirements also get the following benefits:

- At the Bronze level and higher, you get a physical display sign for your place of business or for trade shows, identifying you as an eBay Power Seller.

- $10,000 in monthly gross sales (Silver level) gets you all the benefits of the Bronze level, plus you can access a dedicated team of account specialists to handle your phone support in real-time during eBay business hours.

- $25,000 a month in gross sales (Gold level) gets you Silver and Bronze level benefits, plus eBay gives you a dedicated account manager and a dedicated support hotline, 24 hours a day, 7 days a week!

If you feel that you qualify for eBay's Power Sellers service (eBay knows who you are!) apply at the following URL:

```
pages.ebay.com/services/buyandsell/powersellers.html
```

Appendix A

Computers: How High-Tech Do I Go?

. . . .

*Y*ou don't have to know a lot of fancy computer mumbo-jumbo to do well at eBay, but you do have to have a computer. Read this section for info on what you need and how to get it, and move on to Chapters 12 and 13 if you're looking for advanced technical strategies that can really zip you into the eBay stratosphere.

If you're in the market for a computer, you can buy or lease a new, used, or refurbished system, depending on your computing needs. If you want more information on buying a computer than we give you here, a painless place to find it is in *Buying a Computer For Dummies* by Dan Gookin. If you're in the market for an upgrade, grab *Upgrading and Fixing PCs For Dummies,* 5th Edition, by Andy Rathbone. Both books are published by IDG Books Worldwide, Inc. (Uncanny, isn't it?)

You need access to the Internet to get into the eBay scene, whether you decide to go with a new computer or a used one. Remember that you should find one with a good modem and enough memory and speed to work efficiently on the Internet. See the section "Buying a New Computer," coming up next. You won't have far to look.

Buying a New Computer

Although the following list is geared mainly toward the purchase of new PCs and Macs, which you can get for under a thousand bucks, you should read this info even if you think you may want a used computer:

✔ **Look for a computer with a good memory.** Remember that 1950s horror movie, *The Blob?* The more time you spend using your computer, the more stuff you want to save on your hard drive. The more stuffed your hard drive, the more Blob-like it becomes. A hard drive with at least 4 gigabytes (GB) of storage space should keep your computer happy, but you can get hard drives as big as 20GB. We recommend you buy the biggest hard drive you can afford because no matter how large your hard drive is, you'll find a way to fill it up.

✔ **Make sure you have a fast modem.** Your modem connects your computer to the Internet using your telephone line. The faster the modem, the more information it sends and receives every second (it transfers data over phone lines at a rate called *kilobytes per second* or just plain *K*). With a fast modem, your computer snags a lot more info and makes good use of the online time you pay for. And you don't have to wait forever for your monitor to show you what you want to see. A 56K modem is standard equipment these days, especially if you plan on using a lot of digital images (photographs) to help sell your items (we tell you how to do that in Chapter 13).

✔ **Get a big screen.** A color monitor that has at least a 15-inch screen can make a huge difference after several hours of rabid bidding or proofreading your auction item descriptions. Anything smaller and you'll have a hard time actually seeing the auctions and images.

✔ **Make sure the computer's Central Processing Unit (CPU) is fast.** A CPU is your computer's brain. It should have at least a 333 MHz (megahertz) processor. This isn't as fast as the 700 to 900 MHz processors on the market, but for what you need it to do (create a complete Web page on your monitor with other software running) it's fast enough that it won't choke when you ask it to do some minor multi-tasking. If you want lightning-fast speed (imagine a Daytona 500 race car with jet assist) you have to move up to the 700 to 900 MHz range. Systems with that kind of speed can cost around $2,000 and more.

✔ **Get a CD-ROM drive.** A CD-ROM is standard equipment. You use the CD-ROM drive to load new software programs into your computer from compact discs. The top-end models even play DVD movies on your computer, but we think that you'll be so entertained by eBay, you may as well skip the frills and save the bucks.

✔ **You must have a keyboard.** No keyboard, no typing. The basic one is fine. They do make funky ergonomic models that are split in the middle. But if the good old standard keyboard feels comfortable to you, stick with it.

✔ **You need a pointing device, usually a mouse.** Some laptops come with touchpads or trackballs designed to do the same thing — give you a quick way to move the pointer around the screen so that you can select options by clicking.

Buying a Used Computer

If you don't have a computer yet and don't want to spend a lot of money, you can start by investigating the used market. There are thousands of perfectly good used machines floating around looking for a caring home. You can pick up a Pentium for a few hundred dollars, and it will serve your budding eBay needs just fine. Same holds true for used Apple PowerPCs or 7110/66 models. Make sure a monitor is included in the purchase price; sometimes you need to buy them separately.

If you buy used from a computer reseller, be sure to ask whether there is still a warranty on the system. Also, ask a lot of questions about the potential of upgrading the system with more memory later on.

Buying a Refurbished Computer

If you don't feel comfortable buying a used machine, you may want to consider a factory-refurbished model. These are powerful new machines that were returned to the manufacturer for one reason or another. The factory fixes them up nice and spiffy, and sweetens the deal with a terrific warranty. Some companies even offer optional, extended, on-site repairs. What you're getting is a new computer at a deep discount because they can't be legally resold as "new."

For the most part, refurbished computers are defined as those that were returned by customers, units with blemishes (scratches, dents, and so on), or evaluation units. The factories rebuild them to the original working condition, using new parts (or sometimes used parts that meet or exceed performance specs for new parts). They come with warranties (60 to 90 days depending on the manufacturer) that cover repairs and returns. Warranty information is available on the manufacturers' Web sites. Be sure to read it before you purchase a refurbished computer.

Major computer manufacturers like Compaq, Dell, IBM, Sony, Hewlett-Packard, and Apple provide refurbished computers. Unfortunately, they only ship within the United States.

Because the inventory of refurbished computers changes daily (as do the prices), there's no way of telling exactly how much money you can save by buying refurbished instead of new. We suggest finding a new computer system you like (and can afford) in a store or catalog, and then comparing it with refurbished systems. If you're thinking about buying from the Web or a catalog, don't forget to include the cost of shipping when you add up the total price. Even with shipping costs, however, a refurbished computer may save you between 30 percent and 60 percent, depending on the deal you find.

Upgrading Your System with the Help of eBay

You may think we're putting the cart before the horse with this suggestion, but you can get a new or used computer system at a great price by signing on to eBay *before* you buy your computer. You can get online at a local library or ask to borrow a friend's computer. We've seen eBay listings for Pentium 333 machines with a CD-ROM drive, a modem, a monitor, and a 4GB hard drive, all for $400. Often such systems also come fully loaded with software. And when you've gotten your new system in shape, why not auction off your old system at eBay?

You can also find all the bits and pieces of a computer you need to upgrade at eBay. The items you may find most useful include

- Digital cameras and scanners
- Disk drives, including CD-ROM drives and high-speed compression drives
- Modems
- Monitors
- Printers

If you have a good used computer without a modem (or if you have a really old, obsolete modem with a glacier-like speed of 1,200 baud or even less), you can upgrade to a pretty fast 56K model for about twenty dollars by watching eBay's auctions carefully. If you plan on using a lot of digital images (photographs) to help sell your items (we tell you how to do that in Chapter 13), you're going to need that 56.6K modem. Considering the reasonable price, it certainly makes sense to buy the fastest modem you can afford. (Of course, then you'd have to *have* a modem so you could connect and buy *another* modem. . . .)

If you're interested in blazing speed at a small price, consider buying a second modem, even a 33.6K and a 56K and use two ISP internet connections to double and triple your speed. To accomplish this miracle, you need FatPipe Inc.'s Home Edition of FatPipe Internet. You can find more about this software at www.fatpipeinc.com/home_edit.htm.

You may have to keep checking in and monitoring the different auctions that eBay has going on; listings change daily. Go put in your best bid, and check back a week later to see whether you've won! (If you want to hurry up and register so you can bid, skip to Chapters 2 and 5. We won't be insulted if you leave us for awhile now. Really.)

No Computer? Connect to eBay on the Cheap

Yes, sometimes life is a Catch-22 situation. Say your goal is to make some money at eBay so that you can afford to buy a computer. Because you can't log on to eBay without a computer, you can't make the money, right? Well, not exactly. Here's how you can start selling and bringing in some cold hard cash for that shiny new (or not-so-shiny used) hardware.

Libraries: From Dewey decimal to eBay

If you haven't been to your local library lately, you may be surprised that most libraries are fully wired with computers that can connect to the Internet. Right now, 80 percent of all American libraries offer computer access to the public. They've come a long way since the card catalog file and the Dewey decimal system. (Remember those?) Some libraries don't even require you to have a library card if you want to use a computer. Others limit the amount of time you can spend online and the sites you can log on to (often it's just the "adult" sites that are blocked). eBay is considered fair game, and exploring it is even considered research.

The upside of using the library's computer is that it's free. The downside is you may have to wait for some kid to finish doing research for a term paper on the ceremonial use of yak milk.

WebTV

WebTV connects you to the Internet directly through your TV. You can send e-mail, surf the Web, upload photos, and run your auctions right from your comfy recliner in the family room. You can get all the equipment you need for as low as $149 and the monthly service is competitively priced at $24.95 a month. If you want to use WebTV with your own ISP, it's only $14.95 a month. All you need is a WebTV Plus unit with a remote keyboard and a phone jack, and you're ready to experience interactive TV along with your Internet surfing. Uploading your images with WebTV is a breeze; all you need is a video recorder and you're on your way. Visit www.webtv.net for all the details.

AOLTV

AOL is rolling out its very own form of Internet television. It does everything that WebTV does, but it incorporates all the benefits of AOL on to your TV. AOL members can have AOLTV for an additional $14.95 per month.

Nonmembers have to pay $24.95 a month. The service will be first offered in selected markets — Phoenix, Sacramento, and Baltimore — with the entire country to follow. To find more info on AOLTV, and when it'll be available in your area, visit www.aoltv.com.

Commercial cyber-outlets

If you strike out at the public library (or you're tired of the librarian shhhhshing you as you cheer your winning bids), your friend throws you out of the house, and your boss watches you like a hawk, you can use a commercial outlet to kick off your eBay career.

National chains like Kinko's, or your favorite local cyber-café offer computer usage at an hourly rate. Kinko's offers computers (both PC and Mac) that can get you online for around $12 per hour or 20 cents per minute. No restrictions apply: You get full access to the Internet and can enjoy all the elements of eBay. You can conduct your auctions by posting them and checking back a week later after they close. You can also watch for great computer deals at eBay that you may want to bid on.

Cyber-cafés can be another way to go. If you live near a college, you'll probably find some. Hourly rates are much cheaper, as you end up ordering a cup of joe or a soda. I once checked on my auctions from a cyber-café in Peru, they only charged $1.50 an hour — what a deal!

Time is money, and an hour flies by when you're having fun online. Before you sit down and the clock starts ticking, make sure you're well organized and know exactly what you want to accomplish during that session. At $12 an hour, you don't want to spend a lot of time surfing for items at eBay for fun. You can do that when you own your own system. The money you save now can help you get there.

Hooking up from work

If you get a long lunch at work, or you have to kill time waiting for clients to call back, you may want to get started at eBay from your work computer. But give it a lot of thought before you do. Pink slips can come unbidden to those who run auctions on company time.

Before you even consider tinkering with a workplace computer, check with your boss or MIS person. The last thing you want to do (and it may be the last thing before they show you the door) is crash your company computer system by messing with the hardware.

Choosing an ISP

Okay, so you bought (or found a way to access) a computer, and you're ready to surf eBay. Hold on a minute — before you start surfing, you need access to the Internet. (Details, details. . . .) The most common way to access the Internet is through an *ISP,* or *Internet Service Provider,* such as America Online (AOL), Earthlink, MSN (Microsoft Network), or any of the commercial Internet enterprises out there today. If you don't already belong to one of these, don't worry, they're really easy to join.

Here are some built-in features that big-name ISPs offer to new users:

- ✔ **Powerful Web browsers.** Browsers are software programs that let your computer talk to the Internet.

- ✔ **Local toll-free telephone numbers.** The last thing you want is long-distance charges while connected to eBay for hours.

- ✔ **E-mail software.** Short for *electronic mail,* e-mail lets you send and receive messages electronically.

- ✔ **Easy registration features.** The best are short, sweet, and painless.

- ✔ **A vast database of information and activities.** Each ISP offers chat-rooms, news forums, research areas, online magazines, special events, and shopping sites.

- ✔ **A storage area for your digital pictures.** We explain this in detail in Chapter 13.

To join an ISP, just load the freebie registration disc into your CD-ROM drive and follow the registration steps that appear on your computer screen. Have your credit card and lots of patience handy. With a little luck and no computer glitches, in less than an hour, you'll have an active account and instant access to e-mail and the Internet.

Paying for an ISP service

When you buy a new or factory-refurbished computer, you're hit with all kinds of free trial offers that beg you to "Sign up now, get 30 hours free!" If you already own a computer and need to find an ISP, many of the big commercial ISPs give away millions of free registration CD-ROMs — we're sure you can find a few. They're everywhere! We have a friend who painted all her free CD-ROMs and hung them on her Christmas tree. Another sawed them in half and made a very unattractive cyber-belt. (Ralph Lauren would never approve.) If you're not sure which ISP to go with, your best bet may be to start with America Online. AOL is the largest ISP around, and it's easy to find and easy to use. If you're not happy with AOL down the road, you can easily cancel your membership and sign up with a different company.

Using a free ISP

Looking to save a few bucks? You may want to try one of the free ISPs. There are several big names in the business: Yahoo!, Bluelight.com (Kmart's joint venture — you can pick up a free CD at your local Kmart), NetZero, Juno, or AltaVista's FreeAccess. To find out about the latest in free ISPs, go to www. addlebrain.com. It also has a Search feature that allows you to type your area code at www.addlebrain.com/local/index.php3, and a list of ISPs that service your area with a local phone number appears.

Going digital

If you have a need for speed, and money is no object, you may want to look into getting a digital connection.

DSL

DSL (short for *Digital Subscriber Line*) is your answer. For as little as $39.95 a month, you can get rid of your pokey, analog dial-up connection and always be connected to the Internet. A DSL line can move data as fast as 6MB per second — that's six *million* bits per second, or 140 times as fast as your current 56K modem. At that speed, a DSL connection can greatly enhance your eBay and Internet experience. For more information about what DSL is and how to get it, visit www.dsllife.com.

A DSL service can act as your ISP, so there's no need to pay for one.

Cable

An Internet cable connection is another alternative for Internet access if you have cable TV. Your Internet connection runs through your television cable and is regulated by your cable TV provider. Although it's definitely an improvement over a dial-up connection, your speeds may vary. The more people in your neighborhood that use the Internet cable connection at the same time, the slower your connection is. If you absolutely, positively cannot get a DSL connection, a cable hook-up is the next best thing. Most cable accounts include several e-mail addresses and space to store your images.

Browsing for a Browser

When you join a commercial ISP, those good folks give you a browser for free. A *browser* is the software program that lets your computer talk to the Internet. It's like having your own private cyber-chauffeur. Type in the address (also known as the *URL,* for *Uniform Resource Locator*) of the Web site you want to visit, and boom, you're there. For example, to get to eBay's home page, type **www.ebay.com** and press Enter. (It's sort of a low-tech version of "Beam me up, Scotty!" — and almost as fast.)

The two most popular browsers are Netscape Navigator and Microsoft Internet Explorer. (They are what Coca-Cola and Pepsi are to the cola wars.) Both programs are powerful and user-friendly. Figures A-1 and A-2 show you these browsers. (Sit, browser! Now shake! *Good* browser!)

When you join an ISP, you get either Microsoft Internet Explorer or Netscape Navigator for free. If you need more information (or if you want to make sure you're using the most up-to-date version of the software) you can get it online:

- ✔ For Microsoft Internet Explorer, go to www.microsoft.com.
- ✔ For Netscape Navigator, go to www.netscape.com.

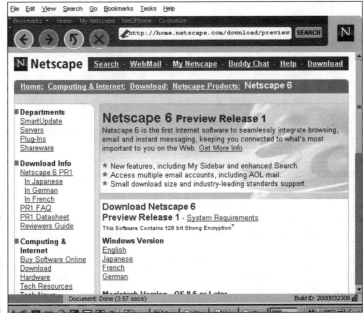

Figure A-1: The Netscape Navigator browser.

Figure A-2:
The
Microsoft
Internet
Explorer
browser.

Hooking Up on E-Mail

After you have access to the Internet, you need access to e-mail. If you have your own computer and an ISP, you probably have e-mail access automatically. But if you're logging on to the Internet from the library or a friend's house, you should look into setting up e-mail for free.

Yahoo! and Hotmail are two of the most popular e-mail providers around. Both are free and secure, and signing up is a snap. We like Yahoo! because it has a Mail Alert feature, which allows you to instruct Yahoo! to contact you via your pager when you have new e-mail.

You can join Yahoo! e-mail at `www.yahoo.com`. You can join Hotmail by going to `www.hotmail.com`.

Whether you sign up for e-mail at Hotmail, Yahoo!, or any other service or ISP, following some common-sense rules can help you protect your account:

✔ **Select a password that's difficult to guess.** Use letter-and-number combinations or nonsensical words that nobody else knows. Don't use common names or words relating to you (like your street name).

✔ **Keep passwords secret.** Nobody will ever ask for your password online — if somebody does, you can bet it's a scam. *Never give it out.*

✔ **Don't open an e-mail with an attachment (another file attached to your e-mail message) from an unknown person.** The attachment could contain a virus.

✔ **Don't respond to spam mail.** *Spam* is online slang for harassing, offensive, or useless-but-widely-distributed messages. If you ignore such junk, the sender will probably just give up and go away.

For more info on using e-mail, a ready resource is (you guessed it) *E-Mail For Dummies,* 2nd Edition, by John R. Levine, Carol Baroudi, Margaret Levine Young, and Arnold Reinhold (from IDG Books Worldwide, Inc. — how *did* we know that?). Also check out Chapter 14 for some additional online privacy tips.

Appendix B

Answers for the Fanatic: Finding More Stuff to Sell

●　●

*A*fter you pick clean everything not nailed down in your house, you may want to broaden your horizons. The key to successfully selling items at eBay is to find things people actually want to buy. (Wow, what an incredible observation.) We know it seems obvious, but having stuff to *sell* isn't always the same as having things people *want to buy*. Using this concept, you can teach yourself all kinds of effective marketing strategies. Finding the item that may be "the next big thing" takes lots of work, timing, and sometimes a dose of good luck.

Knowing the Market

Just as successful stockbrokers know about specific companies, they also need to know about the marketplace as a whole. Sure, we know about the 300 Beanie Babies out there, and so does nearly everyone else. To get a leg up on your competition, you need to know the big picture as well. Here are some questions you should ask yourself as you contemplate making serious scads of money (well, we hope) by selling items at eBay:

✔ **What items are currently hot?** If you see everyone around you rushing to the store to buy a particular item, chances are good that the item will become more valuable as stocks of it diminish. The simple rule of supply and demand says that whoever has something everyone else wants stands to gain major profits.

✔ **Do I see a growing interest in a specific item that might make it a big seller?** If you're starting to hear talk about a particular item, or even an era ('70s nostalgia? Who knew?), listen carefully and think of what you already own (or can get your hands on) that can help you catch a piece of the trend's action.

✔ **Should I hold on to this item and wait for its value to increase, or should I sell now?** Knowing when to sell an item that you think people may want is a tricky business. Sometimes, you can catch the trend too early and find out that you could have commanded a better price if only you waited. Other times, you may catch a fad that's already passé and find that no one's interested anymore.

✔ **Is a company discontinuing an item I should stockpile now and sell later?** Could the manufacturer reissue the item later? Pay attention to items that are discontinued, especially toys and novelty items. If you find an item that a manufacturer has a limited supply of, you could make a tidy profit. If the manufacturer ends up reissuing the item, don't forget that the original run is still the most coveted — and valuable.

✔ **Was there a recall, an error, or a legal proceeding associated with my item?** If so, how will it affect the value of the item? For example, a toy recalled for safety reasons may no longer be appropriate for the kids, but it could be rare and collectible if intact.

Some people like to go with their gut feelings about when and what to buy for resale at eBay. By all means, if instinct has worked for you in the past, factor instinct in here, too. If you've done some research that looks optimistic but your gut says, "I'm not sure," listen to it; don't assume you're just hearing that lunchtime taco talking. Try testing the waters by purchasing one of the prospective items for resale at eBay. If that sale doesn't work out, you won't have a lot invested, and you can credit your gut with saving you some bucks.

Catching Trends in the Media

Catching trends is all about listening and looking. You can find all kinds of inside information from newspapers, magazines, television, and of course, the Internet. Believe it or not, you can even find out what people are interested in these days by bribing a kid. Keep your eyes and ears open. When people say, "That Taco Bell Chihuahua is *everywhere* these days," instead of nodding your head vacantly, start getting ideas.

In newspapers

Newspapers are bombarded by press releases and inside information from companies the world over. Pay close attention to the various sections of the newspaper. Look for stories on celebrities, upcoming movies, and if old fads are making a resurgence. (You can sell as "retro chic.")

On television

No matter what you think of television, it has an enormous impact on which trends come and go and which ones stick. Why else would advertisers sink billions of dollars into TV commercials? And look at the impact of Oprah's Book Club. Just one Oprah appearance for an author can turn a book into an overnight bestseller. Rosie O'Donnell also knows the power of her show. She's turning props and autographed items from guests into cash for charity. (Check out Chapter 17 for more on charity auctions.)

Tune into morning news shows and afternoon talk shows. See what's being featured in the programs. The producers of these shows are on top of pop culture and move fast to be the first to bring you the next big thing. Take what they feature and think of a marketing angle. If you don't, you can be sure somebody else will.

Catch up with youth culture . . .

. . . or at least keep good tabs on it. There's no catching up with it, just as there's no way to say this without sounding over-the-hill: If you remember cranking up The Beatles, James Brown, or The Partridge Family (say what?) until your parents screamed, "Shut that awful noise off," you may be at that awkward time of life when you hardly see the appeal of what young people are doing or listening to. But if you want tips for hot auction items, tolerate the awful noise and listen to the kids around you. Children, especially pre-teens and teens, may be the best trend-spotters on the planet. See what kind of marketing tips you get when you ask a kid:

- **What's cool at the moment?** Or "rad" if you want to sound cool — whoops, that was '80s-speak, wasn't it?

- **What's totally uncool that was cool two months ago?** Their world moves at warp speed!

- **What music are you buying?** Britney Spears, 'NSYNC, and Christina Aguilera — yup, all the hot bands with big hits — but maybe *ewww-that's-so-five-minutes-ago* by the time you read this.

- **What could I buy you at the moment that would make you really happy?** *Hint:* If the kid says, "A red BMW Z-3," or "Liposuction," look for a younger kid.

Collecting magazines

Though not quite a plethora, the number of magazines geared for collectors is definitely approaching a slew. While these won't help you catch a trend (by the time it gets into one of these, somebody's already caught it) they can give you great information on pricing, availability, and general collecting information. And you can follow the course of a trend for a real-life example of how it works.

Here's a list of collectors' magazines we like:

- *eBay Magazine* has all the news on eBay, interesting interviews, what's hot and what's not in all categories . . . and ahem, Marsha Collier's monthly column. Visit them at www.krause.com/ebaymag/.

- *Collector's Mart* is the leading magazine of advertising material in print. Check out the Web site at www.worldcollectors net.com/cmart.

- *Barbie Bazaar* has info on everything related to Barbie. Go to www.barbie bazaar.com.

Check out magazines

Magazines geared to the 18 to 34-years age group (and sometimes to younger teens) can help you stay on top of what's hot. See what the big companies are pitching to this target audience (and whether they're succeeding). If a celebrity's suddenly visible in every other headline or magazine, keep a lookout for merchandise relating to that person. (Are we talking hysteria-plus-cash flow here, or just hysteria?)

The Hunt for eBay Inventory

If you're not sure what you want to sell for profit at eBay — but you're a shop-till-you-drop person by nature — then you've got an edge. Incorporate your advanced shopping techniques into your daily routine. If you find a bargain that interests you, chances are you have a knack for spotting stuff that other shoppers would love to get their hands on.

The goods are out there

When you shop to sell at eBay, don't rule out any shopping venue. From the trendiest boutique to the smallest junk shop, garage sales to Bloomingdales, keep your eye out for eBay inventory. The items people look for at eBay are out there; you just have to find them.

Keep these shopping locales in mind when you go on the eBay hunt:

- Upscale department stores, trendy boutiques, outlet stores, or flagship designer stores are good places to do some market research. Check out the newest items and then head to the clearance area and scrutinize the bargain racks.

- Tour discount stores in your area. Many of the items these places carry are *overruns* (too many of something that didn't sell), *small runs* (too little of something that the big guys weren't interested in stocking), or out-of-date fad items that need a good home at eBay.

- Garage sales, tag sales, and moving sales offer some of the biggest bargains you'll ever come across. Check for vintage kitchen pieces and old toys, and make 'em an offer they can't refuse.

- eBay's Business Exchange has joined with TradeOut, an online exchange where companies buy and sell surplus assets in more than 100 categories. You can purchase merchandise on TradeOut from Fortune 500 industrial companies to mid-sized wholesale distributors. The inventory is sold in bulk.

  Do you have room for 104, 100-percent-cotton women's A-line dresses? If so, here's the place for some great buys. You're able to source large lots of merchandise, such as computers or cosmetics, from TradeOut and resell them in smaller quantities at eBay.

- Thrift stores are packed with inexpensive but well-made items. Feel good knowing that the money you spend in a nonprofit thrift shop is going to a good cause.

- Find going-out-of-business sales. You can pick up bargains if a shopkeeper just wants to empty the shelves, so the store can close.

- Take advantage of any flea markets or swap meets in your area.

- Gift shops at museums, monuments, national parks, and theme parks can provide eBay inventory — but think about where to sell the items. Part of your selling success on eBay is *access*. People who can't get to Graceland may pay handsomely for an Elvis mini-guitar with the official logo on the box.

- Hang on to the freebies you get. If you receive handouts (lapel pins, pencils, pamphlets, books, interesting napkins, flashlights, towels, stuffed toys) from a sporting event, premiere, or historic event — or even a collectible freebie from a fast-food restaurant — they could be your ticket to some eBay sales.

Tips for the modest investor

If you're interested in making money in your eBay ventures but you're start-ing with limited cash, follow this list of eBay inventory Do's and Don'ts:

- **Don't** spend more than you can afford to lose. If you shop at boutiques and expensive department stores, buy things that you like to wear your-self in case they don't sell.

- **Do** try to find something local that's unavailable in a wider area. For example, if you live in an out-of-the-way place that has a local specialty, try selling that at eBay.

- **Don't** go overboard and buy something really cheap just because it's cheap. Figure out who would want the item first.

- **Do** stick to classic and traditional patterns, clothing, and furnishings. They're timeless and rarely go out of style.

- **Do** consider buying in bulk, especially if you know the item sells well at eBay or if the item is inexpensive. Chances are good that if you buy one and it sells well at eBay, by the time you try to buy more, the item's sold out. If an item is inexpensive (say 99 cents), we always buy at least five of it. If no one bids on the item when you hold your auction, you're only out $5. (Anyone out there need any Bicentennial Commemorative coffee mugs?)

Index

• *Symbols* •

& (ampersand), 30, 240
* (asterisk), 89, 174, 240
@ (at sign), 30, 240
, (comma), 89, 240
$ (dollar sign), 171, 182
"" (double quotes), 89
! (exclamation point), 174, 240
/ (forward slash), 240
- (hyphen), 171
– (minus sign), 89–90
( ) (parentheses), 90
% (percent sign), 240
# (pound sign), 240
? (question mark), 240
_ (underscore), 28

• *A* •

abbreviations, 172–174
About eBay area, 45, 286
About eBay link, 45
About Me page(s), 34, 91
   basic description of, 50, 245–248
   creating, 48, 244–248
   layout options, 246–247
   saving, 248
   viewing, 99
Account page, 51–54
Account Status page, 52
Account tab, 49
accounts, setting up, 51–54
Add a New Search button, 301
Add To Description button, 190
Adding To Your Item Description page, 190
address labels, 206
Adult/Erotica category, 175, 186
Adults Only category, 12, 175, 186

advertisements, rules against, 158
Affiliates Program link, 45
age, entering information about your, 23, 252
alcohol, sale of, 157
alerts, non-paying bidder, 52–53
All Categories link, 40
All Featured Items link, 42
All Items Including Gallery Preview link, 44
All Items link, 44
All tab, 49
AltaVista, 79, 328
Amazon Auctions, 302
American Express, 52. *See also* credit cards
Announcements Board, 45, 223–224
   basic description of, 287–288
   reporting of outages on, 287
Announcements link, 223–224
annual household income, 23
Anonymizer.com, 255
antiques, researching, 74–78, 80
Antiquing For Dummies, 80
AOL (America Online), 23, 328. *See also* ISPs
AOLTV, 325–326
Apple Computer, 323
appraisals, 278–280
Ask Seller a Question link, 100, 132
Athletes Direct, 299
attachments, e-mail, 261–262, 331
attorneys, 68
auction(s). *See also* Dutch auctions; reserve-price auctions; auctions, setting up
   abbreviations used in, 172–174
   basic description of, 11–14
   canceling, 220, 222–223
   charity, 13, 32, 44, 286, 292, 297–302
   choice auctions, 158
   duration of, 170, 223–224, 229

auction(s) *(continued)*
  eBay's role in, 15–16
  extending, 223–224
  featured, 34, 39, 42–44, 162–163
  forbidden, 157–158
  interception, 268, 275
  interference, 268
  international, 20, 40, 42, 52, 102–104
  links between Web pages and, 244–245
  -management software, 241–242, 315–318
  pages, 93–97, 130–131, 191, 194
  private, 13, 170, 175, 186
  starting, 186–188
  traditional, 11–12
Auction Confirmation page, 187
Auction Manager Pro Bulk, 312
Auction Tools tab, 137
Auction Web, 11, 29
Auction Wizard, 316–317
AuctionAssistant Classic, 315–316
auctions, setting up. *See also* auctions
  basic description of, 14, 167–190
  choosing item categories, 168, 174–175
  listing acceptable payment methods, 170, 178–179
  making changes to auctions in progress, 188–190
  preparing for, 167–168
  setting minimum bids, 170, 181–182
  setting options, 183–186
  setting shipping terms, 98, 170, 180, 188–190, 196
  setting your auction time, 182–183
  writing item descriptions, 170–177
AuctionWatch.com, 241, 244, 295
  basic description of, 312
  buyer services, 312
  seller services, 312
AuctionWorks, 313
Auctiva.com, 316
Australia, 20, 42
Authentication Services link, 280
authenticity, of items, 98, 278–280, 300
autographs, 154
automobile insurance, 111
Automotive category, 110–111, 161–163

• B •

Back button, 24, 189
back-end deals, 161–162
bait-and-switch tactics, 158
bank(s). *See also* payments
  statements, 58, 192
  transfers, 54
banners, 253
barcodes, 209–210
BBB Online. *See* Better Business Bureau Online
beat-the-clock strategy, 124–127
Bernstein, Lee, 74, 77, 149
Better Business Bureau Online (BBB Online), 255–258
bid(s). *See also* bidders; bidding
  canceling, 220–221
  increments, 109–110
  manipulation, 268
  maximum, 107, 108
  minimum, 11, 12, 160–161, 181–182, 185, 229
  retracting, 63, 112–113
  shielding, 268, 275
  siphoning, 268
  token, 108, 124
  winning, 130, 134, 195, 166
Bid Confirmation screen, 107
Bid icon, 96
Bid History link, 95
bidders. *See also* bids; bidding
  communicating with, 309
  displaying e-mail addresses of, 95
  non-paying, 52–53, 112, 113–115, 268
  researching, 117–119, 213–214
  searching for items by, 37, 86, 117–118
  unwelcome, 268
bidding. *See also* bidders
  abuses, 268
  basic description of, 11, 93–116
  but not responding to sellers, 62
  early and high, 121
  emotional thrill of, resisting, 74–75
  forms, 106–110

history, of items, 119–120, 122
keeping track of an auction without, 96
keeping track of items when, 57–59
lounging-around strategy for, 124
making changes to auctions before the
    start of, 188–190
making changes to auctions during,
    189–190
on your own items, rules against, 222
placing your bid, 106–110
proxy, 108–109
recordkeeping for, 58–59
researching completed auctions before,
    87–88
shill, 266, 267, 275
strategies, 117–128
wars, 122, 124–127
Bidding/Watching area, 49, 96, 129–130
Bidding/Watching tab, 49, 96
Big Ticket auctions, 34
billing inquires, to eBay, 164
Billpoint Service, 54, 83, 102
  basic description of, 136
  specifying, as an acceptable form of
      payment, 170, 179
  transactions, documenting, 192
Bluelight.com, 328
Bold option, 184, 228
bonds, 154
bookkeeping. *See* recordkeeping
bookmarks, 50–51, 81
books, recommended, 2, 80–81, 172, 321
Books, Movies & Music category, 40–41
Browse by Themes link, 39
Browse link, 34
Browse tab, 34
browsers, 327, 329
bubble wrap, 205
Bubblefast.com, 208
Business Exchange, 39, 111, 337
Business members, 192
business Web pages, linking eBay auctions
    to, 244–245

buyer(s). *See also* bidders
  AWOL, 214, 211–218
  communicating with, 131–132, 134,
      193–196
  golden rules for, 305–310
  non-paying, 217–218, 224, 225
  researching, 213–214
  who do not respond, dealing with,
      211–217
  who refuse to meet mutually set
      terms, 272
Buyer Guide page, 104
Buyer Pays Actual Shipping Cost
    option, 180
Buyer Pays Fixed Amount option, 180
Buyer Protection Guarantees, 102
Buying a Computer For Dummies, 321
Buying & Selling link, 112
Buying & Selling page, 137–138,
    224–227, 229
By Bidder search, 37, 86, 117–118
By Bidder Search window, 37
By Item Number search, 37, 81
By Seller search, 37, 81, 84–86, 99, 193

• C •

cable access, 328
Café society, 291
camcorders, 235, 242
cameras, digital, 232–233, 235–236, 324
Canada, 20, 42
Cancel Bid button, 221
Cancel Bids on My Item link, 221
Canceling Bids Placed in Your Auction
    page, 221
capitalization, 30, 90
Cash Out link, 229
cashier's checks, 103
catalogs, sale of, 158
categories
  basic description of, 40
  changing, 188–190, 229

categories *(continued)*
    choosing favorite, for your My eBay
        Favorites page, 54–57
    display of, during auctions, 94
    entering, in the Sell Your Item page, 169
    grading, 77–78
    navigating, 40–42
    searching for items by, 83
    sorting options for, 56
    specialized, 42, 110–111
    viewing options for, 43–44
Category Featured. *See* Home Page
    Featured option
Category Overview link, 40
Category-Specific Chat page, 148
CD-ROM drives, 322, 324
Change Category button, 190
Change My Item's Category link, 190
Change My User ID link, 30
Change User ID button, 30
Changing My Item's Category page, 190
charity auctions, 13, 32, 44, 286, 292,
    297–302
Charity link, 298
chat
    accessing, 34
    basic description of, 16, 286
    category-specific, 148–149, 294–295
    community message boards, 289–290
    discussion boards, 290–291
    doing research through, 80, 148
    privacy issues and, 260, 263
    reporting problems via, 271
Chat link, 293
Chat page, 34
checks, 103, 52–53, 96
    bounced, 62, 218
    personal information revealed by, 252
    specifying, as an acceptable form of
        payment, 179
    tips for making payment with, 135
child pornography, 154, 157
choice auctions, 158
Christie's, 93
CIA (Central Intelligence Agency), 257
COA (Certificate of Authenticity), 154

C.O.D. (Cash on Delivery), 103–104, 178
collectibles
    category, 93
    grading, 172–174
    price guides for, 75
    researching, 73–78, 147–151
commissions, 161–162
Community link, 34, 78, 216
Community Overview page, 148, 223
    basic description of, 286–287
    Help boards on, 288–290
Community Watch, 268
Community Standards, 159, 266
Community Standards link, 159
Community Standards Overview page, 159
Compaq, 323
Complete Your Registration button, 30
Completed Items search, 37, 87–88,
    150–151
Completed link, 56
computers
    buying new, 321–322
    buying used, 322–323
    refurbished, 323
confirmation
    codes, 26–27
    notices, 25–26
Confirmation page, 26–27
Contact Info form, 133
contact information. *See also* privacy
    getting, 131–133
    illegal use of another user's, 269
Continue button, 24
Control Panel, 123
cookies
    basic description of, 32, 194, 253–254
    end of session, 254
    sign-in, 254
Cool Crap auction, 299
Cool Features, 34
Cool Happenings, 288
CooleBayTools.com Web site, 5, 56
copyrights, 155–156, 159
Corel WordPerfect, 209
counterfeit items, 156, 278–280
counters, 313, 316

Country/Region field, 95
court orders, 68
CPUs (central processing units), 322
Create and Edit your Page button, 246
credit card(s), 96, 101–102
  authorization, 52
  information, entering, from your My eBay
    Account page, 51
  information, protecting, 263
  monthly charges on, 52, 53
  PayPal service and, 102
  privacy issues and, 252, 263
  specifying, as an acceptable form of
    payment, 179
  tips for making payments with, 135
Credit Request link, 52–53
Credit Request Process Completed
    page, 226
cropping images, 237, 238
Cultural category, 42
currency converters, 104
Current Issues message board, 291
Current link, 56
Currently field, 94
customer satisfaction, 194–195
Customer Support
  contact information for, 271
  e-mail response form, 271
  message boards, 288–289
cyber-cafés, 326

• *D* •

DAS (Dependable Auto Shippers), 111
date(s). *See also* time
  auction start, 95
  of feedback, 64
  shipping, 178
delivery confirmation, 200
Dell, 323
demographics, 23
Deposits & Fees link, 54
Description icon, 96
descriptions, of items
  adding URLs to, 245
  basic description of, 97–98

care in reading, importance of, 97–98
  changing, 188–190
  displaying, 96
  printing, 191
  researching, 74–78
  writing, 168, 170–177, 229, 308
destination charges, 162
Details link, 59
digital cameras, 232–233, 235–236, 324
Discover, 52. *See also* credit cards
Discuss eBay's Newest Features, 263
discussion boards, 290–291. *See also* chat
Discussion Help & Chat page, 216, 286
dispute resolution services, 273–274
DNF (Discuss eBay's Newest Features)
    message board, 289
documentation. *See* recordkeeping
Dogpile, 79
Don't Miss link, 40
DoubleClick, 253–254
dpi (dots per inch), 233–234, 238
driver's license numbers, 135, 281
drugs, sale of, 154
DSL (Digital Subscriber Line), 328
duration, of auctions, 170, 223–224, 229
Dutch auctions, 13–14, 95, 107
  bidding strategies for, 120–121
  insertion fees and, 161, 228
  non-paying bidders and, 224
  requirements for starting, 181
  reserve price and, 186

• *E* •

Earthlink, 327
eBay Anywhere Wireless, 300
eBay Foundation, 286
eBay Home page
  accessing, 35
  basic description of, 10, 31–46
  categories, navigating, 40–42
  search options, 35–38
  signing in on, 32–33
  welcome mat links, 38–39
eBay ID cards, 63, 96
eBay Insider, 286

eBay Motors, 110–111
eBay Official Time link, 57, 182
eBay Services Overview page, 34
eBay Store, 34, 45, 286, 300–301
eBay Store link, 300
eBay Town Square, 291
eBayla virus, 257
EBayMotors.com, 39
e-commerce
  basic description of, 10
  taxation of, 165, 166
eCommerceTax.com, 166
ECount.com, 136
education levels, 23, 252
Einstein, Albert, 5
eLee.com, 77, 149
E-LOAN, 111
e-mail. *See also* e-mail addresses
  attachments, 261–262, 331
  blocking, 23
  EOA (End of Auction e-mail), 59, 130, 131,
    192, 222
  lists, 154
  notifications, 48
  printing, 192
  querying sellers by, 100–101
  saving, for recordkeeping purposes,
    59, 192
  setting up access to, 330–331
  software, 327
  tips for writing, 134
e-mail addresses. *See also* e-mail
  for the authors of this book, 5
  entering, when registering, 22, 23, 24
  finding, 95, 132–133, 194, 259
  searching for items by, 37, 85–86
  using, in place of User IDs, 48
E-Mail For Dummies, 331
Emergency Contact Board, 215–217,
  292–293
employment information, 252
encryption, 21. *See also* security
End Auction link, 222
End Auction page, 222
End Your Auction Early link, 222

endangered species, 154
Ending Today link, 56
Ending Your Auction form, 222
Enter button, 48
Entire Account link, 53
EOA (End of Auction) e-mails, 59, 130, 131,
  192, 222
ePoster2000, 316
Epson, 232
Equifax, 179, 281
erotica, 157
escrow, 104–105, 111, 134, 170, 306
  basic description of, 278
  forms, 58, 192
  specifying, as an acceptable form of
    payment, 179
Escrow.com, 111
E-Stamp, 209–210, 300
Excel, 192
Excite, 79

• F •

FAQ for the User Agreement, 267
FatPipe Internet, 324
Favorites area
  basic description of, 54–57
  choosing categories for, 54–56
  sorting options for, 56
Favorites tab, 49, 54
featured auction(s), 34, 39
  basic description of, 42–43
  listings, 162–163
  viewing options for, 44
Featured Auctions link, 39
Featured Items area, 42–43
Featured Items link, 42–43
Featured Plus! option, 169, 184
Federal Trade Commission (FTC), 165, 282
FedEx (Federal Express), 105, 197,
  199–203, 208
feedback, 5, 61–68, 140
  on About Me pages, 247
  abuses, 259, 266, 268–269, 272, 275
  basic description of, 15–16, 59–60

color-coded, 64
extortion, 259, 275
Featured Plus! option and, 184
getting and giving, 59–69
hiding, 63
importance of checking, 213–214, 306, 264
leaving, with finesse, 65–68
negative, 61–62, 66–67, 218, 309–310
neutral, 61, 66–67
positive, 61, 66–67, 309–310
privacy and, 63, 66, 264
profiles, 60–63, 67–68, 91, 213
ratings/scores, 15–16, 269, 275
recordkeeping and, 59
removal of, by eBay, 68
responding to, 64–65
tips for writing, 65–68
unwarranted/retaliatory, 272
viewing, 49, 99
Feedback FAQ, 66
Feedback Forum, 34, 39, 45, 63, 65–68
Feedback Forum link, 45
Feedback Profile page, 61–63, 67–68, 91, 213
fees. *See also* Final Value Fee Credit
    attempts to avoid, 268, 275
    basic description of, 160–164
    escrow, 105
    information on, viewing, 49, 52
    insertion, 160, 182, 227–228
    optional, 159, 162–163
    real estate transaction, 159
Fees and Credits link, 52
File a New Complaint button, 277
filenames, for images, 240
Final Value Fee Credit, 52–53, 159, 161–162, 217, 272
    basic description of, 224
    filing for, 224–227
    illegal submission of, 268
Final Value Fee Credit Request page, 52–53, 225
financing, for car purchases, 111
Find Help button, 38
Find It button, 36
Find Members link, 91, 132
Find Members page, 132, 133

firearms, 152
Firefighting category, 42
First Bid field, 95
Fixing PCs For Dummies, 321
forbidden auctions, 157–158
forged items, 154. *See also* fraud
Franklin, Ben, 164
fraud, 226, 274–276
    information resources, 282–283
    insurance, 106, 227, 275, 276–278
    suspension for, 276
Fraud Prevention & Insurance page, 277
FreeAccess, 328
Front Page, 78–79, 148–149
FTP (File Transfer Protocol), 315, 316
Fujifilm, 233

• *G* •

Gallery, 43–44, 169, 186
gender information, 23, 252
General Chat Rooms category, 216
General Support Q&A message board, 289–290
geographic location
    of items, specifying, 170, 178
    searching for items by, 83
    of sellers, 95
Germany, 20, 42
GIF (Graphics Interchange Format), 237. *See also* graphics
GifBot, 315
gigabytes, 321
GIGO (garbage in, garbage out), 234
GivingBoard.com, 292
Global Sites link, 40
glue guns, 206
Going, Going, Gone link, 56
government documents, official, 153
Grab Bag auctions, 34
grading, of items, 77–78, 172–174
graphic(s)
    adding, to your auction, 239–243
    basic guidelines for using, 231–244
    contrast settings for, 238

graphic(s) *(continued)*
  creating high-quality, 234–238, 308
  cropping, 237, 238
  file formats for, 237, 238
  filenames for, 240
  hosting Web sites for, 240, 241–243
  including, in your About Me page,
    245–248
  preparing, for use on Web pages, 238–239
  size of, 238–239
  uploading, 240–243
  URLs for, 169, 188–190, 239–240, 247
Great Collections, 39, 111

• H •

hackers, 257, 263, 269, 276
harassment, 68, 270
hard
  drive space, 321
  outages, 223–224
hardware requirements, 9, 321
Hawaiiana category, 42
Help link, 34
Help message boards, 288–289
Help Overview page, 34
Hewlett-Packard, 323
High Bid link, 96
Highlight option, 170, 184
hits, tracking, 243–244
Holiday board, 292
Home link, 35
Home Page Featured option, 169, 184
Honesty.com, 241, 244
Hot auctions, 34
Hot Picks, 32, 39
Hot Picks link, 39
Hotmail, 330
How Do I Bid? link, 38
How Do I Sell? link, 39
HTML (HyperText Markup Language), 172,
    244–245, 248, 315
HTML 4 For Dummies, 172
HTML Toolbox, 315

human part and remains, sale of, 154
HyperText Markup Language (HTML).
    See HTML

• I •

I Accept button, 25
I Agree button, 138
IBI (Information Based Indicia), 209
IBM (International Business Machines), 323
icons
  basic description of, 83
  for categories, 41
  used in this book, 4
ICQ, 302
ID cards, 63, 96
ID Verify, 280–282
identity. *See also* privacy
  abuses, 269
  misrepresentation, 276
  tests, 281
i-Escrow, 104–105, 137–138, 278
image(s)
  adding, to your auction, 239–243
  basic guidelines for using, 231–244
  contrast settings for, 238
  creating high-quality, 234–238, 308
  cropping, 237, 238
  file formats for, 237, 238
  filenames for, 240
  -hosting Web sites, 240, 241–243
  including, in your About Me page,
    245–248
  preparing, for use on Web pages, 238–239
  resolution of, 233, 237, 238
  size of, 238–239
  uploading, 240–243
  URLs for, 169, 188–190, 239–240, 247
Images/HTML Board, 288–289
income
  levels, 23, 252
  taxes, 165–166
Infoseek, 79
infringing items, 155–156

insertion fees, 160, 182, 227–228
Inside Scoop, 78–79, 148–149
inspection
  periods, 105
  services, 111
insurance
  eBay, 139, 275, 276–278
  collector-car, 111
  forms, 58, 192
  fraud, 106, 227, 275, 276–278
  self-, 199
  shipping, 76, 105–106, 139, 199, 219
intellectual property, 155–156, 159
interest rates, 111
international
  access, to eBay, 20, 40, 42
  message boards, 294
  payment methods, 52, 102–104
  search features, 37, 81, 88
Internet For Dummies, The, 2
Internet Searching For Dummies, 80
Internet Tax Freedom Act, 165
iPix (Internet Pictures Corporation), 240,
    242–243
IRS (Internal Revenue Service), 59, 166,
    192. *See also* taxes
Is My Item Allowed on eBay link, 152
iShip, 202
ISPs (Internet Service Providers), 240–241,
    254, 264, 273, 282, 324–325
  AOL (America Online), 23, 328
  browser software provided by, 329
  choosing, 327
  features offered by, 327
  free, 328
  payments to, 327–328
item(s). *See also* item categories; item
    descriptions
  damaged during shipment, 76, 98, 139,
    218–219
  fielding questions about, 190
  grading of, 77–78, 172–174
  listing the number of, for sale, 180–181
  location, specifying, 170, 178
  numbers, 37, 84, 94

potentially infringing, 151–152
pre-sell, 75
prohibited, 25, 151–155
questionable, 151–152, 157
relisting, 227–229
sorting, 57–59
which are not as described, dealing
    with, 139
item categories
  basic description of, 40
  changing, 188–190, 229
  choosing favorite, for your My eBay
    Favorites page, 54–57
  display of, during auctions, 94
  entering, in the Sell Your Item page, 169
  grading, 77–78
  navigating, 40–42
  searching for items by, 83
  sorting options for, 56
  specialized, 42, 110–111
  viewing options for, 43–44
Item category field, 94
item descriptions
  adding URLs to, 245
  basic description of, 97–98
  care in reading, importance of, 97–98
  changing, 188–190
  displaying, 96
  printing, 191
  researching, 74–78
  writing, 168, 170–177, 229, 308
Item Number field, 84
Item Number search, 84
Items I'm Bidding On section, 108, 130
Items That May Not Be Allowed for Sale
    link, 159

• *J* •

Jan Mayen, 20
Japan, 20, 42
Javascript, 68
Jobs link, 45
joining eBay. *See* registration

JPEG (Joint Photographics Expert Group) format, 237, 238. *See also* images
Juno, 328

• *K* •

Keen.com, 34, 300
Kentis.com, 166
keyboards, 322
kilobytes per second, 322
Kmart, 328
knock-offs, 156

• *L* •

labels, address, 206
laptop computers, 322
lawsuits, 68
Leave Comment button, 67
Leave Feedback icon, 67
Lee Bernstein Antique and Collectibles, 74, 77, 149
libel, 68
libraries, public, 80, 325
Library link, 78
Library section, of eBay, 78–79, 286
license fees, 162
license plates, 153
Link Exchange, 253
links. *See also* URLs
  on About Me pages, 247
  basic description of, 6, 31–32, 35, 38–40
  between Web pages and eBay auctions, 244–245
Listings page, 41
Lloyd, Edward, 278
Lloyd's of London, 106, 276–278
Local Trading, 32
location
  of items, specifying, 170, 178
  searching for items by, 83
  of sellers, 95
Location field, 95
locksmithing devices, 153

logos, 159. *See also* images
lurking, 289
Lycos, 79

• *M* •

Macintosh, 9, 323
magazines, collecting, 336
Mail or Telephone Order Merchandise Rule, 165
Mail This Auction to a Friend link, 96
Make a One-Time Payment link, 53
Make Feedback Changes Public or Private link, 63
ManageAuctions.com, 241, 244, 313–314
March of Dimes auction, 298
MasterCard, 52. *See also* credit cards
maximum bid, 107, 108
media, catching trends in, 334–336
mediation, 273–274
members
  power trading, 299–300
  searching for, 95, 132–133, 194, 214, 259
  specials for, 90–91, 132, 299–300
  suspension of, 217, 270, 272, 275–276
  tracking, 243–245, 258
Memorabilia category, 41
memory, 321
message boards, 80, 289–294. *See also* chat
Message Center, 295
Microsoft Internet Explorer browser, 329
Microsoft Network (MSN), 327
Microsoft Office, 209
Microsoft Outlook, 209
Microsoft Picture It 2000, 237
Microsoft Web site, 329–330
military weapons, 153
minimum bids
  basic description of, 11
  fees and, 160–161
  reserve-price auctions and, 11, 12
  setting, 181–182, 185, 229
Mister Lister, 318
modems, 9, 322, 324

money orders, 52–53, 102–103
  as the safest form of payment, 178
  insurance payments in the form of, 219
  specifying, as an acceptable form of
      payment, 96, 178
  tips for making payments with, 135
monitors, 324
mouse, 322
MoveWithUs.com, 208
movies, sale of, 155–156
MSN (Microsoft Network), 327
MTV auctions, 298–299
music, sale of, 155–156
My eBay link, 35
My eBay page, 10, 34–35
  Account page on, 51–54
  basic description of, 47–50
  changing your User ID from, 30
  Favorites area, 54–57
  Feedback area, 59–69
  Sign In page on, 47–50, 57–58
  sorting items with, 57–59
  tabs on, 49–50
My eBay Preferences, 49, 50–51

• N •

narcotics, sale of, 154
NARU (Not A Registered User), 115,
      270, 271
National Fraud Information Center
      (NFIC), 282
navigation bar, 6, 31, 33–35
NetMechanic, 314–315
Netscape Navigator browser, 329
Netscape Web site, 329
NetZero, 328
New to eBay? link, 38
New Today link, 56
New York City Department of Consumer
      Affairs, 278
newbies, 30, 289
News area, 34, 286–287
newsletters, 34
newspapers, 334

Nikon, 233
noise words, 90
Non-Paying Bidder Alert, 52–53, 224–225
Non-Paying Bidder Alert credit, 225
Non-Paying Bidder Alert Form, 225
Non-Paying Bidder Appeal Form, 114–115
Non-Paying Bidder Appeal Form link, 114
Norway, 20
NR (no reserve), 185
nudge mode, 212–216

• O •

O'Donnell, Rosie, 298
Office (Microsoft), 209
official time, at eBay, 57, 122–123, 182
Official Time page, 122–123
Olympus, 232–233
Omidyar, Pierre, 11, 29
Opinions, Authentication & Grading
      page, 280
optional fees, 159, 162–163
outages, 183, 223, 287
Outlook (Microsoft), 209

• P •

packaging, 61, 98
  basic description of, 197, 204–208
  materials, 204–208
paddle icon, 106
password(s)
  accessing your My eBay page with, 48
  changing, 48, 262
  choosing, 27–28, 262, 330
  entering, avoiding, 49
  entering, in the Sell Your Item page, 169
  hackers and, 257
  protecting your, 64, 307, 331
  signing in with, 33
payment(s). *See also* credit cards;
      transactions
  keeping records on, 192
  methods, importance of
      understanding, 306

payment(s) *(continued)*
  methods, overview of, 101–104
  prompt, importance of, 61, 135–138
  services, 102, 136–137, 179, 192
  terms set by sellers, 49, 96, 178–179,
    188–190
  which do not clear, 58, 62, 66, 103, 218
Payment link, 96
Payment Terms link, 52
PayPal, 102, 136–137
  specifying, as an acceptable form
    of payment, 179
  transactions, documenting, 192
PCGS (Professional Coin Grading Service),
    279, 300
People magazine auction, 298
personal Web pages, linking eBay auctions
    to, 244–245
Personal Shopper, 34, 91, 301–302
Personal Shopper Existing Searches
    page, 301
Personal Shopper link, 91
Personal Shopper login page, 91
pets, 154
Pez, 11
photos. *See* images
physical threats, 276
picture(s)
  adding, to your auction, 239–243
  basic guidelines for using, 231–244
  contrast settings for, 238
  creating high-quality, 234–238, 308
  cropping, 237, 238
  file formats for, 237, 238
  filenames for, 240
  hosting Web sites for, 240, 241–243
  including, in your About Me page,
    245–248
  preparing, for use on Web pages, 238–239
  size of, 238–239
  uploading, 240–243
  URLs for, 169, 188–190, 239–240, 247
Picture It 2000 (Microsoft), 237
pixels, 238
plastic bags, 206
Play Incorporated, 235

Play.com, 235
pointing devices, 322
police badges/IDs, 153
Policies page, 157
pornography, 154, 157
Postal Service (USPS)
  mail-fraud resources, 282
  shipping options, 103, 105, 197–203,
    208–210, 219
Power Sellers service, 318–319
power trading members, 299–300
Preferences page, 50–51
Preferences tab, 49, 50
Premier members, 192
prescription drugs, sale of, 154
pre-sell items, 177
price(s). *See also* bids
  display of, on auction item pages, 94
  guides, 75, 147, 149
  lowest winning, 120–121
  miscalculation of final, 224
  researching, 75–78, 83, 87–88, 147, 149
  searching for items by, 57–58, 83
  start, 57–58, 95
Price Radar, 302, 314
printers, 324
printing documents, 58–59, 87, 130,
    191–193, 324
privacy. *See also* security
  basic description of, 251–264
  cookies and, 253–255
  insuring, 262–264
  registration and, 252–253
  Web servers and, 254–255
private auctions, 13, 170, 175, 186
prizes, 158
Proceed button, 138
profane language, 68
prohibited items, 25, 151–155
promotional priority code, 22
PSA (Professional Sports Authenticators),
    279, 300
PSE (Professional Stamp Experts), 279
public counter programs, 243–244
public libraries, 80, 325

• Q •

quality, sorting items by, 58
Quantity field, 95
questionable items, 151–152, 157
QuickBooks, 192, 209
Quicken, 192

• R •

racist language, 270
raffles, 158
Reagan, Ronald, 280
Real Estate category, 159, 161
real estate transaction fees, 159
receipts, 59, 192
Recent Feedback tab, 49
recordkeeping. *See also* taxes
    after you win an auction, 130–131
    payment methods and, 103–104
    printing documents for, 58–59, 87, 130,
        191–193, 324
Refund link, 53
refunds, 52–54, 62, 227–229. *See also* Final
    Value Fee Credit
    Dutch auctions and, 228
    of insertion fees, 227–228
    for items damaged during shipping, 98
    keeping records on, 59, 192
    making sure to get, 164
    viewing information on, 49
Regional Items link, 39
regions. *See* location
Register link, 39
registration
    basic description of, 10, 19–30
    confirming, 23–26
    creating passwords, 27
    entering general information, 21
    entering required information, 22
    entering optional information, 22–23
    information, changing, 48
    information, privacy of, 252–253, 263
Registration link, 20–21

Reinhold, Arnold, 331
Relist this Item link, 228
Remember My Selling Preferences
    option, 170
Request Final Value Fee Credit link, 225
research. *See also* searching
    basic description of, 15, 72–92
    on bidders, 117–119, 213–214
    on buyers, 213–214
    collectors and, 73–78
    through eBay's online library, 78–79
    importance of, 73–74, 305–308
    on items which are appropriate to sell,
        147–149
    on markets for specific items, 333–334
    on prices, 75–78, 83, 87–88, 147, 149
    on sellers, 75, 96, 98–101
    on trends in the media, 334–336
    on the Web, 79–80
Researching Online For Dummies, 80
reserve-price auctions, 100, 159
    basic description of, 11–12, 94, 185–186
    canceling reserve prices, 229
    Dutch auctions and, 186
    insertion fees and, 160–161
    setting reserve prices, 170, 181, 229
    sorting items by, 58
resolution, of images, 233, 237, 238
restricted-access auctions, 12
Retracting Bid page, 112–113
retracting bids, 63, 112–113
Review and Respond to Feedback
    Comments Left for You page, 64
Review Bid page, 107
Revised User Agreement, 266
riddles, 60
risk reserve, 199
Rules & Safety program. *See also* Rules &
    Safety Overview page; SafeHarbor
    accessing, 34, 45
    abuses you should report to, 267–270
    basic description of, 16–17, 265–284
    mediation and dispute resolution
        services offered via, 273–274
    reporting abuses to, steps for, 270–273

Rules & Safety Overview page, 114, 152.
    See also Rules & Safety program
    accessing, 265
    accessing appraising agencies via,
        279–280
    accessing escrow services via, 278
    basic description of, 265–267
    filing insurance claims with, 277–278
    fraud reporting program, 274–275
    problems which are not handled by,
        271–273

• *S* •

SafeHarbor. *See also* Rules & Safety
        program
    accessing, 34, 45
    accessing appraising agencies via, 279
    basic description of, 16–17, 265–284
    dealing with AWOL sellers through, 139
    fraud reporting program, 274–275
    mediation and dispute resolution
        services offered via, 273–274
    reporting disruptive bidders to, 264
    reporting spam to, 261
SafeWeb Remote Banking Insurance, 102
Saturn, 111
scams, 158–159, 197
scanners, 232–234
    software, 234, 237–238
    tips for using, 236
Search button, 35, 36–37
search engines. *See also* searching
    basic description of, 79
    doing research with, 79–80
    at eBay, 80–91
    how to use, 79–80
Search field, 85
Search for Members link, 132
Search link, 31, 34
search Tips page, 35
Search window, 31, 35–36
searching. *See also* research; search
        engines
    eBay Home page options for, 35–38
    for e-mail addresses, 95, 132–133, 194, 259

for items by bidders, 37, 86, 117–118
for items by item numbers, 37, 81
for members, 95, 132–133, 194, 214, 259
narrowing down the scope of, 88–90
results of, display order of, 83, 85
symbols/keywords for, 89–90
time taken up by, 81
Searching Completed Auctions search, 81
security. *See also* passwords
    encryption, 21
    overview of, 24
    provided by SSL (Secure Socket Layer),
        21, 33, 53, 257, 263
    viruses, 257, 261
See All Feedback about Me link, 61, 62
See Item Description option, 180
Sell link, 34, 169
Sell Your Item form, 34, 39, 43
Sell Your Item page
    adding images to your auction with, 240
    basic description of, 168–186
    checking your entries on, 186–188
seller(s). *See also* selling
    AWOL, dealing with, 138–139
    communicating with, 75, 131–132, 134
    contact information of, getting, 131–133
    failure to respond to, when bidding, 62
    forwarding documentation to, 130–131
    geographic location of, 95
    golden rules for, 305–310
    identity of, authenticating, 63
    other auctions of, viewing, 99–100
    querying, 100–101
    remorse of, dealing with, 219
    researching, 75, 96, 98–101
    resolving problems with, 61, 138–139, 272
    searching by, 37, 81, 84–86, 99, 193
    who refuse to meet mutual set terms, 272
Seller Pays option, 180
Seller (Rating) link, 96
selling. *See also* sellers; setting up auctions
    abuses, reporting, 267–268
    basic description of, 143–166
    comparison, 149–151
    finding items for, 144–145
    keeping track of items when, 57–59

recordkeeping for, 58–59
relisted items, 227–229
rules for, 151–159
timing of, 146–147
Selling tab, 49, 169
servers, 240, 254–255
Services link, 34, 68, 112, 137, 190
Services Overview page, 190
setting up auctions
  basic description of, 14, 167–190
  choosing item categories, 168, 174–175
  listing acceptable payment methods, 170, 178–179
  preparing for, 167–168
  making changes to auctions in progress, 188–190
  setting minimum bids, 170, 181–182
  setting options, 183–186
  setting shipping terms, 98, 170, 180, 188–190, 196
  setting your auction time, 182–183
  writing item descriptions, 176–177
shareware, 238
Shareware.com, 238
shill bidding, 266, 267, 275
Ship to Home Country Only option, 180
shipping. *See also* packaging
  areas, designating, 95, 170, 180
  basic description of, 196–208
  buying postage for, 209–210
  carrier options for, 197, 198–203
  confirmation of, 219
  costs, 105–106, 197, 200–203, 272
  dates, specifying, 177
  etiquette, 196–208
  failures, 62
  handling fees, 197
  importance of prompt, 61, 198
  insurance, 76, 105–106, 139, 199, 219
  international, 96, 198, 201
  items damaged during, 76, 98, 139, 218–219
  methods, specifying, 98, 170, 180, 188–190, 196
  return, payment for, 105
  terms, importance of checking, 96

Shipping link, 96
ShippingSupply.com, 208
Show Me How icon, 94
side deals, 75, 115, 217
Sign In and Display Preferences page, 50
Sign In link, 33, 35, 47
Sign In page, 32–33, 47–50
  personal information required by, 252–253
  sorting items with, 57–58
signing up. *See* registration
Site Map, 35, 132, 182
Site Map link, 35, 132
slander, 68
Smart Search link, 36
Smart Search page. *See also* searching
  accessing, 34
  basic description of, 36–38, 81–83
  criteria for, 82–83
Snappy, 235
sniping, 120, 125–127
Soapbox, 291
Social Security numbers, 27, 135, 263, 281, 307
software
  auction-management, 241–242, 315–318
  free, 238
  image-editing, 237–238
  for offline use, 315–318
  provided by eBay, 318–319
  sale of, on eBay, 156
  scanner, 234, 237–228
Sony, 233, 323
sorting results, 83, 85
Sotheby's, 93
spam, 260–262, 269, 273, 331
spam.com, 261
Special Featured auction area, 184
Specialty Sites link, 39
Spotlight's On feature, 40, 44–45
Spotlight's On link, 40
SquareTrade, 273–274
SSL (Secure Socket Layer), 21, 53, 263
  basic description of, 257
  signing in with the option to use, 33
Stamps.com, 210

Star Chart, for feedback, 60
start price, 57–58, 95
Started field, 95
stocks, 154
stolen items, 155
styrofoam peanuts, 205
Submit button, 53, 55
Submit My Listing button, 187
Summary link, 54
sun icon, 56, 83
sunglasses icon, 30, 52
surveys, 259
suspension, of members, 217, 270, 272,
    275–276
Swoger, Bill, 74–77

● *T* ●

tax(es). *See also* IRS
  agreeing to pay, 25
  federal, 164–165
  getting the latest information on, 166
  income, 165–166
  information, 59
  overview of, 164–166
  recordkeeping for, 164
  sales, 165–166
  state, 166
telephone numbers, 132–133, 327
television, items featured on, 335
thumbnail images, 44. *See also* images
time. *See also* dates
  auction end, 95
  auction start, 95, 182–183
  bidding strategies and, 119–120, 121,
    122–127
  conversion chart, 56
  of feedback, 64
  official eBay, 57, 95, 122–123, 182
  sorting items by, 58
Time Left field, 95
Tips link, 35
title(s)
  of About Me pages, 247
  changing, 188–190

entering, in the Sell Your Item page, 169
  formatting options for, 169–170, 184, 228
  highlighted, 170, 184
  writing, 171–174, 229
To Bidder link, 67
To Seller link, 67
token bids, 108, 124
tracking members, 243–245, 258
trademarks, 155–156, 159
TradeOut, 337
traditional auctions, 11–12
transactions. *See also* payments
  buyers who back out of, dealing with,
    217–218
  documenting, 58–59
  nullifying, 212
Travelers Casualty and Surety
    Company, 102
"trust but verify" option, 281–282
TRUSTe, 255–258
Tucows.com, 238
TurboBid, 124, 317–318
tutorials, 39
TVandMovieStuff.com, 74

● *U* ●

Uline Shipping Supplies, 208
United Kingdom, 20, 42, 103
United Nations, 20
Update Item Information Request Form
    page, 189
Update Your Item Information page, 189
UPS (United Parcel Service), 105, 197–202,
    208, 219
URLs (Uniform Resource Locators). *See
    also* links
  adding, to item descriptions, 245
  basic description of, 329
  for images, 169, 188–190, 239–240, 247
Use a Credit Card for Automatic Billing
    link, 52
User Agreement, 24–25, 266
User Agreement link, 25

User ID(s)
  accessing your My eBay page with, 48
  appearance of, on the Feedback Profile
      page, 63
  availability of, to other eBay members, 259
  changing, 30, 48, 52
  choosing, 28–30, 262, 273
  entering, in the Sell Your Item page, 169
  feedback ratings and, 60
  finding, 133, 194, 259
  forgetting, what to do in the instance of, 48
  rules for, 30
  searching for items by, 37, 85–86
  signing in with, 33
  special characters in, 28, 30
User ID History and E-mail Address
      Request Form, 85–86, 132, 194
User Preferences page, 54
User Profile, 54
user-to-user discussion boards, 290–291
USPS (U.S. Postal Service)
  mail-fraud resources, 282–283
  shipping options, 103, 105, 197–203,
      208–210, 219

● **V** ●

Vanity Items category, 42
verification, 186–187, 280–281. *See also*
      VeRO (Verified Rights Owner) program
VeRO (Verified Rights Owner) program, 24,
      156, 159, 258
videotaping, 235
View a Complaint in Progress button, 277
View Seller's Other Auctions link, 99–100
viewing options, 43–44
Virtual Auction Ad Pro, 317–318
viruses, 257, 261
Visa, 52. *See also* credit cards
vulgar language, 290

● **W** ●

wait-and-see method, 124
wallet information, 281
Wanted message board, 291
warranties, items under, 98
Watch This Item feature, 81, 96–97, 122
Watch This Item link, 81, 96, 122
Web browsers, 327, 329
Web servers, 240, 254–255
WebCrawler, 79
WebTV, 9, 242, 325
WebTV Plus, 242
Welcome Mat links, 20
Welcome messages, 247
Western Union, 103
Why eBay Is Safe link, 39
Weird Stuff category, 42
wildlife, 154
Will Ship Internationally option, 180
Will Ship to United States and the
      Following Regions option, 180
wine, sale of, 157
winning bid, 130, 134, 195, 166
WordPerfect, 209
Wow! effect, 195

● **X** ●

x.com, 102

● **Y** ●

Yahoo!, 302, 328, 330–331
youth culture, 335

● **Z** ●

Zimbabwe, 20
Zoglin, Ron, 81

Notes

Notes

Notes

Discover Dummies Online!

The Dummies Web Site is your fun and friendly online resource for the latest information about *For Dummies* books and your favorite topics. The Web site is the place to communicate with us, exchange ideas with other *For Dummies* readers, chat with authors, and have fun!

Ten Fun and Useful Things You Can Do at www.dummies.com

1. Win free *For Dummies* books and more!
2. Register your book and be entered in a prize drawing.
3. Meet your favorite authors through the Hungry Minds Author Chat Series.
4. Exchange helpful information with other *For Dummies* readers.
5. Discover other great *For Dummies* books you must have!
6. Purchase Dummieswear exclusively from our Web site.
7. Buy *For Dummies* books online.
8. Talk to us. Make comments, ask questions, get answers!
9. Download free software.
10. Find additional useful resources from authors.

Link directly to these ten fun and useful things at **www.dummies.com/10useful**

For other technology titles from Hungry Minds, go to
www.hungryminds.com

Not on the Web yet? It's easy to get started with *Dummies 101: The Internet For Windows 98* or *The Internet For Dummies* at local retailers everywhere.

Hungry Minds™

Find other *For Dummies* books on these topics:
Business • Career • Databases • Food & Beverage • Games • Gardening
Graphics • Hardware • Health & Fitness • Internet and the World Wide Web
Networking • Office Suites • Operating Systems • Personal Finance • Pets
Programming • Recreation • Sports • Spreadsheets • Teacher Resources
Test Prep • Word Processing

FOR DUMMIES
BOOK REGISTRATION

Register This Book and Win!

We want to hear from you!

Visit **dummies.com** to register this book and tell us how you liked it!

- ✔ Get entered in our monthly prize giveaway.

- ✔ Give us feedback about this book — tell us what you like best, what you like least, or maybe what you'd like to ask the author and us to change!

- ✔ Let us know any other *For Dummies* topics that interest you.

Your feedback helps us determine what books to publish, tells us what coverage to add as we revise our books, and lets us know whether we're meeting your needs as a *For Dummies* reader. You're our most valuable resource, and what you have to say is important to us!

Not on the Web yet? It's easy to get started with *Dummies 101: The Internet For Windows 98* or *The Internet For Dummies* at local retailers everywhere.

Or let us know what you think by sending us a letter at the following address:

For Dummies Book Registration
Dummies Press
10475 Crosspoint Blvd.
Indianapolis, IN 46256

...FOR DUMMIES™

BESTSELLING
BOOK SERIES